GLENN R

Studies in Marxism and Social Theory

Rationality and Revolution

Studies in Marxism and Social Theory

Edited by G.A. COHEN, JON ELSTER AND JOHN ROEMER

The series is jointly published by the Cambridge University Press and the Editions de la Maison des Sciences de l'Homme, as part of the joint publishing agreement established in 1977 between the Fondation de la Maison des Sciences de l'Homme and the Syndics of the Cambridge University Press.

The books in the series are intended to exemplify a new paradigm in the study of Marxist social theory. They will not be dogmatic or purely exegetical in approach. Rather, they will examine and develop the theory pioneered by Marx, in the light of the intervening history, and with the tools of non-Marxist social science and philosophy. It is hoped that Marxist thought will thereby be freed from the increasingly discredited methods and presuppositions which are still widely regarded as essential to it, and that what is true and important to Marxism will be more firmly established.

Also in the series

JON ELSTER   *Making Sense of Marx*
ADAM PRZEWORSKI   *Capitalism and Social Democracy*
JOHN ROEMER, ED.   *Analytical Marxism*

Rationality and Revolution

edited by

Michael Taylor

University of Washington

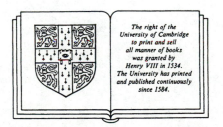

The right of the
University of Cambridge
to print and sell
all manner of books
was granted by
Henry VIII in 1534.
The University has printed
and published continuously
since 1584.

Cambridge University Press

Cambridge

New York   New Rochelle   Melbourne   Sydney

Editions de la Maison des Sciences de l'Homme

Paris

Published by the Press Syndicate of the University of Cambridge
The Pitt Building, Trumpington Street, Cambridge CB2 1RP
40 West 20th Street, New York, NY 10011-4211
10 Stamford Road, Oakleigh, Victoria 3166, Australia
and Editions de la Maison des Sciences de l'Homme
54 Boulevard Raspail, 75270 Paris Cedex 06

First published 1988
Reprinted 1991

Printed in the United States of America

Library of Congress Cataloging in Publication Data

Rationality and revolution.
(Studies in Marxism and social theory).
Includes index.
1. Revolutions and socialism. 2. Social choice.
1. Taylor, Michael. II. Series.
HX550.R48R37 1987 321.09 87-20851

A catalogue record for this book is available from The British Library.

ISBN 0-521-34419-0 hardback
ISBN 2-7351-9211-4 (France only)

Contents

Notes on the contributors

Raymond Boudon is Professor of Sociology at the University of Paris-Sorbonne and a foreign honorary member of the American Academy of Arts and Sciences. He is the author of *Education, Opportunity and Social Inequality* (Wiley, 1974); *The Unintended Consequences of Social Action* (Macmillan, 1982); *The Logic of Social Action* (Routledge, 1981); and *Theories of Social Change* (Blackwell, 1986). He has recently published a book on *L'idéologie ou l'origine des idées reçues* (Fayard) and is currently working on problems related to the philosophy and methodology of the social sciences.

Craig Calhoun has taught comparative and historical sociology and social theory at the University of North Carolina, Chapel Hill, since 1977. His books include *The Question of Class Struggle: Social Foundations of Popular Protest in Industrializing England* (Chicago University Press and Blackwell, 1982) and *Marxism and Sociology* (an edited collection forthcoming from the University of Chicago Press). He is currently studying the legal, political, social and economic origins of the idea that corporations can be autonomous and responsible social actors, and the history of struggles over corporate liability for insidious diseases such as asbestosis and cancer.

Jon Elster is Professor of Political Science at the University of Chicago and Research Director at the Institute for Social Research, Oslo. His publications include *Making Sense of Marx* (Cambridge University Press, 1985); *Sour Grapes* (Cambridge University Press, 1983); *Explaining Technical Change* (Cambridge University Press, 1983); *Ulysses and the Sirens* (Cambridge University Press, 1979, rev. edn 1984) and *Logic and Society* (Wiley, 1978). He is currently working on problems related to bargaining, collective action and social justice.

Samuel Popkin is an Associate Professor of Political Science at the University of California, San Diego. He is the author of *The Rational Peasant: The Political Economy of Revolution in Vietnam* (University of California Press, 1979) and co-editor of *Chief of Staff: Twenty-Five Years of*

Managing the Presidency (University of California Press, 1986). His current research interests include voting behaviour in industrial societies and twentieth-century revolutions. He is co-editor, with Brian Barry and Robert Bates, of the University of California Press Series on Social Choice and Political Economy.

Adam Przeworski is the Martin A. Ryerson Distinguished Service Professor of Political Science at the University of Chicago. His recent publications include *Capitalism and Social Democracy* (Cambridge University Press, 1985) and, as co-author, *Paper Stones: A History of Electoral Socialism*. Currently he is working on a project concerning the relation between governments and private economic actors.

John Roemer teaches economics at the University of California at Davis. He has written many articles and several books, which use standard methods of equilibrium and game-theoretic analysis to study problems in Marxism. This method is followed in, for example, *A General Theory of Exploitation and Class* (Harvard University Press, 1982). More recently, he has been studying problems in political philosophy, and has published a number of papers in journals of economics and philosophy using mathematical models to clarify issues in distributive justice.

Michael Taylor is Professor of Political Science at the University of Washington, Seattle. Previously he taught at the University of Essex, England, where he was Chairman of the Department of Government. His publications include *Community, Anarchy and Liberty* (Cambridge University Press, 1982) and *The Possibility of Cooperation* (Cambridge University Press, 1987). His principal current research interest is in the origins of the state.

James Tong is Assistant Professor of Political Science at the Michigan State University, East Lansing. His current research projects include collective violence in China from the Han to the Song Dynasty (221–1279); a cross-national study of the relationship between economic and political instability; and central–provincial fiscal relations in China from 1950 to 1984.

Michael Wallerstein is an Assistant Professor of Political Science at the University of California, Los Angeles. He is currently studying cross-national differences in the scope and organization of the union movement in advanced capitalist democracies.

Introduction

Revolutions are large-scale and complex events, involving rapid changes in political and social arrangements and characterized by turmoil and violence. It is not surprising that they have generally been thought to be unpromising material for the application of ideas and theories of rational choice. Theoretical studies of revolution have sometimes been psychological (though the psychology is not one of rational choice) and more often structural or functional or both. In the most notable of the recent studies, *States and Social Revolutions*, which adopts a structural but non-functional approach, Theda Skocpol has explicitly denied a useful role to any "voluntarist" or "purposive" ideas in the explanation of revolution. No successful revolution, she says, has ever been "made" by people with revolutionary intentions; actual revolutionary outcomes are neither intended nor foreseen by anyone; and even if revolutionary outcomes are produced by individuals, they act in situations which are not of their making.

These are propositions to which many writers on revolution have subscribed (and *mutatis mutandis* they are the stock in trade of writers on other subjects who are happy with historical macrosociologies lacking microfoundations). But in fact there is nothing in them that is incompatible with intentional explanation. That revolutions are not made by people with revolutionary intentions does not mean that they are not in the first instance the product of intentional action; that they do not turn out as their participants intended or foresaw does not imply that intentional action has no role in their explanation (the unintended consequences of action are in fact the central preoccupation of rational choice theorists); and that the situations in which the participants in revolutions find themselves are not of their making does not entail that rational action had no part in their production.

The essays in this volume begin to show that there *is* a useful role for ideas and theories of rational choice in the study of revolution and rebellion. (Some of the authors might want to put it more strongly than this.) More important, perhaps, than the results they obtain are the possibilities they suggest for fresh lines of attack on what is obviously a difficult, sprawling, subject. These essays also make, for the most part unselfconsciously, a contribution to the newly rekindled debates about "structure" and "action" and their role in the explanation of historical change and the problematic gap between sociological and historical modes of explanation – a gap not bridged in, for example, Theda Skocpol's book referred to above or in Jeffery Paige's *Agrarian Revolution*, whose more-or-less structural theories cannot account for the *changes* they are meant to explain and are supplemented in the detailed accounts of particular revolutions and rebellions by *ad hoc* historical narratives (which are unavoidably littered with statements about or presupposing intentional action). The essays here contribute to these debates not (with one partial exception) by making abstract methodological or philosophical arguments but (for the most part) by showing rational choice theorizing in action.

The first three essays concern rebellion and revolution in essentially pre-industrial settings. Samuel Popkin, building on the account in his well-known book on *The Rational Peasant*, opens with a discussion of the collective action problem and of the crucial role that in some circumstances political entrepreneurs can play in overcoming it. In a detailed study of peasant movements in pre-revolutionary and revolutionary Vietnam he shows how political and religious (or just politico-religious?) entrepreneurs mobilized large numbers of peasants by helping them to solve local collective action problems and in doing so realized a "revolutionary surplus" that could be channelled into national organizations for larger-scale and longer-range revolutionary projects.

This kind of painstakingly constructed mobilization across a whole country or large region – in which the Communists were so successful in the Vietnamese and Chinese revolutions – has not been necessary in every revolution. It was not an ingredient of, for example, the revolutions in France and Russia, where unorganized peasant revolts erupted spontaneously. But if "revolts from below" are one part of what we take a revolution to be, then the collective action or "free-rider" problem which is the central focus of Popkin's essay is a problem which in one form or another has to be solved in all successful revolutions (as well as in rebellions that are not part of a revolution). It is natural, then, that this problem should be addressed in several of the contributions to this volume. It provides the main focus of my attempt in the second essay to show that Skocpol is mistaken in her claim that social revolutions must be explained in purely structural, "non-voluntarist" terms. I argue that it was precisely because peasant collective action in revolutions and rebellions was based on community that it was *rational* for the large numbers of peasants involved to participate. Then, noting that the "thin" theory of rationality which explains such peasant collective action nevertheless fails to explain some kinds of participation in the interest groups and associations which have largely replaced community as the vehicle of movements for change, I try to give a general characterization of the conditions in which the thin theory of rationality is likely to provide good explanations. This general argument about rational choice explanation is finally re-connected to the problem of explaining revolution and to Skocpol's non-voluntarist, structural approach in particular.

The social basis of revolutionary collective action is addressed again in the fourth essay, where Craig Calhoun shows how "conservative" attachments to community and tradition may provide the foundations for rational participation in radical mobilizations. He suggests that Marx was mistaken in his belief that under industrial capitalism a factory-based proletariat with nothing to lose but its chains would eventually come to have the social cohesion necessary to engage in revolutionary collective action; on the contrary, revolutionary mobilizations occur when people *do* have something to defend – a livelihood that is threatened by rapid social transformation – as well as possessing the capacity for sustained collective action. The local community once supplied this capacity for rebel collective action, but it was also its limitation, since it actually inhibited coordination over a large territory. The early nineteenth century is thus of special interest to Calhoun, since it was a time when many workers, above all the artisans, who had much to defend against the incursions of the industrial revolution, were beginning to create political organizations of wider than local scope while still having the traditional local community to draw on. His account of this transitional period leads him, finally, to consider the capacities for collective action and the propensity for radicalism of the modern working class (a theme which is picked up in a later essay).

In the remaining essay of Part I, James Tong sets out to explain the incidence of rebellion and banditry in the Chinese Ming Dynasty. Using an extraordinary collection of data, which he has culled from provincial and prefectural gazetteers giving annual figures on collective violence in all 1,000-odd counties and spanning the entire dynasty (from 1368 to 1644), Tong finds considerable confirmation for a simple model that views rebellion and banditry as rational responses to subsistence crises. More specifically, the incidence of rebellion and banditry is related to the peasant's prospects for surviving as an outlaw (i.e., of escaping government sanctions) and the prospects for surviving the severe hardship that would be his lot if he stayed put.

The four essays of Part II are more purely theoretical. The first of these, by Michael Wallerstein and Adam Przeworski, takes up again the question of the revolutionary propensities of workers under capitalism. Marx and Engels believed that through their struggles for higher wages workers would eventually come to see that they must abolish the wage system itself. This expectation was disappointed, and to see why, we need to view the relation between wages and profits – the game between workers and capitalists – in a more *strategic* light than did Marx and Engels. Workers' and capitalists' interests are not diametrically opposed, for the more moderation workers display in making wage demands today, the greater the amounts available to capitalists for the investments that will benefit workers tomorrow. Wallerstein and Przeworski explore this strategic interaction in two formal models of a stylized capitalist economy: first, an economy with no state intervention and therefore no taxes, then one with a state which imposes a tax on uninvested profits with all the tax receipts disbursed as transfer payments to workers. The outcomes for workers in these two cases are compared to the workers' "bliss point": their lot under a socialist regime in which they alone determine the allocation between wages and investment (a choice between present consumption and future growth). The chapter concludes with some informal comments on the prospects for the social democratic strategy of "functional socialism", which would gradually bring the functions of capital ownership under state control while leaving ownership itself intact.

The argument that we need a more strategic conceptualization of power than Marx provided is taken up in a different though related context by Jon Elster in his discussion of the relation between the state and the capitalist class. The state, in particular, pursues its own goal of raising revenue (which it must first do whatever its further substantive goals) but in doing so must, of course, take account in a variety of ways of the likely responses of capitalists to its policies. How much this strategic interaction constrains the state to pursue policies the capitalists would find optimal is, says Elster, a purely empirical question: the question of the structural dependence of the state on the capitalist class, or contrariwise its scope for autonomous action, is not something that can be decided a priori. In the second half of his paper, Elster critically evaluates Marx's views on the revolutionary transitions from feudalism to capitalism and from capitalism to communism. Marx, he writes, failed to supply an argument supporting his conclusion that classes or individuals would do political battle to give birth to the new relations of production required for the further development of the productive forces. Marx's argument here, and his theory of historical change more generally, lack microfoundations. In fact, Elster concludes, Marx's theory of the communist revolution assumes that workers or capitalists or the state must act irrationally. In his concluding remarks, he links the problematic relation between state and capital with the problem addressed in the preceding chapter, and argues that the situation – characterized as it is by the presence of (at least) three strategic actors (workers, capitalists and the state – though as Elster is aware treating these as actors is problematic) interacting in two interlocking arenas and with much uncertainty about the consequences of adopting alternative policies – is a formidable, perhaps unconquerable challenge for rational choice theory.

John Roemer's essay represents an entirely fresh approach to the explanation of revolutionary ideology. Imagine, he says, a ruler ("the Tsar") and a revolutionary entrepreneur ("Lenin") competing for the support of coalitions of the population. The behaviour of the two protagonists might be viewed as ideologically motivated – irrational inasmuch as it is constrained by given ideological commitments without which purely self-interested actors might have chosen *other* policies better suited to maximizing their appeal. Is it possible that these ideologies have a rational foundation – in the sense that if Lenin (for example) is wholly *un*constrained in his choice of a policy designed to overthrow the Tsar, it will be in his interest to adopt a progressive policy (one favourable to the poor)? It turns out, remarkably, that it is. In a stylized model of the interaction between ruler and revolutionary entrepreneur, Roemer proves that, under certain conditions, a rational Lenin, without necessarily being pre-committed to any particular view of how the poor or the rich should be treated, will find that it pays to be progressive, while a rational Tsar will similarly find it in his interest to adopt a policy of imposing harsher penalties for revolutionary participation on the poor than he imposes on the rich (as Tsars tend in fact to do). In what sense does Roemer's analysis, which is not of course meant to be a descriptively accurate account of interactions between rulers and revolutionary entrepreneurs, "rationalize" revolutionary ideology? Not, says Roemer, in the sense that a clever, rational Lenin would choose a progressive strategy *just because* it is cynically calculated to further his (ideologically unconstrained) ends. Rather, the model suggests that if he does *not* adopt such a strategy, he will not succeed; that is, this strategy (whatever the conscious reasons for which it is adopted) would be selectively adaptive. The formation of ideologies has generally been seen to offer little scope for rational choice explanation; Roemer's essay suggests a possible approach of this kind.

The concluding short piece by Raymond Boudon is not concerned directly with revolution but it intriguingly opens up an avenue of approach to a phenomenon that for many writers is prominent among the preconditions for rebellion (as well as providing another ingenious illustration of what Boudon calls the "perverse effects of intentional action"). He formulates a simple model (as one must in order to *isolate* basic processes) to show how relative deprivation phenomena can be produced out of nothing more than simple structures of competition in which individuals are situated equally. These structures generate deprivation in effect by inciting some individuals to participate in "rivalries". Along the way, this analysis suggests a possible mechanism underlying the effects observed long ago by Tocqueville and more recently by Samuel Stouffer and others: that greater (equal) opportunity for advancement may lead to greater dissatisfaction for more people and that greater frustration and the quarrels consequent upon it can be *increased* by a reduction in inequality.

M.J.T.

Part I

1 Political entrepreneurs and peasant movements in Vietnam*

Samuel L. Popkin

This chapter examines the mobilization of peasants during the Vietnamese revolution. It shows how, out of the rational choices of myriad individuals, peasant society can be restructured and new institutions constructed. It shows in particular how peasant organizers, starting with limited material resources and using only their organizational skills, can "bootstrap" their organizations into existence and so "build something from nothing". Through small interventions in the patterns of daily life these political and religious organizers, here called political entrepreneurs, build institutions which generate a "revolutionary surplus" or profit, and financed by this surplus they then use their local bases to recruit people to a national struggle.

This process of mobilization, in which political entrepreneurs play a crucial role in solving collective action problems (amongst other things) was not peculiar to the Vietnamese revolution; nor is it confined to revolutions in general. But here it will be illustrated in some detail through study of four pre-revolutionary and revolutionary Vietnamese organizations: the Hoa Hao and Cao Dai religions in Cochinchina (the newly colonized Southern region of Vietnam) and the Catholic Church and Communist Party in all three regions of Vietnam (Cochinchina, Annam and Tonkin). These organizations were able to gain control of large sections of the country and to channel significant peasant resources into creating new rural societies. They differed radically in ideology, in national organization, in their definitions of the problems of peasant society, and in their attempts to reorganize rural institutions. There were, however, similarities in the way these four movements attracted support and developed control in the countryside which would be overlooked in a simple division between religious and political movements. Indeed, the differences between them appear much greater today than they did to contemporary observers. Foreign observers, politically active Vietnamese and uneducated, relatively apolitical peasants found many commonalities in the four

---

* Some of the material and ideas in this chapter were originally discussed by the author in *The Rational Peasant* (University of California Press, 1979).

groups. For example, when the Cao Dai religion was first developing in the countryside, many French sought its suppression because it was nothing but "communism masquerading as a religion".[1] Frequently, the Communist leadership had to fight to keep their cadres from joining the exodus to Hoa Haoism or Cao Daism or even Catholicism, when these religions attracted peasants in the Communist associations.[2]

All four movements organized peasants by helping them to break their dependence on, and control by, large landowners and/or village officials. Traditional arrangements were improved on and landlords outbid by organizers who provided the same services at lower cost (and higher dignity).

By undermining the power of village notables, the movements were able to institute village-level insurance and tax, welfare, and communal land procedures that were far more extensive and beneficial than those of either the pre-colonial or colonial periods. But it must be stressed that village officials and landlords had to be undermined; when these movements built their power bases, they were actively opposed by economic and political elites, who had been strengthened by colonial policies.

The organizations provided peasants with mutually profitable sources of insurance and welfare, and helped them overcome the institutional manipulations of market and bureaucracy that had reinforced dependence. These organizations used political skills and bureaucratic connections to give the peasants access to (and leverage against) the institutions that had previously kept them at a disadvantage. By doing so, they helped the peasants to tame markets and enter them on their own.

Economic benefits attracted most peasants but this is often interpreted narrowly as land reform, or a similar redistribution of a fixed pie. In fact, most of the benefits to peasants came not from redistributing land but from reforming the economic institutions within which market society operates. Both the size of the pie and how it is distributed depend upon courts, land-titling procedures, access to bureaucracy, tax collectors, surveyors and a host of other institutions of property rights and contracting. These other institutions determine in large part whether the profits for some upset the livelihood of others or whether there is gain for all.

In all four cases, the initial organization of peasants focused on local goals and goods with immediate payoffs. The profits derived from local organizing were then directed by the leadership to larger, more national, goals and projects. Peasants in the late 1960s still laughed about the early

[1] Virginia Thompson, *French Indochina* (New York: Macmillan, 1937), p. 474.
[2] Mobilizing peasants is but one aspect of a successful revolution so this is not a complete explanation of how and why the Communists triumphed over the other religious and political groups.

attempts by young Trotskyites and Communists to organize them for a national revolution, for industrialization, or even for a world revolution! Only later, when peasants (and workers) were organized around smaller and more immediate goals, were larger organizational attempts successful. This was the strategy used by the Catholics in the seventeenth century, and it proved the most effective strategy again in the twentieth century.

When improved leadership makes possible the incentive systems or cost-sharing mechanisms for self-help projects such as insurance programs and livestock cooperatives, it is possible to produce benefits for the peasants as well as a "revolutionary surplus" which can then be used to support a supravillage organization and applied to broader organizational objectives. All the successful groups, religious and political, developed large-scale, national movements from local organizations that produced a "revolutionary surplus" used for expanding the organization. As Alexander Woodside describes this pattern for the Communists, they perceived

the rather simple sociological truth that a large movement could derive cohesion and even dynamism from multitudes of small-group attachments which fell short, in practice, of attachments to the movement's most complex central ideologies and philosophical doctrines – provided that these small-group attachments were associated with concrete local issues.[3]

A political or religious transformation of society is a collective good which benefits peasants whether or not they participate. Yet, these four groups all elicited resources from rural society with which to wage their national battles over the future of Vietnam. To understand how that was accomplished I begin with Mancur Olson's formulation of the collective action problem.[4]

Peasants are self-interested and that means that they are concerned with individual benefits, not group benefits, when contemplating cooperation. As William Hinton has observed, peasant society exhibits

an all-pervading individualism engendered by the endless, personal struggle to acquire a little land to beat out the other fellow in the market place. Peasants individually driven to bankruptcy viewed economic disaster not as a social but as a personal matter, to be solved in isolation by whatever means came to hand. This essentially divisive and selfish approach made cooperation between peasants on

[3] Alexander Woodside, *Community and Revolution in Modern Vietnam* (Boston: Houghton Mifflin, 1976), p. 179. See also Mancur Olson, *The Logic of Collective Action* (Cambridge, Mass.: Harvard University Press, 1965), pp. 62–3.
[4] Olson, *The Logic of Collective Action*; Norman Frohlich, Joe Oppenheimer, and Oran Young, *Political Entrepreneurship and Collective Goods* (Princeton: Princeton University Press, 1971); Norman Frohlich and Joe Oppenheimer, *Modern Political Economy* (Englewood Cliffs, New Jersey: Prentice-Hall, 1978); Russell Hardin, *Collective Action* (Baltimore: Johns Hopkins Press, 1982).

any level other than the family extremely difficult, greatly increased the leverage of the gentry's divide-and-rule tactics . . .[5]

In particular, whether a self-interested person will contribute to a collective action depends on individual – not group – benefits. Thus, collective benefits from action do not necessarily provide individual reasons to participate. Rational egoists are interested in the benefits that their participation in collective action brings to them individually. If an individual's benefit (more precisely, the individual's utility from the increased collective good that results from his or her contribution to the collective action) does not exceed the cost to the individual of partici- pating, then the individual will want to be a "free rider" – to benefit from the collective action of others (if there is any) while making no contri- bution.

Two of the leading members of the Communist party, Vo Nguyen Giap, who founded the People's Army, and Truong Chinh, who served as Party Secretary, investigated the life of the peasantry and the possibilities for successful Communist political action in the countryside. They found peasants aware of the trade-offs involved when allocating resources to further either individual or common interests:

Peasants also have the mentality of private ownership . . . They are suspicious of talk of collective work. Most of them do not like the idea of contributing money for common goals. Traditional peasant organizations . . . are all characterized by individual profit for each member of the group. None have a social nature, i.e., a common advantage for the entire group or for society . . . We have yet to see peasants spontaneously organize societies which have a common usefulness.[6]

Giap and Truong Chinh had discovered that there is a free-rider problem in peasant society. The common usefulness of organized activity was not sufficient to induce participation. As long as the only results of contributing to common goals were common advantages, peasants left the contributions to others and expended their scarce resources in pursuit of private interests. They opted for individual interests over common inter- ests; they would take part in organizations only when there were benefits contingent upon participation.

Collective action requires more than consensus or even intensity of need. It requires conditions under which peasants will find it in their individual interests to allocate resources to their common interests – and not be free riders. Any attempt to organize for group action must

[5] William Hinton, *Fanshen* (New York: Random House Vintage Books, 1968), p. 55.
[6] Vo Nguyen Giap and Truong Chinh, "The Peasant Question (1937–1938)" (trans. Christine Peltzer White. Data Paper no. 94, Southeast Asia Program. Ithaca: Cornell University Press, 1974), p. 21.

recognize the distinction between individual and group benefits and must provide sufficient incentives to engage in collective action.

Under what conditions can resources for collective endeavor be gathered together? Mancur Olson has stated the argument in its classic form: "unless there is coercion or some other special device to make individuals act in their common interest, rational, self-interested individuals will not act to achieve their common or group interest".[7]

Strictly speaking, this argument, as Olson goes on to argue, typically applies to large groups only. If a group is sufficiently small, then it is likely to be either "privileged" or "intermediate". A privileged group is one containing at least one member who derives so much benefit from the increased supply of the collective good that he or she is willing to provide some of it unilaterally. If a group is not privileged, Olson calls it "latent". Generally, larger groups tend to be latent. But if a latent group is not too large, then some sort of strategic interaction between its members may be feasible and lead to successful collective action: for example, collective action may result from each individual cooperating *if and only if* all the others do, or if *enough* others do. Such a group is called an "intermediate" group. If strategic interaction does not lead to collective action, then the collective good will only get provided if "selective incentives" are brought to bear – that is, benefits are offered only to those who participate (and/or sanctions applied to those who do not). In this case, the collective good is supplied as a "by-product" of the provision of the selective incentives.

This "by-product theory", as Olson calls it, is illustrated by the (simplified) example of the American Medical Association. The Association produces major collective goods, particularly political power, for the medical profession. Since the results of the AMA's influence on tax and health legislation, for example, are available to all doctors, membership in the Association is not required to receive its collective benefits. But a doctor receives selective, non-collective benefits from his membership that justify payment of dues. If the AMA can provide members with valuable information about new medicines or tax loopholes, or if it can monopolize the services of malpractice specialists, then it is in the individual doctor's interest to join the organization.[8]

Earlier theories of interest groups had answered the question "why did this organization form?" or the question "why did these persons join an organization?" with answers that were variants of "because there was a common interest". It was concluded that if organizations did not exist then it was because there was indeed no common interest. "No organizations without interests" led many to conclude incorrectly that there

[7] Olson, *The Logic of Collective Action*, p. 2.
[8] Ibid., pp. 137–41.

were no interests without organizations.[9] Olson's contribution was to show the error of these inferences and to direct attention to collective goods and the problem of free riders. A lack of organization does *not* imply an absence of common interest; and people with a common interest – *especially* if there are large numbers of them – do *not* automatically organize to further it.

Selective incentives and political entrepreneurs

The by-product theory, with its emphasis on centrally supplied incentives, is better at explaining the maintenance of organizations than it is at explaining the origins of organizations.[10] Incentives are necessary to gather the resources to maintain an organization, to prevent people from free-riding on collective benefits; but this does not mean that the by-product theory of selective incentives provides a sufficient explanation of the process of *building* organizations.

There are a number of assumptions implicit in the by-product theory. Examining these assumptions raises questions which lead to the elaborations of the by-product theory which are necessary to account for the cases presented here. The by-product theory assumes:

Individual contributions have an *imperceptible* impact on the contributions of others; each decision whether to contribute is independent of every other decision whether to contribute.

An individual contribution will have an *imperceptible* impact on the level of the collective good supplied; contributions will not be noticed because the collective good is so expensive.

Participating in provision of the collective good has *imperceptible* value; the only benefits come from the collective good itself.

The goals are pure collective goods without excludability; participation will have an *imperceptible* impact on the benefits from the collective good an individual receives from any amount of the collective good because the collective good will benefit or affect everyone equally whether or not they are contributors.

There is no iteration; only one collective action is considered so individual decisions whether to participate have an *imperceptible* impact on future collective endeavors.

When individual contributions have no perceptible impact on the level of the good or on the contributions of others, when participation has no value of its own, and when persons who do not contribute cannot be excluded from benefits, then special incentives are needed to produce any action toward group goals. Yet even when all these conditions hold, the by-product theory still leaves unanswered the question why the collective

---

[9] Ibid., pp. 5–8, 111–31.
[10] Hardin, *Collective Action*, p. 34.

good gets provided at all. If every individual is engaging in self-interested exchanges for selective incentives it is not apparent that the collective goods will be produced even if the organizer is dedicated to producing them for his own reasons. If every individual engages in exchanges which are justified purely on the basis of the divisible and excludable benefits ʾhey receive for the exchange, the entrepreneur provides the collective ϽϽods out of his or her profit on the individual exchanges. But why then ϽϽ the collective goods get produced? If the organizer is motivated to produce the collective goods whether or not they are required to generate the exchanges with individuals, but the others are motivated only by narrow self-interest, then someone should be able to produce the incentives more cheaply by not spending any of the profit on collective goods. If collective goods plus selective incentives cost more to produce than selective incentives alone, why do the goods ever get produced?

Goals, that is the collective goods themselves, matter more to the process of organizing than the by-product theory acknowledges. This is because collective goods and selective incentives *together* can cost less to produce than selective incentives alone.

When studying the peasant movements in Vietnam, a related question arises. Why do the collective goals of the successful movements include goals relating to the *ethos* or culture of society as well as to economic benefits? Why were the only successful organizations those which included in their goals either nationalism or religion, as well as economic changes? To rephrase this question, what role do new conceptions of identify and self-worth play in organizing for economic benefits? Or, what role do economic benefits play in organizing peasants for new conceptions of identity and self-worth?

As we explore these movements it becomes clear that the *ethos* of the organizations, whether in the form of nationalism or religion, is critical to developing careers for political entrepreneurs, developing credibility among the peasantry, altering expectations and creating the boundaries necessary for excludable benefits.

The by-product theory also leaves open the question of where the resources to provide selective incentives come from. Peasant movements are sustained by the contingent benefits they provide, but the leaders of these movements typically start out with little in the way of material resources. How do these entrepreneurs generate the resources with which to provide sustained benefits for peasants? How can free riders be overcome without the initial resources to provide carrots or sticks?

Recall that the by-product theory is brought in by Olson to deal with the large, "latent" group case. In fact, centrally administered selective incentives would *not* be necessary if the (usually large) groups that would otherwise be latent could somehow be, in effect, turned into privileged groups or, more likely, intermediate groups. This would be done if one or more individuals could be got to value participation enough to be willing to contribute unilaterally or if individuals' actions could be made more interdependent. These in turn would be the result of individuals coming to see their contributions as having more impact on the amount of collective good supplied and on the decisions of others. The central issue is development of "mechanisms for coordination of expectations and the pooling of resources".[11]

This is where political entrepreneurs matter. For they can produce these two effects, not merely by administering selective incentives (which they may not be in a position to do initially), but by giving individuals reason to believe that their contributions are significant and making individual contributions interdependent by acting as go-betweens (in effect facilitating conditional cooperation). This they can do by breaking up both large groups and large problems into smaller ones and by institutional design: for example, peasants can be mobilized around pressing, highly local problems, where collective action amongst small numbers of people who already know each other will bring immediate tangible benefits. In such groups, conditional cooperation can be made to work because free riders can be readily detected and because, additionally, social sanctions can be administered easily and effectively by the members themselves.

If political entrepreneurs, in order to do their work, must actually gather resources from the members of the group in question – if, for example, in addition to acting merely as go-betweens to facilitate conditional cooperation they wish to make a "revolutionary surplus" to apply (or pass on to others to apply) to larger and longer-range goals – then they must convince peasants that they are not going to take their money and run, supplying neither the collective goods nor the promised incentives.

Most peasant cooperation, organization, and insurance involves immovable assets – peasants seldom give another peasant money to hold for the future because the peasant could always run away with the money or spend it on himself or his family. Clearly, overcoming this obstacle was for all four organizations a major feat, which could not have been accomplished without trustworthy political entrepreneurs. Organizers have to convince peasants that their goals are credible, that not only can they and will they do what is promised with the peasants' contributions, but that if they do as promised, the peasants' lot will be bettered.

The development of careers for political entrepreneurs was one of the most important steps in the growth of the movements, and an *ethos*, whether religious or political, was necessary to convince the entre-

[11] Frohlich, Oppenheimer, and Young, *Political Entrepreneurship and Collective Goods*, p. 25.

preneurs to dedicate themselves to their organizations. The long-range goals of the organizations and the commitment of the elite to these goals were critical to developing the full commitment of the entrepreneurs.

These entrepreneurs needed above all communications skills to provide peasants with the signals and incentives necessary to collective action and organization-building. In every case the critical village-level entrepreneurs were persons with experience in the few roles in an agricultural society in which communications skills were developed: teachers, bus drivers, river boat pilots, itinerant actors, and NCOs from the French Army.

The by-product theory is a vertical theory of collective action; by assuming that there are imperceptible impacts of contribution on the contributions of others, it concentrates solely on the relations between individual behavior and the central distribution of incentives. Ignoring interactions among persons, it does an inadequate job of explaining situations where collective actions are possible among self-interested persons without centrally supplied incentives. Sustained organization and sophisticated collective actions require elaborate systems of incentives and leadership, but there are a number of limited forms of organization and collective action – boycotts and marches, for example – which require minimal incentives. These situations are important, if limited, because they are part of developing the resources necessary for more sustained actions.

The activities of political entrepreneurs can be leveraged into large-scale collective actions if rules can be developed which can easily be monitored and enforced within a group. If group interactions can be made to provide sufficient incentives for persons to conform to a collective action, then collective action can succeed without centralized incentive systems. This depends upon the benefits of defection, the information required to monitor defections and the ease of communicating the collective strategy.

If all the members of a group, for example, recognize that there is a "united we stand, divided we fall" situation and no one wants to be known as the first defector, then the group can stand together if they know the identify of the first defector will be communicated to the others. When there is widespread recognition that a collective action would benefit all and the common action required can be specified easily then political entrepreneurs can provide the spark by suggesting the specific action upon which to focus.

If peasants see major benefits in talking to their landlords only as a group, or in not talking to anyone aiding the enemy, or in all marching together so that no one can be rewarded for not marching, very little centrally supplied incentives are necessary to produce collective action.

The establishment of collective action in such circumstances may require nothing but an entrepreneur to provide a focal point for the activity, or to suggest the common behavior, or to develop rules which can be easily implemented with the available communications patterns.

Examining alternate forms of community labor pools demonstrates the role of entrepreneurship and design in translating collective agreement into collective action. For example, suppose a village canal becomes choked with weeds unless every villager works one day a month to clear the weeds. One possible arrangement is for each farmer to do one day's work every month. However, this arrangement is vulnerable to free riders; at the end of the month everyone can claim they worked on the canal and no one can falsify their claim unless someone devotes full time to watching the canal and keeping records of everyone's participation. Another possible arrangement is to assign each person responsibility for a specific section of canal. Claims of participation can now be verified without a full-time record keeper if someone checks at the end of the month to see which sections were cleared and communicates the names of free riders through the village so that others can punish them. Yet another possible arrangement is for everyone to agree to do their work *on the same day*; this may be less convenient than allowing farmers to choose their own work time, but identifying free riders and communicating their names to everyone is now nearly costless. Since the common work day makes the identity of free riders easily known to all, a person who scorns or criticizes a free rider can have a perceptible impact on maintaining the work arrangements which lead to the collective good of a clean canal.

The design of such collective actions dependent upon decentralized incentives must balance the incentives to violate the agreement against the incentives to maintain them. An individual contribution may have an imperceptible impact on a collective good; a properly designed agreement to achieve the good, however, may only require contributions to maintaining the procedures, and contributions to maintaining the agreement (sanctioning free riders) may have a perceptible impact on the collective good.[12]

Knowledge conditions are the key to designing and implementing collective action with minimal amounts of centrally supplied incentives. The less one must know about each person, the easier it is to maintain collective actions in large groups. The larger the group, the clearer and simpler the collective actions must be in order to be enforced by indi-

---

[12] This discussion draws extensively upon Russell Hardin's discussion of contract by convention, *Collective Action*, pp. 155–80. Here I am extending his insights about conventions to include the role of entrepreneurs in establishing both collective actions which require no centrally supplied incentives and collective actions which require minimal centrally supplied incentives.

vidually contributed sanctions against would-be free riders. Large group collective action with minimal central direction and incentives will generally be limited to boycotts, marches and very simple forms of festival labor like cutting weeds.

The ease with which defections can be monitored determines the limits to collective action in large groups. It is easy to detect defectors during a labor boycott, and when resources are available the defectors can be dealt with. When it is difficult to detect defections, group solidarity cannot be maintained without extensive organization; collective action to maintain interest rates is an example. If all peasants could agree to borrow only at a given rate and at no higher rate, the interest rate would come down, and non-market methods would govern the allocation of credit. But no one in Vietnam, from the Catholics in the seventeenth century to the Viet Minh during the resistance, was able effectively to put a ceiling on interest rates, for defection (secretly paying the higher rates to get more credit at the expense of the group) was the strategy chosen by enough peasants to thwart boycotts.

Whether an action is self-enforcing depends on how easy it is to monitor free riders and communicate their identity to others. A group is not self-enforcing when a member gains more benefits by dropping out than by voluntarily remaining in the group. If an immediate benefit can be derived from defection, an organization formed to pursue a goal can survive only if there is sufficient coercion available to the leadership to enforce discipline, or enough resources to make defection less valuable than remaining in the group. An insurance scheme, for example, is self-enforcing: when a member fails to pay or do his share, he loses his benefits. In direct contrast is the problem of organizing a work stoppage among laborers in order to raise their wages. If all the laborers in an area were to simultaneously withhold their labor from their fellow villagers who are tenants or smallholders, the laborers' share of the crop could be increased. But such coordinated action is not self-enforcing without some sanctions to apply to the laborer, for there is an incentive for any individual laborer to defect and offer his labor. He will reason that if everyone else withholds his labor, wages will inevitably rise; he will therefore receive the future benefits of the collective action as well as the wages he receives as a strike-breaker.

In developing decentralized collective actions, the obvious approach, the approach which requires the least information, usually dominates the most fair approach because it requires less communication, less organization and less sanctioning than more complicated and more fair arrangements. If every member of the village could choose their own day to work on the canal, many villagers would find it easier to avoid conflicts with other activities, but more sophisticated record keeping and leadership would be required to make the identity of free riders known at the end of the month. It may not be ideal to require everyone to work at the same time, but it makes free riders obvious.

When can collective action most easily occur with minimal leadership or organization? When persons live together in one community or when there are few conflicts of interest in a group, it is easier to decide upon a lowest common denominator for collective action. When defections can be monitored easily it is easier to communicate the identities of free riders to those willing to sanction them. When a job requires a particular skill or a community is isolated it is harder to bring in strike-breakers. If work can be delayed without destroying the product, crucial wages can be deferred but not lost. These conditions all facilitate actions such as boycotts, marches, strikes with little formal leadership to supply incentives.[13]

It is important to emphasize that such collective actions are likely to be limited in scope to the lowest common denominator of the interests within a group; highly visible, universal demands, not the full range of interests of its members or even the most important preferences of the members. Thus, when a group engages in collective action, one should not infer from such demonstrations of collective ability and common interest that the group will be able to function collectively in other more mundane areas of village life. As a colonial newspaper noted in 1896:

A whole village comes to an admirable understanding in order to pillage a convoy of Chinese junks or to plunder the house of a rich neighbor. Discretion will be well guarded even in the case of success. . . . But ask this same village to group together to store their rice in one central warehouse and assure themselves of quick and certain benefits. Disorder and bickering will quickly break out in the midst of the group. In a week they will be calling each other thieves.[14]

We have argued, then, that political entrepreneurs play a critical role in developing coöperation. By focusing on a specific coordination point among many and by coordinating activities and manipulating information they influence the calculations of others. The expected value of an individual action, that is, its perceived efficacy, depends upon expectations of resistance, expectations of the actions of others and expectations of success, all of which are influenced by credible entrepreneurs. An

[13] Note that Cesar Chavez started with vineyard workers in California, where these conditions are met, and not with other groups of agricultural workers among whom it would have been more difficult to develop collective action. These conditions are also met among rubber-plantation workers. Jeffrey Paige, *Agrarian Revolution* (New York: The Free Press, 1975), pp. 50–8; Chandra Jayawardena, "Ideology and Conflict in Lower Class Communities", *Comparative Studies in Society and History*, 10 (1967–8), 418–23.

[14] *Le Courier de Saigon*, quoted in Guy Gran, "Vietnam and the Capitalist Route to Modernity: Village Cochinchina 1880–1940" (Ph.D. dissertation, Department of History, University of Wisconsin, 1973), p. 523.

entrepreneur who can convince persons that everyone else is coming, or that everyone else will come if he comes, or who spreads the names of free riders, thereby raising the costs of free-riding, can leverage large collective actions from his or her efforts.

The goals of the organization and the skills of the entrepreneur play an important part in eliciting contributions. People may need no selective incentives but they do need assurance that their contribution will be effective and the expected value of a contribution depends both upon the value of the goal and upon the effect of the contribution on the probability of success. What must be offered to individuals searching for the best way to expend their contributions is efficacy. A leader must be able to convince people that making the contribution through a particular organization or a particular form of participation is the most effective expenditure of their resources. During the August Revolution, there were many persons in Hanoi and Saigon who felt it their duty to fight for national salvation. Among them, the Viet Minh substantially out-recruited other organizations because it was able to convince them that their contributions would do the most good if channeled through the Viet Minh.

Effective leaders elicit contributions by breaking up a large goal into many steps with critical thresholds. If a large goal can be broken into many small independent pieces, all of which are necessary to the larger goal, the free-rider problem can be overcome, for if each person has a monopoly on a necessary factor for the final goal, all contributions are essential. After land was distributed and rents reduced in Cochinchina, peasants commonly went out of their way to warn Viet Minh cadres that French soldiers or agents were in the area; they did not risk free-riding on warnings by waiting for someone else to notify the cadre. The cadre may not have had a perceptible impact on the entire revolution but the cadre was a critical part of the local benefits received by the peasant.

From local organizations to national movements

Discussions of collective goods usually address the problem of whether a particular good will be provided to a group. In practice, many collective goods can be provided in many different ways. Improving the quality of available leadership, for example, can change the way the good is provided, increase benefits for all participants, and supply large amounts of "profit" for the organizers – profit which the leaders may use to further additional national goals of their own.

Many of the collective goals within peasant society can be achieved within groups of widely varying sizes and structures.[15] *Large* groups are

---

[15] With little savings and money, with a lack of trained leadership, and with costly and unreliable mechanisms for enforcing contracts, it is not surprising to find insurance and

workable, given problems of excludability and defection, only when there is skilled leadership or enforceable contracts. Within a larger group, it is true, the security and viability of the insurance can be improved. A large insurance company is more likely in the long run to provide the promised benefits than is a small company with few members. But large groups require better leadership and record keeping. Although they may be erratic and offer low-quality insurance compared to village-wide or even intervillage associations, the small group arrangements require less capable leadership and are often the only organization possible.

In a small mutual aid group, if one member gains a free ride, the loss of his contribution will be perceptible to all and the group may dissolve. Without skilled leadership or enforceable contracts, exclusion is much easier in small groups. In an eight-man cooperative, if a peasant drops out of the group after the other seven have spent the day helping him plant his crops, he will be blackballed from all similar groups as unreliable. Small groups may be far less rewarding over a number of years than larger groups, but they are viable when there is little or no trusted leadership because there are fewer problems of coordination and incentives. If a skilled leader can convince peasants to join a larger mutual aid group, there is a potentially substantial profit both for the peasants and the leader. The Hoa Hao and the Communists, for example, both established village-wide labor pools to which everyone was required to contribute a few days of labor. This labor was used for emergency purposes to supplement the small labor groups in special situations such as a small local flood or a rampaging water buffalo. Furthermore, all four organizations established supravillage exchange programs whereby resources were transferred to villages in different areas as the need arose, giving local villages or congregations access to insurance for natural disaster or war-related damage in their area.

The acquisition of new skills by peasants and the expansion of communications networks make it possible for small fragmented political and religious movements to be linked into wider, more effective organizations. In 1916, a few years before the Cao Dai began to consolidate many small local religious sects into a region-wide religious movement, the director of the Sûreté Générale described the changes taking place in sects and secret societies. Whereas in the past their activities had been localized, "the new conditions of modern life, the multiplication of means of communications, have favoured the development of broader groups. Better organized or better led associations tend to aggregate and absorb

agricultural cooperatives supplied on a quasi-collective basis rather than on a market basis in peasant society.

the sporadic societies which exist over the whole country."[16] At different times, all four of the groups discussed here expanded by absorbing local groups into a large organizational framework. They were able to do this both because they could manage larger networks and because they had incentives to offer local leaders who joined the larger organization.

Regional variations

The two older regions of Vietnam, which the French called Tonkin or Northern Vietnam, and Annam, or Central Vietnam, differed markedly from the newer Southern region, called Cochinchina. The regions differed not only in their level of wealth and modernization but also in their village institutions. The different institutional frameworks affected the types of organizations and incentives which could operate in the villages.

In Annam and Tonkin, village organizations provided irrigation and were important in determining and adjudicating conflicts over property rights. The villages, through the village notables and the village chief, also parceled out communal land to the members of the village. This communal land averaged one-quarter of all farm land.

Most of the land in Cochinchina had been opened to settlement under the French so the area still had a frontier quality. Irrigation was by rainfall, there was little communal land and property rights were based on French titles rather than local government. Village organizations were much less developed than elsewhere and it was possible for landlords to control/ own huge estates without even living in the villages. These large absentee landlords dominated the administration at the expense of peasants and local smaller landlords as well. Further, Cochinchina was a much wealthier area, which supplied nearly all the colony's rice and rubber exports. There was much less landholding – most peasants were tenants – but the standard of living of laborers, tenants, and smallholders and small landlords was generally much higher than in the older areas.[17]

Catholics

Following the Japanese surrender in 1945, the Viet Minh swept through Vietnam and sought to expand their support. An important element of their coalition were the Catholics who at that time comprised about 10 per

[16] Hue-Tam Ho Tai, "The Evolution of Vietnamese Millenarianism" (Ph.D. dissertation, Department of History, Harvard University, 1977), p. 109.

[17] A detailed analysis of the regional differences before and under colonialism can be found in Popkin, *The Rational Peasant* (Berkeley and Los Angeles: University of California Press, 1979), chapter 4, "Corporatism and Colonialism".

cent of all Vietnamese.[18] Ho Chi Minh himself attended Christmas mass in 1945, there were Catholics in his cabinet, and one of his special advisors was a high-ranking member of the Church hierarchy in Vietnam. The eventual split between Communist-led forces and the Catholics has tended to efface from memory the antagonisms between native Catholics and the French. Even after the split between Catholics and the Viet Minh, no white soldiers were allowed in the areas controlled by the Catholics![19]

The pre-colonial Catholic hierarchy was dominated by Europeans. However, native priests openly struggled for power, and by 1945 the Church had a predominantly Vietnamese hierarchy, and the foreign missions had lost their grip on the native Church.[20]

The organizing power of the Church lay with the priests who were the quintessential political entrepreneurs. There was one fully trained priest for every thousand to fifteen hundred parishioners. Conversions among the elite succeeded, not only because of the appeal of the religion itself, but because of tangible, material benefits – science, cannon, European education – that the priest could offer as proof of the religion's validity. Conversion of the elite gave access to the peasantry and afforded the priests bureaucratic leverage when offering incentives to prospective converts. The priest, moreover, could raise local funds to support his organization by providing more welfare and insurance benefits than could village notables seeking personal profit. Lastly, the priest could provide better adjudication, and at less cost, to the faithful. The faith of Catholicism was attractive, but the material benefits were crucial in solidifying the bonds of the faithful. During the colonial period, for example, when anticlericalism swept the administration of Vietnam, and Catholic ability to manipulate the bureaucracy for the benefit of followers diminished, the Church was threatened by "wholesale defection".[21]

The Church grew because it had an organization that could attract peasants, and because it could further elite ambitions, not because it had official support. If success had been due directly to French policy, then Catholicism would have been strongest in Cochinchina, where French administration was more direct.[22] Catholicism spread among the urban elite of all three areas of Vietnam, but its major numerical growth was in Tonkin and northern Annam. By 1945, 20 per cent of the peasants in these

---

[18] For the early success of the Church in Vietnam, see chapters 3 and 4 of *The Rational Peasant*, in which the incentive system and organizational techniques of the Jesuits are discussed.

[19] Joseph Buttinger, *Vietnam: A Dragon Embattled* (New York: Praeger, 1967), pp. 1021–2.

[20] Thompson, *French Indochina*, pp. 473–5.

[21] Ibid., p. 274.

[22] Gran, for example, notes the opposition among colonists to the Church's acquiring land in Cochinchina. Gran, "Vietnam and the Capitalist Route", p. 291.

poor and harsh areas were Catholics, in spite of the hostility of so many colonial administrators to Catholicism.[23] The number of Catholic adherents increased because the church could effectively manipulate economic and political levers. It attracted the upper-class elite in significant numbers by offering them access to modern education in Quoc Ngu and an advantage over non-Catholics in access to jobs within the bureaucracy. Throughout Vietnam, and especially in Cochinchina, the new "modern" elite was disproportionately Catholic.[24] The church then used its elite contacts for leverage in the countryside.

Most land not under cultivation in Annam and Tonkin was marginal. Such land was worthless to individual entrepreneurs because the capital and labor inputs necessary to put the land into cultivation made such efforts unattractive as short-run profit ventures. The Catholic Church, however, turned vast tracts of swamp and wilderness into land that could support starving peasants. Many peasants abandoned their overburdened villages for the better life the Church was promising on this earth. Dedicated priests provided the moral and social discipline necessary to colonize the new lands; the Church itself provided the necessary financial support:

In the last century nothing existed but marshes, a permanent flood where the reddish waters of the estuaries merged imperceptibly with the tidal flow from the sea. But in this region of mud and brine missionaries dug canals, bringing into existence a checker board of green islands and attracting a population. . . . The very landscape was clerical. . . . Each square, with its Church in the middle as a parish; the curé was the lord and the parishioners his serfs.[25]

Catholicism's rural growth came predominantly from the conversion of the poorest peasants, and Catholic villages often were situated on the most marginal land. Yet, when compared with neighboring villages, Catholic villages were "markedly more prosperous".[26] This emphasizes the tremendous economic benefits that stability could bring to peasants when coupled with a flexible policy of taxation that forgave in bad years. Additionally, aided by Catholic officials, Catholic coolies obtained a disproportionate share of public-works jobs; for the same reason, Catholic villages were less subject to abuse by mandarins. The village priest could

[23] Dennis Duncanson, *Government and Revolution in Vietnam* (New York: Oxford University Press, 1968), pp. 103–4, 390.
[24] Milton Osborne, "Continuity and Motivation in the Vietnamese Revolution: New Light from the 1930s", *Pacific Affairs* (1978), 100–5, 134, 161–2; Duncanson, *Government and Revolution*, pp. 103–4.
[25] Lucien Bodard, *The Quicksand War: Prelude to Vietnam* (Boston: Little Brown, 1967), p. 211.
[26] Thompson, *French Indochina*, pp. 273–4.

blackmail the corrupt, intercede directly with the administration, and dictate to loyal Catholics within the government.[27]

If a Catholic village chief tried to use his powers for personal gain, the priest could bring moral and political power to bear against him. If an outside landowner tried to take over the lands in a Catholic village by bureaucratic manipulation, he faced a priest who could call on an organized church, not an isolated group of notables with limited legal and political resources.

In addition to opening new lands in Tonkin and Annam, priests often gained access to villages by manipulating power struggles within a village. If a rich man, for example, stole the land of a poor man, and if the poor man converted to Catholicism, the priest would then go to court to plead his case. Sometimes, by skillfully utilizing judicial procedures, Catholic villages were able to appropriate the lands and water of non-Catholic villages.[28]

The Catholics did not win as may adherents in rural Cochinchina as they did in Tonkin and Annam. The Church had always seen westward migration as an obstacle to conversion in Cochinchina.[29] Although power struggles within and between villages in the older parts of Cochinchina led to many conversions, the rate was lower than in Tonkin and Annam because it was so much easier for the peasants of Cochinchina to simply "exit" from their villages for the new lands of the western frontier. Once the French canals were dug and the area drained, moreover, emigration to the frontier could proceed at an individual level, without the help of organizers required by the harsher ecosystems of Annam and Tonkin. On the frontier of Cochinchina there were countless small-scale secret societies with their native entrepreneurs to whom the peasants could turn for help and who could successfully compete with the Catholic priests in community formation. Because there were many sources of capital available to the peasants of Cochinchina, they were less likely to need the Church for money and credit. The Church, furthermore, was unable to compete directly with large, private landowners in the new territories because it was denied large concessions of new land.[30]

---

[27] Ibid., pp. 273–4. Also Pierre Gourou, *Les Paysans du delta tonkinois: Etude de geographie humaine* (HRAF no. 1. Paris: Editions d'Art et d'Histoire, 1936), pp. 202–3.

[28] Cao Huy Thuan, *Christianisme et colonialisme au Vietnam* (1847–1914), cited in Christine White, "Revolution and Its Adherents: the Development of the Revolutionary Movement in Vietnam" (unpublished manuscript, 1973), pp. 47–8.

[29] See Popkin, *The Rational Peasant*, chapter 3, pp. 130–1. Also Milton Osborne, *The French Presence in Cochinchina and Cambodia: Rule and Response (1859–1905)* (Ithaca: Cornell University Press, 1969), p. 145.

[30] It is unclear, however, why more peasants in the new territories failed to turn to the Catholics for help after they were fleeced of their land claims by large landowners, who manipulated both titling procedures and French courts to their own advantage. In part, at least, this can be attributed to hostility from French *colons* (who were concentrated in Cochinchina), and to competition from the Cao Dai.

Cao Dai

The Cao Dai have been the least understood of all Vietnamese movements of the twentieth century. Contemporary journalists, to whom they revealed nothing, describe the Cao Dai as a comical syncretic sect combining the beliefs of all the world's major religions and worshiping a pantheon of saints that included Victor Hugo, Joan of Arc, and Charlie Chaplin. Such journalists were so ethnocentric that they even failed to note the common radical–political streak in the three saints.[31]

The Cao Dai was a syncretism of the Vietnamese Three Religion system (Tam Giao), which stressed a merger of Confucianism, Buddhism, and Taoism. It combined the vocabulary of religious Taoism and Taoist techniques of spirit mediumship with the essentials of apocalyptic Buddhism, in which the day of judgment – the future epoch – was imminent. Formally organized in 1926, its adherents included Vietnamese from every socioeconomic class and numbered in the hundreds of thousands within a few years.

There were many similarities in organizational form between Cao Dai, with its Pope and Holy See, and the Catholic Church, on which the early Cao Dai consciously relied for a model. Between 1926, when the first group of Cao Dai sought to win legal status from the French (and the concomitant right to open oratories, own property, and receive certain tax protections), and the Second World War, when nearly a million of the five million-plus Cochinchinese were members, an elaborate hierarchy of over eleven thousand offices (not all filled at one time) developed. Headed by the Pope, the executive branch (Altar of the Nine Spheres) controlled the temporal organization – and eventually the armed forces – of the sect. Nine ministries, including health, agriculture, and education, supplemented the executive branch. There was also a major welfare agency that administered charitable houses for the old, disabled, poor, and orphaned throughout Cao Dai areas. These charitable houses also functioned as recruitment agencies. All members of a local congregation had a role in selecting their leader, who was their link with the higher organization. Local taxes financed the welfare activities and supported the hierarchy.

Cao Dai was based on long-standing beliefs and small local sects and

---

[31] The author has relied heavily for this account of Cao Dai organization on the following works: Jayne S. Werner, "Cao Dai: The Politics of a Vietnamese Syncretic Movement" (Ph.D. dissertation, Department of Politics, Cornell University, 1976); Ralph Smith, "An Introduction to Caodaism, Part I: Origins and History", pp. 335–49, and "Part II: Party Beliefs and Organization", pp. 573–89 (*Bulletin, School of Oriental and African Studies*, University of London, vol. 33); Tai, "The Evolution of Vietnamese Millenarianism". The last contains important revelations about Cao Dai.

secret societies that pre-dated the French conquest, which were introduced into Cochinchina from China. Binding their members with religious oaths and rituals, and offering them self-help and protection, these
sects proliferated until, as estimated by the governor-general of Cochinchina in 1916, they comprised as many as two hundred thousand
Vietnamese in Cochinchina.[32] Indeed, it was acknowledged by the French
that all rebellions in the region between 1860 and 1916 sprang from one or
more of the sects identified with the Tam Giao tradition.

Over 60 per cent of the original Cao Dai elite were administrative
employees of the French, and many of the key founders of the organization were among the highest-ranking Vietnamese in the colony.[33] Their
goals when founding Cao Dai were twofold: (1) to restore the political and
economic influence the French had deprived them of in Cochinchina, and
(2) to restore pride in Vietnamese culture. As Pham Cong Tac, an early
pope, stated, the Cao Dai would "no longer accept the spiritual humili-
ations of before".[34]

How were the men who founded Cao Dai able to further their economic
and political interests? What incentives could they provide to bring the
small organizations into one large organization that could then attract
hundreds of thousands of new members?

With their level of administrative and linguistic competence, and with
their positions in the French colonial system, the Cao Dai founders were
able to provide significant economies of scale and benefits for the small
sects simply by being able to legalize the sects.[35] The scope of the
small-scale organizations could easily be increased by legalization, which
afforded them considerable protection from local enemies. Cao Dai
leaders converted droves of monks and their followers once they began to
win French acceptance of their religion.[36]

With a base in the sects, the Cao Dai were able to attract large numbers
of small landowners and tenants. The religion's success can be attributed
in large part to the organization's ability to offer peasants protection
against the inequities of French courts, marauding notables, and large
landlords.

Under the colonial system entrepreneurs had created vast landholdings
by taking advantage of the sociopolitical incompetence of the majority of
peasants. It was easy to prevent peasants from becoming landowners –

[32] Gran, "Vietnam and the Capitalist Route", p. 517. The Heaven and Earth Society, for
    example, dropping its emphasis on China and opening separate branches for
    Vietnamese only, organized eighty branches in 1900–20 in the region around Saigon
    (Werner, "Cao Dai", p. 123).
[33] Werner, "Cao Dai", pp. 9, 95–6.
[34] Ibid., p. 296.
[35] Tai, "The Evolution of Vietnamese Millenarianism", p. 131.
[36] Werner, "Cao Dai", p. 58.

easy even to steal the land of peasants who did not have the skills to understand and use the French titling procedures and courts. Many landed fortunes were built on the wealth and contacts acquired by interpreters for the French, because such jobs provided a Vietnamese with the knowledge to use the system against others. In Cochinchina capitalism did not threaten the peasants because they lacked the economic competence to handle markets, risk, and entrepreneurship; rather, the problem was that a colonial dual-language system with extreme inequality of access to courts and property rights provided enormous uncertainty for peasants.

In many areas of Cochinchina, there were large landlords whose landholdings and fortunes were gained and/or solidified by using the French courts against their neighbors. As a French administrator reported of one such large landowner:

Thefts of fish from the ditches, expulsion by force of smallholders, the burning of harvests belonging to his neighbors, and physical attacks by hired assailants at his command have served in the preceding years to intimidate the population of the region who dread this man. Brought to the tribunal, [he] always succeeded in squashing the affair by buying witnesses and intimidating his adversaries.[37]

Village officials often attempted to block surveyors and thereby maintain peasant dependency and insecurity. Peasants complained to journalists that surveying was to their advantage, that if their lands were surveyed, then village chiefs could not take them. The courts were always available to peasants seeking redress against such manipulations, but the expenses of a dual-language system gave considerable advantage to the more affluent. As one newspaper noted, a court suit is "all that is necessary to worry an adversary for long years, force him to onerous expense, and even ruin him completely unless the latter, better advised, decides to come to terms".[38] This was no minor problem: at least 30 per cent of all land in Cochinchina is estimated to have been subject to title contest![39] And the success of many of the small sects that preceded the Cao Dai was directly linked to struggles against large concessionaries trying to steal lands via legal manipulations and deed-juggling.[40]

With so many adherents in high-level administrative positions, the Cao Dai protected their members from landlords whose initial opposition to the movement was strong.[41] In 1928, two years after Cao Dai was founded, and when membership was already over two hundred thou-

---

[37] Gran, "Vietnam and the Capitalist Route", p. 332.
[38] Ibid., p. 199.
[39] Ibid., pp. 172, 318.
[40] Tai, "The Evolution of Vietnamese Millenarianism", pp. 143–4.
[41] Werner, "Cao Dai", pp. 68, 162.

sand, a French inspector toured many of the frontier areas of western Cochinchina. He found Cao Dai successful among only the poor tenants and small landholders and actively opposed by the rich landowners.[42]

The emphasis on protection for the members had considerable appeal to the peasantry. The easy communication among all levels of the organization also resulted in a sense of equality and brotherhood. Cao Dai leaders were selected with far wider participation than were the leaders of village political or religious bodies. Cao Dai's branches throughout Cochinchina enabled peasants to travel and expand their contacts within a context of familiarity and security far broader than that of family or village. "Don't call me a great mandarin", one high-ranking, civil servant Cao Dai told the peasants, "let's be brothers."[43] In another instance, a retired administrative deputy recruiting for the Cao Dai moved among the peasants addressing them as "brother" (instead of the usual "child" or "boy") and preaching equality and a future without maldistribution of wealth. The contrast between the Cao Dai official's emphasis on equality and protection and the patriarchal deference demanded by the notables and large landholders was not lost on the peasants. The former administrator's egalitarian approach undermined the current administrator's status and prestige.[44] The success of the Cao Dai among peasants also led to the recruitment of educated Vietnamese. Many village schoolteachers, who were generally hostile to, and in rivalry with, landlords and notables seeking to control access to literacy, aided or joined Cao Dai.[45] Indeed, the Cao Dai saw themselves as a modernization of and improvement on past sects; they boasted of being the religion of the educated.[46]

The emphasis on local communities with local collective welfare systems contrasted directly with the dyadic *charity* of the landlords. Cao Dai communities restrained the ability of large landlords to forcibly maintain the dyadic pattern of landlord–tenant relationships whereby landlords played tenants off against one another – distributing resources unequally and developing close relations with some tenants to control others and prevent collective bargaining. Using taxes and dues to build a system of crisis aid for its adherents, Cao Dai weakened tenants' dependence on landlords, as well as the ability of large landowners, through control of notables, to dominate small landowners. This mediation of agrarian relations through the local Cao Dai community with its graduated hierarchy was a distinct change from dyadic, unmediated relations and prompted beneficial changes in the way landlords treated their

[42] Gran, "Vietnam and the Capitalist Route", p. 545.
[43] Werner, "Cao Dai", pp. 115–16.
[44] Ibid.
[45] Author's fieldwork. See also Werner, "Cao Dai", pp. 114–15.
[46] Tai, "The Evolution of Vietnamese Millenarianism", p. 138.

tenants. When landlords follow their tenants into Cao Dai, a French report noted:

The poor classes of the population who practice this religion are flattered to number among their coreligionists their own bosses – members of the bourgeoisie and high functionaries – who treat them with more humanity, benevolence and generosity than in the past. Indeed, one witnesses everyday a rather remarkable change in the attitude of landowners toward their share-croppers and tenants, for instance, when they all belong to Cao Dai.[47]

As the religion developed, some landlords joined the religion for purely instrumental reasons, as a way to stabilize their estates by establishing a religious and social community. A French report noted, for example, of the conversion of Cao Trieu Phat, a Cao Dai leader in the remote southern peninsula:

His conversion seems to have been dictated by considerations of personal interests rather than by sincere religious conviction. It consolidates his position as land-owner in Ca Mau by assuring him of an incontestable moral authority over the population of the region, which is partly a floating population without strong familial and communal traditions.[48]

Cao Dai leaders were searching for forms and methods that would grant them equivalence with Western organizations.[49] The Cao Dai was inspired by the forms of the Catholic Church and competed with it for membership and influence. Its welfare activities – granting persons aid as a matter of right and not as a matter of charity or dependence – were attractive, and in a period when the Catholic Church had not yet Vietnamized its hierarchy, the overtly nationalist, cultural content of the Cao Dai program was an important source of satisfaction and attraction to its membership. Whereas both the Cao Dai and the Catholics could offer welfare and protection against the divide-and-conquer tactics of landlords and notables, only the Cao Dai could immediately offer positions of power

[47] Ibid., p. 135.
[48] Ibid., pp. 135–6. These Cao Dai allied with the Viet Minh in 1945 and retained control of their areas against all opposition throughout the resistance. Although Cao Dai is sometimes called a patron–client system, it has more in common with corporate systems. The value to large landlords of using Cao Daism, instead of a pure dyadic patron–client system to rule estates, is indicative of the management problems involved in trying to extend agrarian management techniques used with a handful of tenants to large estates involving intermediary agents, contracts and clienteles. The example of Cao Trieu Phat deserves extended comment. Despite the French cynicism about him, Phat was both the entrepreneur *par excellence* and a left-wing activist who was influential in earlier political parties before joining the Cao Dai, reminding us that not all landlords were conservative. The example of Phat also reminds us that although I have emphasized the political manipulations of large landowners and their attempts to structure their relations with their tenants so as to keep tenants at a decided disadvantage, there were indeed many landlords who were true economic entrepreneurs and popular leaders of their tenants, men who mobilized land, labor, and capital to benefit landowner and tenant alike.
[49] Woodside, *Community and Revolution*, pp. 186–7.

and influence to local bonzes, administrators, and teachers; the Catholics could offer such positions only after a decade or more of special training, at best.

The Cao Dai built a court system copied from the French. Just as peasants in the seventeenth century searched out Jesuits to hear their court cases and dispense a more equitable and economical justice than the native mandarins were dispensing, so the Cao Dai leadership often was sought by its adherents to hear cases and dispense justice.[50] This is a clear example of how an entrepreneur can increase profit for himself and for all the members of his religion and strengthen the bonds of the religion by increasing contacts among members. Along with better justice for commercial transactions than could be obtained from the French, there was also less uncertainty and risk in dealings among members of the Cao Dai, as well as some profit to the religion from court fees (whether in gratitude or in actual payment). This was an incentive for Cao Dai adherents to deal only with one another and was an economic benefit for the organization, as well as for its peasant supporters.[51] It is, therefore, no coincidence that in time many rural businessmen and large landowners, seeing the advantage to themselves of being part of a more stable administrative system than the French provided, joined the Cao Dai.

In some areas, Cao Dai membership was so widespread that it threatened a breakdown of the French administrative system. So successful were they at recruiting the administrative elite that in some districts the French found that the Cao Dai hierarchy and the provincial administration were almost one and the same.[52] One report to the Minister of Colonies complained that in areas where Cao Dai was growing in strength the idea of non-collaboration was spreading – administrative contact was becoming more difficult, notables were turning indifferent, and bailiffs were even being threatened.[53]   The success of Cao Dai challenges the popular belief that the growth and expansion of the modern state strips away and destroys traditional organizations – leaving the peasant naked and defenseless in the face of capitalism and colonialism. On the contrary, Cao Dai is an example of how the skill and resources of the modern administrative system can be a stimulus to the expansion and improvement of traditional organizations. The robes and ceremonies, the spiritualism of the Cao Dai, should not obscure the political importance of the institu-

[50] Werner, "Cao Dai", p. 125.
[51] This point is made by Max Weber in his discussion of Protestant sects. See "The Protestant Sects and the Spirit of Capitalism", in *From Max Weber*, translated and edited by H.H. Gerth and C. Wright Mills (New York: Oxford University Press, 1958), pp. 320–2.
[52] Werner, "Cao Dai", p. 113.
[53] Ibid., pp. 130–1.

tional framework that the religion developed to deal with peasant problems, nor the improvement it represented over dependence on village landlords and notables. Cao Dai was a religious movement, but it served other interests as well. Some of the Cao Dai elite were interested in a political base for the long-run battle against colonialism and political dependence; others were interested only in the profits to be made from operating a large-scale religious/insurance/protection system. In either case, there was a nonzero-sum situation in which enough resources were generated to grant benefits to both the elite and the members. As Tran Van Giau, one of Vietnam's most prominent Marxist historians, summed it up for Jayne Werner, the Cao Dai "had a bit of something for everybody."[54]

Hoa Hao

The Hoa Hao religion takes its name from the Cochinchinese village Hoa Hao, birthplace of Huynh Phu So, who founded a peasant-oriented religious movement that combined a "Calvinistic", this-worldly Buddhism with virulent anticolonialism. It is a far more explicitly millenarian, anti-colonial, and egalitarian religion than Cao Dai.[55] So built his movement on the teachings of Phat Thay Tay An, the Buddha of Western Peace and the founder of a religious organization called the Buu Son Ky Huong.[56] During the uncertainty and disorder of the Second World War and the Japanese occupation, So used his writings and personal magnetism to transform a small religious organization based on long-standing ideas into a fervid following of more than a million adherents (mostly in the newer, "pioneer" areas of western Cochinchina) in less than five years.

The Hoa Hao never developed more than a rudimentary national structure before the Communists assassinated So in 1947. The heart of the

---

[54] Ibid., p. 52, n. 87.

[55] Francis Hill, "Millenarian Machines in South Vietnam", *Comparative Studies in Society and History*, 13 (1971), 331.

[56] Phat Thay Tay An founded Buu Son Ky Huong in 1849. The Buu Son Ky Huong advocated remaining within society (**nhap the*) not withdrawal into monastic life. Its heroes were Buddhist emperors who could make the transition from monk to warrior as the nation's problems demanded. Tay Son ideology was also an influence, in large part because many Tay Son soldiers from Annam had been demobilized in western Cochinchina, where the religion was based. (Tai, "The Evolution of Vietnamese Millenarianism", *passim.*) The religion stressed the accumulation of merit for future life, but its definition of merit was revolutionary: merit was acquired by performing good deeds, not by supporting the monastic order. Followers were not to be guided by monks, but were to guide themselves. The traditional Buddhist indebtedness to an emperor, moreover, was changed to indebtedness to one's country. Opposition to French rule was an article of faith. (Tai, "The Evolution of Vietnamese Millenarianism", p. 126.)

organization was the Hoa Hao council in every village of converts. Above these men was a civil–religious hierarchy concerned with social welfare and propagation of the faith, as well as a military "self-defense" organization. After So's death the military forces split into four groups led by his four main military lieutenants, so that the basic organizational units for the sect were the village and province for welfare activities and the military region for political affairs. In contrast to the Cao Dai's elaborate system of titles and ranks, the Hoa Hao functioned with only village and provincial committees, a small national committee, and the four armies.

Huynh Phy So, the "mad bonze", was born in 1919 and exhibited no particular ambition or talent in his youth.[57] Son of a village notable, he failed the French-oriented primary school and spent his days aimlessly wandering through the village, his nights catching crickets. So fell ill and was treated at length by doctors, soothsayers, and mediums – none of whom was successful. His illness was apparently a dual disease of malaria and spermatorrhoea, a combination that left him frail and in a constant state of nervous exhaustion. Villagers assigned various causes to the disease, and one belief common at the time was that a goddess was in love with So and wanted his death to have him to herself. Later, it was decided that this three-year illness was a series of trials to mortify his fleshly body – purify it, sanctify it, and enable it to receive and spread communications from the beyond. Whatever the cause, the disease left So pale, emaciated, and with the intense, illuminated stare of a visionary.

When all other cures failed, So's father sent him to a monk where So learned acupuncture, hypnotism, folk medicine, and the history and philosophy of Buu Son Ky Huong. When the monk died in 1939, So returned to his family; still uncured, he projected "light" and a "holy spirit". Soon thereafter, So was cured, whereupon he established next to his family altar a second altar dedicated to Buu Son Ky Huong and began to spread his message.

Word of his new preaching spread quickly throughout the area, and people flocked to hear So speak. His preaching was a poetic, vernacular form of the Buu Son Ky Huong teachings of Phat Thay Tay An. Spreading everywhere by word of mouth, it almost immediately brought tens of thousands of persons to follow So's teachings.

So was aware of the political impact of his actions and of the social significance of his religious appeal. His aim was to create a Buddhist society of this world and not of the next:

[57] A.M. Savani, "Notes sur le Phat Giao Hoa Hao" (unpublished manuscript, 1951). Major Savani was the key source of data on the Cao Dai and Hoa Hao for the French. As head of French intelligence in Cochinchina, he collected and translated much valuable material. (See Werner, "Cao Dai", pp. 33, 52.) Unless otherwise specified, Major Savani's work is the source for this summary of So's life.

According to observations the Buddhist teaching founded by the Sakyamuni Buddha has as its foundations the doctrines of compassion, altruism and universalism with regard to all living creatures. I see him as a radical ideological revolutionary because of the following sentences:

"All living creatures are endowed with a Buddha nature",

and

"Buddha is the same and equal to all living creatures."

Being equal in nature, the reason living creatures are not equal with Buddha is due to their level of enlightenment and not that they cannot advance on the same level of the Buddha. If in this world the advanced peoples still oppress backward peoples, this is contrary to Buddha's teachings. The Sakyamuni Buddha could not practically apply his teachings during his lifetime due to the unfavorable environment in India at that time. Thus, he just elucidated the spirit of his teachings. Presently the development of mankind has reached a satisfactory level. Along with scientific advances, we can put into practice those teachings and realize an equal and humane society. Thus I will coordinate the altruistic, compassionate heart I have absorbed with a method to organize a new society to practically serve my compatriots and mankind.[58]

So began with attacks on the waste, ritual, and superstition in the daily life of the peasant. The stress was on interior faith not impressive appearance. Offerings were to consist only of water, flowers, and incense, and were to be made only to ancestors, national heroes, and Buddha – it was not necessary to make offerings to other spirits or to monks. Sacrifices to gods were not necessary, he explained, for "gods are not like the functionaries here below, corrupt, dishonest, and extortionary, distributing their favors for recompense".[59] He attacked monks who tried to convince people that the way to earn merit and prepare for the millenium was through gifts to them, not through good deeds.[60]

Simplicity and sincerity were central to So's preachings. His religion was also called Buddhism of the Home, because of its emphasis on obligations to fatherland or family. Four prayers a day were said at home – for family, for nation, for Buddha, and for the little people "to free themselves from profound ignorance".[61] Funerals were to be simple, for "what use is the expenditure of much money on the pretext of materializing feelings of filial piety, fidelity, and friendship toward the dead, when it would have been better to express these same feelings when they were living?"[62] Similarly, there was to be no haggling or bargaining over

[58] Huynh Phu So, *Sam Giang Hue Duc Huynh Giao Chu* (compiled by Hoa Hao faithful. Saigon, 1962), p. 450. The author is deeply grateful to Hu-Tam Ho Tai for translations from So's works.
[59] Savani, "Notes", pp. 64, 72.
[60] So, *Sam Giang*, p. 9.
[61] Savani, "Notes", p. 65.
[62] Ibid., p. 64.

marriage; the emphasis was on free choice. Alcohol, opium, and gambling were to be abjured.

So was interested in liberation and social change, and there is a veiled anticolonialism in his preachings. Much of his hostility was directed at what he derisively called "civilization":

> In the cities, people rush to produce bad habits
> For boys and girls.
> People smoke opium, drink liquor,
> Prostitutes and pimps pump away your blood
> Whoever takes a careful look at society
> Cannot help but wail for the decadent nation.[63]

> Civilized people change their faces [makeup],
> Wearing bright clothes they enjoy themselves day after day.
> They display voluptuous figures
> And in the streets say amorous words.
> In their hearts are evil things,
> Their words, their speeches are too tricky.[64]

> Our ancestors were ignorant
> But they were more honest and sincere than people today.[65]

So made his sympathy for the poor and his derision of the rich abundantly clear in his vernacular style. His poems ridiculing the rich and their adoption of French ways were particularly popular:

> As for the rich, they are busy competing with others
> To fill up their coffers and their safes.
> They amass worldly goods and try to hold on to them,
> Afraid that they will be stolen by thieves.
> They worry about becoming famous and powerful,
> They fear that the poor will not be able to pay them
> Back their money.[66]

Although So decried the callousness of the rich and favored ending class distinctions by treating all alike and abolishing special privileges, he did not preach the class struggle or attack religion. His opposition to Marxist ideology was explicit:

---

[63] Huynh Phu So, *Suu Tap Thi Van Giao Ly Cua Duc Huynh Giao Chu* (compiled by Hoa Hao faithful, Saigon, 1962), p. 81.
[64] So, *Sam Giang*, p. 65.
[65] Ibid., p. 66.
[66] Ibid., p. 108.

In this twentieth century,
People try to get rid of religion.
Credulous people think that
One must compete through force.
Thus one can get power and fame
By preventing religious people from doing good.
People are welcoming this new wave in great numbers.
Their spirits are aroused,
They despise the old national customs
And say that religion is an opiate
And that whoever tastes it becomes addicted to it
And no longer cares to struggle.[67]

Because So "did not submit to the politically strong or scorn people in difficulties", and because he rejected class distinctions and treated everyone equally, he was called "the general of the common people".[68] So effective were his teachings at winning converts and so frantic and devoted his followers that urban Communist orators, "impressed and annoyed by his power and ability to hypnotize peasant audiences by 'speaking volubly without end'", made "shameless pilgrimages" to ask So for his secrets and to study his techniques.[69]

The rapid success of the Hoa Hao must be understood within the context in which it flourished. Western Cochinchina was an area where violence and instablility were more widespread than in other parts of Cochinchina, particularly during the Second World War.

Most of the rice exported from Cochinchina came from the western part of the colony, where there had been only scattered settlements before the French drained the area. Vast concessions had been granted in this area, and the landowners, some with as many as three thousand tenants, expended considerable effort to keep the peasants in a state of dependency and prevent them from buying themselves out of tenancy into small ownership. The scarcity of labor (compared to the rest of the colony) made population control essential to profit maximization for the land lords; as in the older areas of the colony, peasant access to new lands or mini-frontiers was often blocked. Provincial officials were sympathetic to the landowners who tried to keep lands either in their own hands or in wasteland. Peasants who occupied and sought to cultivate new lands were constantly harassed; often the lands were seized from them and given to large landowners.[70] The fight to control tenants and maintain landlord domi-

[67] Ibid., p. 99.
[68] Toan Anh, *Tin Nguong Viet-Nam* (Saigon: Khai-Tri, 1968), p. 386.
[69] Woodside, *Community and Revolution*, p. 189.
[70] Gran, "Vietnam and the Capitalist Route", pp. 325–8. In addition to the sources cited, much of this material was developed in interviews conducted by the author with the Hoa Hao in 1966, 1967, 1969, and 1970.

nation also meant an active opposition to the development of any communal land sources.

The grand landowners also discouraged any peasant action likely to increase their personal sociopolitical competence to deal with collective action or markets. Peasants were usually forbidden to sell any excess paddy themselves; they were required to have the landlord sell it for them.[71] Tenants were provided with buffalo, tools, and food; their taxes were paid for them by the landlords.[72] Tenants who preferred to obtain these resources on their own in the market were sent away. The large lords clearly did not want tenants to develop their own contacts and skills.[73] In addition, tenants were not allowed to organize themselves to provide additional drainage or irrigation ditches for the large estates. Although additional drainage and irrigation often would have been of great profit to the landowners, there was clear aversion to any development of horizontal organization among the tenants. There was, furthermore, a general pattern of opposition and hostility by these large owners to the establishment of schools. Peasants often were forbidden even to make improvements in their own tenancies if these improvements could be interpreted as a long-term, secure claim to the tenancy. Peasants could recall being forbidden to plant fruit trees: the trees were of value only after many years, and many landlords refused to guarantee the long-term tenancy – dependence was to be wholly upon the estate owner. In short, landlords would not make long-term commitments to tenants even for the prospect of increased profits.

In this western area there were always transients and drifters. Except for the early years of the Depression, there was always money to be made in the frontier areas. Coolies and tenants from the Saigon area, for example, could slip away for five or six years, earn some money, and then return to pay their debts and rejoin their families.[74] In addition, there was a steady stream of men heading West to escape criminal charges, and orphans with nothing to lose by migrating.

Regardless of the fluctuation in international prices, the general level of subsistence in western Cochinchina was comparatively high, as the migration from older areas would suggest. But many people, although secure against a true subsistence crisis of the kind so often faced in Annam or Tonkin, found themselves with a surplus, but with few or no ways to

---

[71] Pierre Gourou, *Land Utilization in French Indochina* (HRAF no. 2. Washington: Institute of Pacific Relations, 1945), p. 353.

[72] Pierre Melin, *L'Endettement agraire et la liquidation des dettes agricoles en Cochinchine* (HRAF no. 121. Paris: Librarie Sociale et Economique, 1939), p. 23. The landlords then retained the identity cards to restrict peasant mobility (personal research).

[73] Gourou, *Land Utilization*, pp. 352–4, and author's research.

[74] Ibid., p. 521.

slowly or marginally increase their standard of living by investment. It is not surprising, therefore, that Pierre Gourou found a passion for high-stakes gambling: a large stake was needed to buy one's way through the system. Similarly, losses could be easily tolerated because basic subsistence was certain.

The area had a decidedly rough-and-tumble, "wild-west" atmosphere. This unsettled air was most prominent near the Cambodian border, where the vast wilderness area was dominated by gangs fighting for control of smuggling routes and the protection money extorted from residents of the area.

The Japanese occupation of Vietnam in 1940 increased the violence and instability. As administrative controls collapsed, the area became increasingly disorganized. As the credit and market system fell apart, and as production ceased on vast tracts of land, the Japanese tried to extract rice and jute from the area by force of arms. By 1943, bands of smugglers and pirates kept entire villages in a state of constant terror. These were not rebels who robbed only the rich: if they robbed only the rich, it was because the poor had nothing left to give.

Fortune-tellers, small sects, and "prophets" sprouted everywhere. Huynh Phu So was but one among the many prophets to whom the peasants turned for advice, and his was but one of many "messages" that abounded. But the small prophets to whom peasants turned generally held only small followings, no more than a few hundred faithful, attracted over a long period. So was able to expand his following because he had a message that was credible in the abstract and did not require personal transmission by him to win adherents.

So had a talent for organization which facilitated the dissemination of his message. Squads of peasants were taught So's sayings and poems and fanned throughout the area to spread his message. So differed from other prophets because he knew how to "mass merchandise" his message – and how to build a powerful organization from a mass following.

Despite its emphasis on home-centered religious practices, and despite its origins among peasants lacking the skills of the Jesuits, Cao Dai elite, or Communist cadres, the Hoa Hao developed a strong village-centered organization. Its leadership accomplished this by offering peasants resources which lessened their dependence on and control by the large landowners; guaranteeing and adjudicating local property rights and disputes; and collecting local taxes, which were then used to provide both insurance and welfare benefits. Moreover the movement's non-Communist and anti-French position interested the Japanese and allowed for expanded operations and continued growth of the movement during the occupation.

So's early aides came from two sources. In most villages at least a few of the Buu So Ky Huong faithful were willing to take part in a peasant-oriented movement with patriotic and radical overtones. Throughout the area, furthermore, So attracted many outsiders – orphans, retainers of the rich, and others with no place in any village.[75] Many of these followers were directed to become friendly with the Japanese or to work for them, and they later provided the Hoa Hao with many weapons.

With the Buu Son Ky Huong and others as a core, So organized village congregations that charged high taxes.[76] In return, the illiterate adherents received instruction in the teachings of the Hoa Hao. The money was used secretly to build local self-defense forces that would protect the congregations from the turmoil before the coming millenium (as well as from the French). Most important, tax money was used to claim and put into production abandoned land, which was then sold or rented cheaply to believers. The income from such sales and rentals, in turn, supported the supravillage organization. As congregation funds helped to finance agricultural improvements, peasants who belonged to a Hoa Hao congregation became increasingly free from their former total dependence on landlords. Dependence on landlords was further weakened by the establishment of stock-farm cooperatives that provided another source of draft animals.[77] By these means, the leadership acquired great power almost overnight.

Fearful of the fanaticism – ritual murders were not unknown – and the mutual support of congregation members, landlords began to loosen their control over tenants and permitted them to enter the rice market on their own. They finally contented themselves with merely collecting rents, but little or no rents were paid as the peasants began to give their rice to the congregations – in effect daring the landlords to object. Alarmed by the threat of their power, the landlords soon sought to slow it by "finding faith" and joining congregations. By the Second World War, however, neither the landlords nor the French were able to slow Hoa Hao forces, which were powerful enough to prevent village authorities from harassing adherents or acting for large landlords.[78]

Soon the security teams emerged from underground. Effectively controlled by the Hoa Hao committees, they began to protect harvests and property; the Hoa Hao displaced French courts as adjudicators of contes-

[75] Author's research.
[76] The exact rate of taxation has not yet been determined. The variation between areas and the general inflation of that period make accurate information difficult to obtain or assess.
[77] Author's research.
[78] Author's research; see also Pierre Dabezies, "Forces politiques au Viet Nam" (thèse de droit, Université de Bordeaux, 1955), pp. 138–9.

ted land. The security teams also defended against piracy: as the self-defense movement developed into actual armed units, the more adventurous military leaders (such as the legendary Ba Cut) raised a fortune for their religion (and themselves) by charging rich landlords and merchants huge sums to track down and destroy pirates and bandits. Pirate heads were hung on stakes around villages to serve notice that the Hoa Hao armed forces were in the area and protecting their own.

Money was available among the peasants to finance a major organization. The peasants willingly paid heavy local "taxes" in a situation where they were able to place long-run faith in the credibility and viability of the movement and its leaders and to expect a return on their investment via insurance, protection, and welfare benefits.

As the movement increased in numbers, frequent conversions among the French-controlled provincial troops nullified or hindered the ability of the French to move against the Hoa Hao. Their several attempts to detain or deport So, for example, were unsuccessful. They were equally helpless to prevent the Hoa Hao from restoring and using as resistance centers the pagodas destroyed by the French in the nineteenth century.[79] The Japanese and So, on the other hand, exploited each other to mutual benefit. Desperate to obtain for their war effort as much rice as possible from Cochinchina, the Japanese willingly permitted So to travel the western region as long as he calmed the anxieties of the peasants and urged them to continue rice production. (The Japanese, of course, were by no means entirely hostile to non-Communist, anti-French movements.)

As So's fame spread he began to attract urban activists searching for a movement. After the Communists destroyed the urban Trotskyite movement in 1945–6, many Trotskyites sought to work with the Hoa Hao.[80] In 1945, So had standardized rules for local Hoa Hao communities. Now, due perhaps to Trotskyite influence, he undertook the formation of a political party. Disturbed by the fanaticism of his followers, So argued that "to lead a crowd by religion is to lead it by fanaticism, while [to lead] it by politics is to appeal to reason".[81] The platform of Dan Xa Dang, or Social Democratic Party, advocated socialism, large, commonly owned farms for those who wanted them, and a rejection of inequality. But So did not change his stance toward Marxism.

The formation of the party finally convinced the Communists that So had to be eliminated. Shortly after the party's formation, he was assassinated by the Communists. As a precaution to ensure against his return to life, So's body was hacked into three pieces, and each portion was buried

[79] Savani, "Notes", pp. 14–15.
[80] Author's research. Also Savani, "Notes", pp. 11, 26.
[81] Ibid., p. 24.

in a separate grave. Still uncertain, and still apparently imbued with the local fear of spirit vengeance, the Communists later dug up the pieces to make sure that So was, indeed, dead.[82]

Communists

Thousands of Vietnamese joined the Communist Party before 1941, and most of them had their determination reinforced by French prisons. But whatever the intensity of their determination and their previous efforts, there is no reason to believe that they would have so dominated Vietnamese politics after 1945 had the Japanese not occupied Indochina, and had the Communists not fundamentally changed their approach after 1940.[83] Communist success ultimately depended on Ho Chi Minh's change from a "cosmopolitan ideologue" emphasizing global imperialism, class struggle, and the proletariat to a "back-woods insurrectionist" who dropped earlier views about culture and religion as nothing but tools with which people were oppressed.[84]

When Ho Chi Minh returned to Vietnam in 1941 after roaming Asia for years as a Comintern delegate, the preoccupation of the Soviet Union with the war in Europe gave him a freer hand to develop a local Communist strategy than at any previous time. The weaknesses that were the result of rigid Comintern directives and that had kept the Communists in a precarious position could now be overcome, and Ho, drawing on his

[82] Ibid., p. 29.
[83] This is not intended as a comprehensive history of the Communist Party; I have concentrated on rural organization. For fuller accounts, on which this summary has relied heavily, see Huynh Kim Khanh, "Vietnamese Communism: The Pre-Power Phase (1925–1945)" (Ph.D. dissertation, Department of Political Science, University of California at Berkeley, 1972); William Duiker, *The Rise of Nationalism in Vietnam 1900–1941* (Ithaca: Cornell University Press, 1975), *The Communist Road to Power in Vietnam* (Boulder, Colorado: Westview Press, 1981), "The Revolutionary Youth League: Cradle of Communism in Vietnam", *China Quarterly*, 13 (1962), 475–99, "The Red Soviets of Nghe-Tinh: An Early Communist Rebellion in Vietnam", *Journal of Southeast Asian Studies*, 4 (1973), 186–98, "Building the United Front: The Rise of Communism in Vietnam, 1925–1954", in Jospeh Zasloff and McAlister Brown (eds.), *Communism in Indochina* (Lexington, Massachusetts: D.C. Heath, 1975), pp. 3–26, and "The Comintern and Vietnamese Communism" (Southeast Asia Program, Monograph no. 37. Athens, Ohio: Ohio University for International Studies, 1975). Additional information on the Second World War comes from John T. McAlister, *Vietnam: The Origins of Revolution* (New York: Alfred A. Knopf, 1969); King Chen, *Vietnam and China 1938–1954* (Princeton: Princeton University Press, 1969); Archimedes Patti, *Why Vietnam?* (Los Angeles and Berkeley: University of California Press, 1980); and David Marr, "World War II and the Vietnamese Revolution", in Alfred W. McCoy (ed.), *Southeast Asia Under Japanese Occupation* (New Haven: Yale University Southeast Asia Studies, 1980). Unless expressly cited, all information on the policies followed in urban and rural areas is from personal research.
[84] Woodside, *Community and Revolution*, p. 220.

Leninist training and Comintern experience, could reorient his strategy to local conditions.

The Viet Nam Doc Lap Dong Minh Hoi (Alliance for Vietnamese Independence), or Viet Minh Front, was formed by the Communists in 1941 at a low point for Vietnamese communism. All that remained was the skeleton of an underground party throughout the three regions of Vietnam, scattered cells in provincial capitals and industrial areas, and a small organization among tribal groups in the mountainous highlands between Vietnam and China.[85] Expecting a Japanese defeat, the Front was oriented to the postwar period and to the rising tide of Vietnamese nationalism. It reflected a willingness by the Party to work more seriously than in the past with intellectuals and the middle class and to develop a mechanism for the more effective mobilization of "reformist" possibilities among the peasantry.

From the very first days of the Revolutionary Youth League there had been distrust of intellectuals. Although intellectuals had been among the first to sacrifice themselves, they had nevertheless been viewed as "opportunists" and their grievances against the French either downplayed or ignored. Similarly, because the emphasis on workers had been paramount, there had been uneasiness after championing or allying with bourgeois groups.[86] The grievances of the middle class had been ignored, culture and religion had been seen as "weapons to keep the Vietnamese stupid",[87] and nationalism had been seen as "archaic".[88]

Now the Party emphasized national liberation. The move toward nationalism enabled the Communists to tap the growing national awareness among intellectuals and the middle class that was stimulated by the wartime environment. Once-hostile writers, often uninterested in communism or class struggle, were more than willing to propagandize for national liberation and allied themselves with the Communists, who were then the only party interested in mobilization. Soon Viet Minh propaganda, drawing on Vietnamese legends and nationalist feelings, spread throughout the country.

Under the regnant Japanese, the French administered the country until 1945. But throughout the period of occupation, the Japanese constantly encouraged anti-French and non-Communist groups, such as Hoa Hao and the Cao Dai, and parties friendly to Japan such as the Dai Viet. The French responded by doubling the number of Vietnamese in high-level administrative positions and by beginning programs for mobilizing the

[85] Khanh, "Vietnamese Communism", pp. 349–56.
[86] Ibid., pp. 88–9.
[87] Woodside, *Community and Revolution*, p. 169.
[88] Duiker, "Red Soviets", p. 196.

student population before the Japanese could sway them. The Communists directed their members and friends toward many positions in the provincial capitals, especially those directly concerned with mobilizing youth. Leadership of the enormously popular youth and sport program that the French developed throughout Cochinchina (the first legal youth program of any import) was dominated by Communists and their sympathizers. This program and its paramilitary successor under the Japanese were directed by three men, who were either Communists or strong sympathizers from the beginning, and who served in Ho Chi Minh's government after 1946.[89]

By 1943, Viet Minh propaganda was spreading throughout the country, Communists and Communist sympathizers were being placed in strategic locations throughout the administration, and servicemen's groups were being organized in many regiments.[90]

One area where the Communists had survived suppression was among the mountain minorities of Tonkin. The other parties concentrated on the urban Vietnamese elite and rarely bothered with workers or peasants, but the Communists were developing a large following in tribal areas, which were also right on the edge of the Tonkin delta.[91] Indeed, when the Viet Minh entered Hanoi in 1945, non-Vietnamese troops were a large element of the small Viet Minh army, and Chu Van Tan, one of the key Communist military leaders, was himself a Tho-Ti who led the first guerilla band in the mountain base area.

The mountain base so near to the Tonkin delta grew in importance as the Japanese occupation continued. As large tracts of land were forcibly diverted from rice production to jute, and as large quantities of peanuts and rice were commandeered for the war effort, famine entered Tonkin. As early as 1943, with American planes bombing the rail lines to Saigon and preventing the shipment of food, there was starvation in the North. By 1944, there was mass starvation that took between five hundred thousand and two million lives in Tonkin. The Communists were the only political group willing or able to aid the Tonkinese peasantry, and they used the famine to build organizations in villages of Tonkin. With a few weapons, often with nothing but spears or an occasional grenade, Communists organized bands of desperate peasants to attack the Japanese granaries; the distribution of Japanese rice among the participants in the raids was a powerful incentive for peasants to gather to the Viet Minh banner.

When the Japanese staged a coup against the French in 1945, member-

---

[89] White, "Revolution and Its Adherents", p. 27.
[90] Woodside, *Community and Revolution*, p. 227.
[91] McAlister, *Origins of Revolution*, chapters 10 and 12, and "Mountain Minorities and the Viet Minh: A Key to the Indochina War", pp. 771–844.

ship in all political parties swelled; the increase was clearly related to heightened expectations of victory over a debilitated France. The Communists outpaced their rivals by using those national salvation organizations that formed part of the Viet Minh Front as half-way houses to coopt thousands of people. Eager to help their country and/or themselves, doctors, poets, soldiers, and bureaucrats attended the meetings of their respective national salvation associations to discuss what their members could do to create a new Vietnam and what role their professions should play in an independent society. By July 1945, the Viet Minh presence was "ubiquitous": its flags were everywhere; Viet Minh songs were sung in schools and in the streets; and the Association of Vietnamese Students was leaning toward the Viet Minh.[92]

Then in late summer, after the Japanese surrender to the Allies, the Viet Minh, with a Communist Party now "swollen" to nearly five thousand, emerged from the backlands and mountains to mount the August Revolution. Over a period of weeks, they disarmed the Japanese, took over government buildings in regional and provincial capitals, and proclaimed a broad-based government of all Vietnamese. Soon thereafter, Vietnam was occupied by the Allies – the Chinese occupying the northern half of the country, the British the southern half. The next year was the most difficult of all for the Communists. In the north they confronted Chinese-supported groups like the VNQDD as well as rampaging troops of Chinese warlords.[93] In the south they soon confronted the French, returned to power by the occupying British, who helped them drive the Communists from Saigon.

But in the South, in the center, and in the North, the Communists – through the Viet Minh – were able to develop sufficient rural support to gain control of large areas of the countryside and to hold those areas against all other forces, Vietnamese or French, through a long war of resistance. The August Revolution was the beginning, not the end, of

[92] Khanh, "Vietnamese Communism", p. 423.
[93] The VNQDD arrived back in Vietnam with the KMT army and tried to mobilize a following. Although they were able to build a party, their inexperience and incompetence prevented them from attracting an elite via intermediate organizations. With no plans for the future, they were unable to give patriotic but apolitical members of the elite a conviction that alliance with the VNQDD would be efficacious. The Communists even managed to hinder their party-building at times, by setting up dummy parties with coopted ex-members to draw people away (Chen, *Vietnam and China*, p. 124). Despite their friendly feelings for their (Vietnamese) ideological brothers, the KMT forces found themselves working most closely with the Viet Minh (and therefore with the Communists), who were best able to meet the demands of the occupying forces – both the "legal" demands for food and support and the *sub rosa* demands for gold and opium. Indeed, the Viet Minh ended by purchasing substantial numbers of weapons from KMT troops with opium they obtained in the highlands and donations they collected in Hanoi (McAlister, *Origins of Revolution*, pp. 228, 246–55).

peasant mobilization. Thus, during the Japanese interlude and after the August Revolution, while Dai Viet and VNQDD members worried about personal power, cabinet seats and portfolios in a joint government of all parties, the Communists developed meaningful and exciting activities for those eager to secure the future. This allowed them slowly to recruit the best of the elite for their government and party and to make an alliance with those who, although unwilling to become Communists, *were* willing to work with them at a different level of activism and commitment.

These fronts were crucial, not only because they coopted persons from other parties, but also because many of these people were willing to leave the cities and join the Viet Minh in the countryside when the postwar Chinese occupation of the north and the truce with the French came to an end. These allies helped to build the army and administration that were essential for the mobilization of the villages following the August Revolution. By devoting attention to nationalism, culture, and the middle class, the Communists attracted an elite, its "revolutionary friends", whose energies could be channeled into mass organization.

Village mobilisation: Annam

Except for a few key ports and other strategic points along the coast, the greater part of central Vietnam was never reoccupied by the French after the Second World War. The Party, through the Viet Minh, still did not achieve firm control of village administration until after 1950. Seizing power, in other words, was but the beginning of the process of gaining control of the villages and of bringing about economic and political redistribution in the countryside.

Seizing power in the provincial and district capitals did not produce a lasting surge of volunteers among the peasantry. After the August Revolution, as the major Communist theoretician Truong Chinh noted, there were still many areas where even the young "consider the sabotage of roads, the building of earthen barricades, helping the army, as they did forced labor under the imperialist regime".[94] The problem of building support and overcoming free riders was as central to Viet Minh strategy as it was to Cao Dai, Hoa Hao, and Catholics: "How many able people still consider that the resistance war is the affair of the government and the army, and maintain the indifferent stand of 'doing nothing while your neighbor's house goes up in flames'".[95]

During the Second World War, both the VNQDD and the Dai Viet were able to build contact nets of party members in Annam, nets that included

---

[94] Truong Chinh, "The Resistance Will Win", in Truong Chinh, *Primer for Revolt* (New York: Praeger, 1963), p. 206.
[95] Ibid., p. 207.

the major provincial and district capitals, as well as scattered members in many villages. At the time of the August Revolution, they undoubtedly had as many weapons and more party members in the areas studied than did the Communists. Following the revolution, however, the Viet Minh quickly surpassed opposition membership with the support of province- and district-level front organizations. Whereas the Dai Viet and VNQDD limited their appeals to educated members of the elite – particularly administrators and officers of the militia – the Viet Minh targeted other groups in the population. Although they too sought to win members of the elite, they also made concentrated efforts to attract enlisted men and non-commissioned officers, locally powerful guilds like the weavers and fishermen, and machinists and skilled workers at scattered railroad yards and industrial sites. Of particular strategic importance for the Viet Minh's campaign to mobilize the peasantry was their success with the technical cadre who built and maintained the sea walls, bridges, dams, and irrigation works on which many villages depended for survival. The opposition attracted members from the militia, but the Viet Minh was particularly successful with the soldiers who returned to Vietnam following the defeat of France.

The Viet Minh were not sufficiently integrated into the provinces at the time of the takeover to place their supporters in every village administration, nor did they have enough power to ensure that the existing village leadership would carry out their orders. As an intermediate step, they formed intervillage administrations, combining all the villages within a local market area into a larger "supervillage". Through these intervillage Viet Minh administrative committees, the Communities gradually developed the general support and organizational strength with which they were later able to take control of the individual villages and break the control of the notables. But the policies that were first implemented were chosen to be – and were – so popular that little external power was needed to carry them out.

Immediately after the takeover, all schoolteachers and educated youth were "drafted" to begin literacy campaigns throughout the countryside. Sometimes, villagers were not allowed to enter the market-place until they had learned the new words for the day. This was an important policy identifying the Viet Minh with progress and a generalized "antifeudalism", and it was overwhelmingly popular. Both teachers and peasants remember the literacy program for its contrast with the opposition of the previous mandarin bureaucracy and village administrations, which had so often – despite the Confucian respect for literacy – tried to stop the spread of education for the masses as threats to their own power. It is not clear how many older peasants learned to read, but many young persons did, and there is no doubt that teachers developed strong attachments to a regime that encouraged them. The Viet Minh collected large "donations" from the well-to-do (protection money, in the eyes of the rich) and used some of this money to support the teachers, which meant that for the first time the poor in many villages were able to afford education.

Immediate changes were made in the communal land system. Wives of men absent from the village were, for the first time, given land. Before, when the men away from the village had been only poor laborers, their wives' demands had been scorned; now the absentees were often armed and members of the Viet Minh. Communal land that had been diverted to private use by notables was returned to the village.

The bidding system for the communal lands that were auctioned off for village expense money was then reformed. Only small parcels were auctioned, and payments for the parcels were made after the harvest, not at the time of auction. This broke the back of the system whereby only the rich had benefited from the auction; it also added to the money realized from the lands for the village treasury. Both the poor and the villages gained at the expense of the rich. Even more revolutionary (and somewhat controversial) was the policy of giving everyone who had lived in a village more than five years the right to a portion of the communal land.[96]

When the bidding system was changed to increase the benefits for the poorer peasants, an even more drastic, and more popular, change was made: the customary ladder of rank and seniority by which communal lands were distributed was replaced. First, equalization committees carefully reorganized the parcels to make them as equal in value as possible (which, of course, coopted a few villagers and heads of family into close working relationships with the intervillage committees). Then, random lotteries were instituted for the distribution of the communal land. Instead of a regressive system in which the rich picked first, in most villages a new system was introduced in which everyone had an equal chance for every parcel.

This new lottery system, after a period of confusion and tension, gained widespread support for the clear increase in equity and benefits for so many villagers. In addition, it wrested a major source of power from the village notables without exposing the Viet Minh committees to charges of power-grabbing.

Some villagers and administrators fled the area when the Viet Minh took over. These "traitors" left behind them both land and animals, which were promptly appropriated by the intervillage committees. Unlike the communal lands, however, these were distributed by a committee selec-

[96] It is not unreasonable to assume that there might have been serious resistance to this enfranchisement. It is hoped that further research will supply details.

ted at the intervillage level and stocked with Communists and "progress-ive" elements. These resources became a source of patronage by which a small and loyal following in the villages could be built. As a village base in each area began to develop through the favors and patronage of the intervillage committee, the standing notables were replaced by notables elected in open meetings by all villagers. Repeatedly, the Communist candidates overwhelmingly defeated their opposition, which lacked the sophistication to arrange agendas, stack meetings, or prepare slates.[97]

When the Viet Minh gained administrative power within the villages, the body and land taxes were replaced with a single, progressive income tax based on total family productivity and providing a standard exemption for every adult and child.[98] This meant that tax demands would never again squeeze anyone below subsistence. Ultimately, it also meant that when the pressures of war were most severe, the Viet Minh could extract more taxes from the villages than the French had ever done – and without reducing anyone to starvation. By judicious selections to the village committees in charge of assessments, the Communists were able to increase their control of the villages dramatically. The program itself won wide popular support, and serving on the assessment committee enhanced and prestige and following of its members.

Soon after the August Revolution, all debts for which the interest on the original loan exceeded 200 per cent were declared paid in full by the Viet Minh. In reality, the debts were cancelled because the creditors – often outside landlords who had built landed fortunes by manipulating taxes and assessments – fled. The Viet Minh also made serious attempts to impose maximum allowable interest rates, but the attempts were as unsuccessful as others had been in the past. An intermediate result was obtained, however, when village officials ceased to permit evictions before the· harvest. The Viet-Minh-controlled administration was also unwilling to evict persons for small debts.

The results of a campaign to limit all rents to 25 per cent of the crop are more ambiguous, and it is not clear how frequently the Viet Minh were able to control the transfers between tenant and landlord. In some

[97] There was wide support for a lottery system to replace the ranking system for distributing communal lands, but every other issue involving the communal lands ended in either stalemate or unresolved conflict. There were attempts in some villages to turn all lands into communal lands, and this met with opposition from all classes (but not from all persons in each class). There were attempts to limit the distribution of communal lands to only the poor and landless. These also met with widespread opposition and conflict, as did the attempts to convert the communal land into private lands for the laborers, landless, and families of Communists and soldiers.

[98] Supposedly, this change was instituted effectively in 1945, but the data suggest that it took several years before the administrative capacity and credibility to make the change actually existed.

villages, the Viet Minh collected the rent and paid the landlords in an attempt to prevent side payments, but in at least some such cases landlords were still able to demand under-the-table payments.

Viet Minh taxes had clear and negative effects upon landlords. As the demands of war led to tax increases, many landlords found it to their advantage to sell most of their lands to tenants or poor relatives to avoid the increasingly confiscatory taxes for the upper-income brackets. This brought about a *de facto* land-to-the-tiller program even before the Communists organized any campaign against large landowners.

The Viet Minh also subsidized such village-level improvements as increasing the water storage and irrigation facilities. Many of the poorest smallholders could not afford either time or money to dig or improve water ponds on their property. Village neighborhoods often lacked enough ponds to store water for later release into the fields because no one in the neighborhood had time, money, or leadership skills. Now the Viet Minh helped to finance and coordinate extensive additions to waterworks in poor neighborhoods; they even subsidized improvements on small parcels of land held by the poor. The long-run increases in productivity, to say nothing of the support such policies generated, more than repaid the small expenditures of the Viet Minh.

The Viet Minh's prestige as the group responsible for declaring a free and independent Vietnam did not easily translate into the rural support necessary for the resistance. That support was gained by slowly restructuring village government to create a positive system of exchanges between village leaders and peasants that could be tapped for the resources and manpower necessary to build an army. The Communist/ Viet Minh success, therefore, was also due more to the stripping of power from the notables and to progressive taxation than to any land redistribution, as narrowly conceived.

Village mobilization: Cochinchina

The Communists were more active in the rural areas of Cochinchina than they had ever been in the rural areas of Annam and Tonkin (except for Nghe An and Ha Tinh). At the time of liberation, furthermore, the peasants of Cochinchina were by far the most militant. Yet the Communists were not able to duplicate their successes of the other regions; they had fewer Party members and controlled fewer villages in Cochinchina than elsewhere. Whereas in Annam and Tonkin they could capture villages and then remake them, in Cochinchina they had faced a far more complicated task of creating villages. Such a task was hampered by many factors that did not prevail in the other regions. In 1945, for example, their central organization was in almost complete disarray. Moreover, they had to be content with both a stronger French presence and the powerful forces of the Hoa Hao and Cao Dai.

The Communists were active in the peasant movements and tax protests of 1930–1. Throughout Cochinchina, these demonstrations led to violence against landlords and village offices and to the burning of tax rolls and land records. The protests covered most provinces of Cochinchina and involved tens of thousands of peasants; six of these protests even led to the creation of nascent "soviets".

From 1936 to 1939, the Communists, building on old contacts, used the new, more liberal Popular Front standards of political activity to again develop extensive rural ties. When a call was raised in Saigon for an Indochina Congress to discuss the future of the colony, the Communists used the planned Congress – which never occurred – to re-establish rural networks. In 600 of the 1,300 villages of Cochinchina, Committees of Association were formed with the ostensible purpose of discussing grievances to be brought before the Congress. The Communists were forming small self-help fraternal organizations, one-fourth of whose members had been political prisoners. These organizations were built around friendship associations, groups to build straw huts, associations to celebrate the cult of the genii, and insurance systems. So quickly did these groups develop, and so popular were they in the countryside, that the official press was soon referring to them as the "new soviets" and saw in them a portent of future uprisings.[99] After the collapse of the Popular Front, these associations were smashed and many of their members arrested. Still more Communist organizations were smashed and more peasants arrested following the abortive 1940 uprising at the start of the Second World War, but the prisoners from that period were freed in 1945.

Yet another source of Communist support was the youth movement. During the Second World War the key leaders of the French youth and sports movement were either Communist or pro-Viet Minh, and many chapters of the village youth associations were organized by underground Communists or their supporters.[100]

Cochinchina was the area with the most anti-landlord hostility and the greatest demands for "land to the tiller". In much of the region, the August Revolution of 1945 was a widespread agrarian revolt during which

[99] Daniel Hemery, *Revolutionnaires vietnamiens et pouvoir colonial en Indochine: Communistes, trotskyistes, nationalistes, à Saigon de 1932 à 1937* (Paris: François Maspero, 1975), pp. 318, 287, 327. Seventy per cent of the committees were in villages around Saigon, Cholon, Hoc Mon, and Thudaumot; in Gia Dinh from Saigon to Hoc Mon nearly all villages had committees. This suggests the need for further study of the links between these committees and earlier Nguyen An Ninh Association. On committees, see also Khanh, "Vietnamese Communism", pp. 263–6.

[100] Werner, "Cao Dai", p. 255; Khanh, "Vietnamese Communism", pp. 345–6.

land seizures were common.[101] By then many of the large estate owners had lost control of their tenants. In areas where there were smallholders and local landlords, as well as large estates, a credit and marketing infrastructure independent of the large landlords had developed. This gave peasants access to alternate sources of credit, and to rice markets, which meant that any forced dependence on the large landlords was harder to maintain, particularly in the aftermath of the Japanese coup, when administrative breakdowns made it harder for big landlords to rely on village officials to police their tenants. Throughout Cochinchina, there was widespread retaliation against landlords, their clients, their agents, and the village officials with whom they had connived.

Lands were also seized by peasants who had been deprived of what they felt was their legitimate right to ownership of land. During the settling of Cochinchina, large portions of land had been subject to ownership disputes that arose from manipulations of French title processes. This was repeated during the depression of 1930–1, and bureaucrats in the administrative centers profited from their fixed salaries to buy up land from smallholders who could not meet their tax payments (often because of manipulations by these same bureaucrats). Many of these smallholders now moved to reclaim their lands.

But in spite of widespread agrarian hostility to the landlords and bureaucrats, and in spite of the Communists' past political efforts and their many rural contacts, Cochinchina proved to be the weakest of the three areas of Vietnam for them, and they ended up controlling and organizing only about one-third of the population. If the Communists had done as well in Cochinchina as they had in Annam and Tonkin, there would have been no second Indochina war, for there would have been no conceivable base for a non-Communist government.[102]

One obstacle to their success in Cochinchina was the situation following the abortive uprising of 1940, which left the regional committee in disarray and without control of the provincial and local party apparatus it required to proceed effectively during the August Revolution. The distance of Cochinchina from the Party's mountain base in northern Tonkin, moreover, posed severe problems of communication and coordination.[103]

Another obstacle was French power in the south, restored almost immediately after the Second World War. Whereas the Chiang Kai-shek troops who occupied the northern half of the country were visibly anti-French, the British who reoccupied Saigon immediately released

[101] Donald Lancaster, *The Emancipation of French Indochina* (London: Oxford University Press, 1961), p. 421.

[102] Werner, "Cao Dai", pp. 353, 339–44.

[103] Truong Chinh, "The August Revolution", pp. 35–6, in Truong Chinh, *Primer for Revolt*.

French officers and administrators from prison and helped them re-establish an administrative presence in Saigon and the provinces. This drove the Communists out of the cities and into remote areas before they could either ally themselves with (and dominate) or eliminate all their competition. Many of the Trotskyite leaders who were released from prison in 1945 (or who had managed to avoid imprisonment in 1939) were assassinated; many, however, escaped to plague the Communists. As Truong Chinh reviewed the August Revolution in the south, "because of the extremely intricate situation . . . it was not possible to carry out a systematic elimination of the counter-revolutionary elements on Jacobin or Bolshevik lines. . . . For a new-born revolutionary power to be lenient with counter-revolutionaries is tantamount to committing suicide."[104]

Although the Trotskyites had no mass base of their own after 1939, they added to the troubles the Communists had with the Hoa Hao and Cao Dai. Because they sought to hold together all three regions of the country, and because they wanted to be *the* political party to deal with France over the future of Vietnam, the Communists were restrained in their attitudes toward future relations between Vietnam and France. Lacking these prospects, the independent Trotskyites were bound by no such constraints. The moderate behavior of the Communists cost them little in the north, where the pro-Chinese VNQDD and the pro-Japanese Dai Viets were too incompetent at rural mobilization or alliance formation to pose a threat to the Viet Minh; nor did the behavior of either the Japanese or Chinese troops add to the power or prestige of the respective parties. In the South, however, where the competition was keener, Communist moderation was costly, and only one faction of the Cao Dai was willing to align itself with the Viet Minh.[105] With their rabid anti-French stance, the Trotskyites persuaded the remaining Cao Dai and the Hoa Hao sects to form their own front with them.[106]

Furthermore, while the Communists were having trouble establishing an effective alliance with the Hoa Hao and Cao Dai, many areas of Communist strength and many past and former Communists and militants were joining the competition. In the province-by-province history of the August Revolution compiled in Hanoi, a persistent Communist comment on the South was that participants in the 1930 and 1940 uprisings were being lost to the sects and that, for example, Hoa Hao propaganda was attracting "a number of our comrades, whose consciousness was

[104] Ibid., pp. 40–1.
[105] Werner, "Cao Dai", p. 256.
[106] Tai, "The Evolution of Vietnamese Millenarianism", p. 230. The Trotskyites also had developed extensive personal contacts with the rural elite during their electoral campaigns for seats on the colonial council (see Hemery, *Revolutionnaires Vietnamiens*, pp. 248–75).

inadequate".[107] When they formulated their plans for seizure and consolidation of rural power, the Communists emphasized the districts with the strongest tradition of protest and revolution. When the moment came, however, the areas where protest had been most extensive and rabid in 1930 – the areas where soviets had been formed – were solidly Hoa Hao.[108]

There were many other groups in the region, all armed with weapons obtained from the Japanese. Besides the Hoa Hao, Cao Dai, Catholics, and Communists, there were many local sections of the youth movement that the Communists, despite their top-level infiltration of the youth movement, had not been able to control. Some of these groups were controlled by landlords and village officials who had placed their retainers in them to receive military training; others were little more than freelance extortion and protection groups who terrorized all sides equally. There were also sections of the Heaven and Earth Society that had never joined the Cao Dai; some VNQDD, Dai Viet, and Tan Dai Viet; the White Lotus Society; Trotskyites; groups of Chinese (who were Communist, but not yet allied with the Vietnamese Communist Party); the French-Vietnamese Colonel Jean LeRoy, who organized a Catholic militia and controlled (and sometimes terrorized) large parts of the Tan An-Ben Tre area; a brotherhood of railroad workers; gangs of rubber plantation workers; and even armed Boy Scouts.

An important part of Communist strategy was to bring as many of these groups as possible into the Viet Minh, but here too they faced competition. For a while, the anti-Communist Nguyen Hoa Hiep was able to organize a division in the area near Saigon by attracting many of these small groups to his side.[109] In Bien Hoa province, for example, the railroad workers had for years maintained a secret brotherhood associated with the Vietnamese branch of the Heaven and Earth Society. During the war, they raided several French armories and developed a small military force with which they attacked recalcitrant colonial administrators. After 1945, the workers were attracted to the Resistance; hostile at first to the Communists, they allied themselves loosely with a division formed by Nguyen Hoa Hiep from groups similar to their own. Hiep, however, was unable to maneuver politically and create a large and powerful military force. Nor was he able to use his military forces to take control of villages and develop new administrations. Disillusioned, the railroad workers – and the relatives and neighbors they had recruited – allowed themselves to be integrated into a Communist-controlled force. With their back-

---

[107] Tai, "The Evolution of Vietnamese Millenarianism", pp. 221–2, 184, 170, 205.
[108] Ibid., pp. 167–8, 225–6.
[109] Werner, "Cao Dai", pp. 277–8; Tai, "The Evolution of Vietnamese Millenarianism", pp. 236–7.

ground of industrial discipline and organization, and with their secret society experience, three of the men from the railroad workers brotherhood – which never numbered more than a hundred men – soon rose to command their own Viet Minh military units.[110]

In addition to the areas controlled by the Hoa Hao and Cao Dai (both of which eventually made peace with the French in return for control of their own territory), as well as the Catholics, the Communists faced opposition from landowners, many of whom actively collaborated with the French to protect their lands. French outposts and hostile landlords kept the Communists off balance in many areas where the peasantry was sympathetic to the Viet Minh. In an effort to gain effective control of such areas, they sought to reduce the strength of the opposition by appeasing the landlords. In short, they reversed their usual tactics and declared that anyone who seized private property would be severely punished. But the declaration went unheeded.[111] With no effective regional organization to control their own supporters, much less the many competing groups, the Communists were unable to stem the cries for agrarian reform and redress of grievances. "Land to the tiller" was the most potent slogan in the countryside, and some local Communist groups began to redistribute land, cattle, and tools immediately following the August Revolution.[112] Even the Catholic Colonel LeRoy instituted land reforms in the areas he controlled.[113] The Communist attempt to curtail land seizures and defuse the opposition failed: it was unacceptable to a militant peasantry that found ready support from so many other political/religious groups.

In Annam and Tonkin the challenge to the Communists was to restructure villages. In Cochinchina the challenge was to create villages. In the corporate areas of Annam and Tonkin villages controlled large amounts of water and land, as well as dikes, sea walls, irrigation or drainage canals. Political control of a neighborhood, of a few notables, or of lineages generally led either to the splitting of the village or to the support of the whole village. In the open villages of Cochinchina, however, where the public sector was small and the mode of production required little or no widespread cooperation, all the contending groups – Hoa Hao, Cao Dai, Catholics, Communists – had to create their villages, household by household, to control areas.

As many large landlords began to side with the French, the Viet Minh

[110] Author's research. By 1970, at least three of these men had reached the level of regimental commander or provincial Party secretary.
[111] Ellen Hammer, *The Struggle for Indochina 1940–1955* (Stanford: Stanford University Press, 1955), p. 108.
[112] Tai, "The Evolution of Vietnamese Millenarianism", pp. 230, 329, n. 27.
[113] Bernard Fall, "The Political Development of Vietnam: V-J Day to the Geneva Ceasefire" (Ph.D. dissertation, Department of Political Science, Syracuse University, 1954), pp. 444–7.

village committees, reversing their former policy, ratified and defended (as well as extended) the distribution of property seized from collaborators. They also supervised the collection of rents by patriotic landlords to enforce rent ceilings. Although few large, urban-based landlords or landowning bureaucrats supported the Viet Minh, many village-based landlords with 20 to 100 hectares did. Hating the large landlords and the French for pushing them around, many preferred a future of reduced landholdings under the Viet Minh to the colonial situation. Clearly, some of these land lords were protecting themselves against a Communist future. (Many of them, however, never tried to reclaim their lands after 1954, and many of their sons chose to become Viet Minh cadres instead of landowners under the French.)

These economic benefits resulted in many small-scale, voluntary actions for the Viet Minh. When the Viet Minh kept landlords, their clients, and their agents out of power, the peasants benefited economically. It was, therefore, important to the peasants that Viet Minh cadres not be captured. Indeed, the latter travelled almost everywhere in their villages unarmed, confident that someone would make the effort to alert them if the French entered the area. By contrast, village officials siding with the French could operate in most villages only when accompanied by several armed guards.[114]

But far more than either land reform or meeting subsistence requirements was required to develop a power base for the Viet Minh. The decline of the export trade meant that many villages had surplus land. With land uncultivated – over 35 per cent of the land in Cochinchia went out of production in 1946[115] – hunger and land shortages were not important short-run problems for most peasants. What attracted many unorganized peasants to the Viet Minh and gave the Party its entry into many areas was cotton cloth and cotton seeds for planting. Although there was enough to eat in Cochinchina during the period of instability that followed the Second World War, Japanese requisitions of fibre and disruption of international trade had produced a shortage of cloth. It was so complete that large amounts of rice could not be transported because there were no sacks to hold the rice. As will be noted in the following quotation, the cloth shortage even limited the time peasants could spend outside their houses. Just as the Viet Minh distributed sweet potato and manioc seeds to peasants in Tonkin to help them back on their feet after the floods, so the Viet Minh in Cochinchina signaled their concern for the

[114] Jeffrey Race, *War Comes to Long An* (Berkeley and Los Angeles: University of California Press, 1972), p. 3.
[115] Davy Henderson McCall, "The Effects of Independence on the Economy of Viet Nam" (Ph.D. dissertation, Department of Economics, Harvard University, 1961), p. 125.

peasantry with cotton seeds and attacks on stores of textiles. As one peasant recalled his first contact with the Viet Minh:

[During the war] we had money but there were no clothes available to buy anywhere. We had one pair of pajamas. . . . When my wife went to the market I would stay in the house and then when she came back I would wear the pajamas to the field . . . The pajamas wore out and all we had was a single rice sack. . . . When she wore the sack to market I stayed home. . . . Then I wore the sack to the fields. The only time we could go to the fields together was at night when no one could see us . . . we were so ashamed . . . then the Viet Minh came to our village. . . . They had some cloth and a few sacks and they brought some cotton seeds and taught us how to plant them.[116]

Another popular action was the local court the Viet Minh established in each village to arbitrate disputes. Localizing and "Vietnamizing" the courts gave the thousands of peasants engaged in land disputes with large landowners an opportunity for local hearings in a language they spoke and without intimidation of witnesses. The comparative advantage of well-connected and powerful landowners declined, and there were countless reversals of earlier decisions of village councils or French courts. Reversals occurred even in intrafamily disputes:

When Ba Qui's father died he left him six hectares of ricefield, but Mr Ca Dau, a relative of his, seized the land and made it his own . . . When the Viet Minh arose, Ba Qui sued Ca Dau. The Viet Minh invited all the [prestigious men] in the village to a meeting, and they testified that the land belonged to Ba Qui's father and that Ca Dau had seized the land and enjoyed the yield of the land for many years. Then the Viet Minh authorities ordered Ca Dau to return the land to Ba Qui. This was done and Ba Qui didn't demand any compensation payments. So the case was settled very nicely. While Ca Dau had the land and enjoyed the yield of the six hectares of ricefield, he used part of the income to worship Ba Qui's parents, and this is why the authorities sympathized with him and didn't punish him.[117]

In the villages the Viet Minh organized peasants' and women's associations. To pump life into them and to give villagers an incentive to join and to deal with the leaders of these associations, they were given an important voice in all village decisions about land, taxes, and marriage disputes. The peasants' association, for example, had a voice in arbitrating tax disputes and in assessing labor drafts. The women's association was assigned a role in marital disputes; it also gave land and support to households headed by women. The activities of the new local courts also served to increase the prominence of the associations. Because their leaders represented the defendants in all court cases, the villagers had still another reason to remain on friendly terms with the leaders, building up

[116] Author's research.
[117] Rand Corporation interviews with the NLF, interview DT-49, p. 2.

obligations by attending meetings, contributing labor to group projects, and so on.

As in Annam, educational opportunities were greatly expanded. The literacy classes were enormously attractive and demonstrated to many the Viet Minh's break with the "feudal" past. One program was called "Six Months in Two Years": providing basic literacy adapted to the rhythms of rice agriculture, it spaced the six months of teaching over the slack portions of two years. Further, both to make the classes more attractive and to develop exchange relations with the Viet Minh that would continue after the end of classes, the classes were organized as vehicles of collective action and insurance for the students:

We put them into groups of 20 or 30 people. Besides teaching them to read and write, we also helped them with their family or economic problems. For instance, if the house of a student has burned down, then the whole class and the whole unit will devote its effort to helping that particular student. Therefore the students are responsive to the class: they are eager to attend the class because the class is not only where the people learn, but also the place where we discuss other problems of collective interest.[118]

The literacy and self-help programs became an important recruiting ground for lower-level officials and Party members. A major source of personnel for higher branches of the Viet Minh were the two large high schools (Thai Van Lung and Nguyen Van To) they established.

A people's culture and art movement was founded which recruited from the wandering troupes that performed traditional Sino-Vietnamese shows at village festivals, from vagabond musicians, and from village guitar teachers. Much like the bands at Tammany Hall election rallies, these groups helped attract large crowds for Viet Minh village rallies. With their traditional arts and their newly developed skits and songs, they glorified the Resistance and ridiculed the basket carriers (the flatterers and clients of the rich) and Francophile Vietnamese.

These programs demonstrated the concerns of the Viet Minh for the peasantry and were essential to the development of their armed forces. They led many young people to see a bright future with the Viet Minh, and the local cadres helped release youth for full-time participation in the struggle by taking care of their families. As one man who had spent his youth living as a buffalo boy in the home of a landlord recalled:

The Viet Minh came through on their promises. They actually took the land from the landlords and distributed it among their followers. Their propaganda struck a responsive chord in me because I hated the French . . . who were in league with

---

[118] Simulmatics Corporation, "Studies of the Chieu Hoi Program", interview CH-5, 1966. This person was one of the organizers of the education and literacy programs during the Resistance and later became a member of a provincial Party committee.

the landlords that had oppressed and beaten me . . . I thought in following them that I would have a brighter future . . . that I would get land to till, and my family could break out of its poverty . . . [Before joining] I thought about my grand-mother. I worried that she would live in misery if I went off and joined the army because no one would be left to look after her. I brought these apprehensions up with the cadres and they said that they were certain that the village authorities would take care of my grandmother. After I left my grandmother was given 0.6 hectare of ricefield.[119]

Despite their eventual success in many villages, the national Commun-ist leaders, most of whom came from Annam or Tonkin, found problems in Cochinchina that they did not encounter elsewhere. Ho Chi Minh's 1949 complaint about the failure to eradicate individualism in Cochinchina indicates the hold of a market orientation among the peasantry.[120] In some areas, the Viet Minh tried to treat confiscated lands as communal land, allocated by the village Viet Minh committee. This was a decidedly unpopular measure among the peasantry – who demonstrated a marked preference for private property – and the Viet Minh quickly reverted to allotting confiscated lands to their supporters without placing any time limits on the allocation. The Viet Minh preferred communal land as a prelude to collective agriculture, but as the head of Viet Minh economic and financial services for Cochinchina stated, "the system [private prop-erty] is far from perfect. . . . It leads to over-fragmentation of property and to a very definite decrease in output. However, we have been obliged to stick to it because our entire political action among the peasants is based upon the right of each to individual property. We would have risked losing their support had we stopped breaking up landholdings."[121]

Furthermore, there was tension between the Viet Minh leadership and the peasantry over increased consumption. With surplus rice, many peasants in liberated areas resumed trade with the French-occupied cities for kerosene, cloth, fish sauce, and bean curd. Other peasants began to raise pigs and ducks for urban markets. The Viet Minh wanted to isolate the cities and keep the liberated areas autonomous. They even killed ducklings and piglets in order to curtail trade, although these measures only aroused strong resentment and evasion. Eventually they had no choice but to allow the trade and relied instead on taxing it – tacitly ignoring the circulation of French piastres alongside their own Ho Chi Minh currency in liberated areas.[122] Paradoxically, this tension between peasant "bourgeois" economics and national liberation efforts was vastly ameliorated by French action. Concerned that the international rice trade

---

[119] Rand Corporation interview DT-101, p. 4.
[120] Lancaster, *Emancipation of French Indochina*, p. 420.
[121] Nguyen Than Vinh, quoted in Hammer, *The Struggle for Indochina*, p. 340.
[122] Author's research. See also Rand Corporation interviews DT-148, DT-145.

was providing an important source of taxes for the Viet Minh, the French instituted an economic blockade of most of Cochinchina and severely cut rice exports.[123] Because there was less money, and therefore less interest in market goods among the peasantry, it was easy for the Viet Minh to manage (and isolate) the subsistence economy that ensued from the French action.

Given its competition, the disarray of the Communist Party in 1945, and the distance from the liberated areas of Tonkin, the success of the Viet Minh in developling liberated government in the south can be considered an achievement. The rural institutions that the Communists developed helped create villages in the liberated area, as well as remarkable support among non-Communist peasants and cadres. As Joseph Alsop wrote in 1954 when he visited a Viet Minh liberated area in Cochinchina:

> The thing that impressed me most, in fact, was not the Communists' extraordinary feat of organizing, maintaining and expanding an independent state in southern Indochina without exterior support and in the teeth of French power. What impressed me most, alas, was the moral fervor they had inspired among non-Communist Viet Minh cadres and the stout support they had obtained from the peasantry.[124]

Conclusion

As these movements developed, they changed authority relations in peasant society. The changes in authority relations, in turn, spawned new conceptions of identity and self-worth among the peasantry. For example, adopting Catholicism was comparable in its effect to acquiring a new "occupation"; it was a change in lifestyle and status not just a change in beliefs.[125] After the Communists controlled Annam, the paternalistic terms of address between common peasants and village leaders changed; village officials and peasants began to address each other in fraternal terms, "younger brother" to "older brother".[126]

When these changes in authority relations occurred, great passions were expressed, but the passions did not precede the movements. These movements were not created by passionate and outraged peasants. Great works need not require great leaps by impassioned or outraged peasants. Peasants unleashed passions and let rage out when new contexts decreased the risks of expressing age-old angers or when new options led

---

[123] Lancaster, *Emancipation of French Indochina*, p. 415. The blockade also caused nearly one million peasants to leave Viet Minh areas for Saigon or areas controlled by the sects.
[124] Joseph Alsop, *New York Herald Tribune*, 31 December, 1954.
[125] Thompson, *French Indochina*, p. 274.
[126] Author's research.

to a re-evaluation of old procedures as onerous, humiliating, and illegitimate.

It is a mistake to assume that peasants ready and willing to make great leaps are a necessary condition for revolutionary movements. The changes these movements wrought were large, yet peasants did not start out conscious that they were about to accomplish large works. The four movements studied here were built upon countless small steps that had a large cumulative impact on society.

These movements depended upon organizers, whom I have called political entrepreneurs, who built their prestige and the legitimacy of their movements from small collective actions which solved local problems for the participants. With few resources but their own skills they provided coordination which brought immediate benefits to peasants.

When Viet Minh organizers provided the plans and coordination for starving peasants to raid Japanese granaries during the famine; when Hoa Hao leaders convinced peasants that enough other tenants were boycotting the landlord and that there was no risk in withholding grain; when Cao Dai and Catholic priests adjudicated disputes so peasants would not have to risk French justice, they were creating something from nothing. They were building their influence and prestige, and organizing collective actions and new institutions with few material incentives of their own to dispense.

Marches, boycotts, and strikes require significantly more interaction among participants and can occur with far less organization and special incentives than the by-product theory suggests, but even in these forms of collective action, the entrepreneurs were critical. As entrepreneurs provided the coordination and information to make collective actions credible and possible, they developed the influence they needed to gather resources from the peasantry for further national activities. As a Communist Party document noted:

Staging demonstrations is like conducting military operations. You should march in certain ways and advance and retreat on command. Only through this kind of disciplined action will you be able to extend your influence.[127]

Even though peasants' initial involvements may have been motivated by local concerns and not a commitment to national or radical change, the ethos of the organizations, their visions of the future and their moral codes, mattered. When assessing whether their efforts would contribute to collective goals or bring enough individual benefits, peasant calculations were affected by the visions and moral codes of the organizations.

---

[127] As quoted in Ngo Vinh Long, "Peasant Revolutionary Struggles in Vietnam in the 1930s" (Ph.D. dissertation, Department of History, Harvard University, 1978).

Visions of the future affected calculations of the efficacy of contributions. The religious movements brought visions of the future consonant with peasant beliefs, and peasants were able to relate these visions to their contemporary actions. When the goals of the entrepreneurs were credible, it led to increased estimates of the probability that contributions would result in the immediate local goals claimed.[128] The great success of religious movements *vis-à-vis* the Communists before the latter began to incorporate cultural themes and nationalist appeals underscores this point even more than do the failed appeals of Westernized organizers. So long as the Communists neglected ethnic Vietnamese content, they were unable to present a credible vision of the future to the peasants; hence, their early organizational efforts failed. Peasants did not understand why organizers were offering to help them and were reluctant to join with them even for small local projects.

Moral codes raised the credibility of the entrepreneurs. A major factor in the credibility of both the Communist and religious movements over the century, in contrast to the failed bourgeois organizations, was the self-abnegation of the leadership. The self-denial of Communist organizers, the celibacy of missionary priests, the scorn of conspicuous consumption by Hoa Hao organizers, were striking demonstrations to peasants that these men were less interested in self-aggrandizement than were the visibly less self-denying organizers from other groups.

[128] Woodside, *Community and Revolution*, p. 188.

2 Rationality and revolutionary collective action

*Michael Taylor**

In a much-praised book on *States and Social Revolutions*, Theda Skocpol announced her commitment to a strongly "nonvoluntarist, structural" methodological programme. Social revolutions are to be explained, she argued, as the product not of individual actions but of structural and situational conditions. In particular, "the sufficient distinctive causes" of the social-revolutionary situations commencing in France, 1789, Russia, 1917, and China, 1911 can be located in the relations of each of these states to other states and to its own domestic social classes (and I take a set of relations to be a structure) together with the country's "agrarian sociopolitical structure".[1] Skocpol's work on revolution is the most purely "structuralist" of the best recent work on revolution and peasant rebellion. Neither rational action nor any attitudes, interests, goals, beliefs, etc., are to have any explanatory role (at least in her statements of her methodological programme and general theoretical argument; they creep back in, as they have to, in her narrative histories of the three revolutions). Structural outcomes ("basic transformations of a society's state and class structures") are explained directly in terms of structural causes.

I shall take issue here with this one-sided structuralism, amongst other things, and try to show how rational-choice theory can contribute to our understanding of large-scale historical change. But although I share the view of those who believe that explanations of "macrophenomena" should be provided with "microfoundations", I do not believe that this is all that explanation should consist of and I wish to argue for a methodolo-

* I would like to thank the people who read and commented on, or listened to and discussed with me, the earlier versions of this paper which were presented at a seminar in 1982 at the Australian National University, Canberra, at the Western Political Science Association conference at Seattle in 1983, and at the Public Choice Institute at Halifax, Nova Scotia in 1984. They are Brian Barry, Stanley Benn, Alan Carling, Jon Elster, Alan Gibbard, Bob Goodin, Russell Hardin, Margaret Levi, Daniel Little, Howard Margolis, Douglass North and Hugh Ward. I am also grateful to Yves-Marie Bercé for his help. I am sadly aware that I have not resolved all the problems raised by these people.
1 Theda Skocpol, *States and Social Revolutions: A Comparative Analysis of France, Russia, and China* (Cambridge: Cambridge University Press, 1979), p. 154.

gical perspective which is both individualist *and* structuralist (though *not* in the manner of Bhaskar and Giddens).

To this end, I first argue (in sections I–V) that peasant collective action in revolutions and rebellions was based on community (as many historians have argued) and this is mainly *why* the large numbers of people involved were able to overcome the free-rider problem familiar to students of collective action (which has *not* been recognized by the historians). In establishing this I will have shown that revolutionary and rebel collective action is the product of rational action and in fact is explained by what I will call the thin theory of collective action (since it rests on the thin theory of rationality). There are many who reject this theory – and who will therefore be sceptical about my argument on revolutionary collective action – on the grounds that there is much collective action which the theory cannot account for, including some participation in interest groups and other associations, which have largely replaced community as the vehicle of movements of social and political change. I comment on this in section VI and go on to examine briefly (in section VII) some alternative accounts of individual rationality or motivation which might form the basis of a better theory of collective action. This will leave me convinced that no such theory is yet available, while agreeing that there are indeed facts about collective action which the thin theory is unable to account for. It would therefore be useful to know when the thin theory is applicable, to characterize the conditions in which it is likely to provide good explanations. I try to do this in section VIII. In the final section, after what may seem to have been a long detour, I connect this argument about the applicability of the thin theory to the question of explaining revolution, to Skocpol's "nonvoluntarist, structural" method in particular, and to social explanation in general.[2]

I

Social revolutions, whose origins and development it is Skocpol's aim to explain, are defined as "rapid, basic transformations of a society's state and class structures . . . accompanied and in part carried through by class-based revolts from below".[3] The revolts (which in the three historical cases Skocpol considers are agrarian revolts) can be successfully mounted only if certain structural preconditions are met, preconditions having to do with the social structure of the class in revolt and with its relations to

---

[2] I begin and end this essay with discussion of Skocpol's outstanding work because I think that it does in fact provide an important part of the explanation of the French, Russian and Chinese Revolutions. But it does not provide the whole of the explanation even of these cases (as I shall argue) and its applicability to other revolutions is another matter.

[3] Skocpol, *States and Social Revolutions*, p. 4.

other classes and to the state. It is also a condition of their success that the old regime's state repressive capacity has been weakened. The initial weakening of the state's repressive capacity, which provides the opening for peasant revolt, is the product of a political crisis whose causes lie in the state's relations to its own domestic classes and its position within international structures: finding itself under intensifying military pressure from more economically advanced and hence more militarily powerful foreign nations, the state's attempt to cope by trying rapidly to extract extraordinary resources from its population and to carry out basic reforms was impeded by a backward agrarian economy and powerful landed upper class, with the result that the regime collapsed.

In the final section I shall return briefly to this question of the emergence of revolutionary situations, of breakdowns in the repressive apparatus which provide openings for sustained revolutionary collective action by the peasants. The image of a structure of competitive international relations in which a state is enmeshed and which compel it to behave in certain ways towards its own population may seem to offer especially persuasive support to Skocpol's structural position, though here too I shall argue the need for rational choice explanation. But my main concern in this essay is with the explanation of the sustained peasant revolts which took advantage of the collapse of state power and which are a central part of most social revolutions.[4]

At first blush it would appear that the participation of vast numbers of peasants in collective action contradicts the familiar "logic of collective action". But I shall argue that this is not so, if we take the "logic" to encompass (to put it very loosely) the argument advanced by Mancur Olson in *The Logic of Collective Action*, as clarified, qualified and extended by a number of people (especially Russell Hardin in chapter 4 of his *Collective Action*); the theory of conditional cooperation;[5] and the impli-

---

[4] "Peasant revolts have been the crucial insurrectionary ingredients in virtually all actual (i.e., successful) social revolutions to date" (cases like Cuba and Yugoslavia providing the exceptions, though not because urban workers played the crucial role), and certainly in the French, Russian and Chinese cases "peasant revolts against landlords were a necessary ingredient . . . Whereas successful revolts by urban workers were not" (Skocpol, *States and Social Revolutions*, pp. 112–13 and 318 n. 2). I shall not discuss urban collective action here; but it is worth noting an important contrast between urban workers and peasants. Communities of peasants – and the more their production is already geared to subsistence the more this is true – are, or can often quickly become, "self"-sufficient in food. They can thus survive for some time independently and often they can also support guerrillas and revolutionary armies (who may take advantage of, or strengthen, pre-existing community in order to expand subsistence food production). This is of course not possible for urban workers, who are necessarily parasitic on the countryside.

[5] See Michael Taylor, *Anarchy and Cooperation* (London: Wiley, 1976). Robert Axelrod's work, as reported most fully in *The Evolution of Cooperation* (New York: Basic Books, 1984), gives some support to the conclusion of this theory. It demonstrates the success of the "tit-for-tat" strategy which was shown in *Anarchy and Cooperation* to be the most rational

cations which can be informally drawn from these two bodies of theory about the intervention of political entrepreneurs (which I will discuss in connection with collective action in the Chinese and Vietnamese revolutions).

I call this collection of arguments the thin theory of collective action to emphasize that it is founded on the thin theory of rationality. (There are, so far as I am aware, no other, elaborated, "thicker" theories of collective action founded on broader accounts of rationality. The alternative accounts of rationality which will be discussed briefly in section VII do not, in my view, provide foundations for superior explanations of collective action). By the "thin theory of rationality" I mean the familiar account of rationality which also provides the foundation for conventional neo-classical microeconomic theory. I emphasize (with no attempt at precision) three features of the thin theory: (i) Rationality is relative to *given* attitudes and beliefs (which are each assumed to be consistent) and the agent's actions are *instrumental* in achieving or advancing the given aims in the light of the given beliefs. It is for this reason alone that Jon Elster has called the theory "thin".[6] (ii) The agent is assumed to be egoistic. (iii) In applications of the thin theory the range of incentives assumed to affect the agent is limited. Olson, for example, limits them to the increase in the supply of the public good caused by the individual's action, the resources he must devote to the action, and "selective incentives" which themselves are limited to economic or material incentives and "social sanctions and social rewards".[7] Other theories limit them even more, for example to profit alone.[8] Without such limitation, a thin theory is liable to become a tautology. The ends which are limited in this way are not themselves assumed to be rational in any sense.

strategy under certain conditions. But it must be borne in mind that Axelrod treats only tournaments in which players interact in pairs, so that his results have doubtful application to most public goods situations involving more than two people. On this and on the other work referred to in this paragraph, see my *The Possibility of Cooperation* (Cambridge: Cambridge University Press, 1987).

[6] Jon Elster, *Sour Grapes: Studies in the Subversion of Rationality* (Cambridge: Cambridge University Press, 1983), p. 3. For a fuller discussion of the thin theory, see chapter 1 of *Sour Grapes* generally. In place of the usual "preferences" or "desires", I prefer "attitudes", a broader category including but not restricted to preferences, desires, goals, etc. (as in Donald Davidson's "Actions, Reasons and Causes", reprinted in his *Essays on Actions and Events*, Oxford: Clarendon Press, 1980).

[7] Mancur Olson, *The Logic of Collective Action* (Cambridge, Mass.: Harvard University Press, 1965), pp. 60–1, n. 17 on p. 61 and n. 91 on p. 160.

[8] In fact, *most* if not all explanatory rational choice theories assume agents to be motivated either by economic/material incentives alone or by these together with social incentives based on the desire to avoid disapprobation. They take for granted Harsanyi's "postulate" that "People's behavior can be largely explained in terms of two dominant interests: economic gain and social acceptance" (John C. Harsanyi, "Rational Choice Models of Behavior versus Functionalist and Conformist Theories", *World Politics*, 22 (1969), 513–38).

Action which is rational according to the thin theory of rationality will be said to be "thin-rational" and in the agent's "thin self-interest".

It is important to bear in mind that most successful collective action takes place in what Olson calls intermediate groups or succeeds in large groups because they are made up of intermediate subgroups. Olson provided no theory of strategic interaction in these groups. If agents are thin-rational and there are no selective incentives (unless tacit selective incentives are said to be entailed in conditional cooperation itself), successful collective action outside of privileged groups must result from some form of conditional cooperation. At a minimum, an individual would not contribute or participate if nobody else did.

For my purposes in this chapter, I need to emphasize certain properties of conditional cooperation. As intuitively we would expect and as we can prove in the case of the n-person Prisoners' Dilemma super game, conditional cooperation is more likely to be rational (before selective incentives are brought in) in small groups than in large ones. It is also more likely to succeed in conditions where relations between people are those characteristic of *community* – not just because individual behaviour can more easily be monitored, but because a strong community has at its disposal an array of powerful, positive and negative social sanctions which were highly effective in maintaining social order and in the provision of other public goods in all precapitalist societies and continued to play an important role subsequently, though sometimes in atrophied and attenuated forms.[9] An important point here is that these sanctions can be used as selective incentives, not only to induce individuals simply to contribute or participate, but also to bolster conditional cooperation – which is always a precarious business. Political entrepreneurs also have an important role to play here. Usually thought of as "an innovator with selective incentives",[10] the political entrepreneur also organizes collective action by facilitating conditional cooperation.

It might be argued that a community member would not take the trouble to implement sanctions against a free rider (and hence that nobody would find the threats to use the sanctions credible), since punishing a free rider is itself a public good for the community and each individual would therefore prefer others to do the job. Against this I suggest that the cost of applying a sanction is typically slight, and if a general argument about thin rationality which I make in section VIII is right, it will follow that in making *this* choice (to participate in community sanctioning of free

[9] There is a detailed treatment of these and of their use in the provision of certain public goods – especially in "primitive" and peasant communities – in Michael Taylor, *Community, Anarchy and Liberty* (Cambridge: Cambridge University Press, 1982).
[10] Olson, p. 177 of Appendix added in 1971 to *The Logic of Collective Action*.

riders), the individual does not act thin-rationally.[11] This argument should hold for the cases I will be concerned with here.

One final preliminary: I take the core properties of *community* to be: (i) its members have beliefs and values in common; (ii) relations between members are direct and many-sided; and (iii) its members practise "generalized" as well as merely "balanced" reciprocity.[12] Each of these criteria can be satisfied in varying degrees, so that a collection of individuals may be more or less of a community, and I shall speak of "weak" and "strong" communities. One important way in which some of the peasant communities I shall discuss are "weak" is that relations between their members are in certain spheres not direct, as required by the second criterion, but mediated – for example through the intervention in community affairs of local landlords and state officials. To the extent that people do not deal with each other directly but pursue their common ends through the agency of such outside parties, to that extent (other things being equal) they are diminished as a community.

When the peasant community was sufficiently strong, then, it provided a social basis for collective action, including revolutionary collective action and rebellions and other popular mobilizations. Revolutionary or rebel mobilization built on and used the existing network of local communities. The individual participated as a member of a community. These communities provided conditions in which spontaneous conditional cooperation could succeed or, failing that, could provide and effectively use against most of their members all the sanctions which are characteristic of the traditional community. Sometimes, mobilization was assisted by a political entrepreneur. And in some cases, where the local community was less strong (because there was little cooperation amongst its members in the agricultural work which dominated their lives, for example, or relations between members were too much mediated by landlords or officials), revolutionary mobilization could not occur without entrepreneurs – who set about their work, however, by building or strengthening the local community through organizing mutual aid and undermining the dependence of the villages on local landlords.

In arguing that community facilitates revolutionary collective action by making conditional cooperation rational and the use of social sanctions effective, I am assuming that the peasant rebellion is, in effect, embedded in a larger iterated game. Participation in rebellion is conditional on others continuing to participate (rebellions are not instantaneous events), but the

[11] Or as Olson (*The Logic of Collective Action*, p. 164 n. 102) says, "there is a 'threshold' above which costs and returns influence a person's actions, and below which they do not".

[12] For a more detailed discussion of "community", see Taylor, *Community, Anarchy and Liberty*, section 1.4.

experience of conditional cooperation, the knowledge conditions which are necessary for successful conditional cooperation (e.g. knowing that others are cooperating) and the effectiveness of social sanctions used during a rebellion all derive from the fact that the participants in the rebellion are members of a pre-existing community and will continue to be members of the same community after the rebellion.[13]

Part of this argument about community and revolutionary collective action has been made by numerous historians and by Skocpol. They have correctly seen in the peasant community the social basis of revolutionary collective action, but have not recognized that it is precisely in virtue of the peasant's membership of a community that it is *rational* for him to participate. Skocpol is prevented from understanding fully this connection between community and revolution by her anti-voluntarist and structuralist methodological commitments, as we shall see later. The general argument that supplying the motivational link – in this case, explaining collective action in terms of individual motivations and these in terms of social structure – makes for better explanation will be made in the final section.

II

Skocpol argues that although there were widespread peasant revolts against landlords in the French, Russian *and* Chinese Revolutions – far transcending the localized revolts or disturbances which these countries had experienced previously and far more successful in bringing lasting radical transformations – there was nevertheless an important difference between the French and Russian cases on the one hand and the Chinese on the other. In the former cases, the peasant community was still strong and "the peasant village assembly, relatively autonomous as it was from outside control, provided the organizational basis for spontaneous and autonomous revolts" (p. 138). The peasantry of China, on the other hand, during the revolutionary interregnum between 1911 and 1949, "lacked the kind of structurally pre-existing solidarity and autonomy that allowed the agrarian revolution in France and Russia to emerge quickly and relatively spontaneously in reaction to the breakdown of the central governments of the Old Regimes" (p. 148). The consequence was that, compared with the French and Russian Revolutions, the Chinese Revolution was much more protracted and peasant collective action had in effect to be organized, village by village, by the Communists.

[13] This is, I think, a good example of Russell Hardin's argument about "overlapping activities". See Hardin, *Collective Action* (Baltimore: Johns Hopkins Press for Resources for the Future, 1982), chapter 11.

Let us put some flesh on the rather abstract skeleton of the arguments made in the last section by looking at these three cases in more detail.[14]

In FRANCE, all through the eighteenth century, there had been bread riots in town and country. But in 1789 the peasants went much further. Across the country, they launched an assault on the seigneurial system itself, refusing to pay seigneurial dues, tithes and royal taxes and often destroying the local seigneur's feudal records and sometimes his chateau too, as well as seizing local grain stores. The direct end result of their actions was the radical transformation of the class structure through the abolition of seigneurialism, and an indirect result, through the effects of the peasant revolts on the behaviour of the Constituent Assembly, was the emergence of a new type of state. Though the final outcome may not have been intended by them, the peasants made a social revolution.

That the peasant revolts issued in this successful outcome was due to conjunctural factors. But the peasants' collective action was made possible in the first place by the pre-existing framework of village communities, which provided a foundation of long experience of reciprocity and acting together in the collective control of their agricultural and pastoral activities and of their common property and public facilities.

Albert Soboul has emphasized how much the cohesion and unity of the pre-revolutionary peasant community owed to its universally shared opposition to the lord.[15] It is true that within the community, inequality – especially differentiation into possessors and non-possessors of a plough-team – was well developed by 1789. Peasants could freely sell or bequeath the land they possessed (more than a third of French soil was in this category; and more than another third owned by the lords was used by the peasants as sharecroppers or tenants). But the resulting differentiation amongst the peasants was overshadowed by their common subjection to the lord, who exercised with respect to peasant land tenures a right of overlordship marked by the peasant's payment of seigneurial dues (in addition to royal taxes, tithes, and rents or crop shares), a crippling burden that was actually worsened during the eighteenth century by the "feudal reaction". One effect of this seigneurial regime, then, was to produce a defensive unity of the rural community in the face of the lord's depredations.

This unity was enhanced by a measure of communal self-government,

14 On the peasant village community in the European cases generally (this section and sec. V), two articles by Jerome Blum are very useful: "The Internal Structure and Polity of the European Village Community from the Fifteenth to the Nineteenth Century", *Journal of Modern History*, 43 (1971), 541–76; and "The European Village as Community: Origins and Functions", *Agricultural History*, 45 (1971), 157–78.
15 Albert Soboul, "The French Rural Community in the Eighteenth and Nineteenth Centuries", *Past and Present*, no. 10 (1956), 78–95.

exercised through the assembly of the community's heads of households, which met in the church (parish and community usually coinciding) and was assisted by the local priest. "The assembly dealt with all that concerned the community: sale, purchase, exchange or leasing of communal property; the maintenance of the church, of public buildings, roads, and bridges; the election of the communal syndics, of the schoolmaster, the communal shepherd, the hayward, the collectors of tithes, the assessors and collectors of the taille."[16]

But, as Soboul and Marc Bloch before him emphasized, the real foundation of the rural community's unity was its economic system, and in particular its collective possession of important resources and its communal regulation of the use of certain private possessions and of access to collective possessions in the common interest of all the inhabitants. Individual villagers were restrained from enclosing their land, were obliged to conform to the communal pattern of crop rotation, and were constrained by communal rules concerning such things as harvest dates, use of woods, rights of gleaning, of pasturing on the fallow and on communal lands, and so on.

A dispersed settlement pattern – as in the forest areas of Normandy and Brittany – was not necessarily a barrier to communal cohesion (as some writers have maintained). Though there was less collective organization of agriculture in such areas than in the open-field country of the North and East, there was often more communal land, especially pasture land and woodland, to defend and regulate in the common interest, and mutual aid was practised amongst the peasants at key points of the agricultural cycle.

On the eve of the Revolution, then, the great majority of the French people lived in cohesive communities, long used to meeting together in their assemblies, regulating their life together and working together. It was as the member of such a community that each individual participated in the revolt against the seigneurial regime.

Skocpol's analysis of the peasant revolution in RUSSIA during 1917 is confirmed by the account given in Graeme Gill's *Peasants and Government in the Russian Revolution*, which was published at the same time as Skocpol's book and appears to be the fullest account of the peasant land seizures in English to date.[17] After the fall of the Tsar in March, the peasants at first supported the provisional government and were willing to have local government bodies work out a solution to the land question. But they were not impressed with the government's feeble tinkering with the existing system of government in the countryside and soon became

---

[16] Ibid., p. 81.
[17] Graeme J. Gill, *Peasants and Government in the Russian Revolution* (London: Macmillan, 1979).

impatient with its temporizing over the redistribution of land. "The widespread peasant rejection of the emerging administrative structure was linked with the strength throughout the countryside of traditionally-based peasant organizations rooted in the fabric of village society".[18] Before long the peasants began to meet in their village assemblies and proceeded to create organizations of their own to put in the place of the official structure. The local functionaries of the old regime were driven from the villages and in their place the village assemblies or the entire village elected committees at village and district levels. The unrest which followed, especially in the first part of 1917, was usually organized by these new bodies, propelled and radicalized in many cases by outside agitators.

Attacks on landowners and seizures of land were generally carried out by each village acting separately, though sometimes there was collective action at district level involving coordination between neighbouring villages. The decision to move against the local landowner was usually taken at a meeting of the village assembly or the new committees at village and district level.[19]

At first, in March, the peasant assaults on landowners were typically destructive, with peasants arresting and sometimes killing the local landowners, seizing grain, cutting down and carrying off timber, destroying grain-stores and equipment. But from April to August, the peasants turned mainly to seizing and redistributing land, which they began immediately to use. Private lands were integrated into the land already controlled by the *obshchina*, their owners and workers sometimes driven from the area. In some cases landowners were compelled to surrender land which was not being used or was already on a short lease in exchange for low rents decreed by peasant committees or assemblies.

In all this activity the individual participated as a member of an *obshchina* – typically a territorial community corresponding to a village or small settlement, exercising a considerable measure of self-government through the assembly of heads of households (*skhod*). Politically, it was the lowest-level local government authority, with a wide range of administrative, fiscal and law-enforcement responsibilities. Economically, it was the legal owner of most of the peasant land. It allotted portions of arable land to the peasant households, keeping some land, especially pasture and forest, for collective use. Peasant households did, however, have small hereditary plots around the house and could buy land for private ownership from outside the commune. In many areas, the *skhod* exercised the right to reallocate the communal land periodically between house-

---

[18] Ibid., p. 29.
[19] Ibid., pp. 149–50.

holds in order to re-establish a fairer distribution. Such repartitional communes were weakest in the northwest, southwest and parts of the southeast. But even in the hereditary communes the work of the peasants was subject to extensive collective regulation. As in similar regimes in other countries and at other times, "the prevailing open-field system, with its formal three-field cycle of farming and the division of land into strips, made agricultural cooperation of all the members of the commune mandatory at the major stages of the farming year".[20] Many other economic functions were exercised by the commune.

It is scarcely surprising that the peasants of such a commune were able to act as one in the assault on the landlords. The *obshchina* was a genuine community, whose members would find conditional cooperation rational, especially when it was organized by the *skhod* or the new committees, and if they did not they could be subjected effectively to the selective incentives which characterize peasant communities nearly everywhere.[21]

It is interesting to note that the unrest was greatest in the areas where the traditional repartitional commune was strongest. But it was also in these areas – especially the Central Agricultural Region and the Middle Volga Region – that the peasants owned least land and were therefore most obliged to rent non-peasant land in exchange for money, labour or a share of the crop.[22] So the firmest social foundation for collective action was combined here with the greatest need for it.

The situation of the peasants in CHINA at the fall of the Manchus differed significantly from that of the peasants of pre-revolutionary France and Russia. In the first place, the Chinse peasant community was normally more "open" than its French or Russian counterparts (in the sense of Eric Wolf's well-known contrast between open and closed communities): it was less self-sufficient, more a part of a larger economic system, more exposed to alien ideas and values; there was more mobility out of and into the community. The peasant was in fact a member of two "communities": his village and the marketing "community" composed of a market town and its dependent area containing perhaps 15 to 25 villages.[23] It was the market "community" which constituted the peasant's social world. Its size alone would have made it weak as a community. It was, in addition, characterized by very considerable social, economic and political stratification. In particular, the gentry took a leading role in these local "com-

---

[20] Teodor Shanin, *The Awkward Class: Political Sociology of Peasantry in a Developing Society: 1910–1925* (Oxford: Clarendon Press, 1972), p. 37.

[21] For evidence on this from the 1905 revolution, see Maureen Perrie, "The Russian Peasant Movement of 1905–1907", *Past and Present*, no. 57 (1972), 123–55.

[22] Gill, *Peasants and Government in the Russian Revolution*, pp. 157–69.

[23] G. William Skinner, "Chinese Peasants and the Closed Community: an Open and Shut Case", *Comparative Studies in Society and History*, 13 (1971), 270–81.

munities", organizing and managing clans, peasant associations and secret societies. They *mediated* relations between peasants.

Finally, the agricultural work of Chinese peasants involved much less cooperation than it did in France and Russia. Households worked independently; there was no collective regulation of the village agriculture and no common lands to manage; and there was only limited mutual aid between households – principally in connection with water storage and irrigation, which in any case gave rise to as much conflict as cooperation.

The Chinese peasant community, then, was far weaker than its counterpart in France and Russia, too weak in fact to provide a foundation for a spontaneous revolution in the countryside. It had to be mobilized by the patient efforts of political entrepreneurs.

There were, it is true, many peasant rebellions before the Chinese Revolution. Some were on a great scale and a few even succeeded in installing new regional governments for a time or causing the ruling dynasty itself to be replaced.[24] Skocpol recognizes this, but believes that even the most sustained of these rebellions could not have led to social revolution because they were all eventually infiltrated by non-peasants – local gentry or those, like merchants or would-be literati, who aspired to the gentry. The peasants, she concludes, "lacked the local community-based autonomy to render their resistance even potentially revolutionary" (p. 151), and certainly it is true that these rebellions, far from having revolutionary outcomes, invariably had the end result of strengthening or re-establishing the traditional system. Presumably, Skocpol's view must be that these peasant insurrections would have been doomed to terminate in non-revolutionary outcomes (because they were infiltrated and coopted by gentry, etc.) even if the conjunctural factors had been propitious. But since many of them were so massive and sustained (especially in the period 1850–70 when great waves of rebellions, including those of the Taipings and the Nien, involved millions of peasants and engulfed large areas of the country), the question arises of how the peasants managed to get so far as to mount them in the first place. Some of them were, indeed, more successful in reaching their own goals than many of the European peasant insurrections which did not have revolutionary outcomes but which were nevertheless made possible by the existence of strong peasant communities.

Skocpol, in her discussion of "Agrarian Structures and Peasant Insurrections", has I think overstated the case against the Chinese community, as her own later discussion of the Communist Party's mobilization efforts itself suggests. There *was* a non-negligible degree of community, sufficient

[24] See for example Jean Chesneaux, *Peasant Revolts in China, 1840–1949* (London: Thames and Hudson, 1973).

to provide a foundation for collective action. It would of course have been stronger if much of the cooperation amongst peasants had not been mediated by non-peasants; but there was *something* there, especially in the North, for the CP cadres to go to work on, when they had displaced the local gentry as political entrepreneurs. This slightly different emphasis finds support in the work of Elizabeth Perry and Philip Huang. Huang shows how in the 1930s villages on the North China plain were more closed, less integrated into wider trading networks and possessed of greater "communal solidarity" than is portrayed in the influential analysis by William Skinner which is accepted by Skocpol.[25] Perry, in her discussion of the massive Nien Rebellion (1851–63), for example, stresses the importance of communal connections and especially the success that clans sometimes had in coordinating their members from many villages: "families, clans, and lineage settlements were at the heart of Nien organizational strength". She writes of the Red Spear Society, which came to have three million followers and attempted takeovers of entire county administrations during the republican period, that it was a "community-based movement" and "although rural villages constituted the basic organizational unity of the Red Spears, in Honan the movement expanded to encompass a network of village alliances".[26]

But she goes on to say that the village chapters which were the cells of the Red Spear movement were organized at the initiative of village notables. Clans, too, and the secret societies which often played an important role in the organization of rebellions, were led by gentry or merchants; and Skocpol is undoubtedly right to argue that for this reason the peasant movements could not have been revolutionary. Nevertheless the Chinese Communist Party did succeed in making a revolution in part by building on what there was already to hand in the way of village communities. In the militarily secure base areas the Party's cadres immersed themselves in the life of the villages, extending traditional forms of mutual aid and introducing new ones, forming peasant associations, and putting these new practices and groups to work to bring tangible economic benefits to the peasants.[27] In order to do this, the CCP had to displace the existing village elite, taking over its role as political entrepreneur, though putting it to different uses of course. My point is that they could not have done this successfully unless there was already

---

[25] Philip C.C. Huang, *The Peasant Economy and Social Change in North China* (Stanford, California: Stanford University Press, 1985), Part 3.

[26] Elizabeth Perry, *Rebels and Revolutionaries in North China, 1845–1945* (Stanford, California: Stanford University Press, 1980), pp. 128 and 155. See also her "Collective Violence in China, 1880–1980", *Theory and Society*, 13 (1984), 427–55.

[27] See for example Perry, *Rebels and Revolutionaries*, chapter 6, and Mark Selden, *The Yenan Way in Revolutionary China* (Cambridge, Mass.: Harvard University Press, 1971).

some degree of community amongst the peasant members of the village.[28]

III

It should be clear from this brief review that the account given by Skocpol and others of the social–structural preconditions for successful peasant insurrections in three great social revolutions is quite compatible with the rational choice theory of collective action if what I had to say earlier about community is accepted. But I am saying something stronger than this, namely that the thin theory of collective action provides part of the explanation of social revolution. This is not Skocpol's view. For her, as we have seen, a proper understanding of social revolutions requires the adoption of a "nonvoluntarist, structural perspective". In particular, she says (at p. 115), peasant insurrections were caused by "structural and situational conditions" – those I have discussed above together with others whose effect was a weakening of the state's control of the countryside. (I return to the second group below.)

We can accept Skocpol's view that "no successful revolution has ever been 'made' by a mass-mobilizing, avowedly revolutionary movement". The actions of revolutionary groups and of peasants (who may not have revolutionary aims) can produce a revolutionary outcome only in the right conditions. It is true that neither the revolutionaries nor the peasants produce these conjunctures (which are characterized especially by state crises); and it may be true that no one intended or foresaw the outcomes. But it does not follow that what happens in these revolutionary situations is not in part explicable by rational choice theories. Nor does it follow that the conjunctures themselves were not in turn the products of rational choices.

Skocpol points to the correlation between pre-existing social structure and the behaviour of entire villages or local populations; without the intervening links showing the effect of social structure on the individuals and the interactions between the individuals, this is, I submit, at the very least an incomplete explanation.

In the case of China, the peasants did not rebel spontaneously, even though they were given the right sort of revolutionary "opening". But the explanation for this failure to rebel is in the first place that it was not rational for the individual peasant to participate in rebellion, and it was

---

[28] This point is neglected by two earlier writers who recognize the importance of political entrepreneurs and the use of selective incentives, especially in the Chinese and Vietnamese revolutions: Jeffrey Race, "Toward an Exchange Theory of Revolution", in John Wilson Lewis (ed.), *Peasant Rebellion and Communist Revolution in Asia* (Stanford, California: Stanford University Press, 1974), and Joel S. Migdal, *Peasants, Politics, and Revolution* (Princeton, N.J.: Princeton University Press, 1974), chapter 10.

not rational because his relations to other potential rebels were not those of a strong community. The Chinese peasants' attacks on their landlords came only after the CCP had penetrated their villages and helped them to organize collective action. The CCP chose consciously to do this, to pursue "the Yenan Way". Why? And why did this strategy succeed? Certainly, as Skocpol in effect says, the Communists chose in circumstances which were not of their choosing; their options were conditioned, both limited and opened up for them – as by the Japanese invasion for example – but nothing she says proves that the CCP had to do what it in fact did. To argue that what the CCP chose to make of its opportunity is explicable without reference to its leaders' preferences and beliefs is implausible. But this is only Skocpol's methodological position; the detailed account she herself gives of the Chinese Revolution shows plainly the crucial role of the Communists' aims and beliefs in its making. It would be equally implausible to claim that the success of the Communists' strategy – which, as Selden, Perry and others have emphasized, required the use of selective material incentives in a reconstructed community setting – is explicable without reference to the peasants' preferences and beliefs.

It might be argued that this much can be conceded without damage to a "non-voluntarist, structural" position if it is reckoned that action is always mechanically caused by structural and situational factors and/or by preferences and beliefs which themselves have causes external to their possessor. In this case, the argument would go, the (thin) rational choice theorist as we know him is reduced to the minor supporting role of a technician and the serious part of the business is to explain the evolution of structures and situations and/or to find the causal origins of attitudes and beliefs; or, more strongly, that individuals are nothing more than bearers and transmitters of structural and other causal forces and therefore make no independent contribution to the explanation. I deal with these views in the final section below.

IV

I am aware of only one writer who, in methodological contrast to Skocpol, has taken a rational choice approach to peasant collective action. This is Samuel Popkin, in his extremely valuable book *The Rational Peasant*.[29] But he does not argue, as I wish to, that pre-existing rural *community* made it rational for the individual peasant to participate in revolutionary collective

[29] Samuel L. Popkin, *The Rational Peasant: The Political Economy of Rural Society in Vietnam* (Berkeley: University of California Press, 1979). An interesting forerunner of Popkin's analysis of political entrepreneurs and revolutionary mobilization is Jeffrey Race, "Toward an Exchange Theory of Revolution". But unlike Popkin, Race does not develop his argument systematically out of the free-rider problem.

action; indeed, as part of his sustained attack on the "moral economy" approach to peasant society he argues that there was little community to be found in the Vietnamese countryside at the time of the revolution. What he does do is to show that because peasants were (thin-) rational there was a problem about collective action, that the problem was overcome by political entrepreneurs, and that the ways in which they overcame it are consistent with the rational choice theory of collective action. So, while he makes no general argument about rationality and community, he provides the part of the argument (the part concerning individual motivation) which is missing in Skocpol's treatment of the Chinese Revolution – for, so far as peasant collective action is concerned, there are important similarities between the Chinese and Vietnamese cases.

In imperial times and even (but decreasingly) under French colonial rule, there was some degree of local community amongst the peasants, especially in the Northern and Central provinces of Tonkin and Annam. In these areas, peasants lived in nucleated villages which were closed corporate communities, though they lacked some of the communal features that characterized the closed corporate communities of, say, much of Eastern and Western Europe before the twentieth century, including the Russian *mir* described earlier. The village had *some* autonomy, with its own village council to manage local affairs, including the collection of taxes, the distribution of communal lands, the adjudication of disputes within the village, and the organization of religious rites and festivals; it possessed *some* communal land – more than a quarter of all agricultural land in precolonial times but a declining proportion under French rule; the villages engaged in *some* mutual aid, including cooperative labour, and collectively they maintained part of the local irrigation, flood control and drainage system.

But against these signs of community we have to set the facts of considerable stratification and mediation in the village: within each village there was a hierarchy of notables determined by education, wealth and age; the village council was made up of senior notables and a junior notable served as village "chief"; landholdings were very unequally distributed and there was intense competition for land with frequent boundary disputes; the communal lands, far from occasioning cooperation, produced conflict, as the notables, who controlled their periodical redistribution, used the distributions to enrich their relatives, their supporters and themselves; and most of the work of cultivation was carried out by individuals and families acting alone, with only limited cooperative labour restricted to small groups practising balanced reciprocity of well-defined specific tasks, despite the enormous scope for enhanced production through greater cooperation to improve irrigation systems.[30]

In the South, in Cochinchina, the peasant community was even weaker. The economy here was dominated by large estates, divided into small holdings worked by sharecroppers and tenants producing rice for export. The villages were open and less compact than in Annam and Tonkin; many of them were frontier settlements of recent foundation, with less ramified kinship links and a shallower tradition of cooperation.

There was, besides, an almost total absence of farm cooperatives, peasant associations or any other kind of supravillage formal organization or voluntary association in the Vietnamese countryside.[31]

In these circumstances, the Communists had to *build* a revolutionary movement village by village, and their approach was similar in some respects to the strategies pursued by the Chinese Communist Party. In this, they were of course assisted by the presence of an alien colonial power (though also impeded by its weakening of the village communities) and hugely assisted by the Japanese occupation of Vietnam in 1940, their displacement in March 1945 of French rule, and their own withdrawal in August 1945, paving the way for the Communists' "August Revolution".

The Communists were not alone in trying to build movements among the peasants during this period. The Catholic Church and two native politico-religious organizations – the Hoa Hao and Cao Dai – also had considerable success, using many of the methods adopted by the CP.[32]

In 1930–1 there had been large-scale peasant *jacqueries* against landlords and notables in Cochinchina (following a plunge in the price of rice caused by the world depression) and in Annam (following catastrophic famine). Both were organized by the recently formed Communist Party. In Cochinchina, the sporadic unrest was not coordinated over a large area and was quickly crushed. In Annam, the rebels actually took control of two provinces and held out for nine months. It seems clear that the leadership provided by the CP was crucial. In Cochinchina, the rapid defeat of the movement seems to have been partly due to the CP's failure to provide more coordinated leadership; while in Annam, in James Scott's view, "there is little doubt that the rebellion would not have taken on quite the dimensions of size and cohesiveness that it attained had it not been for the role of the Communist party", which was particularly strong

[30] Pierre Gourou, *The Peasants of the Tonkin Delta* (New Haven, Conn.: Human Relations Area Files, 1955); Popkin, *The Rational Peasant*, pp. 88–109.
[31] Alexander B. Woodside, *Community and Revolution in Modern Vietnam* (Boston: Houghton Mifflin, 1976), pp. 142–7.
[32] See Popkin, *The Rational Peasant*, chapter 5.

in the affected provinces.[33] (An even worse famine at the turn of the century provoked little protest.) We should also recall that the village community was much stronger in Annam than in Cochinchina.

But it was not until after 1940 that the Communists really began to succeed in mobilizing the peasantry. After the destruction of their urban cells in 1940 – undoing much of the rebuilding that had gone on since the French suppression following the uprisings of 1930–1 – the CP under Ho Chi Minh's leadership began to embrace something like Mao's "Yenan Way". From their mountain base near the Chinese border, the Viet Minh began to build peasant organizations in the villages first by taking advantage of the famine that Tonkin suffered in 1943–4: they alone brought help to the peasants by organizing bands to attack Japanese rice granaries, with participation in the attack bringing an immediate benefit in the form of a share of the rice that was seized. The support which the Viet Minh mobilized in the countryside after the August Revolution of 1945 enabled them to control large areas of all three regions (though less successfully in Cochinchina). As Popkin explains,[34] they did this by organizing the peasants in each village around pressing local problems, winning their support not in the first instance (or perhaps at all) for highly uncertain, large-scale, long-run goals but for less risky, small-scale goals whose achievement brought immediate concrete benefits. They subsidized and organized improvements in the local irrigation and water-storage system; they instituted popular literacy campaigns – using the classes to promote self-help and mutual aid as well; they made changes in the system of allocating communal land and of taxation, benefiting the poor and the village at the expense of the rich; they established village courts to arbitrate disputes, enabling the peasants to defend themselves against landowners in their own language; and they organized labour pools and enlarged the scope of mutual aid. In all this, the entrepreneurial role of the Communist cadres was crucial: by disaggregating the big overall goal of building a revolutionary movement into many smaller ones, by localizing the effort, by facilitating conditional cooperation, by enhancing the individual peasant's appreciation of the importance of his contribution and his valuation of the public good, and by the use of selective incentives, the Communists made it *rational* for the peasant to participate.

All this entrepreneurial organizing effort was in part made necessary by the relative weakness of the village community. But I want to argue – as I did in the case of China – that it would not have succeeded if there had

[33] James C. Scott, *The Moral Economy of the Peasant: Rebellion and Subsistence in Southeast Asia* (New Haven: Yale University Press, 1976), p. 147.
[34] Popkin, *The Rational Peasant*, chapters 5 and 6.

been no community at all for the cadres of the CP to work on, once they had weakened the hold of the existing oligarchy of notables. Most peasant members of the village shared the same values and beliefs and had common enemies; they practised *some* reciprocity; they had lived and worked together in one place for many years. In this setting, the peasants of a single village were not so numerous and not such strangers to each other that conditional cooperation could not be made to work with a little help from political entrepreneurs; monitoring of participation and contributed effort was possible; and informal social sanctions could be effective.

V

Successful social revolutions have so far occurred only prior and during the transition to industrial capitalism. There have also been in this period countless peasant rebellions, some of them large-scale and sustained, which were not part of a revolution. The argument I have made about rationality and the role of community in revolutionary collective action applies also to these other forms of peasant collective action. Again, the historians of these rebellions have had a lot to say about community but nothing about rationality.

There seems to be wide agreement amongst historians that the local communities provide the social basis and organizational framework of peasant rebellion (and a variety of other kinds of popular disturbance as well). This is a refrain of Perez Zagorin's *Rebels and Rulers, 1500–1660*, for example. Writing generally of peasant rebellion in early modern Europe he says: "Agrarian rebellion almost invariably began in the mobilization of village communities, their members summoned to rise by the violent ringing of church bells in the parishes and then flowing together in growing crowds from all parts of the countryside . . . The village community contained the main potentiality of joint action. It was the elementary cell from whose coalescence with other similar cells peasant struggles, whether against the state or landlords, developed."[35]

For example, in the Croquant revolts in southwestern France in the 1590s and again in the 1630s and 1640s "the community in village and parish became the institutional cellule of revolt" and "Agrarian rebellion was thus sustained by the structure, action, and values of the peasant community."[36]

---

[35] Perez Zagorin, *Rebels and Rulers, 1500–1660*, 2 vols. (Cambridge: Cambridge University Press, 1982), vol. 1, p. 86; see also p. 182.
[36] Ibid., pp. 220 and 223. For a detailed treatment of the Croquants revolts, which establishes the community basis for rebellion and reproduces interesting documentary evidence of their organization and of the use of threats of sanctions against

Of the biggest peasant rebellion of the early modern period, the German Peasant War of 1525–6, which was really a whole series of rebellions, Zagorin writes that "Mobilization followed communal lines as crowds of peasants belonging to a particular lordship, district, or jurisdiction streamed together carrying arms. Communities seem sometimes to have decided as a body to rebel. They then formed bands . . . which were organised and chose leaders parallelling the familiar *Dorf*, or village organisation."[37] The Peasant War was confined almost entirely to western Germany. This was one aspect of a broad divergence between Germany east and west of the Elbe in the later middle ages – the late development of serfdom in the east compared with its decline in the west as the peasants successfully struggled to limit the lords' powers – which was due, Robert Brenner has argued, to the great difference in the strength of the village community. Economic cooperation, village self-government and communal control of common resources were all much less developed in the east.[38]

The case of England is peculiar and controversial. Rodney Hilton seems to believe that the argument about community and rebellion applies to the medieval period in Europe in general and to the Great English rising of 1381 in particular.[39] Of Kett's rebellion of 1549, which was the biggest peasant rebellion of the early modern period in England, Zagorin again argues that the village community played an important role in the mobilization.[40] And even as late as the early nineteenth century, in the machine-breaking and rick-burning of "Captain Swing", in most of the actions, according to Hobsbawm and Rudé, "the typical basic unit was a village group, composed of neighbours or bound by family ties, which took the initiative in organizing their own and neighbouring villages for common action by persuasion, the force of example, or impressment".[41] Nevertheless, Kett's rebellion was localized and short-lived and the Swing riots, though widespread, were not long sustained. More significantly,

non-participants, see Yves-Marie Bercé, *Histoire des Croquants*, 2 vols. (Geneva and Paris: Droz, 1974).
[37] Zagorin, *Rebels and Rulers*, vol. 1, p. 194.
[38] Robert Brenner, "Agrarian Class Structure and Economic Development in Pre-Industrial Europe", *Past and Present*, no. 70 (1976), 30–75.
[39] Rodney Hilton, *Bond Men Made Free: Medieval Peasant Movements and the English Rising of 1381* (London: Maurice Temple Smith, 1973), and "Peasant Society, Peasant Movements and Feudalism in Medieval Europe", in H.A. Landsberger (ed.), *Rural Protest* (London: Macmillan, 1974). In the latter (at p. 70) he writes of the peasants' "communal regulation of vital aspects of economic life" that "these necessary functions of economic life were the basis of the cohesion of the village community. The capacity for organisation in pursuit of social and political demands arose from the day-to-day experience of peasants" and peasants were thus "capable of tenacious common action".
[40] Zagorin, *Rebels and Rulers*, vol. 1, p. 211.
[41] E.J. Hobsbawm and George Rudé, *Captain Swing* (Harmondsworth: Penguin, 1973), p. 174.

even when, during the English Revolution, political circumstances were more propitious for large-scale, sustained rebellion, there was none at all – only scattered, short-lived rioting. Even if we do not accept Alan Macfarlane's controversial judgment that the local community in England had already begun to decline (and the peasantry to disappear) by 1381,[42] it is nevertheless probably true that, after the sixteenth century, though there was *some* rural community, it was not sufficiently strong to provide the necessary basis for really sustained, large-scale revolutionary collective action, even when the repressive capacities of the state were temporarily weakened.[43]

VI

Some people may be sceptical about the argument I have made to the effect that revolutionary and rebel collective action has rational foundations and conforms to the thin theory of collective action. The sceptics presumably would include those (and there are many of them) who reject this theory on the grounds that "it's obvious" that there is in reality much participation in collective action which, if the theory were correct, ought not to occur, and this includes participation in interest groups and other associations, which have of course largely replaced community as the vehicles of movements for social and political change. A brief comment on this position will lead to an assessment of the applicability of the thin theory of rationality.

The first point is that in fact there is now a great deal of evidence on such

[42] Alan Macfarlane, *The Origins of English Individualism* (Oxford: Blackwell, 1978).
[43] According to Craig Calhoun (*The Question of Class Struggle*, Oxford: Blackwell, 1982, especially p. 72), the potential of the English community for sustained collective action did not crumble until the early nineteenth century. He argues that up to and including the Luddism of the 1810s, popular protest in England had been made possible by the small community – based on propinquity or, in the towns, on a common craft, or on a combination of these. But while community was the foundation of rebellious collective action it was also its limitation, since it provided no means of – was indeed an obstacle to – coordination over a large territory. What was needed was a combination of the small local communities and a national *organization* to coordinate them. Only then would revolution be possible. This combination made a brief appearance in England, beginning with the end of Luddism and fading already in the 1830s. This is Calhoun's argument.

Two comments on this argument are relevant here. First, revolutions can be made – and not only in the predominantly peasant societies I have considered here – without effective national organization or nation-wide coordination of local communities. Second, the period of about two decades, which on Calhoun's account had most revolutionary potential, was a very brief moment of time when artisans still lived or worked in quasi-communities *and* began to organize nationally, and this might indeed have been a potent mixture if only it could have developed and been sustained. But the rise of organizations on a national scale, and for that matter of formal organizations of all kinds, was precisely prompted and to some extent facilitated by the developing conditions which had undermined the village communities and the quasi-communities based on craft. The combination could not last long.

associations which supports the thin theory of collective action (bearing in mind the modifications referred to in section I above): where large numbers of people share a common interest in a public good, relatively few do anything about it, and where an association or organization exists to further such an interest, of those who do join or participate or make donations, very many, perhaps most, are induced to do so by selective incentives admissible in Olson's theory, namely, "economic" and "social" incentives (or by a combination of these and the expected net subjective benefit arising from their contribution).[44] A number of studies have shown how important "social" incentives are in mobilizing people to contribute to collective action. An individual joins or contributes or participates because he is asked and tacitly or overtly pressured by friends, colleagues, workmates, or co-members of the association's local branch or cell. He cannot say "no" to them; he is afraid of losing their approval, respect or cooperation. "Social" incentives of this kind are especially effective in relatively small and stable groups. Hence, many large associations have a federal structure and mobilize support through their local branches.[45] Often these local cells will be small enough for conditional cooperation to be rational for their members and the conditional cooperation will be bolstered by the operation of the informal social sanctions. Hence, too, an individual can more readily be mobilized in the first place if he works with others or has friends sharing the common interest, or is part of an existing social network linking him to members of the association in question. In other words, in the absence of genuine community, associations can sometimes mobilize people by trading on the remnants or surrogates of community.[46]

---

[44] A good brief review of evidence on labour unions, farm groups and business associations is Terry M. Moe, *The Organization of Interests* (Chicago: Chicago University Press, 1980), chapter 7. There is also much interesting evidence scattered throughout James Q. Wilson, *Political Organisations* (New York: Basic Books, 1973), despite the author's disavowal of Olson's theory.

[45] Olson himself pointed this out: *The Logic of Collective Action*, p. 68.

[46] A number of studies showing this are discussed by Wilson in *Political Organisations*, though he fails to see that they give support to the thin theory of collective action. If some people join associations as a result of pressure brought to bear on them by existing friends and associates, it is also true, I would argue, that others join in part because of the prospect of *making* friends or having company. It also seems to me likely that *some* people, already sympathetic to a cause or to the goals of some association but not so strongly that they are prepared to do anything about it, join the association in order to put themselves in a position where they will be subject to the informal social sanctions exercised by their new associates and friends. There is in this bootstrapping operation a weaker version of the precommitment described by Jon Elster in *Ulysses and the Sirens* (Cambridge: Cambridge University Press, 1979): the precommitment does not actually eliminate options but makes the individual more vulnerable to pressure and coercion. The individual is committed to the cause enough to feel guilty about being a free rider but recognizes, in effect, that the commitment is too weak to overpower thin rationality. Another interesting possibility is that an individual with only a weak commitment joins

But associations are not communities, and only sometimes – and then only in highly attenuated forms – do they have available to them the positive and negative sanctions which a strong community can wield against its members with such extraordinary effectiveness. Failing these, an association must normally apply "economic" sanctions, for which (barring gifts like the state's backing for closed shops in trade unions) it must first gather the necessary resources, usually from its own members (though not of course at its founding and in its early days), and this puts a limit on the resources it can devote to producing the public good or on the resources it can devote to selective incentives to attract and retain supporters – a limit, either way, to its effectiveness in achieving its ends.

Although the evidence suggests that most collective action and failures of collective action are consistent with (thin) rational choice theory, there is clearly much collective action which is *not* explicable by the thin theory. People send dues to large associations without their contributions even being known to any one they know; they participate in massive demonstrations and movements *not* as members of a local branch or cell; they vote secretly in large constituencies; they contribute as isolated individuals to the provision of public goods by quietly refraining from various kinds of pollution without any social sanctions or pressure being applied or threatened; and so on. If these actions are not *thin*-rational, are they rational in some other sense, or are they simply not rational at all? If the latter, what explains them and why are people apparently sometimes thin-rational, sometimes not?

VII

In the thin theory, it will be recalled, rationality is relative to *given* aims and beliefs, and the agent's actions are *instrumental* in achieving or advancing the given aims in the light of the given beliefs; the agent is assumed to be egoistic; and the range of the agent's aims or the range of the incentives affecting the agent is limited, for without such limitation a thin theory is liable to become a tautology. It follows that, if a thin theory is to have much explanatory power, there are at least three general kinds of motivation which have little force. Since a thin theory requires action to be instrumental, it must be the case, first, that the pleasure or benefits of any kind which are got in the process of *doing* the action, as opposed to the value of the *consequences* of the action, must be unimportant; and second,

---

in the hope that this will strengthen the commitment, out of a sense that he or she ought to have proper commitments, ones strong enough to issue in action. I will have more to say in a later section about commitment and problems of the "self". The decision to join in these last two cases is not of course rational on the thin theory.

that *expressive* motivations – the desire to be "true to one's self", to act consistently with one's deeply held commitments, and so on – play no important role. And since, in a thin theory, action must be instrumental in bringing about benefits to the agent himself, *altruistic* motivations must be relatively unimportant.

Each of these three kinds of motivation has been made the subject of alternative accounts of rationality or models of motivation. The authors of two of these models – Margolis's "new model of rational choice" incorporating altruism and Scitovsky's model of motivation incorporating in-process benefits[47] – believe that they have greater power than the thin theory to explain the whole range of facts about collective action; to explain, that is, both the facts which the thin theory seems able to account for (such as peasant revolutionary collective action, if my argument is correct) and those which it is not (such as those referred to at the end of the last section). If this were true, we would presumably have reason to abandon the thin theory of rationality and build an explanation of collective action on one of the alternative theories or a synthesis of them. Then we would have a unified theory of collective action consistent with community-based revolutionary collective action *and* with *all* forms of association-based revolutionary or reformist movements.

Unfortunately, neither Scitovsky's nor Margolis's theory (nor any other alternative to the thin theory that I am aware of) will do the job. I have set out elsewhere the reasons why in my view Margolis's theory (though it is the most interesting attempt to date to incorporate altruistic motivations systematically into a model of individual choice) is unusable[48] and I will not repeat them here. In Scitovsky's theory, contributing to the provision of a public good may not be a "cost", as it is in the thin theory of collective action; it may on the contrary bring what he calls "pleasure", which is derived essentially from stimulation, often the product of doing as opposed to *having*. This is true of the participatory or active forms of collective action – such as active participation in a political movement or in a protest demonstration. *These* kinds of collective action – some of which may not be consistent with the thin theory – are consistent with Scitovsky's theory. But it is hard to see how this can be claimed of non-participatory or non-active forms, such as charitable donations and subscription payments to associations. And of course the theory does not explain why someone would choose public rather than private forms of "pleasure" – political activity rather than mountaineering.

[47] Howard Margolis, *Selfishness, Altruism and Rationality* (Cambridge: Cambridge University Press, 1982); Tibor Scitovsky, *The Joyless Economy* (New York: Oxford University Press, 1976).

[48] Michael Taylor, review of Margolis, *Selfishness, Altruism and Rationality*, Ethics, 94 (1983), 150–2.

Both Margolis and Scitovsky's theories are incompletely specified, hence difficult to assess properly. Margolis's theory in particular is premised on the belief that the conventional model of rational choice is generally "unreliable in the context of public goods". Since in this context there *is* in fact very little participation in collective action (relative to the vast unrealized potential for collective action to provide public goods), it is doubtful that these two models can do better than the conventional theory. They would almost certainly predict *too much* collective action. As I suggested earlier, most cases of collective action that do occur can be explained by the conventional theory if we remember that it encompasses conditional cooperation and the use of selective social incentives, which are often ignored, as well as economic incentives. And if it turned out (as I think it would) that Margolis's and Scitovsky's theories were inferior to the simple thin theory in this vast majority of cases, then we should be wary of using them for the residue.

There is a more radical alternative to the thin theory, which claims to explain, or at least to understand or interpret, this residue – as well as much other collective action which its authors seem to believe is not explained by the thin theory (perhaps again because they neglect the possibility that it is explained by the theory of conditional cooperation together with the use of informal social sanctions in subgroups). This alternative bears on the issue of "structural" and "voluntarist" explanation with which I began and to which I will shortly return, so I will set it out more fully.

The approach differs radically from the thin theory (and also from Margolis's theory) in that it takes an *expressive* rather than an instrumentalist or consequentialist view of rationality. A relatively clear statement of one version is due to Stanley Benn.[49] "Action", he says, "is rational if it manifests attitudes, beliefs, or principles that it would be inconsistent in a person, under appropriate conditions, not to give expression to, given the character he is generally content to acknowledge as his own." This allows rationality to the expression of mere attitudes and beliefs as well as principles and appears to put little restriction on their content. But Benn later adds that the rational actor should be a "morally responsible person" who acts autonomously, that is, who has and uses standards which are "his own" in the sense that he subjects them to a continuing process of critical scrutiny. "In such ways he makes himself a person of some particular kind defined by the things he cares about." Action is rational, then, only if it is consistent with these autonomously derived *commitments* to the values, principles and ideals the individual cares about.

[49] Stanley Benn, "The problematic rationality of political participation", in P. Laslett and J. Fishkin (eds.), *Philosophy, Politics and Society*, 5th series (Oxford: Blackwell, 1979).

It is clear that rationality in this sense would often require the individual to do things which the thin theory would deem non-rational. If someone is deeply committed to, say, certain environmentalist ideals, and these commitments are part of the individual's "nature" or "identity" and it is the case in some particular time and place that all true environmentalists should join in a certain protest demonstration, then rationality as moral self-expression requires that he participate, even if the costs of participation are much greater than his likely benefits (but not, of course, if the individual's participation made no difference whatever).

A variant of this approach, sharing its general view that the thin theory provides a daft account of the concept of rationality, is due to Martin Hollis, who argues not that the thin theory of rationality does a relatively bad job of explaining the facts but that it is doing no explanatory work at all.[50] If I understand Hollis's elusive *Models of Man* at all, he too, like Benn, reckons that (fully) rational action has to be autonomous. But he arrives at this position from a different direction.

According to Hollis, the thin theory makes of the individual a *Plastic Man*. He is a causally determined automaton who (which?), faced with externally given opportunities and subject to externally given constraints, simply translates into action given preferences and beliefs which themselves have causal origins external to him. In which case, says Hollis, "rationality" is doing no explanatory work. (Presumably, the explaining is being done, if any is being done at all, by the causes of the constraints and opportunities and the individual's preferences and beliefs.)

The actions of *Autonomous Man*, on the other hand, "cannot be explained by causal laws and conditions". But in Hollis's view this does not make Autonomous Man's action altogether inexplicable, as some writers would have it, for Autonomous Man is "the explanation of his own actions". Unfortunately, the nature of this form of explanation is never made entirely clear.[51] Hollis's argument seems to be roughly as follows. By definition an autonomous man acts freely (his actions are not causally determined) and this he does only if he has good reasons for his actions; he has good reasons only if he acts in his "ultimate" or "real" interests and these are "bound up with" or "derive from" what he "essentially is". The "real interests" are never clearly defined but they come with the characters or roles which the individual autonomously chooses or affirms and which thereby give him his identity – give him a

---

[50] Martin Hollis, *Models of Man* (Cambridge: Cambridge University Press, 1977). See also Hollis's "Rational Man and Social Science", in Ross Harrison (ed.), *Rational Action* (Cambridge: Cambridge University Press, 1979).

[51] Nor, likewise, is the idea of "agent causation", to which Hollis's notion bears a resemblance. See, for example, Roderick Chisholm, "Human freedom and the self", reprinted in G. Watson (ed.), *Free Will* (Oxford: Oxford University Press, 1982).

"self" which he expresses in his actions. Without autonomy, he would not be giving expression to a self but to external causal forces operating through him. On this account, then, to act *rationally* is to act in one's "real" or "ultimate" interests and this is to give expression to what one is. And it is this identity which in some sense *explains* its possessor's actions.

If an action is done just because it is required by a role or in some way expresses a "self" which is entirely determined by its bearer's social positions, then it is not of course autonomous, and on Benn's or Hollis's account it is not rational. Thus, an individual who is a roaring success as a capitalist entrepreneur, maximizing profit as (let us suppose) the role requires, cannot act rationally if he came to and performs this role uncritically and the role is not one he identifies with. Acting in this role cannot be *self*-expressive, for being a capitalist is not part of his identity.

A lot of collective action occurs precisely in situations where people act heteronomously. (The peasants whose revolutionary collective action I described earlier are surely in this category.) In such cases, I think Hollis would say, what explains the collective action are the causes determining the framework of opportunities and constraints in which the individuals act and the causes which move them to act. In these cases, I would at least agree, it is especially obvious that a theory of collective action which takes the individual's reasons for acting (his attitudes and beliefs) as unexplained givens is a radically incomplete explanation; but I want to insist that it is still a non-trivial *part* of the explanation.

In any case, there is, it seems to me, an analogous problem, if it is a problem, about explanations founded on a presumption of autonomy. Here, on Hollis's account, the explanatory buck, as it were, stops at the individuals' selves or identities. These are constituted by the characters or roles and the principles, ideals and projects which the individual has chosen to commit himself to or identify with. Without an explanation of how such commitments and identifications are made, this explanation of actions and their interaction is incomplete too.[52]

If I am not persuaded by Benn or Hollis to abandon the thin theory in favour of an expressive account of rationality, I do nevertheless take seriously the idea, or rather the range of ideas, of self-expression and I do believe that *expressive motivations* are important *in some contexts*. Undoubtedly some people are motivated to put their beliefs into practice; to act consistently with deeply held commitments to values, ideals and principles or simply to what is of central importance to them; not to be deterred from the pursuit of long-term projects; to make something

---

[52] *Some* of these commitments may be *rationally* chosen, taken on in order to protect the individual from the temptations of short-run gain and bring him greater gain in the longer run.

coherent out of what remains of their lives; and to search for their "real selves" or even try to construct identities (however problematic the idea and however self-defeating the endeavour). All these (overlapping) things can come into conflict with what is rational on the thin theory, can require the individual sometimes to act against his or her narrow self-interest as it is defined by the thin theory in question.[53]

VIII

If we accept, then, that expressive motivations – as well as altruistic motivation and perhaps some Scitovskian pleasure-seeking – exist as well as the motivations of thin self-interest, we need, in the absence of an empirically well-founded or at least applicable general theory of motivation which incorporates all these sorts of motivation, to have some general idea of the conditions under which these other kinds of motivation are important relative to thin self-interest, or, equivalently, to be able to say when the thin theory of rationality alone is likely to provide a good foundation for explanatory theories.

I suggest, first, that behaviour is *most likely* to be thin-rational (and hence a thin theory is most applicable) where: (i) the options or courses of action available to the individual are limited; (ii) the thin incentives (or some of them at least) affecting the individual are to him well defined, clearly apparent and above all substantial; (iii) the individual's choice situation and the thin benefits and costs together are such that a lot (for him) turns on his choice, that is, there is a course of action available to him which if followed would bring him very much more (in thin terms) than at least one of the alternative available courses of action;[54] and finally, and

---

[53] My point here is analogous to Bernard Williams's well-known argument against Utilitarianism ('A Critique of Utilitarianism', in J.J.C. Smart and B. Williams, *Utilitarianism: For and Against* (Cambridge: Cambridge University Press, 1973)). The good Utilitarian must act so as to maximize the sum of everyone's utilities, or at least of everyone who could be affected by the decisions available to him. This might require him to do something which conflicts with his projects or is inconsistent with his beliefs; to the Utilitarian it is enough that the utility of these things, which may be very great, has been entered into the aggregate utility calculation. But what if the right Utilitarian decision requires a man to turn aside from projects or ideals he is deeply committed to and identified with, that are part of what his life is about? (Such is the case, in Williams's example, of George, a chemist deeply opposed to chemical and biological warfare, who by taking a research job at a CBW laboratory could clearly increase the total utility of all those in any way affected by his choice, even after the great dis-utility attached to all the subsequent misery that would accrue to George if he took the job is taken into account.) To ask a man to do this, says Williams, is absurd; it is "to alienate him in a real sense from his actions and the source of his actions in his convictions"; it is "in the most literal sense, an attack on his integrity".

[54] Harsanyi, "Rational Choice Models", makes a similar point. Something like this point is also made in connection with the decision to vote by Robert E. Goodin and K.W.S. Roberts in "The Ethical Voter", *American Political Science Review*, 69 (1975), 926–8.

more weakly and uncertainly, (iv) prior to the choice situation in question there have previously been many similar or analogous occasions.

These conditions are neither necessary nor collectively sufficient. I make only the weaker claim that, other things being equal, the more any one of them is met, the more purchase is a thin theory likely to get.

The final condition is the one I feel least sure of. The idea here is that, if this condition is satisfied, then non-rational behaviour is likely to have been selected out or filtered out (or both).[55] But I would guess that this condition could readily be overridden by the other conditions.

A special case which satisfies both (ii) and (iii) – which are the most important conditions – is that of credible, substantial, explicit threats and offers (and throffers). Where selective incentives affect an individual's decision whether or not to participate in collective action, there are always at least tacit threats or offers (and this could also be argued of conditional cooperation). If these are explicit and substantial, they are even more likely to make the individual "think thin-rationally".

Of course, the extent to which the first three conditions are satisfied – the extent to which the agent's options are limited, or any of the incentives facing him are substantial, or a great deal turns on his choice – depends on the agent's resources of the relevant kinds. If the range of incentives specified in the thin theory is limited to monetary incentives, for example (or to any material things which money can buy), and the agent has already an abundant stock or supply of money, then he is less likely to be affected by threats and offers involving these incentives, and more likely not to act thin-rationally at all. In fact, thin theories invariably limit the incentives either to material incentives alone or (like the thin theory of collective action) to material incentives and "social" incentives based on the desire to avoid disapprobation. Now of course a person may be materially rich but not "rich" with respect to the "social" incentives, for there is a limit to how much approval, friendship, and so on, can be bought by money (or by food or other material goods), and approbation is not, like money, something of which one can accumulate a large stock that can then be spent over the rest of one's life; it has to be almost continuously earned. Furthermore, even in the sorts of societies in which these social incentives get most purchase, it seems likely that they are less

---

[55] On selection and filtering mechanisms, see Jon Elster, *Explaining Technical Change* (Cambridge: Cambridge University Press, 1983), p. 58 and chapter 6. The general idea can be found in several places in Joseph Schumpeter's writings; for example: *Capitalism, Socialism and Democracy*, 3rd edn (New York: Harper and Row, 1950), pp. 25 and 122–3; and *The Theory of Economic Development* (Cambridge, Mass.: Harvard University Press, 1934), p. 80. My attention was drawn to the last of these passages by the discussion of it in Richard R. Nelson and Sidney G. Winter, *An Evolutionary Theory of Economic Change* (Cambridge, Mass.: The Belknap Press of Harvard University Press, 1982), at p. 40. The passage is also quoted by Elster, at p. 114 of *Explaining Technical Change*.

fundamental motivators than the material incentives in the sense that they have much less force than material incentives when an individual is very poor materially.

So that, as long as material incentives are the only or the dominant motivators, it follows from conditions (i)–(iii) that the very poor are more likely to act thin-rationally than the relatively rich. Motivations *other* than those of thin self-interest will affect the rich more than the poor. Among these other motivations I would include pleasure in the technical sense of Scitovsky, altruisim in Margolis's sense, and the expressive motivations mentioned at the end of the last section. Pleasure, altruism and "moral self-expression" are, as it were, luxuries.

It would of course be nice to have a general theory of motivation, with the thin theory dropping out as a special case applicable especially to zones of "scarcity" and "constraint" (see conditions (i)–(iii) above). But we do not have such a theory and I doubt if we ever will.

The relevance of all this to mobilization for revolutionary collective action – in community and association – should be apparent.

The situation of the poor peasant member of the traditional communities which provided a basis for peasant collective action in the revolutions and rebellions of the past was just the kind of structured, constrained and stable situation which, I have argued, tends to make the individual act thin-rationally. By "situation" I mean not just the peasant's poverty but also the effects on him of the community and of the social and political environment without which community could not flourish. Scarcity and the coercive potential of the community tend to put the peasant in mind of his narrow self-interest and to leave little scope for such motivations as pleasure, genuine altruism (as opposed to reciprocity) beyond the household, or moral self-expression.

The world of the traditional community gave way, as everyone knows, to a world of associations and organizations. It is especially the better-off members of such societies who are disproportionately most likely to make donations to, join or participate in voluntary associations of all kinds, and I am suggesting that this is *because* they tend not to act thin-rationally. The theory of collective action based on the thin theory of rationality should not be applied to them. Unfortunately we do not have a workable theory that *can* be applied to them. We have, as I have said, neither a general theory of motivation of which the thin theory is a special case, nor any alternative explanatory theory that is applicable to the residue of non-thin behaviour. It is quite likely that most of the cases of participation in collective action and other kinds of contribution to public goods provision that cannot be explained by the thin theory can be understood, *one by one*, as pleasure-seeking, altruism, or some form of self-expression, but the available theories that include these motivations are a long way from providing a foundation for a testable theory of collective action. And the prospects are not good, for pleasure-seeking and the search for self and its expression take myriad idiosyncratic forms, lacking any predictable regularity.

The destruction and decay of community in modern societies removes the most important social basis for collective action; it is also part of an historical process which makes non-thin-rational behaviour more common and the success of collective action less predictable.

IX

The argument made in the last section about the applicability of the thin theory of rationality seems to have returned us to the starting-point of Hollis's argument (section VII). For if the thin theory is applicable only in structured and constrained situations of the sort I have indicated, then, it might be argued, it is precisely in these situations that the "structure" or situation is doing all the explaining because it limits the actors' options, provides or makes possible the use of non-trivial sanctions, and powerfully shapes the actors' attitudes and beliefs. If this is so, then, as I said earlier in discussing Skocpol's "anti-voluntarism", it would seem that the role of the rational-choice theorist is that of mere technician, the serious part of the business being left to those who can explain the causal origins of attitudes and beliefs and the situations in which they operate. This conclusion, I shall argue in this final section, is mistaken.

Let us go back to peasant rebellion (whether part of a successful social revolution or not). It is undeniably the product in the first place of individual actions. The actions are caused by attitudes and beliefs (including attitudes to and beliefs about structures) and these in their turn have causes. Amongst the causes of peasant attitudes and beliefs are surely *structures* (by which I mean sets of relations) – most obviously, the relations of production (the economic structure) whose terms are productive forces and persons, including peasants; the political relations between peasants and their landlords and the state; and other social relations amongst the peasants themselves, including aspects of the social structure of the village community not included in the economic or political structure. (I emphasize that I am not supposing that *abstract* structures – that is, sets of relations defined independently of specific relata – can be causes, even of attitudes to and beliefs about structures. But what can be causes, surely, are *specific* structures, that is, structures with specific relata, or those parts of them which impinge on, say, the attitudes and beliefs in question.)

But the fact that individual actions, attitudes and beliefs are caused – by structures or by anything else – does not make them explanatorily irrelevant, any more than the fact that structures are in part the product of individual actions makes structures explanatorily irrelevant. We need, then, both individualist explanation of structures (and other macrophenomena) *and* structuralist explanation (amongst other kinds of explanation) of individual attitudes and beliefs. To deny either side of this supposition is to deny *any* causal force either to structures or to individuals, to attach *all* the explanatory power to one or the other. This is what is proposed by, on the one side, structuralists who would treat individuals as nothing other than the "effects" of structures or as mere "supports" or "bearers" of functions determined by structures, and history as "process without a subject"; and on the other side, those methodological individualists who suppose that all social phenomena can be reduced without residue to individual action and that explanation should always start with individuals (or stop with them, depending on which direction you look in). Either attitude, it seems to me, rests on a dogma, an unproven assertion that flies in the face of common sense.

By *structuralist explanation* I simply mean causal explanation of social phenomena, or of attitudes and beliefs, in terms of social structures – including economic and political structures – or aspects or properties of such structures. Much structuralist "theory" or argument is or crucially relies upon some form of functionalist "explanation", and is therefore not a valid form of explanation.[56] But not all structural explanation is functional. Skocpol's explanation of social revolutions is not. Nor is the general theory proposed by Jeffery Paige in *Agrarian Revolution*, which gives us in effect a causal explanation of some of the attitudes, beliefs and options that would be relevant to an explanation of revolution, rebellion, etc., in terms of their bearers' locations in an economic–political structure.[57]

A pure individualist explanation would have the field to itself *only if* the causes of the attitudes and beliefs which cause action are themselves nothing but actions and properties of individuals. Certainly, individuals' actions and properties can be causes of attitudes and beliefs: a person's attitudes and beliefs can be caused (perhaps without his knowing it) by other attitudes and beliefs of his own; they can be produced directly by others' actions or behaviour; and they may even in part be *self*-made – the intentional products of the individual's own actions. But, as I have said, attitudes and beliefs, *including attitudes to and beliefs about structures*, can also be the products of the individual's situation or position in a social structure. So (if we set aside direct causation by the individual's physical

56 See Elster, *Explaining Technical Change*, part 1.
57 Jeffery M. Paige, *Agrarian Revolution* (New York: The Free Press, 1975).

environment) methodological individualism would have the explanatory field to itself only if structures (or all those aspects of them which could affect individuals' actions via their attitudes and beliefs) were *nothing but* individual (inter-) actions. Now a social structure might be, as Bhaskar and Giddens would say, the medium of action. And certainly, a structure typically emerges as a result of, and is maintained or transformed by, the actions of individuals. But it is not *the same thing as* these actions.

The methodological position I am here advocating (or supporting), though it involves attempting to supply causal links beginning and terminating at *individuals*, does not commit me to pure methodological individualism any more than it commits me to any version of methodological holism. To repeat: individuals – their actions or properties – are no more "rock-bottom" than (for example) structures. I am therefore not committed to certain views with which methodological individualists are customarily (though in most cases unjustly) saddled. Skocpol shares some of these misconceptions of methodological individualist practice. Most obviously, she seems to believe (as many sociologists persist in believing) that the position she attacks is destroyed by the obvious fact that outcomes are rarely the ones intended by the actors producing them. (In fact, of course, most rational choice theorizing outside of economics is centrally concerned with problems of unintended consequences.) A related mis-understanding, shared (I think) by Skocpol and very relevant to the argument of this essay, concerns the issue of the role of the individual in history, which is sometimes confounded or conflated with various other issues, including that of determinism. As Elster has argued,[58] the distinct-ive issue involved here is one of *stability*: whether a society, after any small "deviation" from its course brought about by the action of a single individual, will eventually resume the course it would have taken in the absence of the perturbation. But such stability entails nothing about how best to *explain* the course of history. (This, I *think*, is not Elster's view, but his brief discussion is unclear.) The historical path taken by a society may depend very much on what individuals do yet be immune to the effects of what is done by any individual, even (though I doubt it) an outstandingly creative or powerful or critically placed individual. Suppose that a rebellion is precipitated by a single act: a soldier fires on a crowd perhaps. It may be true (though impossible to prove) that the rebellion (or rather one like it) would have occurred even if this act had not been performed

---

[58] Elster, *Explaining Technical Change*, pp. 32–3. My general methodological position is probably very close to that of Elster, to whose work I am indebted. I say "probably", because he apparently sees his approach as that of methodological individualism. See especially "Marxism, Functionalism, and Game Theory: the Case for Methodological Individualism", *Theory and Society*, 11 (1982), 453–82. See also *Making Sense of Marx* (Cambridge: Cambridge University Press, 1985).

(indeed even if no act like this one had been performed), because there were underlying "social forces" which would (sooner or later) have produced the rebellion anyway. (Each of the clauses in parentheses in this sentence signals an obvious difficulty with specifying statements of this kind satisfactorily.) But it does not follow that the explanation of the rebellion and the historical path leading up to it must be non-individualist or that it cannot take the general form suggested earlier for good causal-cum-intentional explanation in the social sciences.[59]

Now it may be the case that, although the rebellion would *not* have occurred without the crucial precipitating act, this single act was sufficient to precipitate the rebellion only because of some underlying condition(s). Again, this does not oblige us to embrace purely structural explanation or some other form of holism.

Whichever of the two kinds of cause mentioned in the last two paragraphs – "unnecessary" or "necessary but superficial" – is the precipitating cause, the analysis of the *underlying* causes should in any case meet the criteria for good explanation. And I take it that good explanation should be, amongst other things, as *fine-grained* as possible: causal links connecting events distant in space–time should be replaced wherever possible by chains of "shorter" causal links.[60] This is an important reason for supplying explanations with causal links beginning and terminating at individuals. Structuralist and other holistic theories, where they take a causal form, are typically coarse-grained in this sense: they relate macrostates directly to macrostates without supplying a "mechanism" to show how the one brings about the other.

I have concentrated in this chapter (which is long enough as it is) on revolutionary collective action amongst peasants. But Skocpol's structuralist case may seem more persuasive when she argues that, whatever revolutionaries or peasants want, believe or do, they will not make a revolution unless the right sort of situation presents itself, and the production of such a situation is beyond their control, since it is in large part the consequence of the state's position in an international structure. I think we can accept this argument about the influence of international structures (at least in the cases of France and Russia) without, however, embracing Skocpol's resolute rejection of "voluntarist" and "purposive" explanation. For these structures, too, though they may have been intended or foreseen by no one, have to be explained in their turn and I see no reason why they should not in part be explained in terms of the rational

---

[59] The latest writer to draw this incorrect inference in support of holistic theorizing is Richard W. Miller in *Analyzing Marx: Morality, Power and History* (Princeton: Princeton University Press, 1984), p. 289.

[60] Elster, *Explaining Technical Change*, pp. 24, 28–9.

actions of states (or state managers) and other actors. (There is no hint of *proof* in Skocpol's book that these were not the important proximate causes.) Indeed, I think there are more compelling reasons for believing that individuals in state managerial roles act (thin-) rationally, especially in response to economic and military competition and pressures from other states, than there are for believing that most other kinds of agents act rationally.[61] (This follows from the general argument about the applicability of the thin theory which I made in section VIII.) In fact, much of what Skocpol herself has to say about the historical behaviour of actual states seems to presuppose that they act rationally; and her general characterization of the state (pp. 29–32) attributes to it broad *aims* – above all in the maintenance of domestic order and defence against other states – which give it specific *interests vis-à-vis* domestic actors, including both dominant and subordinate classes, as well as foreign actors, including states. Skocpol rightly emphasizes how revolutionaries, on seizing state power, themselves quickly adopt these basic interests of the state – and shows too how they also have other, ideologically inspired aims, not shared with the old regime managers, which seem to cause them to act in certain ways. Indeed, in her detailed historical accounts of the French, Russian and Chinese Revolutions – which are littered with statements about, or presupposing, intentional action – Skocpol fails quite generally to live up to her "nonvoluntarist, structural" methodological ideals.[62]

What of the other structural and situational conditions that Skocpol sees as necessary for social revolution? Like the state's international situation, these too have to be explained in their turn and again I see no reason why the explanation should not be at least partly intentional. Though intended by no one, these structures and situations are themselves in significant part the products of intentional actions. The peasant community, the relative power of the landed upper class and indeed the whole pre-revolutionary class structure, as well as the economic and military backwardness of the state relative to its competitors, and other character-istics of the international situation in which the state finds itself – *all* of these, as I hope to show in another place, are *precipitates* of past intentional actions.

---

[61] For a stimulating discussion of the state's pursuit of its self-interest, see Anthony de Jasay, *The State* (Oxford: Blackwell, 1985). See also Fred Block, "Beyond Relative Autonomy: State Managers as Historical Subjects", in Ralph Miliband and John Saville (eds.), *The Socialist Register, 1980* (London: Merlin Press, 1980).

[62] Something similar occurs in Paige's *Agrarian Revolution*, referred to earlier. Though not as coarse-grained as Skocpol's, Paige's general theory is similarly radically incomplete and ahistorical and cannot account for change, as it is supposed to do. But, as with Skocpol, history creeps back in, as it has to, when Paige turns to detailed study of cases.

3 Rational outlaws: rebels and bandits in the Ming Dynasty, 1368–1644

James Tong

In this study, we will construct and test a rational choice model of collective violence in a premodern society, using rebellions and banditry in the Ming Dynasty of China (1368–1644) as the empirical referent. This model views rebellions and banditry as a rational response in a subsistence crisis, in the same family of survival strategies as migration, pawning of children or wives, or becoming monks, eunuchs, and cannibals. It postulates that the decision to become an outlaw is a function of (1) the likelihood of surviving severe hardship; and (2) the likelihood of survival as an outlaw. And it predicts that there would be more rebellions and banditry when the times were bad and, at the same time, when government punishment was uncertain. As will soon be evident, the empirical pattern of collective violence in Ming appears to fit these predictions closely.

In the pages that follow, we will begin with a description of the empirical pattern of Ming collective violence, in particular, its spatial–temporal distribution. To account for the empirical pattern, we will examine two dominant approaches – class conflict and social change explanations, which we found to be incongruous with the Ming configuration. This will be followed by a discussion of survival strategies in agrarian crises in premodern societies. Having thus prepared the setting, we will turn to an exposition of the rational choice framework and a presentation of the empirical findings.

The empirical pattern

Before we describe the empirical pattern of Ming collective violence, some comments about our data collection effort are in order. To begin with the *spatial–temporal domain*, our study includes eleven of the fifteen Ming provinces, and spans the entire Ming Dynasty (1368–1644). Four provinces in southwestern China are excluded because of data problems.[1]

[1] The four southwestern provinces (Sichuan, Yunnan, Guizhou, Guangxi) are excluded primarily because of data problems. Whereas each of the other eleven provinces has at

Our choice of Ming rests on the fact that few premodern systems have the systematic, annual, county-level data on collective violence as well as on a whole array of explanatory variables that Ming had. It is the first Chinese dynasty that had such systematic disaggregated data, and the last one before social change, foreign wars, and Western contact deprived China of its innocence as a premodern society.

Second, the unit of analysis is an *event* rather than an incident.[2] In all, we counted over a thousand violent events, but only 630 of these met our criteria for inclusion. To articulate our counting procedures, we included those acts of collective, organized, and armed resistance, or attacks on constituted authority that were recorded in local gazetteers (a) as an uprising (*qi*) or a disturbance (*luan*); (b) at a specific county and year; (c) with an identifiable leader or group designation; and (d) perpetrated by Han Chinese groups. Our selection criteria are restrictive so that the cases included would be relatively homogeneous. Excluded from our universe are: (1) foreign invasions; (2) uprisings of non-Han ethnic minorities; (3) non-violent collective action; (4) acts perpetrated by small, nameless brigand groups; and (5) those for which we cannot identify either the location (county) or the time (year) of the uprising. In addition, we have excluded all interregnum violence accompanying the birth of new dynasties. For most provinces, we began counting in 1371, the year after the civil examination was inaugurated, an event indicating that equilibrium had been basically restored in the province. For similar reasons, we have also excluded all anarchic violence that took place after the Ming capital was overrun by rebel forces in the third month of 1644.

Third, each *case of observation* in our study is a county-year. Since there are 1,097 counties and 277 years, our universe thus consists of 303,869 cases of observation. We combed through local gazetteers for data on collective violence as well as explanatory variables for each county year. The local gazetteers that served as the main data sources are provincial and prefectural gazetteers published during the Ming Dynasty, and the Qing Dynasty (1644–1911) that came after it. All extant Ming and Qing editions of provincial gazetteers, numbering around 100, in major collections in the U.S., Japan, and China were examined. In addition, we also consulted at least one Ming or Qing edition of the prefectural gazetteer, totalling around 130 titles. Only in the very rare instances when data

---

least one Ming or early Qing *provincial* gazetteer, and at least one Ming or Qing edition of the *prefectural* gazetteer, the same is not true for the four southwestern provinces. We have only mid or late Qing editions of Yunnan, Guizhou, and Guangxi provincial gazetteers, and we do not have any gazetteer for several prefectures in the four provinces.

[2] An event is made up of incidents. Our choice of an event is based on the fact that it is more comparable and identifiable, and less sensitive to the problem of underreporting.

were unavailable in provincial and prefectural gazetteers, were county gazetteers consulted. Data were also collected from the primary and secondary sources noted below. For data on violent events, the chronology (*jishi*) and military affairs (*bingshi*) sections of these local gazetteers are used.

Fourth, we will use *frequency* and *extent* as two measures for the level of rebellions and banditry. We are aware that other studies (Richardson, 1960; Russett, 1964; Tilly and Rule, 1965, and Sugimoto, 1973) have employed severity (number of people killed) and magnitude (number of man-days of participation) as measures of levels of violence.[3] However, reliable, interval data for severity and magnitude measures are unavailable for the Ming data. Most accounts of rebellions and banditry in local histories or special histories do not provide rough estimates, still less precise figures of the number of rebels, their casualties, or the duration of their activities. And when they do, the reliability of some of their estimates are highly suspect.[4] Thus, our choice of the appropriate measures is seriously constrained by available reliable data.

For the present, we have chosen frequency and extent as our measures of the level of violence. To be specific, we will use the number of rebellions and cases of banditry that began in a particular county in a particular year as the frequency count. Note that this is a measure of violence *begun* rather than violence *under way*. That is, if a given rebellion began in year one and persisted till year five, it will only be counted once, that is, only in year one. Note that this is also a measure of the *source location* rather than the *total affected area*, as we are attributing these uprising acts only to those counties in which they arose rather than those to which they spread. To control for the magnitude of violence, we will also use an *extent* measure, by counting the number of counties affected by each rebellion or banditry event.

Fifth, within our universe of rebellions and banditry, we have further distinguished among the following three subtypes. Rebellions can be staged by *dynastic contenders* or *military challengers*. The former refer to those uprisings that manifest dynastic ambitions or proclaimed sover-

---

[3] See Lewis Richardson, *Statistics of Deadly Quarrels* (Pittsburg: The Boxwood Press, 1960); Bruce Russett, "Inequality and Instability: The Relation of Land Tenure to Politics", *World Politics*, 16 (April, 1964), 442–54; Charles Tilly and James Rule, *Measuring Political Upheaval* (Princeton: Princeton, N.J.: Center for International Studies, Princeton University Monograph (1964), no. 19); Yashio Sugimoto, "Equalization and Turbulence: The Case of the American Occupation of Japan" (Ph.D. dissertation, University of Pittsburg, 1973).

[4] For example, it has been pointed out that the *Ming Shi* figure that 600 million people were slaughtered during the rebel Zhang Xianzhong's occupation of Sichuan in late Ming was 200 times the total population of the province as listed in the geographical chapter of the same book; see James Parsons, *The Peasant Rebellions of the Late Ming Dynasty* (Tucson: University of Arizona Press, 1970), p. 186.

eignty by (a) declaring the founding of a new dynasty; or (b) claiming a sovereign title for its leader or official titles for his entourage; or (c) establishing a bureaucracy or inaugurating the civil examination to recruit new officials; or (d) renaming cities and prefectures under their control; or (e) adopting symbols of soveriegn rule – government seals, new coat of arms, standard, or currency. Second, *military challengers* were those uprisings that launched a military offensive against the state, by (a) attacking seats of the county, prefectural, or provincial government, or (b) assaulting military garrisons or police check-points, or (c) raiding county or prefectural treasury, or (d) releasing county prison inmates, but short of manifesting dynastic ambition or proclaiming sovereignty. Third, *banditry* refers to those armed groups that pillaged villages, raided stores and provisions, robbed travelling merchants, or captured hostages for ransom, but fell short of launching a military offensive against the government, or manifesting dynastic ambition or proclaiming sovereignty. In Ming, we counted 37 cases of dynastic contention, 57 cases of military challengers, and 536 cases of banditry.

In our larger research project, we have kept these three subtypes as well as other classifications of local disturbances analytically distinct, depending on the research task at hand. For our present purpose, however, we will treat them as an undifferentiated universe of cases, and refer to them as "rebellions and banditry", "armed uprising", "armed disturbance", and "violent incidents" or "acts of collective violence" interchangeably. We will do so because the small number of cases of dynastic contentions and military challenges would present statistical problems if analyzed separately. In addition, they share a common denominator of armed defiance that scholars, administrative historians, and Ming authorities have treated as a similar class of events. They were listed in the same section in local gazetteers under the rubric of "Military affairs" or "Banditry". They were considered to be the same class of serious threats to peace and order in Ming that local officials were required to report to higher hierarchical levels and take suppressive actions, and all such offenders would be sentenced to capital punishment. In fact, in Ming administrative lexicon, there was no separate terms for "rebel" and "bandit". The leaders as well as the rank and file of major rebellions in Ming (e.g. Li Zicheng, Liu Liu, etc.) were referred to as "bandits" or "rebellious bandits". Elsewhere, Hobsbawm has also noted that banditry tends to flourish in the same areas as rebellions, and indeed would usually merge with the more ambitious types of rural endemic insurrections, millenial or messianic rebellions or revolutions.[5] In Ming as

[5] Eric Hobsbawm, "Social Bandits", in Henry A. Landsberger (ed.), *Rural Protest: Peasant Movements and Social Change* (London: Macmillan, 1974), pp. 146–7.

Table 1. *Frequency of rebellions and banditry in 11 provinces in Ming*

Province	First Half (1368–1505)	Second Half (1506–1644)	Total Period (1368–1644)	% of Total
Beizhili	4	21	25	4
Shandong	1	22	23	4
Henan	0	23	23	4
Shanxi	1	24	25	4
Shaanxi	2	40	42	7
Huguang	5	33	38	6
Jiangxi	19	34	53	8
Nanzhili	5	24	29	5
Zhejiang	5	21	26	4
Fujian	19	88	107	17
Guangdong	47	192	239	38
Total	108	522	630	101

in Europe then, rebellions were considered as an extension or a variant of banditry.

An overview of the empirical pattern

To summarize the broad features of the empirical configuration, there were distinct patterns of spatial and temporal distribution of rebellions and banditry in Ming. In the whole period, a total of 630 rebellions and banditry events erupted in the 11 provinces, affecting 1,089 counties. Temporally, the second half of the dynasty (1506–1644) was much more rebellious and bandit-ridden than the first half. Less than a fifth (108 of the 630, or 17.1%) of the total number of violent events occurred in the first half, and the remaining four-fifths (82.8%, or 522) events occurred in the second half. The same pattern of preponderance of the second half was observed regardless of the different measures, different regions, or levels of aggregation used.[6] Spatially, the south had more rebellions and banditry than the north. More than three-quarters (78.1%) of the rebellions and banditry, or 492 of the 630 incidents were found in the 6 provinces in the south. The dominance of the south also persists even when time periods and levels of aggregation are controlled. On the province level, the southern provinces of Guangdong and Fujian were the

---

[6] We have used both the frequency of occurrence, as well as the number of counties victimized, as two measures of the level of rebellions and banditry. For regional stratification, we have divided the provinces into five northern and six southern provinces, using the Yangzi River as the line of demarcation. The analysis was performed on both the empire, regional, and provincial levels.

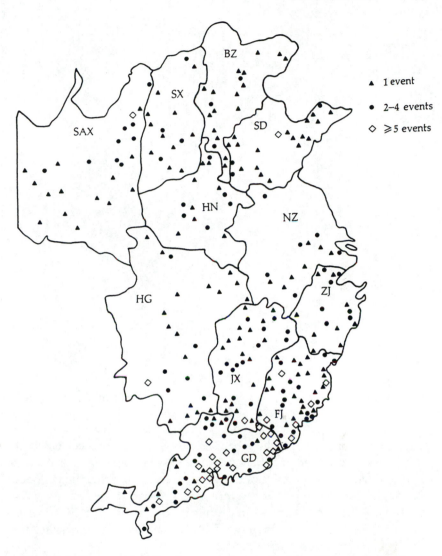

Fig. 1 Rebellions and banditry in 11 provinces in the Ming Dynasty, 1368–1644

leading collective culprits, while the two northern provinces of Henan and Shanxi were least rebellious. A more detailed picture of the spatial–temporal pattern is given in table 1 and figs. 1 and 2. Table 1 presents the frequencies of rebellions and banditry in the eleven provinces in the first and second half of the dynasty. The first five are provinces in the north. Fig. 1 presents the geographical location as well as the size of rebellions and banditry. Each point on the map represents the seat of a county from

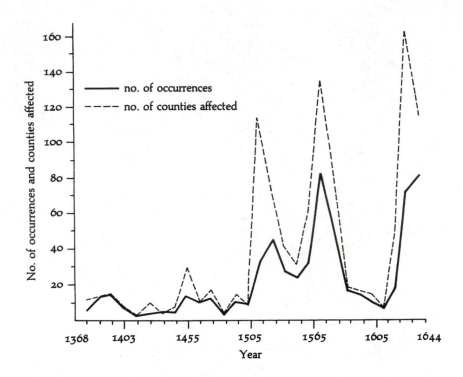

Fig. 2 Rebellions and banditry in 11 provinces in the Ming Dynasty, 1368–1644

which rebellions and banditry had arisen. A cross denotes that such incidents had occurred once in that county in the entire period, a star two to four times, a diamond five or more times. Fig. 2 presents the temporal distribution of rebellions and banditry aggregated to 10-year periods. The continuous line represents the total number of such incidents in the given decade. The dotted line represents the total number of counties affected by such incidents in the same period.

The class conflict and social change approaches compared

Having thus described the empirical pattern of premodern collective violence in Ming, we turn to the task of constructing and testing a rational choice approach to explain the above pattern. To underscore the significance of the present effort, let us begin with the observation that there is as yet no theoretical attempt to describe and explain collective violence in a premodern society. In Eckstein (1980), Zimmerman (1983), as well as

Tilly's (1978) catalogs of leading brands in the market,[7] major works on collective violence either adopt a Marxian paradigm, attributing collective violence to antagonistic class conflict, or follow the Durkheimian tradition, emphasizing the effect of rapid social change on social disintegration and anomic violence. The major problem with applying these two frameworks to collective violence in premodern societies is their anachronism. Class conflict approaches cannot adequately account for political violence in a premodern society where intraclass solidarity and interclass antagonism have not yet been intensified by urbanization and industrialization. Nor can we attribute collective violence to mass anomie, before urbanization uproots traditional communities, industrialization accelerates social differentiation, and commercialization aggravates relative deprivation. We thus need to construct a model that will specify conditions for the outbreak of collective violence in a premodern society. Before we do so, let us briefly examine our Ming data to see whether they do in fact fail to support these two theoretical approaches.[8]

Social change

To begin with social change approaches, many theorists have attributed the occurrence of collective violence to rapid social change, as the effect of social disintegration (Durkheim, 1933; Smelser, 1963); mass mobilization (Kornhauser, 1959; Huntington, 1968); structural strain (Parsons, 1966); system disequilibrium (Johnson, 1966); social comparison and relative deprivation (Davies, 1969; Gurr, 1970).[9] If the social change model is operative, then we would expect higher levels of collective violence to be found in regions and periods that are more commercialized, urbanized, or industrialized, or where the rate of change is more rapid. Such, however, is not the case in Ming.

[7] Harry Eckstein, "Theoretical Approaches to Explaining Collective Political Violence", in Ted Robert Gurr, *Handbook of Political Conflict: Theory and Research* (New York: The Free Press, 1980), pp. 135–66; Ekkart Zimmermann, *Political Violence, Crises, and Revolutions: Theories and Research* (Cambridge, Mass.: Schenkman Publishing Co. 1983); Charles Tilly, *From Mobilization to Revolution* (Reading, Mass.: Addison-Wesley, 1978).

[8] For a more detailed treatment, see James Tong, "Collective Violence in a Premodern Society: Rebellions and Banditry in the Ming Dynasty, 1368–1644" (Ph.D. dissertation, University of Michigan, 1985).

[9] See Emile Durkheim, *The Division of Labor in Society* (New York: Macmillan, 1933); Neil Smelser, *Theory of Collective Behavior* (New York: The Free Press, 1963); William Kornhauser, *The Politics of Mass Society* (Glencoe, Ill.: The Free Press, 1959); Samuel Huntington, *Political Order in Changing Societies* (New Haven: Yale University Press, 1968); Talcott Parsons, *Societies: Evolutionary and Comparative Perspectives* (Englewood Cliffs, N.J.: Prentice-Hall, 1966); Chalmers Johnson, *Revolutionary Change* (Boston: Little Brown, 1966); James Davies, "The J-Curve of Rising and Declining Satisfaction as a Cause of Some Great Revolutions and a Contained Rebellion", in Hugh D. Graham and Ted R. Gurr (eds.), *Violence in America: Historical and Comparative Perspectives* (New York: Bantam, 1969), chapter 19; Ted R. Gurr, *Why Men Rebel* (Princeton: Princeton University Press, 1970), chapter 4.

First, the social change model cannot explain the spatial–temporal distribution of collective violence in Ming. In terms of spatial distribution, the Jiangnan region, which included the most commercialized and urbanized prefectures in Ming, was not one of the more rebellious regions. Conversely, Guangdong and Fujian, the most rebellious provinces, were not among the more industrialized, commercialized, and urbanized regions. In particular, the many instances of banditry in predominantly rural, uncommercialized, sparsely populated mountainous counties in Guangdong and Fujian remain unexplained. Temporally, the pattern of industrial and commercial expansion in Ming is generally considered to be in the shape of a gradually rising curve, beginning at mid-Jiajing (1522–66), and continued through the Longqing and Wanli period (1567–1620).[10] Such a pattern does not correspond to the trimodal distribution of rebellions, peaking at 1506–25, 1556–75, 1626–44, and dropping off for the Wanli period (1573–1620). It certainly does not explain the first hump of rebellions in 1506–25, a time before the first spurt of commercial, industrial, and urban expansion occurred.

In addition to the above lack of fit between the spatial–temporal distribution of collective violence events on the one hand, and areas with higher levels of social change on the other, we have also collected data on various measures of commercialization, urbanization, and social change. We then correlated the level of collective violence with: (1) the level of commercial tax in 1,097 counties; (2) the level of commercialization in 289 counties in Huguang, Nanzhili and Jiangxi, measured by the number of market towns (zhen), markets (shi), and periodic markets, (ji, qu); (3) the level or urbanization in 316 counties in Huguang, Nanzhili, and Jiangxi, measured by the number of boulevards (dajie), streets (xiaojie), and alleys (xiang). In all these three cases, we did not find higher levels of collective violence in the more commercialized and urbanized counties.

Thus far, the above two tests employ a cross-sectional design correlating the level of collective violence with the *level*, not the *rate*, of social change. To scrutinize the effect of the rate of social change, we have examined the critical period in the 214 counties around the time when imperial sales tax offices were abolished in these counties. We reason that since they were abolished in different years,[11] this meant that there was a

[10] See Zheng Tianting (ed.), *Ming Qing Shi Ziliao* (Tianjin: Tianjin Renmin Chubanshe, 1980), p. 252; Fu Yiling, *Mingdai Jiangnan Shimin Jingji Shitan* (Shanghai: Shanghai Renmin Chubanshe, 1957), pp. 16, 20, 81, 102, 105; articles by Shang Yue, Han Dacheng, Wang Fangzhong, Huang Peijin, in *Ming Qing Shehuijingji Xingtai di Yanjiu* (Shanghai: Shanghai Renmin Chubanshe, 1957); and articles by Liu Yongcheng, Qin Peiheng, Kong Jingwei, Liu Yuncun, and Li Hua in *Ming Qing Zibenzhuyi Mengya Yanjiu Lunwenji* (Shanghai: Shanghai Renmin Chubanshe, 1981).

[11] The earliest abolition of an imperial sales tax office was recorded in 1490, in Shandong's Renping, En, Xiajin, and Wucheng counties, and Gaotang zhou. The Zhengyangmen

significant decline in tax receipts in these counties in the period preceding the abolition. This reflects a downturn of the local economy and higher levels of frustrated expectations that Davies's (1969) J-curve suggests. If the social change hypothesis is true, then we could find significantly higher levels of collective violence *around the time* of the abolition of the sales tax offices in these 214 counties. Our examination of the data also shows that within the group of 214 counties, there were no significantly higher levels of political violence in the 10 years before and after the abolition, than the other 200 (220−20) years.[12] Second, comparing the critical period of this vulnerable group, a total of 4,280 (20×214) county-years with the remaining cases in the total universe, or [(277×1,097)−(20×214)] county-years, there were also no significantly higher levels of collective violence among this critical group. In short, the results do not support the hypothesis that higher *rates* of social change led to higher levels of collective violence. None of the four sets of tests turned up evidence that the level of collective violence is related to either the *level* or the *rates* of social change.

Class conflict explanations

Turning to class conflict models, we have also found the following anomalies. First, those who subscribe to class conflict explanations, especially Chinese and Japanese historians, often allude to the presence of armed conflicts between antagonistic classes as evidence of class conflict in Ming. In particular, they have often cited revolts of commoners against aristocrats, tenants against landlords, bondservants against masters, and employees against employers. These four forms of antagonistic class conflict, however, constitute less than 10 of the 630 cases of armed disturbances in our universe. By our count, there were only 3 incidents of revolts against the aristocracy, 2 cases of bondservant revolts, and 5 tenant revolts that would fit our criterion of inclusion.[13] As less than 2% of the total cases, they are numerically insignificant to constitute a general explanation of the occurrence of collective violence in Ming.

Second, while there were only three incidents of revolts of commoners against aristocrats, it could be argued that the proliferation of the size, power, and privilege of the imperial aristocracy had three major effects on

---

office of Shuntian prefecture was recorded as the last being abolished in 1583: see *Daming Huidian*, ch. 35: 9–31.

[12] The 220-year period represents the period from 1368–1587, the cut-off point for data on the abolition of imperial sales tax offices listed in the *Daming Huidian*, ch. 35.

[13] Although we have counted three cases of armed conflict between employees and employers, they do not qualify for inclusion as there was no report of armed confrontation between these groups and government authorities.

the rise of rebellions.[14] First, their numerical increase in geometric progression from 58 in the first reign to over 80,000 in the last decades of the dynasty meant ever-increasing grain drain to feed these aristocrats.[15] Indeed, close to a third of the empire's total grain tax went to provide for emolument of the imperial clansmen,[16] and the total disposable grain revenue of the province of Shanxi and Henan was insufficient to feed the aristocrats in residence.[17] Second, coupled with drastic increase in expenditure was a sharp decrease in government tax revenue, as more taxable government land became non-taxable feudal estates.[18] To meet increasing aristocratic consumption and to compensate for loss of revenue, the state increased the tax burden on peasants. Third, driven away from their native villages by the oppressive land-tenure system, the original tenants in feudal estates became displaced peasants and easy recruits for incipient rebel groups.

We have found little systematic evidence to support the above contention. Spatially, the two most rebellious provinces were Guangdong and Fujian, which accounted for more than half of the violent incidents and victimized counties. There were, however, no feudal aristocrats in residence, nor feudal estates in these two provinces. Conversely, Shanxi and Henan, which had the heaviest burden in feeding the aristocrats, were the least rebellious and bandit-ridden among the 11 provinces.[19] Temporally, the shape of aristocratic proliferation is unimodal. The number of feudal aristocrats rose steadily through the dynasty till the reign of Shizong (1522–66), when it began to dip till the end of dynasty. However, as noted earlier, the shape of rebellions and banditry was *trimodal*, and peaked at 1506–25, 1546–75, and 1626–44. It thus appears that there is no relationship between the proliferation of aristocrats and increasing collective violence.

Third, it is conceivable that although the presence and proliferation of

[14] For arguments that came close to this view, see Gu Cheng, "Mingdai di Zongshi" (The Imperial Clansmen in Ming) in *Ming Qing Shi Guoji Xueshu Taolunhui Lunwenji* (Tianjin: Tianjin People's Press, 1982), p. 109; Wang Yuquan, "Mingdai di Wangfu Zhuangtian" (Aristocratic Estates in the Ming Dynasty), *Lishi Luncong*, 1 (1964), 227. Sato Fumitoshi, "Guanyu Mingmo Zhoufanwangfu di Datudisouyou" (On the Great Landholdings in Aristocratic Estates in Late Ming), in *Ming Qing Shi* (1982), 555.

[15] *Ming Shi*, ch. 116–18; *Ming Jingxiwenbian*, ch. 491.

[16] *Ming Shi*, ch. 82.

[17] *Ming Jingxiwenbian*, ch. 491; *Ming Shi*, ch. 82.

[18] See James Tong, "Collective Violence in a Premodern Society", dissertation, ch. 3.

[19] There were fifty feudal estates in Ming. Only twenty-eight, however, survived till the end of Ming. They were distributed in four provinces in the north: Shandong (Princes De, Lu, Heng); Shanxi (Princes Jin, Dai, Shen); Henan (Princes Zhou, Cheng, Tang, Zhao, Chong, Lu, Fu): Shaanxi (Princes Chin, Qing, Han, Su, Rui); and three Yangzi valley provinces: Huguang (Princes Chu, Min, Xiang, Jing, Rong, Hui, Gui); Jiangxi (Princes Huai, Yi); and Sichuan (Prince Su). There were no feudal aristocracy in the two capitals (Beizhili and Nanzhili), or the southern coastal provinces (Zhejiang, Guangdong, Fujian); or the three southwest provinces (Guangxi, Yunnan, Guizhou). See *Mingshi*, ch. 100–104; *Guangyutu*; Wang Yuquan (1964), pp. 299–305.

feudal estates did not account for rebellions and banditry in the south, they might still be related to these violent incidents in northern and central China. To put this proposition to the test, we have examined data on the duration and locality of enfeoffment of the highest 2 of the 14 ranks of Ming aristocrats, and the size of feudal lands.[20] Correlating the frequency of rebellions and banditry with the number of higher-order aristocrats listed in *Mingshi*, and using each of the 277 years as the unit of analysis, we have found no significant correlation between the two variables. That is, years with more enfeoffed aristocrats were often not the years that were more rebellious, and vice versa.[21]

To offset possible source and indicator bias, we have also examined the same set of relationship with data on aristocratic land endowments in *Mingshilu*, compiled by Li Longqian (1982). Correlating the size of aristocratic land endowments with the frequency of rebellions in the 28 decades in Ming, we have also found no significant relationship.[22] To examine a related hypothesis that the effect of proliferation of aristocratic privileges may be delayed rather than immediate, we have lagged the frequency of rebellions by 10 and 20 years, and the correlation between the size of aristocratic endowments and the frequency of rebellions and banditry remains insignificant.

The above two tests were performed on longitudinal data. The same lack of relationship is observed in cross-sectional analysis. Cross-tabulating the presence and absence of rebellions with Wang Yuquan's (1964) data on the size of aristocratic landholdings on 97 counties in Shanxi, using 10,000 *mou* as the cutting-point between high and low levels, the tau-B obtained is −0.004, showing no relationship between the two

[20] These were (a) *qinwang* (imperial princes); and (b) *junwang* (sons of imperial princes). They are either sons or grandsons of the ruling or deceased emperors, ten years old or above, and constitute a special upper class of aristocrats listed in the table on imperial aristocrats in the official *Ming Dynastic Annals*. They represent the highest two of fourteen ranks of Ming aristocrats. Systematic data for the lower twelve ranks are not available. Since these two ranks of aristocrats receive much more in the way of land grants and emoluments than the other ranks, our data thus include the more important aristocrats. Further, since most aristocrats, high and low, resided in palaces in provincial and prefectural capitals, even lower-order aristocrats would be indirectly included in our data set.

[21] The correlation coefficient is 0.082, insignificant at both the 0.05 and 0.01 levels of confidence. Using the number of counties affected by rebellions as an alternative measure, there is also no significant correlation between the two variables. The correlation coefficient is 0.0473.

[22] Since many years passed with no land grants, and such missing data would introduce bias into the analysis, we have to collapse the annual units into ten-year periods. The correlation coefficient, −0.1169, is insignificant at both the 0.05 and 0.01 levels of confidence. There is also no difference when we used the number of counties affected by rebellions as an alternative measure for the level of rebellions. The data are from Li Longqian, "Mingdai Zhuangtian di Fajan He Tedian", *Zhongguo Shehui Jingjishi Luncong*, vol. 2 (Taiyuan: Shanxi People's Press, 1982).

variables. In other words, counties with greater acreage of aristocratic landholdings did not have significantly higher levels of collective violence. Using the *Mingshilu* data on aristocratic endowments in the 11 provinces, the same pattern is observed.[23] The tau-B obtained is −0.031, also insignificant at the 0.05 level. Lowering the size threshold of the aristocratic landholdings from 10,000 to 5,000 *mou* has not affected the relationship significantly. All these tests, then, have not found any significant correlation between the level of collective violence with aristocratic presence and the size of their landholdings. We thus conclude that we have found no systematic evidence from the empirical pattern of Ming rebellions to support class conflict explanations.

The rational choice explanation

Having discussed the inadequacy of the social change and class conflict approaches as an overall framework for describing and explaining premodern collective violence in the Ming Dynasty, we now turn to the attempt to construct a rational choice explanation of premodern collective violence, using rebellions and banditry events in the Ming Dynasty as the universe of observation. Before we articulate the research design and describe the data manipulation procedures, let us first consider hardship conditions in a subsistence economy, the survival strategies given such hardship conditions, including rebellions and banditry, and official sanctions against such outlaw behavior.

Survival strategies in hardship conditions

In premodern China, as well as in other agricultural societies, economic well-being was contingent on the size of harvests, which in turn depended on the vagaries of nature. Floods, drought, locusts, early frost or hail, typhoon or sandstorm, could ruin the harvest of the season, and successive crop failures brought about by continuous bad weather would lead to widespread starvation. By our count there were more than 10,000 calamities (measured in county-years) in the entire 277-year period recorded in provincial and prefectural gazetteers in the 11 provinces included in the study. In other words, for any given year during the Ming dynasty, close to 40 counties had one kind or other of natural calamities. To illustrate with an example of extreme hardship, in this case a famine in Qingzhou, Shandong in 1615:

---

[23] Of the 43 counties and areas with more than 10,000 *mou* of aristocratic landholdings, only 6 had armed uprisings. Conversely, of the 144 counties that had uprisings, 138 counties had less than 10,000 *mou* of aristocratic landholdings.

There was no rain since the fourth month, and no maize, rice, or beans were harvested. In the eighth and ninth month, locusts covered the ground and devoured all the wheat seedlings. Consequently, the price of grain soared and bandits roamed like bees . . . There was also no snow in winter, and one *dou* of grain was sold for 300 *wen*. Hungry peasants stripped the bark off trees and ate it with the chaff. All the trees died in this way. People who starved to death were piled up along the roadside. People first ate flesh cut out from corpses, and then they devoured one another . . . Human flesh was sold in the market for 6 *wen* per catty or they were salted and kept in storage in case of need.   (*Qingzhou Fuzhi*, vol. 20, p. 28)

Given the severity of hardship conditions where their own lives were at stake, peasants turned to survival strategies they abhorred at other times. Historians of famine have documented how proud men begged for alms, chaste women were driven to prostitution, close families practiced infanticide, and non-cannibalistic societies permitted the abandonment and killing of the aged or the sick.[24] In Ming, we found the following behavior emerging in times of severe hardship. Some migrated out of the disaster area. Others sought alternative means of livelihood as monks and eunuchs. Some of those that stayed behind pawned their children or wives, or resorted to cannibalism. Others became rebels and bandits. Each of these alternatives will be illustrated in greater detail below.

Migration
To begin with a phenomenon that can also be observed in our own day, migrations often accompany economic recessions, wars, or famine. To name but a few of those large-scale migrations, the Minister of Public Works reported in 1428 that there were more than 100,000 hungry Shanxi migrants in Henan's Nanyang prefecture that year. Not long afterwards, in 1443, the imperial emissary for Shanxi requested famine relief for 200,000 wandering Shandong and Shanxi migrants in Henan. In 1465, Jingzhou and Xiangyang prefectures of Huguang province were devastated by epidemic rebellions, and a million peasants migrated from the area. More than 100,000 of these went to Nanyang prefecture of Henan province. Another 120,000 households were settled in Yunyang prefecture, a new administrative district that the empire created to accommodate these wandering migrants.[25] These migrations in Ming then, were comparable in scale with the largest migrations in European history. The Irish migration after the great potato famine of 1846 unleashed 400,000 emigrants in two years, and 2 million in the thirteen-year period from

[24] Pitirim Sorokin, *Man and Society in Calamity* (New York: E. P. Dutton, 1942), p. 69.
[25] *Ming Huiyao*, Section 51.

1847 to 1859.[26] Elsewhere, local Ming gazetteers also recorded many migrations of a lesser magnitude out of famine-stricken communities.

Monks

A second survival strategy is to seek alternative employment. In a premodern, agricultural economy as in Ming, there was little demand for unskilled labor. Nevertheless, two occupations existed which required no special skills, though they demanded special sacrifices. First, thanks to imperial largesse, the Ming government gave monks their daily bread. An annual stipend of 6 *tan* of rice (approximately 0.3 metric tons) was given to each ordained Buddhist monk or Taoist priest.[27] In early Ming, there was a quota of 20 monks and priests per county, 30 for each *zhou*, and 40 for each prefecture. The total number then should amount to only 37,080, since there were only 147 prefectures, 277 *zhous*, and 1,145 counties. By the time of Emperor Zhengtong (1436–49), or a century later, the number of ordained monks and priests far exceeded ther quota. In 1466 alone, 132,200 were ordained, another 113,300 in 1476, and another 224,500 in 1486.[28] To be sure, not all became monks to avoid hardship. Many might have chosen monastic life out of religious commitment. Yet there were indications that a substantial number sought ordination for worldly reasons. Among those that were ordained, for instance, many immediately sold their ordination papers for a price.[29] Many others indulged in sins that flesh was heir to. Most monks in Shanxi, for instance, would neither abstain from meat nor wine,[30] while many monks in Beijing led such scandalous lives that a decree was promulgated in 1469 prohibiting women from visiting temples in the imperial capital.[31] A decree in 1474 restricting the number of ordinations in the Empire concluded: "Monks who are ascetic and closely follow monastic rules are fewer than one in a hundred."[32] In this respect, it should be noted that the same mixture of spiritual and materialistic motives can also be found in European cloisters. Prior to ecclesiastical reforms in the twelfth century, European monastaries were depositories of superfluous and handicapped children.[33] In

[26] Sorokin, *Man and Society*, p. 109.
[27] *Ming Huiyao*, Section 39.
[28] *Daming Jiuqing Shili Anli*, Section 6.
[29] Ibid., Decree of 1475.
[30] Ibid., Decree of 1492.
[31] Ibid., Decree of 1492.
[32] *Daming Jiuqing Shili Anli*, Section 6.
[33] For instance, the new abbot who arrived at the Abbey of Andres in the Diocese of Arras in 1161 was shocked at the deformity of his flock. "For some were lame, some were crippled, some were one-eyed, some were cross-eyed, some blind, and even some missing a limb among them." Elsewhere, William of Auvergne, Bishop of Paris from 1228 to 1249, wrote that "[other] monks are cast into the cloister by parents and relatives just as if they were kittens or piglets whom their mother could not nourish", see Joseph

England, royal and episcopal visitations testify to the "manifest sin, vicious, carnal, and abominable living" in English monasteries in the years immediately preceding their dissolution by the Parliament in 1536.[34]

Eunuchs

Second, and more indicative of the painful choices that had to be made in times of hardship, it was not uncommon for people to make the unmanly decision to castrate themselves so that they could qualify to be employed as eunuchs, usually as gardeners or custodians, either in the imperial court in Beijing, or in feudal courts in the provinces. The number of castratees was ever on the rise throughout the dynasty. In the first century of the dynasty (1368–1464), the largest number of castratees recorded in any single entry in the *Ming Veritable Records* was only 58. Each of the following three reigns of Emperor Xianzong (1465–87), Hongzhi (1488–1505), and Zhengde (1505–21) had reports of thousands of castratees beating the drum outside the Forbidden City, demanding to be employed as court attendants. In 1479 and 1487, 2,000 were reported; 2,246 in 1492; 3,468 in 1516, and 5,030 in 1517. More than 10,000 were reported in 1522, the first year in the reign of Emperor Jiajing (1522–66). The number of castratees reported during Emperor Wanli's reign ranged from 2,000 to 6,000. The record year was 1621, when 20,000 castratees applied for 3,000 eunuch attendant positions in the imperial court.[35] While some could be well-to-do people motivated not so much by hardship as by perceived opportunity for wealth and status, many were simply driven by desperation and destitution. In 1532, more than five thousand of the 8,072 castratees seeking employment were skinny and starving vagabonds.[36] They chose castration despite the fact that such practices were contrary to the traditional emphasis on patrilineal procreation, and despite the Ming Law that prescribed the death penalty to both the castrater and the castratee, and banishment of the offender's entire family to frontier areas.[37]

H. Lynch, *Simoniacal Entry into Religious Life from 1,000 to 1,260: A Social, Economic, and Legal Study* (Columbus: Ohio State University Press, 1976), pp. 42–5. The same author also presented empirical evidence to show that many families offered their younger sons to religious orders as oblates.

[34] For accounts of alcoholism, gambling, and homosexuality among monks, and pregnancies among nuns, see G. W. O. Woodward, *The Dissolution of The Monasteries* (London: Blandford Press, 1966) and an identical title by Joyce Youings (London: George Allen and Unwin, 1971); and Dom David Knowles, *The Religious Orders in England* (Cambridge: Cambridge University Press, 1959).

[35] Zhou Long, "Mingdai Di Huanguan" (M.A. thesis, National Taiwan University, 1959), pp. 14–47.

[36] *Daming Jiuqing Shili Anli*, decree of 1532.

[37] *Ming Huiyao*, Section 52, p. 97.

Pawning of family

Becoming either monks or eunuchs involved decisions that were more or less irreversible. Ordination would require a change of household classification, and a period of noviceship, while castration meant a permanent physiological change. Thus both were responses to more long-term deprivation. There were other kinds of behavior that appear to be responses to more short-term, intense, subsistence crisis. When harvests failed, peasant families often had to borrow grain from usurers, and offer children, or sometimes wives, as collateral. According to a memorial by the Minister of Households dated 1466, the worth of a 5- or 6-year-old as collateral was only 5 *dou* (56 lbs) of rice in a famine in Huaian prefecture in the same year. The extent of such practice can be seen in the scope of famine relief programs, which often included funds to bail out family members being pawned this way. For instance, Emperor Hongwu in 1386 decreed the redemption of children from creditors in a famine in Henan. Emperor Yongle did the same for famine-stricken peasants in the Jiangnan area in 1410.[38] In one instance, where actual figures are available, the government redeemed 4,263 children and wives pawned during a single famine.[39]

Cannibalism

A yet more extreme form of survival behavior was cannibalism, which was found in many non-cannibalistic societies that otherwise regarded such practices as unpalatable or in bad taste. The Book of Deuteronomy tells us what we should expect in starvation, "Thou shalt eat the fruit of thy own body, the flesh of thy sons and daughters", and describes how starvation would transform an angel to a beast:

The tender and delicate woman among you, who would not adventure to set the sole of her foot upon the ground for delicateness and tenderness, her eye shall be evil toward the husband of her bosom, and toward her son, and toward her daughter . . . for she shall eat them for want of all things.[40]

Reports of cannibalism in Ming bear close resemblance to what social historians and anthropologists found in other premodern societies, in particular those in Europe between the ninth and the seventeenth centuries.[41] There was the same tragic tales of vulturism – of the snatching of corpses from cemeteries or gallows, or dismembering cadavers on the

---

[38] *Mingshi*, ch. 6.

[39] *Jiufang Tushuo.*

[40] Book of Deuteronomy, 28:53. Elsewhere in the Old Testament references to cannibalism can be found in Leviticus 26:29; 2 Kings 6:28; Jeremiah 19:9; Lamentations 2:20, 4:10; Baruch 2:3; and Ezekiel 5:10.

[41] See Sorokin, *Man and Society*, pp. 50–81; Reay Tannahill, *Flesh and Blood: A History of the Cannibalism Complex* (New York: Stein and Day, 1975), pp. 35–55.

roadside, as some peasants in Wuding county of Shandong were doing in 1554.[42] There was the same poignant account of public sale of human flesh on the market, as reported in Burgundy in 1030–1, and in Weihui prefecture in Henan in 1579 or Qingzhou, Shandong in 1616.[43] There were the same sad stories of parents killing and eating their children and vice versa, and husbands slaying and devouring their wives and vice versa, as in Jending prefecture in Beizhili in 1527 and 1528, Baofeng county of Henan in 1594, Jinan prefecture in Shandong in 1615, or Yanzhou prefecture in 1638.[44] Finally, there was the same pathetic report of two parents in Gaoping *zhou* of Shanxi in 1462 swapping sons to be devoured, an event that has a striking parallel with the story in the Second Book of Kings, 6:28.

The above reports were by no means isolated incidents. In Ming, we found cannibalism reported in 377 county-years. More than three-quarters (257 of 337) were found in the five northern provinces. This should not surprise us, as the shorter growing season and lower precipitation in the north made harvests more vulnerable to the effect of calamities. Temporally, as in the case of rebellions and banditry, most of the cannibalism incidents (250 out of 337) were found in the second half of the dynasty.

Bandits and rebels

Two implications may be drawn from the foregoing discussion on survival strategies in chronic hardship. First, hardship desocializes, demoralizes, suppresses taboos and inhibitions against unethical conduct, and provokes antisocial and brutal behavior. As hardship becomes protracted and intensified, more and more of the immiserated population would override moral considerations and social sanctions to follow their survival instincts. The second implication, and a corollary of the first, is that rebellions and banditry would increase as hardship becomes more severe. If famine can transform a caring mother into a cannibal, drive a man to abandon, sell, or slay his closest kin, compel men to castrate themselves, and cause communities to disintegrate, it would also lead men to banditry and rebellion.

There is also no lack of contemporary Ming accounts linking the rise of banditry and rebellions to hardship caused by famine. To begin with illustrations from local gazetteers, the following record in the Guangping prefectural gazetteer was rather typical: "In 1640, the year of great famine,

[42] *Jinan Fuzhi*, vol. 20, p. 28.
[43] *Qingzhou Fuzhi*, vol. 20, p. 28; *Weihui Fuzhi*, in *Gujin Tushu Jicheng*.
[44] See *Jending Fuzhi*; *Jinan Fuzhi*, *Ruzhou Fuzhi*, *Yanzhou Fuzhi*, sections on Portents and Calamities.

most of the old and weak died, and the able-bodied followed each other to become bandits." The only two extant Ming merchant manuals also counselled itinerant salesmen against travelling to certain areas in bad years. The *Survey of Merchant Routes* warned, "Bandits often appear from Huguang to Ichen, especially around Jiazhou where bandits abound in famine years",[45] and again, "from Jiangxi to Raozhou, bandits roamed among the lakes, especially in famine years."[46] The *Pictorial Record of Roads in the Empire* also states, "There is no need to worry about bandits from Hengzhou prefecture to Zhenjiang prefecture. But one should be alert in Pengmen, Wulong Bridge . . . and several other places. There are bandits along the small rivers in bad years."[47]

The authorities were also aware of the connection between banditry and hardship. Li Zhai from the Ministry of Defense described the situation in Xinxing county during a famine in the late Wanli period (1573–1619): "Local elders Zhen Weizhong and others reported that around a thousand hungry civilians in Magang and other places joined the bandits *en masse* and brought their wives and children with them."[48] A Kaifeng official cited the following deterministic law in his memorial: "When the crops fail the people will be hungry; when the people are deprived bandits will rise. This is an inevitable trend."[49] A Minister of Households not only observed that he has "heard that affluence breeds propriety, and poverty breeds banditry," but also predicted, "we have famine [in Shandong] this year. There will be plenty of bandits."[50] Blessed with hindsight, Chin Weitian, a Qing scholar-official concurred, "The Demise of Ming was due to banditry. The rise of banditry is due to famine."[51]

Within the imperial bureaucracy, officials in charge of famine relief were most cognizant of the connection between banditry and hardship. Practically every manual on famine relief in Ming attests to this relationship. Lin Xiyuan in his *Collected Words on Famine Relief* stated that "Hunger and cold make a bandit", and attributed the disappearance of banditry in famine-stricken Xizhou to his provision of relief.[52] Tu Long, in his *Study of Famine Relief*, agreed: "In famine years, if there is no government relief, and tax collection is not relaxed, . . . those who did not die of famine will rise to become bandits."[53] Zhou Kongjiao echoed the same rationalist logic: "In years of famine, civilians who refused to die of starvation will inevitably

[45] *Shangcheng Yilan*, vol. 1, p. 24.
[46] Ibid., vol. 2, p. 49.
[47] *Yitong Lucheng Tuji*, p. 19.
[48] *Bingzheng Jiilue*.
[49] *Kaifeng Fuzhi*, Kangshi edn, vol. 35, p. 9, Memorial of He Chutu.
[50] *Anli*, memorial by Minister Yang in 1473.
[51] *Wuli Tongkao*.
[52] *Fangzheng Chongyan*.
[53] *Fangzheng Kao*.

become bandits." Zhong Huamin saw the relationship in time-series terms, "There will be more banditry when we have successive years of famine."[54]

The decisional calculus: to rebel or not to rebel

To summarize the preceding discussion, we have attempted to show that in subsistence crises, when famine stalked the land, it would not be irrational to be an outlaw, given that the alternative was death or starvation. We have further noted that to survive in severe or extreme hardship, sizeable segments of the rural population made the painful choice to migrate out of their communities, to pawn their children or wives, or to be monks, eunuchs, or cannibals. The likelihood of surviving hardship, however, is not the only factor in the decisional calculus to be an outlaw. Two other considerations are also part of the calculus. First, what are the chances of being caught? And second, what are the sanctions against rebels and bandits? In other words, how *certain* and *severe* will be the punishment against rebellions and banditry?

Severity of sanctions against rebels and bandits
To begin with the simpler of the two considerations, official sanctions against rebellions and banditry were severe. To quote from the Ming Penal Code:

(1) All participants of a rebellion, including the leader, co-conspirators, and the led, will be sentenced to immediate execution by quartering;[55]
(2) All male relatives of the clan of rebels up to second cousins, 16 or above, whether they be able-bodied, handicapped or invalid, will be decapitated;
(3) All male relatives under 16, and female relatives up to second nieces will be given to high meritorious officials as slaves;
(4) Those who knowingly conceal rebels will be decapitated; those who know and do not inform the authorities will be given 100 lashes and banished 3,000 *li* (1,500 km) away.

The following regulations stipulated sanctions against bandits:

(1) Armed bandits who have robbed in daylight, regardless of their numbers or whether they have assaulted victims, will be sentenced to capital punishment and their heads spiked on poles at the site of robbery for public edification;
(2) Bandits who (a) have killed, raped, or engaged in arson; or assaulted government prisons, stores, offices, and city walls; or (b) numbered over a hundred

---

[54] *Zhen Yu Jilue.*
[55] The Ming had more lenient kinds of capital punishment for lesser offences – immediate decapitation; immediate hanging; commuted decapitation (to be carried out after the Fall harvest) and commuted hanging.

regardless of whether property have been seized, will be sentenced to capital punishment and their heads spiked on poles.

Uncertainty of sanctions

Sanctions against rebels and bandits were thus severe. Given the severity of sanctions, rebellions and banditry did not pay. Even if the individual peasant did not care about his own life, or those of his clan, his clansmen would try to restrain him. However, even the most severe sanction may not be an effective deterrent, if it is not *certain*. The degree of certainty of sanction would be contingent on the following factors. First, it would depend on the *accessibility and strength of government forces*. We can reason that the farther away the government forces and the smaller their size, the easier it would be for outlaws to rebel or raid, and get away. In Ming, the bulk of government troops were clustered in military garrisons (*wei*), or its subdivision, the fort (*qianhusuo*), each with 1,200 troops, usually located around provincial and prefectural capitals. Aside from these troops, which were under the jurisdiction of the provincial military command, Ming counties also had local militia and police checkpoints, but these were not equipped to deal with disturbances of a larger scale.

Other than the distance to the location of disturbance, the coercive capability of these government forces could also be diminished by rugged terrain, concurrent outbreaks of disturbances, and troop mutinies. To elaborate, the *rugged terrain* of mountain ranges could impede government forces from locating rebel hideouts, and make them vulnerable to rebel ambush. Further, being more familiar with the terrain, the rebels could choose to hide or attack, and if they should choose direct confrontation, they could first occupy strategic hilltops and mountain passes. Similarly, water margins of lakes overgrown with reeds could camouflage rebels, and the vast expanses of the ocean would also make it difficult for government naval forces to locate and pursue pirates. Second, *concurrent outbreaks of armed disturbances*, namely, rebellions and banditry, or foreign invasions in the vicinity could tie up or split the strength of government troops. In the same vein, such outbreaks in the recent past could have decimated government forces or damaged defense installations like fortresses, guard houses, or city walls, and exposed the weaknesses of the regional defense system. Third, and no less serious, *troop mutinies* could not only paralyze local defense, but also engage other government forces in the region. Even after the event, troop morale would suffer if the leaders of the mutiny were sanctioned, or military discipline would be low if the latter got away unpunished.

Aside from the coercive capability of the government, the rebels would also have to reckon with *local civilian defense efforts*. The more common form was the organization of armed self-defense units, either fighting independently, or in cooperation with the local military commander or civilian official, or acting as supportive units in surveillance, fire-fighting, and transportation. Less overtly, the local populace might also contribute material for self-defense, or raise bounties to reward soldiers distinguished in combat.

Model construction and research design

Having thus discussed the factors that might enter a peasant's decisional calculus, let us now turn to the operational task of constructing and testing our explanatory model. To show rational choice in such events, we have to postulate goals for the actors, specify the choices to be made, and relate alternative decision rules to these choices. The goal we postulate is survival in an agrarian society. The choice is to be or not be a rebel or bandit. The decision rule we specify is to rebel when the times are bad and when it is easy to get away; and to stay put when otherwise. To show such rational choice, we will devise a research design that would: (a) specify quasi-experimental conditions wherein the given population is confronted with a choice to rebel or not to rebel; or to be or not be an outlaw; and (b) construct a payoff matrix by manipulating a different mix of incentives and sanctions for rebellion and banditry in each condition.

The logic underlying our research design is simple. To deter rebellions and banditry, the Ming Penal Code prescribed the death sentence to rebels and bandits, and death or enslavement to rebels' families. Given such draconian penalties, the rational peasant would not resort to rebellion or banditry unless he calculated that the likelihood of survival as an outlaw was greater than the likelihood of survival if he chose to stay put. Under normal economic and administrative circumstances, the choice of remaining a law-abiding citizen seemed most rational. But in times of famine, the likelihood of his survival would be low. If, at the same time, government forces were rendered ineffectual by distance, terrain, mutinies and defeat, or preoccupied with concurrent uprisings or foreign invasions; and also at the same time local defense was not mobilized, then he might evaluate the likelihood of survival as a rebel or bandit as greater than the likelihood of survival if he chose to stay put. The basic logic of the main argument is schematized in fig. 3.

In fig. 3, if our rational choice model is operative, then we would expect to find the following: first, the highest proportion of rebellions and banditry will be found in the lower left corner of the diagram, where there is *minimum* likelihood of surviving hardship but *maximum* likelihood of survival as an outlaw. Second, the lowest proportion of collective violence

LIKELIHOOD OF SURVIVAL AS OUTLAW

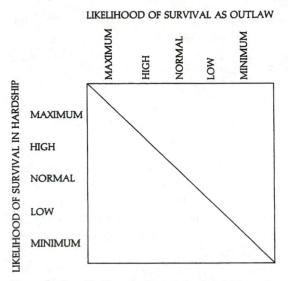

Fig. 3 Scaling likelihood of surviving hardship and survival as an outlaw

events will be found in the top right-hand corner, since the conditions are reversed. Third, in general, rebellions and banditry are more likely in the area below the diagonal line, and less so in the area above it. As will soon be made clear, empirical evidence does, in general, support these expectations.

Before we turn to empirical operationalization of the foregoing argument, let us address two related theoretical issues. First, the alert reader would have noted that in the above rational choice framework, severity of punishment is not part of the decisional calculus. This is at variance with studies on the economics of crime (Becker, 1968; Becker and Landes, 1974; Witte, 1983),[56] which include both the severity of punishment and certainty of sanctions in the calculations of the criminal. Our justification for such omission lies in the assumption that there is little meaningful variation in the severity of punishment meted out to rebels and bandits. As noted earlier, the sanction against rebels, both for leader and led, was immediate execution by quartering; and for bandits, decapitation.[57] Given

---

[56] See Gary Becker, "Crime and Punishment: An Economic Approach", *Journal of Political Economy*, 76 (1968), 169–217; Gary Becker and W. Landes, "Participation in Illegitimate Activities: An Economic Analysis", in Gary Becker and W. Landes (eds.), *Essays in the Economics of Crime and Punishment* (New York: Columbia University Press, 1974); Ann D. Witte, "Crime Causation: Economic Theories", *Encyclopaedia of Criminal Justice* (New York: The Free Press, 1983), vol. 1, pp. 316–22.

[57] The Ming penal code allows for less severe punishments for bandits belonging to small bands not guilty of robbing in broad daylight or assaulting victims. This study's restrictive criteria for inclusion, however, ensures that for most the the cases included, the perpetrators, if caught, would have faced capital punishment.

such draconian sanctions for both rebels and bandits, it is reasonable to assume that rational individuals would consider either punishment unacceptable. The decisional calculus for becoming rebels or bandits would then rest, not on weighing which punishment was less severe, but on the likelihood of being caught.

Second, the above conceptualization of rational choice and our research design also provides a solution to the free-rider problem that has plagued the study of collective action. The problem arises if one assumes that the goal of participating in collective action is to seek public goods. Since the individual's contribution to the outcome of collective action is small but the cost to him may be great, he will be better off as a non-participant. The rational person will thus choose to be a free rider and collective action is unlikely to take place.[58] The problem can be circumvented by postulating that people seek private gains rather than public goods in collective action. This, however, will also raise a problem as it cannot be easily shown that private gains would outweigh costs for participants in collective violence. Participation in such actions are inherently costly, since authorities generally impose severe sanctions on those seeking to overthrow the government or undermine public order. On the other hand, selective incentives like promise of high office and other material rewards are generally insufficient and uncertain. Thus it would be difficult to maintain that participants in those activities will be better off or at least not worse off than non-participants.[59] In sum, then, whether one conceives the motive of such action as seeking either public good or private gain, it would be problematic to argue logically and demonstrate empirically that participation in collective violence is rational.

In the rational choice framework articulated above, we make no claims on whether Ming rebels and bandits seek public or private goods. Nor will we attempt to show that the private gains of participating in collective violence will always exceed costs. We do attempt to show that the occurrence of rebellions and banditry is related to the structure of incentives and disincentives of being an outlaw on the one hand, and to staying put on the other. To state our basic argument simply, given varying degrees of hardship and uncertainty of punishment in a pre-modern economy, the incentive to be an outlaw is the enhanced likelihood of survival, the disincentive is the risk of arrest, execution, and getting

[58] Mancur Olson, *The Logic of Collective Action: Public Goods and the Theory of Groups* (Cambridge, Mass.: Harvard University Press, 1965).

[59] For the conceptual and empirical studies premised on selective interests in revolutionary participation, see Gordon Tullock, "The Paradox of Revolution", *Public Choice*, 11 (1971), 89–99; Morris Silver, "Political Revolution and Repression: An Economic Approach", *Public Choice*, 17 (1974), 63–71; Philip Roeder, "Rational Revolution: Extension of the 'By-Product' Model of Revolutionary Involvement", *The Western Political Quarterly*, 35, no. 1 (March 1982), 5–23.

Hardship level	Scope
Low	Ordinary calamities, without extensive and intensive qualifiers, and without accompanying report of damage of human lives, crop, livestock, and property
Moderate	Extensive or intensive calamities with accompanying reports of limited damage to human lives, crop, livestock, and property
High	Famine, or extensive or intensive damage to human lives, crop, livestock, or property
Severe	Extensive or prolonged famine, or widespread death due to starvation, or outward migration from famine-stricken area
Extreme	Abandonment, sale, or pawning of children or family, cannibalism, public sale of human flesh

Fig. 4 Scale of hardship levels

hurt in action. The incentive to stay put is to avoid combat injuries and legal sanction, the disincentive is to suffer starvation or death. The crucial variables then, are the likelihood of surviving hardship and the likelihood of survival as an outlaw. On one end of the range of possibilities, when unmitigated hardship is combined with ineffective deterrence, it would be more rational to be an outlaw than under reversed conditions. On the other end, when the absence of life-threatening calamities coexists with swift and certain punishment, it would be more rational to abide by the law. By systematically varying the mix of incentives and disincentives, we can demonstrate the extent to which the outbreak of rebellions and banditry corresponds to rational expectations.

Scaling likelihood of surviving hardship
Turning to how we operationalize our model, let us begin with a description of how we construct the scale of likelihood of surviving hardship. First, we have ranked all calamities in the following 5-level hardship scale, in ascending order of intensity, from low to maximum. Thus a *low* level of calamity would be any record in the local gazetteer referring to an ordinary calamity (locusts, earthquake, etc.) without any intensive or extensive qualifiers (prolonged drought, a series of earthquakes, swarms of locusts, etc.) and without accompanying reports of damage to human lives, crops, livestock, and property. On the other end

of the scale, an *extreme* level of calamity would be one referring to (a) abandonment, sale, or pawning of children or family; or (b) various forms of cannibalism described earlier; and (c) public sale of human flesh. A sketch of the coding scheme is shown in fig. 4.[60]

The level of hardship, however, is not totally determined by natural calamities, the effects of which could be ameliorated by at least three factors. First, we can reason that counties with bumper harvests in the preceding year would have stacked away some surplus grain for use during lean years. Second, government famine relief could alleviate some of the misery caused by natural calamities. Third, local construction projects could also have a beneficial effect on the suffering population. In much the same way as a public jobs program does in recession, local construction provides alternative employment and means of livelihood for the deprived segment of the population.

For *size of good harvests*, we have conformed closely to the description in local gazettes, which distinguished between: (1) bumper harvests and (2) greater bumper harvests. *Famine relief* is coded in a 7-level scale of descending order of efficacy: (1) central government relief in grain or cash; (2) local (provincial, prefectural, county) government relief in grain or cash; (3) total tax exemption; (4) partial tax exemption; (5) exemption of corvee labor for monumental government projects; (6) commendation for private relief; (7) construction of granaries. *Local constructions* include both the construction and major repairs of (1) government buildings (administrative buildings and city wall); (2) schools; (3) irrigation canals and bridges; and (4) Buddhist and Taoist temples, ancestral halls and shrines.

To construct the composite index of likelihood of survival in hardship, these 4 sets of data (hardship, harvests, relief, and constructions) are manipulated as follows. Ascending levels of hardship (from low to extreme) are combined with data on harvests, relief, and construction to form a scale of likelihood of survival during hardship. In this new scale, for instance, a given county-year will be considered as having maximum likelihood of surviving hardship if it had (1) no hardship at all; or (2) a low level of hardship but also had a bumper harvest in the current of previous year, or received government relief, or had reports of local construction, or (3) a moderate level of hardship but also any two reports of government relief, local construction, or bumper harvests. This is shown in fig. 5.

---

[60] A more detailed discussion of a more elaborate coding scheme and coding rules is given in James Tong, "Collective Violence in a Premodern Society", ch. 5.

Level	Likelihood of survival	Hardship level[a]	Harvest/relief/ construction
1	Maximum	(A) None (B) Low (C) Moderate	None/anyone Any one Any two
2	High	(A) Low (B) Moderate (C) High	None Any one Any two
3	Probable	(A) High/severe (B) Extreme	Any one Any two
4	Low	(A) High/severe (B) Extreme	None Any one
5	Minimum	(A) Extreme	None

Fig. 5 Scale of likelihood of survival in hardship
[a]See fig. 4.

Scaling likelihood of survival as an outlaw

Turning to the likelihood of survival as an outlaw, we have noted earlier that the peasants' decisional calculus would take into account (1) the proximity of the outlaws to mountain and water sanctuaries; (2) the coercive capability of the government forces; (3) the concurrence of armed disturbances; (4) the existence of troop mutinies; and (5) the mobilization of local defense. To construct the scale, each of these 5 factors will be operationalized and an ordinal scale constructed. Next, the 5 factors will be combined to form a cumulative composite index of the likelihood of survival as outlaws in rebellions and banditry.

For *proximity to mountain and water sanctuaries*, we will use the following 5-point scale: where the distance from the county seat to a mountain range with an absolute elevation of 500 meters, or the ocean, is (1) 0–24 km; (2) 25–49 km; (3) 50–74 km; (4) 75–99 km; and (5) >100 km. The operational definition for a mountain is adopted from a recent Chinese atlas.[61] The intervals are based on an estimate of multiples of distances covered in a day, calculated from (a) official Ming regulations stipulating the maximum period of time that local officials could spend between different locations on official business,[62] and (b) *Where the Boat and Coach Sojourned*, a

[61] *Zhonghua Renmin Gongheguo Dituji* (Beijing: Ditu Chubanshe, 1979), Map 9.
[62] *Daming Huidian*, Section 220.

travelogue in early Qing listing the distances covered each day in a tour throughout the empire.[63]

For *government coercive capability*, a composite scale based on both the distance to, and the strength of, government troops is used. For each county, we will divide the number of forts by the distance (in *li*, or 0.5 km) from the county seat to the location of the troops, which were usually clustered around provincial and prefectural capitals in multiples of 5 forts. Thus, county A that was 100 *li* away from a cluster of 20 forts will have a government coercion score of 0.2, and county B 200 *li* away from 10 forts will score 0.05. All counties will then be ranked in the following 5 levels, as those that score between (1) 0.01 or less; (2) 0.01 to 0.04; (3) 0.05 to 0.10; (4) 0.11 to 0.14; and (5) 0.15 or greater.

For *concurrence of local disturbances* in the vicinity, counties are classified as those that had (a) any other armed disturbance (rebellions, banditry, and in this case, foreign invasions) in the same prefecture, or (b) three or more armed disturbances in adjacent prefectures within (1) the same year; (2) previous 2 years; (3) previous 3 years; (4) previous 4 years; (5) previous 5 or more years. Similar scales for the effects of *government troop mutinies* and *local defense mobilization* will be used. With respect to the latter, counties will be ranked as those that had no report of local civilian population resisting the rebels or bandits in the previous (1) 5 years; (2) 4 years; (3) 3 years; (4) 2 years; (5) 1 year.

Finally, these five separate scales will be combined to form a composite scale of likelihood of survival as an outlaw, which has a range of values from 5 to 25. A minimum value of 5 means the county scores 1 in all the 5 separate scales, that is, it was closest to a mountain refuge, where government coercion capability was weakest, the impact of concurrent local disturbances and troop mutinies strongest, and local defense least mobilized. That is, the likelihood of surviving as an outlaw in that county in that year would be high. Conversely, a score of 25 would mean that the reverse conditions obtain in all the 5 factors, and hence the likelihood of surviving as an outlaw would be minimum. Cutting-points are drawn around scores of (1) 5–14; (2) 15–16; and (3) 17–25, denoting respectively maximum, moderate, and minimum likelihood or surviving as an outlaw. These cutting-points are chosen so that (a) there is no zero entry in each contingent condition; and (b) the distribution of the sample population of county-years across contingencies is fairly even.

Data on rebellions and banditry are then cross-tabulated with those on the likelihood of surviving hardship and survival as an outlaw. Since the 5-level hardship scale in fig. 2 also resulted in several zero entries, some statistical procedures cannot be used. To overcome this problem, adjacent

[63] *Zhoujusuozhi.*

Table 2. *Frequencies of rebellions per 100 county-years by likelihood of surviving hardship*

	Survival as outlaw			
Hardship survival level	Maximum	Moderate	Minimum	Row total
Maximum	0.39	0.11	0.12	0.19
Moderate	1.32	0.53	0.20	0.59
Minimum	1.79	0.90	0.82	1.15
Column total	0.41	0.13	0.12	0.21

Table 3. *Frequencies of rebellions by likelihood of surving hardship and survival as outlaw*

	Survival as outlaw			
Hardship survival level	Maximum	Moderate	Minimum	Total
Maximum	330	103	141	574
Moderate	16	8	4	28
Minimum	14	6	8	28
Total	360	117	153	630

Table 4. *No. of county-years by likelihood of surviving hardship and survival as outlaw*

	Survival as outlaw			
Hardship survival level	Maximum	Moderate	Minimum	Total
Maximum	84,910	90,621	121,145	296,676
Moderate	1,215	1,510	2,045	4,770
Minimum	780	664	979	2,423
Total	86,905	92,795	124,169	303,869

levels of the hardship scale relating to the high and probable conditions (2nd and 3rd row) as well as the low and minimum (4th and 5th row) levels were merged. The new contingency table thus has 3 levels on each dimension, to which we will refer as maximum, moderate, and minimum. The results are displayed in table 2, which shows the *proportion* of rebellions and banditry in each specified condition. These values are obtained through dividing the frequencies of rebellions and banditry shown in table 3, by the number of county-years that fall into each contingent condition shown in table 4. For instance, there were 780 county-years where the chances of surviving hardship was minimum but the likelihood of survival as an outlaw was maximum (lower left cell of table 4). In these 780 county-years, 14 rebellions and banditry events actually occurred (lower left cell of table 3). This amounts to 1.79 events per 100 county-years (lower left cell of table 2).

Findings

Before we summarize our findings, let us recall the logic of our rational choice model, which predicts that there would be more rebellions and banditry where the likelihood of surviving hardship is minimum but where the likelihood of survival as an outlaw is maximum. That is, we would find more rebellions and banditry in those counties and during those years when extreme hardship was not ameliorated by government relief, previous bumper harvests, and local construction; and, at the same time, the long arm of the law had difficulty in reaching them. Conversely, the model predicts that there would be fewer incidents of rebellions and banditry when the conditions are reversed, that is, when hardship was negligible and retribution was almost certain. More specifically, if the model is operative, we would expect to find: (1) the minimum–maximum cell (bottom left) would have the highest level of rebellions and banditry per 100 county-years; (2) conversely, the maximum–minimum cell (top right) would have the lowest level; and (3) in general, cells lying above the diagonal line would have lower levels of such violent events than those below the diagonal line.

As shown in table 2, the observed pattern matches these theoretical predictions rather closely. First, the minimum–maximum cell, registering 1.79 violent events per 100 county-years, did have the highest level of rebellions and banditry. Second, while the maximum-minimum cell (0.12 events) was not the lowest level, it was nevertheless the second lowest level, and very close to the lowest level (0.11 events) among the nine sets of conditions. In fact, the former is 9.4 times more violent prone than the latter. Third, cells lying below the diagonal line do have a higher proportion of outlaw incidents (0.90, 1.32, and 1.79 per 100 county-years) than cells above the diagonal line (0.11, 0.12 and 0.20 per 100 county-years). Looking down the row totals on the 4th column, the proportion of rebellions and banditry consistently *increases* (from 0.19 through 0.59 to 1.15 per 100 county-years) as the likelihood or surviving hardship *decreases* from maximum to minimum. Looking within each column, the same relationship obtains. That is, irrespective of whether the likelihood of survival as an outlaw is maximum, moderate, or minimum, there are always *more* rebellions and banditry per 100 county-years as it becomes less likely to survive hardship.

With respect to the relationship between rebellions and banditry on the one hand and the likelihood of survival as an outlaw on the other, the model also predicts the direction of the expected relationship. Looking across the column totals on the 4th row, the proportion of rebellions and banditry consistently decreases from the first (0.41) to the third column (0.12). The only exception was the small anomaly noted in the middle and right cell in the first row, which shows a slightly higher level of rebellions and banditry in the latter.

Conclusions

To summarize and conclude, empirical evidence suggests that the rational choice model we have constructed can predict the different levels of collective violence on the basis of (a) chance of surviving hardship; and (b) chance of surviving as an outlaw. In particular, we have found higher levels of rebellions and banditry in those counties and during those years where there were unmitigated hardship, and when government sanctions were uncertain. Conversely, we found lower levels of collective violence when conditions are reversed, namely, when hardship was ameliorated or tolerable, and when punishment appeared indubitable. This suggests that the rational choice model is operative, and that participating in a violent anti-government act can be understood as a rational choice rather than as aberrant and anomic behavior. We suspect that differentiating outlaw groups and specifying decisional calculus for each would improve the conceptual rigor and predictive validity of the model. In addition, it is conceivable that fine-tuning the data manipulation procedures on the one hand, as well as decomposing the composite index and correlating levels of violence with calamities, famine relief, ruggedness of terrain, etc. may squeeze more analytical mileage out of the present data. These tasks, however, must be deferred to another occasion.

4 The radicalism of tradition and the question of class struggle*

Craig Jackson Calhoun

That revolutions are risky undertakings poses a problem for theorists of popular insurrections. Why, it has often been asked, would reasonable people place their lives and even their loved ones in jeopardy in pursuit of a highly uncertain goal? Neither the success of uprisings nor the desirability of post-revolutionary regimes has appeared likely enough to outweigh the probability of privation and the physical harm. A conservative view, as old as Plato but more recently argued by LeBon, Smelser, and others, concludes simply that revolutionaries must not be very reasonable people.[1]

Revolutionaries and their defenders have, of course, disagreed. Most famous among them, Marx offered an important argument for the rationality of revolution. This argument combined a notion of necessary historical progress with the assertion that revolution would be in the rational interest of the class of workers created by industrial capitalism. It turned in part on the expectation that progressive immiseration of the proletariat would eliminate other possibilities for self-improvement and leave the workers of the world with "nothing to lose but their chains". Conservatives have sometimes been sympathetic, suggesting that desperation might make revolt understandable if not quite reasonable.

Long arguments have pursued the question of whether the position of workers deteriorated during the industrial revolution.[2] A more recent line of historical research has shown that, whether or not overall standards of living improved, the people in the forefront of European revolutionary mobilizations, while often workers, were seldom either the most miser-

---

* This paper includes revised versions of "The Radicalism of Tradition", *American Journal of Sociology*, 88, no. 5 (1983), 886–914, and selections from *The Question of Class Struggle* (Chicago: University of Chicago Press, 1982).

[1] Gustav LeBon, *The Crowd: A Study of the Popular Mind* (New York: Viking, 1960 [1909]); Neil Smelser, *Theory of Collective Behavior* (New York: The Free Press, 1962).

[2] On England, compare, among many, A.J.P. Taylor (ed.), *The Standard of Living in the Industrial Revolution* (London: Methuen, 1975); Brian Inglis, *Poverty and the Industrial Revolution* (London: Panther, 1971); A. Seldon (ed.), *The Long Debate on Poverty* (London: Institute of Economic Affairs, 1974); E.P. Thompson, *The Making of the English Working Class* (Harmondsworth: Penguin, 1968 [1963]).

able or the members of the modern proletariat.[3] The most radical workers were usually artisans, sometimes peasants, and most always those with at least some prosperity and often many privileges to defend. Their identities and aspirations were largely traditional; they drew much of the social strength of their mobilizations from communal bonds, a good deal less from membership in the new "working class".

Marx himself recognized the ambiguity of the ideological orientation of nineteenth-century revolutionaries; he correctly saw early radicals to be ambivalent about visions of a better past to which they wished to return and visions of an emancipatory future which they wished to create. But Marx wrongly took the popular appeals to tradition to be mere epiphenomena which would have to be swept away before revolutions could accomplish their truly great historical destinies. As he wrote of the 1848 revolution in France:

Men make their own history, but not of their own free will; not under circumstances they themselves have chosen but under the given and inherited circumstances with which they are directly confronted. The tradition of the dead generations weighs like a nightmare on the minds of the living. And, just when they appear to be engaged in the revolutionary transformation of themselves and their material surroundings, in the creation of something which does not yet exist, precisely in such epochs of revolutionary crisis they timidly conjure up the spirits of the past to help them; they borrow their names, slogans and costumes so as to stage the new world-historical scene in this venerable disguise and borrowed language.[4]

Marx's insights in this passage are profound, and yet, like many heirs of the Enlightenment, he cannot accept the intrusion of seemingly irrelevant tradition into the rationality of the future. He does not grasp the changing significance of tradition as it enters into different practices in different historical contexts. Unlike the revolutionary French workers who found in the attenuated institution of *compagnonnage* a potent model of social solidarity – fraternity – Marx does not recognize any valid continuity

---

[3] R.D. Price, *The French Second Republic: A Social History* (Ithaca, New York: Cornell University Press, 1972); Charles Tilly and L.H. Lees, "The People of June, 1848", in R.D. Price (ed.), *Revolution and Reaction: 1848 and the Second French Republic* (New York: Barnes and Noble, 1975), pp. 170–209; B.H. Moss, *The Origins of the French Labor Movement* (Berkeley and Los Angeles: University of California Press, 1976); Barrington Moore, *Injustice: The Social Bases of Obedience and Revolt* (White Plains, New York: Sharpe, 1978); M. Traugott, "Determinants of Political Organization: Class and Organization in the Parisian Insurrection of June 1848", *American Journal of Sociology* 86 (1980), 32–49, and *Armies of the Poor* (Princeton, New Jersey: Princeton University Press, 1985); C. Calhoun, *The Question of Class Struggle: Popular Protest in Industrializing England* (Chicago: University of Chicago Press, 1982).
[4] Karl Marx, "The Eighteenth Brumaire of Louis Bonaparte", translated by D. Fernbach, in D. Fernbach (ed.), *Surveys from Exile* (Harmondsworth: Penguin, 1973 [1852]), p. 146.

between the corporatism of the past and the socialist future.[5] For him the fullness of revolution can be only radical novelty: completely new thoughts and acts in dialectical opposition to old.

In the same way, the beginner who has learned a new language always retranslates it into his mother tongue: he can only be said to have appropriated the spirit of the new language and to be able to express himself in it freely when he can manipulate it without reference to the old, and when he forgets his original language while using the new one.[6]

Generations of analysts of revolutions and radical mobilizations have shared Marx's orientation. Like him, they have inherited from the Enlightenment a sense of inherent opposition between rationality and tradition. I think this is a false opposition. It is linked to the overly simple equation of tradition and community with order, in contrast to the apparent disorder of revolution. The political right and left have engaged in a common misunderstanding, for both have failed to recognize the paradoxical conservatism in revolution, the radicalism of tradition.

In this chapter I propose to examine this paradox and to argue that "reactionary radicals" have been at the center of most modern social revolutions and a much larger number of other radical mobilizations in which revolutionary outcomes were precluded. I shall argue that traditional communities provide the social foundations for widespread popular mobilizations and that traditional values are key ingredients to their radicalism. But tradition, I shall suggest, has been misunderstood as Bagehot's "hard cake of culture" or as mere continuity with the past. For example, the foremost contemporary analyst of tradition sees it as anything "handed down from the past".[7] Shils follows Weber in an analysis of the variable importance of tradition in social action, emphasizing that we must go beyond Weber's opposition of traditionalism and rationalism to see the importance of tradition in rationalism itself and in all societies.[8] I shall ask that we go still further beyond the Enlightenment's historicist opposition of tradition to modernity and see tradition as grounded less in the historical past than in everyday social practice. This fully sociological concept of tradition I see as inextricably linked to communal social relations. In the following pages, then, I shall comment briefly on Marx's theory of proletarian collective action and identify the reactionary radicals, focusing on early nineteenth-century France and England. I shall then develop my concepts of tradition and community

[5] On *compagnonnage*, see William H. Sewell, Jr., *Work and Revolution in France* (Cambridge: Cambridge University Press, 1980).

[6] Marx, "Eighteenth Brumaire", p. 147.

[7] E. Shils, *Tradition* (Chicago: University of Chicago Press, 1981), esp. pp. 12–21.

[8] Shils, *Tradition*, p. 9; see also M. Weber, *Economy and Society* (Berkeley: University of California Press, 1968 [1922]), pp. 24–6.

and show how "conservative" attachments to tradition and community
may be crucial bases for quite rational participation in the most radical of
mobilizations, sometimes culminating in revolutions. Last, I shall offer a
few suggestions as to why the modern working class has not shown the
propensity for radicalism that artisans showed during the period of
European industrialization and why reformism rather than revolution is
its "natural" form of action.

Marx

In the mid-nineteenth century Marx argued a case for the iminence of
social revolutions in which the new, factory-based proletariat which was
growing up within industrial capitalism would be the protagonist. Past
revolutions, he suggested, had been primarily the products of the bourgeoisie struggling to free itself from the fetters of feudal restraints on
capital accumulation. Such revolutions had mobilized popular support,
but only as an adjunct to their bourgeois thrust. The lower classes had
grown stronger and more able to recognize that they must act independently of the bourgeoisie at the same time that the socioeconomic
structure had shifted to make exploitation by the bourgeoisie rather than
oppression by feudal lords their major enemy. This was not just a process
of learning, then, but a transformation of the class structure.[9] The new
relations of production which created the modern proletariat gave it a
radicalism and a potential for social revolution which Marx thought
peasants, artisans, and other earlier groups of workers lacked. On the one
hand, the proletariat would be radical because of the extreme misery to
which it was reduced and the absolute polarization of classes in bourgeois
society. On the other hand, the proletariat would be capable of sustained
revolutionary mobilization because it was unified with an unprecedented
social solidarity.

The main thrust of Marx's argument focused on the structural identifi-

[9] It is essential to the Marxian argument that both class structure and class formation (in
E.O. Wright's terms, *Classes* [London: New Left Books, 1985], ch. 3) be recognized as
changing, and that neither be reduced to the other. The focus of this paper is on class
formation – the historically concrete processes by which collectivities are created and
develop the organization necessary for action and the consciousness to guide it. Though I
agree with Wright as to the importance of structural analysis of the capitalist totality, I am
arguing precisely (a) that capitalism's totalizing tendency is not so great as to reduce
non-class determinants of collective action to insignificance, and (b) that an argument
based on the rational recognition of interests by putatively discrete individuals is
necessarily an insufficient basis for explaining the creation of fundamental social
solidarities and collective action on their basis – in other words, that an argument from
class structure to class interests to collective action cannot in principle succeed for any
action of great moment or any structural class faced with competition from other practical
identities.

cation of the proletariat as a class created by capitalism, defined as a unit in the totality of capitalism. On this basis, Marx believed he could deduce the inescapable and rational reasons the members of the proletariat had for uniting in revolutionary collective action. But even this was a secondary concern. Marx's main deductions concerned the reasons why the workers' collective action would be revolutionary, not why the workers would act collectively. History and structure seemed to Marx to exert sufficient compulsion over the proletariat as a whole so that he treated social relationships among members of the proletariat only incidentally. Thus, "It is not a question of what this or that proletarian, or even the whole proletariat at the moment regards as its aim. It is a question of *what the proletariat is*, and what, in accordance with this being, it will historically be compelled to do."[10] In other words, Marx moved rather casually and problematically from the identification of "objective interests" to collective action in pursuit of those interests. The particularities and idiosyncrasies of different individuals and groups did concern Marx in such concrete historical analyses as "The Eighteenth Brumaire of Louis Bonaparte", and in considerations of political strategy, but they played no constitutive role in his more abstract theory of class struggle.

Marx's presumption of rational action on the basis of objective interests seems to be based on a theory of knowledge which leaves little room for the incompletely determined creation of interests in the course of human activity.[11] In the long run, outcomes are definite not only because people

[10] Karl Marx, *The Holy Family*, translated by R. Dixon and C. Dutt, in *Collective Works*, vol. 4. (London: Lawrence and Wishart, 1975 [1845]), pp. 5–211.

[11] Or, perhaps even more to the point, Marx shares in the Enlightenment tendency to suppress ontology in favor of epistemology. For Marx's version of a practice theory, thus, the question is still primarily how one knows one's interests rather than how those interests are constructed in practical existence. This is true of Marx's writings on politics and class struggle despite his profound critique in *Capital* of the tendency of capitalism to quantify everything and devalue the purely qualitative. Though Marx's critique implies a need to recover the purely qualitative (e.g. in use values and labor not dominated by the demands of commodity production) his positive theory of class struggle presumes the determination of workers' action within the rationality of the capitalist totality, negating it not through any immediate qualitative content, but only in the ultimate impossibility of completely subsuming the human being to that rationality. In his main writings on class struggle, Marx seems to vacillate between a Hegelian historicism and a reflection theory of knowledge. See, among many instances, Marx's appropriation of Hegel's assertion of the identity of the rational and the actual (Marx, "Contribution to the Critique of Hegel's Philosophy of Law", translated by M. Milligan and B. Ruhemann, in *Collected Works*, vol. 3 (London: Lawrence and Wishart [1927] 1975), p. 63); G.W.F. Hegel, *Philosophy of Right*, translated by T. Knox (Oxford: Oxford University Press [1821], 1967), p. 10, and his contrast of Feuerbachian materialism to the rest of German philosophy (Marx, *The German Ideology*, translated by C. Dutt, W. Lough and C.P. Magill, in *Collected Works*, vol. 5 (London: Lawrence and Wishart, [1932] 1976), pp. 36–7). Of course, Marx's materialism stressed, not the externality of material phenomena, but their incorporation into human life through practical activity, of which conscious control and awareness are always a part ("Theses on Feuerbach", in *Collected Works*, vol. 5 (London: Lawrence and Wishart, [1845], 1976), p. 4), but capitalism appears to constitute a sort of limiting case in

are rational but because history – working at a supra-individual level – is rational. In the short run, therefore, real people must be in error; Marx, like "scientific Marxists" after him, introduced the notion of "false consciousness" as the complement to that of "true interests". This was necessary in order to explain why action theoretically regarded as rational did not empirically occur. Had Marx not been prone to hypostatize the proletariat on the basis of his structural deductions, he might have seen more reason to develop a substantial theory of collective action. As it was, he (and many later Marxists) avoided such a theory either by hypostatization, or by attribution of false consciousness to actual workers. Non-Marxist accounts of collective action reveal, however, that rational individual actors fully conscious of their shared interests may fail to secure goods in their greatest interest both as individuals and as collectivities. The key reason is because they are sure of their interests, they are not sure of each other's action. Collective action is thus problematic in itself. Marx, however, does not see as problematical in this sense the question of how the objective class of proletarians becomes the subjective actor "the proletariat". As a result, he asserts, but does not demonstrate the transition from "class in itself" to "class for itself".[12]

Together with Engels, Marx argued that the concentration of workers in factories and large towns and the increasing organization of the workplace itself would help to mold the workers together and provide the social basis for their activity.[13] The leveling effect of industrial capitalism would give all workers the same poor standard of living and the same

which the material conditions for practical activity become maximally external. Marx rejects the abstract, ahistorical conception of human nature common to many rationalists, such as Bentham (*Capital*, vol. 1, translated by B. Fowkes (Harmondsworth: Penguin, [1867] 1976), p. 571; *The German Ideology*, p. 571). The 1844 manuscripts insist on the social and historical embeddedness of all "real" examples of humankind. In some contexts, thus, Marx thus appreciated the rootedness of action which I shall stress, but in his specific arguments concerning the revolutionary potential of the working class he focused on an account of rational interests which even his own sociological observations suggest is inadequate (see, e.g., both "The Class Struggles in France, 1848–1850", translated by P. Jackson, in Fernbach (ed.), *Surveys from Exile*; and "The Eighteenth Brumaire").

12 Marx, *The Poverty of Philosophy*, in *Collected Works*, vol. 6 (London: Lawrence and Wishart [1847], 1976), p. 211. Of course, this may be because Marx is not interested in an empirical, sociological shift in capacity for collective action, but in a dialectical transformation from a passive sum of individual existences to a single active collective existence, on the pattern of Rousseau's distinction of the will of all from the general will. This suggests, however, a much stronger holism to the notion of class for itself than is generally implied in modern "analytic Marxist" treatments of class formation (cf. Wright, *Classes*, chapter 3), or than is readily subject to empirical analysis.

13 Marx, *The Poverty of Philosophy*, p. 211; *Capital*, vol. 1, chapter 14; F. Engels, *Socialism: Utopian and Scientific*, in R. Tucker (ed.), *The Marx–Engels Reader* (New York: Norton, [1880] 1978), sec. 2.

desperate wants.[14] Through everyday interactions based on their common interests, and especially through continuous political activity in opposition to their exploiters, the workers would develop a class consciousness.[15] This class consciousness would provide an accurate understanding of external circumstances and thus of collective interests; these would provide sufficient rational reasons for unification in revolutionary collective action.

Marx was thus not without a sociological argument as to the sources of proletarian solidarity. It was an inadequate argument, though, as both logical and empirical counter-arguments suggest. Logically, Mancur Olson has shown that some structure of selective inducements is necessary to make it rational for an individual to participate in collective action even when the collective good sought is in his interest.[16] This is particularly so the larger and more "latent" the group and the more costly and widely dispersed the good sought. The reason is that individuals may choose to expend their limited resources in the pursuit of other, perhaps lesser, goods in ventures the success of which they can better control. At the same time, they may try to be "free riders", allowing others to pursue a good from which they will benefit but toward which they do not contribute.[17] Marx, neglecting such considerations, assumes that the very large class of workers will unite to seek a very uncertain collective good in a highiy risky mobilization, without much control over each other. To improve Marx's argument we need to identify a sociological source for selective inducements to collective action. Olson suggests that we may find this in social pressure within certain kinds of pre-existing organizations.[18] I concur, and this chapter expands the argument, particularly by suggesting that such pre-existing organizations need not be formally constituted or created for the purpose of pursuing the collective good at hand. Rather, the informal bonds of community relationships may

---

[14] Karl Marx and F. Engels, "Manifesto of the Communist Party", in *Collected Works*, vol. 6 (London: Lawrence and Wishart [1848] 1976); *Capital*, vol. 1, chapter 23, 32).

[15] Marx, "The Class Struggles in France", "Eighteenth Brumaire".

[16] M. Olson, *The Logic of Collective Action* (Cambridge, Mass.: Harvard University Press, 1965), pp. 2, 51, 134.

[17] Ibid., pp. 105–10.

[18] Others have stressed pre-existing organization even more, e.g. T. Moe, *The Organization of Interests* (Chicago: University of Chicago Press, 1980). Olson (*The Logic of Collective Action*, p. 63) argues that large "organizations that use selective *social* incentives to mobilize a latent group interested in a collective good must be federations of smaller groups" (emphasis added). I have developed this idea elsewhere (Calhoun, "Democracy, Autocracy and Intermediate Associations in Organizations", *Sociology*, 14 (1980) 345–61); here I would argue that while a class is nearly always a large, latent group, communities within it may provide strong social incentives to mobilization and therefore members of a class may best be mobilized for risky and radical pursuits through such intermediate associations as pre-existing communities.

provide powerful selective incentives, and a form of pre-existing organization ready to mobilize in a variety of actions.

Empirically, Marx's argument runs up against the relatively low rate of participation of members of the modern proletariat in revolutionary mobilization and the relatively high rate of such participation among artisans and other pre-industrial workers. Whereas Marx is emphatic in holding that proletarian unity arises out of new conditions of social existence, I suggest that pre-existing communal bonds are at issue. Further, the new proletariat, generally speaking, has had less of this pre-existing social organization on which to draw than have groups of workers challenged by industrialization. This helps to explain why craftsmen and peasants, rather than factory workers, form the majority of revolutionary crowds of early nineteenth-century Europe.[19] From the point of view of objective interests, Marx finds the proletariat to be bound by "universal chains".[20] By contrast, the radical mobilizations of actual history have come more often from those bound by very particular chains.

In the famous last pages of *The Poverty of Philosophy*, Marx sums up his argument. He indicates that the rise of capitalist domination created the class of workers as a mass of individuals. "Large-scale industry concentrated in one place a crowd of people unknown to one another."[21] Under such circumstances, the competition created among the workers by capitalists "divides the interests" of members of this class (more precisely, Marx should have said that *similar* interests within the competitive job market divide the workers). Despite advice from all quarters to the contrary, the workers act, not on the interests which divide them, but increasingly on those collective interests they share. Implicitly, Marx holds that they do so because the collective interests are greater. Shared or collective interests (such as maintaining high wages) lead the workers to form combinations against their employers; such combinations grow in direct proportion to the growth of industry. By uniting to compete against the capitalists, workers are able to secure a collective good apparently more valuable to each than the private goods to be secured by some through competition with others. The initial basis of this combination,

[19] Of course, the same argument divides even more starkly the relatively advanced industrial societies of the world from those just undergoing a transition to capitalism, or suffering under capitalist economic exploitation managed from abroad or from narrow and non-transformative urban enclaves. The heritage of colonialism and the workings of the modern world system sufficiently alter certain aspects of economic life and revolutionary politics in these societies that it is worth reiterating that this argument applies most directly to the narrower range of differences found among groups of workers during European industrialization (and to a lesser extent, that of North America).

[20] Marx, "Contribution to the Critique of Hegel's Philosophy of Law", p. 186.

[21] Marx, *The Poverty of Philosophy*, p. 210.

thus, is "a common situation, common [i.e., shared, not just similar] interests".[22] This is why it is so important that workers are drawn from rural isolation into urban concentration. The working class enters increasingly into struggle with the capitalists (who already constitute a class for itself) and takes on an existence of its own. As a class for itself, "the interests it defends become class interests"; simultaneously, it becomes a political actor, because "political power is precisely the official expression of antagonism in civil society".[23] The unclear point in the argument is the nature of the social relations which turn the class in itself into the class for itself, which make the proletariat the class of associated producers, not simply the aggregated producers.

In the following pages I present an argument that pre-existing communal relations and attachments to tradition are essential to revolutionary mobilizations. By the last phrase I mean radical movements which, whether they intend to transform society, to topple a government, or to extract a few concessions, pose such fundamental challenges to existing social trends that those in power can make them no meaningful concessions. Obviously revolutionary outcomes have a great deal to do with other structural factors, notably the circumstances of state power and international relations, as Skocpol has recently observed.[24] Nonetheless, revolutions are not simply spontaneous collapses of state power; regimes are pushed, even when they seem to topple like houses of cards. Movements resisting industrial capitalism may more readily give such a push than movements of workers within industrial capitalism. This has been obscured by Marx's stress on the radical novelty of revolution.

Reactionary radicals

There is no principle, no precedent, no regulations (except as to mere matter of detail), favourable to freedom, which is not to be found in the Laws of England or in the example of our Ancestors. Therefore, I say we may ask for, and we want *nothing new*. We have great constitutional laws and principles, to which we are immovably attached. We want *great alteration*, but we want nothing new.[25]

William Cobbett, author of the appeal to tradition just quoted, was the most important publicist and one of the most important popular leaders of the rising tide of protest and insurgency which marked the first decades of the nineteenth century in England. His words are salutary for those who would understand radical popular mobilizations, including those which

[22] Ibid., p. 211.
[23] Ibid., pp. 211–12.
[24] Theda, Skocpol, *States and Social Revolutions* (Cambridge: Cambridge University Press, 1979).
[25] W. Cobbett, *Political Register*, 2 November, 1816.

have produced revolutions, in other times and places as well. Cobbett voiced a critique of the existing social and political structure in the name of traditional rights and values. He fought against economic trends which were disrupting established ways of life, not in favor of an abstractly conceived future. This English populism was not statist or supportive of reactionary elites, in the manner of some Latin American populisms. Rather, it was a genuine and radical insurgency. It spoke primarily on behalf of "the people". It was against those who would abuse the people, but not necessarily in favor of any specific segment of the population. By the 1830s, this emphasis on the people was competing with a growing analysis of the distinctive interests of the working class.[26] Before then, a common populist ideology had tended to obscure the divergent social foundations on which artisans, outworkers and some rural insurgents on the one hand and members of the emergent modern working class on the other joined together for collective action.

English populism had a strongly negative ideology; it was much concerned with a critique of corruption in favor of some postulated prior and better state of society.[27] Its aims were consistently to restore society to this blessed state. Images of this golden age embodied the values of contemporary community life at least as much as an amalgam of actually remembered virtues of the past. Based on this foundation, the populist movement resisted the industrialization of England. It resisted most of all the particular paths this industrialization was taking, and the injustices which were embodied in the system for reasons of the self-interest of elites rather than the demands of production or the benefit of the nation. But it also resisted the whole transformation of social life which industrialization implied or required. As such, this populist movement was fundamentally conservative. Its strength and its aims sprang from the communities in which its proponents actually lived and worked, not from an abstractly imagined or rationally determined future.

At the same time, this populist agitation was very radical, because it demanded things which could not readily be incorporated within the emerging framework of industrial capitalist society. Indeed, it demanded an organization of productive and distributive relations which could fit

[26] Hollis observes, for example, that "Place spoke the language of aristocracy and People, and within the People there could be no division of class. Hetherington spoke the language of class": *The Pauper Press: A Study in Working-Class Radicalism in the 1830s* (Oxford: Oxford University Press, 1970), p. 8. Though his rhetoric retained populist overtones, the more Francis Place become a Utilitarian, the less he fitted the model of populist outlined here.

[27] "For it was always the abuse of authority, not the authority itself, that was the immediate target of attack, even although other targets might present themselves as a campaign progressed", A.P. Thornton, *The Habit of Authority: Paternalism in British History* (London: Allen and Unwin, 1965), p. 14.

well into neither capitalist economics nor modern industrial processes. It is in this sense that I have termed the participants in this movement (or movements) "reactionary radicals". They called for changes which were at once founded on traditional aspirations and almost diametrically opposed to the dominant economic and social trends of their day – that is, the development of industrial capitalist society. The chances of their movement's being socially revolutionary were in direct proportion to its relative social strength, not its ideological clarity. Such strength was to be found most of all in local communities, least in national organization. Populist pressure from below competed in a zero-sum game, as it were, with the forces pushing for the dominance of capitalist industry. Each side's victories had to take something directly from the other side; there was virtually no ground for compromise. This is not to say that elites did all they could to ameliorate the plight of those who suffered from the growth of capitalism; they did precious little. But even if they had done more, it would have been only amelioration or an easing of the transition away from valued traditions, crafts, and communities. Neither charity nor constititional reform, paternalism nor liberalism offered the possibility of saving what capitalist industrialization threatened. The new working class could fight through Chartism and a variety of more narrowly focused struggles for improvements within the capitalist system, without forfeiting its basic identity. The new working class could even make alliance with the liberalism of old Whigs and some new Utilitarians, but the populist craftsmen of the intervening period could not. Even democracy, however damnably insubordinate and threateningly unstable it might seem to elites, could not in itself solve the problems of handloom weavers and others like them (though many thought it could). Democracy could be granted in an extended (and reluctant) series of reforms without sacrificing the capitalist industrial society, or even most of the cultural hegemony and material power of the elite strata.[28]

In the 1810s, Cobbett spoke to the bulk of the English people in a shared populist rhetoric of traditional glories and present-day theft and corruption. He and other reactionary radicals already had their critics on the left, however, such as John Wade, a pro-union journalist and publisher of *The Gorgon*. Wade stressed "the relative degree of comfort and importance enjoyed by the labouring classes of the present day, compared with former periods".[29] He, and others of similar ideological bent, were particularly conscious of the emergent class of factory workers, and of the

[28] Similarly, of course, capitalists could grant better wages and working conditions without fundamentally jeopardizing capitalism, though they were not always aware of this fact or eager to do so.
[29] *The Gorgon*, 23 May 1818, p. 8.

position of strength which growing numbers and importance gave to this newer laboring population by contrast to the older and more precarious movements of journeymen. Cobbett, however, was convinced like most of his readers in craft communities, of the virtues of tradition and the real existence of a golden age, the rules of which were preserved in England's ancient Constitution (as suggested in the quotation given above). He had little confidence in new possibilities opened up by reason (which might have been a Jacobin consciousness) or by technological or social-organizational advance (the developing consciousness of both the bourgeoisie and the nascent working class). Cobbett indeed thought it a pleasant and quite possible prospect that commerce and manufactures could be greatly diminished, the clock turned back, and the factory system averted.[30] This was a vision which held out a good deal to artisans and outworkers but very little to the factory workers. Wade's reply was scathing:

The Cause of reform has been injudiciously betrayed by reverting to the supposed rights and privileges enjoyed by our ancestors. We are no sticklers for precedents, nor for dead men's Government; neither do we wish to revert to the institutions of a barbarous age for example to the nineteenth century. Englishmen of the present day can have no more to do with the Government of the Saxons, than of the Romans, the Grecians, or the Carthaginians.[31]

Wade was perhaps a realist where Cobbett indulged his fantasies, but Wade was also a rationalist (and indeed, almost a Utilitarian) in a way Cobbett never was. But Cobbett was neither unreasonable nor without profound insight. He thought and argued in a different way, however, to and for a fundamentally different population. The populist radicalism of craftsmen and outworkers, which reached its height between 1816 and 1820, was revealing ever more sharply the discontinuities between its social foundations and those of the increasingly trade-union oriented and pragmatic movements of factory workers. In 1818, this was visible as Wade devoted considerable attention to the Manchester factory spinners' strike, while the spinners' organization, perhaps the strongest trade union of the time, pointedly held itself aloof from the radical and reform agitations of Cobbett and the other reactionary radicals.[32]

There are, of course, continuities in English political radicalism throughout this period, as working-class movements inherit concerns from populist predecessors and both develop themes that date back at

---

[30] See, e.g., *Political Register*, November 1807.
[31] *The Gorgon*, 23 May 1818.
[32] R.G. Kirby and A.E. Musson, *The Voice of the People: John Doherty, 1789–1854* (Manchester: Manchester University Press, 1975), pp. 18–22; Thompson, *The Making of the English Working Class*, pp. 706–8.

least to Locke.[33] But the discontinuities are important. Cobbett and a number of his followers idealized the small farmer and petty commodity producer; hopes for a chance to own a few country acres and achieve self-sufficiency in vegetables lingered among urban workers long after the demise of the Chartist Land Plan. Artisans similarly emphasized the maintenance or re-creation of a traditional craft autonomy. Indeed, ideas of autonomy were considerably more prominent amongst them than notions of exploitation, such as that which Marx would show to be appropriate to free wage-labor.

Though it strained against this ideoogy of autonomy, artisans did sometimes recognize the importance of division of labor and the fact that all workers in modern society live by the exchange of their products and by cooperation in combining individual acts of production into larger wholes. Wheelwrights recognized that they did not make whole carriages. But accepting a division of labor did not mean accepting either a centralization of control or a concentration of all production in a single workplace – a factory. Craft workers in England resisted the transition from payment for products to wage labor.[34] Even where their products were manifestly only parts of a larger whole, craft workers preferred piece-rates to payment for time. Well acquainted with acting as their own supervisors and managers, the artisans were quite prepared to grant these activities a share in the produce of socially organized labor.[35] They were less convinced about the claims of those who merely owned property in the means of production and claimed a share in the products on this basis rather than any contribution of their labor or ingenuity.[36] They were not by any means unanimously opposed to such private property,

[33] See G.S. Jones, "Rethinking Chartism", in *Languages of Class: Studies in English Working Class History, 1832–1982* (Cambridge: Cambridge University Press, 1983).

[34] The same was true, perhaps even in greater degree, in France. See William Reddy, "Skeins, Scales, Discounts, Steam and Other Objects of Crowd Justice in Early French Textile Mills", *Comparative Studies in Society and History*, 22 (1979), 204–13.

[35] Thomas Hodgskin (*Labour Defended Against the Claims of Capital*, New York: Kelley, [1825], 1963, pp. 86–91), for example, noted the importance of ensuring the maximal level of cooperation and finding the best way of judging the contributions of each worker. He therefore distinguished between the capitalist as manager and as mere middleman. The term "middleman" itself is instructive, for it suggests something of the way old mercantile categories were carried into the analysis of capitalist industry.

[36] On the other hand, the main brunt of their criticism was directed against grossly unequal distributions of wealth, not of capital specifically. As one sophisticated advocate of the framework-knitters' cause argued, depressed wages lead to depressed prices which benefit all those who have the wealth to purchase. Thus unequal condition in the market causes the transfer of wealth from those who labor to those who do not, whether or not there is exploitation in the labor process: R. Hall, *A Reply to the Principal Objections Advanced by Cobbett and Others against the Framework-Knitters' Friendly Relief Society* (New York: Arno, [1821] 1972). Hall was writing, as it happened, to take Cobbett to task for failing to apply his general principles to the case of the framework-knitters. From Cobbett's point of view, the knitters' relief society looked too much like a union.

however; at least as many simply wished to see the craftsman's skill recognized as a property right. They wanted to see government and law defend the prerogatives of skill (what later economists would call human capital) just as they did the fixed capital of proprietors. The result of all this was that artisans generally resisted the notion of a single homogenous class of workers, even when they presented the claims of those who labored to those who did not. The artisans continued to think of working classes in the plural; indeed, England's present-day trade-union structure reflects this traditional legacy in the extent of its craft organization.

During the 1820s factories came for the first time into ascendancy over domestic and small workshop production in the Lancashire textile industry; most of the rest of English industry gradually followed. This decade, coming between Peterloo (the brutal suppression of a public rally in 1819) and the "last labourers' revolt" (the rural incendiarism of 1830–1) marked the close of the great wave of locally based, communitarian populism which ushered in capitalist industry in England. By the end of the first third of the nineteenth century, the predominantly traditional "old radicalism" was virtually past. It lingered a bit in the opposition to the new Poor Law and the agitation for electoral reform, but in Chartism and the factory agitations of the 1830s and 1840s a new generation of leaders came to the fore and the problems of common people began to be conceptualized in new and different ways. Perhaps most importantly, a greater division among political, industrial, and social problems (and mobilizations to solve those problems) began to emerge. This was especially the case at the level of formal organizations extending across the boundaries of local communities; these were themselves assuming an increasing importance.

The age of Chartism and the early factory agitations was dominated, as far as working people's collective action was concerned, by the split between the older artisan and outworking populations and the newer factory and laboring populations. This is not to say that there were simply two opposed camps, but a great many of the partially ideological divisions of the period are easier to understand when seen in the light of the divergent interests and social strengths of these two broad populations. Trade unionism was the great survivor of the period, not political radicalism. Though a number of artisan trades retained their place in production throughout the nineteenth century, from late Chartism onwards the artisans lost their position of pre-eminence in workers' movements.[37] The political radicalism of the early part of the century had

[37] R. Samuel, "Workshop of the World: Steam Power and Hand Technology in Mid-Victorian Britain", *History Workshop Journal* 3 (1977), 6–72; C. Calhoun, "Industrialization and Social Radicalism", *Theory and Society*, 12, no. 4 (1983), 485–504.

been very strongly tied to these artisans, to their local and craft communities, and to the traditions which they maintained. Much of this was lost or deeply submerged during the Victorian era. The social foundations which had sustained the mobilizations of artisans were transformed. Chartism needs to be seen, in important ways, as an ending as much as a beginning. It was an ending not just of this phase of protest against incipient industrial capitalism, but of the long reign of a directly political (rather than political because economic) radicalism forged in the English Civil War.[38]

It was during the Chartist movement and the factory agitations that Marx and Engels came to examine English society and take the mobilizations of English workers as central to their theory of working-class radicalism. They, like most analysts since, saw the period almost entirely as one of beginnings. These, to be sure, were many. This was the period in which popular politics and the trade-union movement as we now know it both got seriously under way. it was after surviving the crises of 1837 and 1847 that industrial capitalism developed the sense of confidence which characterized it throughout the Victorian era. But Marx's hoped-for and predicted working-class movement did not mature as clearly or continuously as capitalism. Marx failed to foresee this development partly because he had not realized how much of the radicalism he observed among English workers (and workers of other nationalities) was part of the resistance waged by artisans and small producers of many sorts against large-scale industrial capitalism. And he had not realized the extent to which the demands of the new factory population could be incorporated within capitalism, unlike the demands of the artisans. By understanding why so much of what Thompson calls "the making of the English working class" is the reactionary radicalism of the threatened artisanate, we are better placed to understand the problems which were incorporated from its beginnings into Marx's theory of revolutionary class struggle.

The form and content of populist radicalism in industrializing England was distinctive, but Cobbett's claims for tradition have much in common with the ideologies characteristic of many popular struggles against emergent or imposed capitalism. These struggles have been at once radical and reactionary; their radicalism has been based on tradition and in immediate social relations supporting and supported by such tradition. It is within an unwarranted rationalism that Marxist (and some other) analysts have attempted to assimilate these movements to the category of class. Engels, indeed, did this when he analyzed the fifteenth- and sixteenth-century German peasant wars as primitive revolutionary mobil-

[38] Jones, "Rethinking Chartism".

izations based on poorly understood class interests.[39] Some modern writers would go further and argue that the analytic framework of class struggle can be applied to such precapitalist movements without having to use qualifiers like "primitive". Others, though, are more cautious and suggest that such mobilizations are neither revolutionary nor class-based in the sense in which Marx used those terms to describe modern movements.

For example, in summarizing his argument concerning "primitive rebels," Hobsbawm observes that "the political allegiance and character of such movements is often undetermined, ambiguous or even ostensibly 'conservative'". Their participants are generally "*pre-political* people who have not yet found, or only begun to find a specific language in which to express their aspirations about the world. Though their movements are thus in many respects blind and groping, by the standards of modern ones, they are neither unimportant nor marginal."[40]

What Hobsbawm means by pre-political has been fairly clear throughout his work: it refers to the ideologically uncertain and ephemeral, rather than the analytically sound and historically transformative among orientations to collective action. In contrast, it is organized, self-conscious action which makes a collectivity's struggle to achieve control over its own fate political. "The poor," Hobsbawm has written more recently, "or indeed any subaltern group, become a subject rather than an object of history only through formalized collectivities, however structured. Everybody always has families, social relations, attitudes toward sexuality, childhood and death, and all the other things that keep social historians usefully employed. But, until the past two centuries, as traditional historiography shows, 'the poor' could be neglected most of the time by their 'betters,' and therefore remained largely invisible to them, precisely because their active impact on events was occasional, scattered, and impermanent."[41]

Hobsbawm's work emphasizes the disjuncture between millenarian movements, rebellions, and related events in precapitalist societies and the more formally organized and rationally self-conscious activity of the modern working class. And yet, in a preface to the third edition of *Primitive Rebels*, he suggests that, if anything, he underestimated the revolutionary significance of both organized millennial sects and communities and relatively unorganized millennial movements.[42] I think he is

[39] F. Engels, *The Peasant War in Germany*, in *Collected Works*, vol. 10 (London: Lawrence & Wishart, [1850] 1978), pp. 397–482.

[40] Eric Hobsbawm, *Primitive Rebels* (Manchester: Manchester University Press, 1959), p. 2.

[41] "Should the Poor Organize?" *New York Review of Books* (23 March, 1978), p. 48.

[42] Hobsbawm, "Preface", *Primitive Rebels*, 3rd edn (Manchester: Manchester University Press, 1971), pp. xi–xii.

right because, when societies are rapidly changing, commitment to tradition can be a radical threat to the distribution of social power. And communities in which interpersonal relations are densely knit, many-faceted, and organized in harmony with traditional values can be potent informal organizations on which to base sustained insurgency.

Traditional communities

The idea of contrasting modern society to an earlier age of traditional communities has been roundly criticized in recent years. The *Gemein-schaft–Gesellschaft* opposition, to be sure, was somewhat vague and ill-defined, and, in Tonnies' version, was sentimental and full of personal evaluations which are hard to substantiate empirically.[43] Other dichoto-mous renderings of modern history have fallen on similarly hard times, and for good reason: history is more complex. I think, however, that our rejection of the contrast which shaped sociology's vision of modernity may have become as categorical and simplistic as the original contrast itself. What we need is to conceptualize a cluster of variables measuring traditionality and community.[44] Not only would such variables get us away from false dichotomization, they would also allow us to treat variance directly rather than through the often spurious indicator of historical dates. We could see that at any one time different social groups might be organized more or less traditionally, more or less communally, without treating them as more or less advanced. This would avoid the romanticism of the *Gemeinschaft* notion. Moreover, we could recognize that binding relationships may be full of conflict. As the Arab proverb has it, "I against my brothers; I and my brothers against my cousins; I, my brothers and my cousins against the world." Solidarity is not the same as harmony. While village England may never have been characterized by blissful unity, it did offer certain forms of mutual support, and it did knit even many enemies together as insiders who clearly understood their distinction from outsiders. To challenge the relevance of this concept of traditional community would require more than evidence that people are selfish or hostile to each other even in tribes and small villages.

We shall need to see tradition as more than a collection of ideas or artifacts transmitted from generation to generation. Shils emphasizes the basic etymological sense of tradition (*traditum*) as anything "handed down from past to present",[45] but in his book discusses tradition in a variety of

[43] Ferdinand Tonnies, *Community and Association (Gemeinschaft und Gesellschaft)*, translated by C.P. Loomis (New York: Harper, [1887] 1957).

[44] By convention, let "traditionality" indicate a pattern of social organization rather than the ideological value suggested by "traditionalism".

[45] Shils, *Tradition*, p. 12.

senses which go far beyond this usage. I suggest that, in order to make full sense of tradition, we shall have to see the acts of transmission as all social interaction, with the validity of traditional ideas or practices coming not just from their antiquity but from the element of consensus and universality of their use. I shall focus on traditionality as a mode of organizing social action rather than on traditionalism as an abstract ideology venerating the past. This language is Weberian, and I have in mind the Weberian notion of social action as subjectively meaningful behavior taking account of the behavior of others and thereby oriented in its course,[46] but not the Weberian notion of tradition. Weber saw traditional action as "determined by ingrained habituation", and thought that it lay very close to the borderline of what could be called meaningfully oriented action.[47] Like most thinkers since the Enlightenment, he opposed traditionalism as mere unconscious reflex or unexamined inheritance to rationality as conscious and sensible action. Traditionalism was, for Weber, "piety for what actually, allegedly, or presumably has always existed".[48] Such a conceptualization ties tradition too closely to history.[49] I suggest that we see tradition less in terms of antiquity and communication across generations than in terms of practical, everyday social activity. The traditional construction of social reality takes place as people in manifold interactions produce and reproduce shared understandings of their behavior. As Shils has put it:

A society to exist at all must be incessantly reenacted, its communications must repeatedly be resaid. The reenactments and the resayings are guided by what the individual members remember about what they themselves said and did before, what they perceive and remember of what other persons expect and require of them: they are guided too by what they remember is expected or required of them, what they remember to be claims which they are entitled to exercise by virtue of particular qualifications such as skill, title, appointment, ownership which are engrained in their own memory traces, recorded in writing and in the correspondingly recorded qualifications of others. These particular qualifications change and the responses to the changes are guided by recollections of the rightful claims and rights of the possessors of those qualifications.[50]

This is all true, but we need to complement Shils's stress on memory with more focus on practical activity, taking place amid specific material needs

---

[46] Weber, *Economy and Society*, p. 4.

[47] Ibid., p. 25.

[48] "The Social Psychology of World Religions", in H.H. Gerth and C. Wright Mills (eds.), *From Max Weber* (London: Routledge and Kegan Paul, [1925] 1948), p. 296.

[49] It also presumes the possibility of something close to "traditionless" thought and action, failing to consider the extent to which all activity is grounded in shared and/or inherited "prejudices", to use H.-G. Gadamer's phrase (*Truth and Method*, New York: Seabury, [1960] 1975). Rational thought cannot escape prejudgments, whether understood ontologically or hermeneutically.

[50] Shils, *Tradition*, pp. 166–7.

and social circumstances. It can involve habits, to be sure, but socially conditioned habits. Tradition is the tacit knowledge which allows participation in social life.[51] As such it is hardly rigid. On the contrary, tradition must often be interpreted and reshaped to fit the exigencies of contemporary situations.[52] Strategic reinterpretations of "that which has always been"[53] are common. They are not, however, evidence for either the insignificance of tradition or the universal predominance of self-interested individualism.

The continual reproduction of tradition necessarily involves many minor and some major revisions of it. These are signs that tradition remains vital and has not become a mere crust of ceremonial lore. But such reinterpretations are not the products of discrete individuals acting quite self-consciously; they are, instead, collective interpretations produced or acquiesced in by people who take such social constructs as materially real. Drawing on, but modifying, Durkheim, I suggest not that society is ontologically prior to individuals, a phenomenon *sui generis* in some absolute sense, but that societies vary in the extent to which their members must take them as "naturally" given (rather than contingently constructed and modifiable by human choice).[54] Traditional societies are those in which they must do so.

That people should take their social contexts to be as immutably "real" as their physical contexts is the result of the special power which those social contexts have over them. Closely knit into webs of communal relationships, individuals are committed to the long-term view of their activity which is implied by the notion of moral responsibility.[55] Choices are still to be made, but they must take social relationships very closely into account. Tradition is the medium in which interactions take place. Like language, it is at once passed from individual to individual through use and given much of its substantive meaning by the particular instances of its use. Changes in social or natural context often require impro-

---

[51] Michael Polanyi, *Personal Knowledge: Towards a Post-critical Philosophy* (Chicago: University of Chicago Press, 1958).

[52] This is a point frequently noted by anthropologists, perhaps because it is easier to demystify the claim to complete continuity of an oral tradition than it is of one which actually passes down the same written documents. See Pierre Bourdieu, *Outline of a Theory of Practice*, translated by R. Nice (Cambridge: Cambridge University Press, 1972), chapter 2; Nur Yalman, "Some Observations on Secularism in Islam", *Daedalus* 102 (1973), 139–68, esp. p. 139; E. Colson, *Tradition and Contract* (London: Heinemann, 1974), p. 76.

[53] Weber, *Economy and Society*, p. 36.

[54] Emile Durkheim, *The Elementary Forms of the Religious Life* (New York: The Free Press, [1915] 1965); see also T.M.S. Evens, "Logic and the Efficacy of the Nuer Incest Prohibition", *Man*, 18, no. 1 (1984), 111–33.

[55] Marc Bloch, "The Long Term and the Short Term: The Economic and Political Significance of the Morality of Kinship", in Jack Goody (ed.), *The Character of Kinship* (Cambridge: Cambridge University Press, 1973), pp. 75–87.

visations on the part of actors. But these improvisations, too, are constructed according to the rules of tradition; they take their meaning from their relationships to the rest of the active tradition as well as from practical circumstances, and they are validated by communal acceptance.[56]

Traditions do not reflect the past so much as they reflect present-day social life. Only to the extent that such social life is coherent and consistent across the membership of a given society or subsociety can tradition be very effective in ordering people's actions.[57] Moreover, it is the repeated practical use of traditions in relating to important others that gives the traditions their deep psychological importance. Community is thus a central medium for transmitting tradition and a large part of what tradition is about.

Such a view clearly implies a special definition of community. Essentially, I take community to be a complex variable measuring the extent to

[56] See Bourdieu's discussion of the "habitus", the source of regulated cultural improvisation (*Outline of a Theory of Practice*, pp. 78–87). A key distinction of what Bourdieu calls archaic societies is the narrow range (by contrast with capitalist societies, at least, and possibly a wider and less clearly demarcated modernity) within which self-conscious and explicit strategizing and innovation are acceptable. The habitus functions to provide social actors with a "sense of the game" which is an essential complement to formal rules, but which cannot be rendered explicit. Thus much of the strategizing and improvization which does exist in archaic societies must be "misrecognized". It is treated as what must be done and what always has been done even when it is optional and new. This requirement of misrecognition, however, is also a constraint. It inhibits a free play of improvisation and militates in favor of reproduction of existing, collectively understood strategies and patterns of action. By extension, we can read the argument as suggesting that capitalist societies are characterized by the reproduction of certain large-scale forms of social relationship (commodity production and capital accumulation) which necessitate constant variation in more immediate patterns of social relations and constant innovation in technique. Noting the historical and cross-cultural differences reminds us that the conceptualization is a sociological, not a psychological, universal proposition. It is, however, in accord with social psychological arguments that individuals act to preserve the consistency of their thoughts, feelings, and behavior; see L. Festinger, *A Theory of Cognitive Dissonance* (Stanford, California: Stanford University Press, 1962), and *Conflict, Decision and Dissonance* (Stanford, California: Stanford University Press, 1964); Fritz Heider, *The Psychology of Interpersonal Relations* (New York: Wiley, 1958). In terms of Heise's distinction of fundamental and transient elements of individuals' "control systems" (D. Heise, *Understanding Events* (Cambridge: Cambridge University Press, 1979)), I suggest that (perhaps barring psychopathology) most "fundamentals" are products of traditional culture.

[57] Thus, although Shils points out that nineteenth-century liberals were right "to see traditions as limitations on human freedom", we might accurately see a "chicken and egg" situation. On the one hand, "tradition hems an individual in; it sets the condition of his actions; it determines his resources; it even determines what he himself is" (Shils, *Tradition*, p. 197); on the other hand, changing practical circumstances demand innovation within tradition, some social organizations support stable traditions better than others, and individuals vary in the novelty and disruptiveness of their interpretations of tradition. Capitalism acts against much of traditional social organizations by creating a totality the reproduction of which demands the constant production of novelty in productive technology and in many social interactions.

which people are knit together by direct social relationships.[58] To speak of "a community" is thus only shorthand for referring to a population characterized by a considerable extent of community. Variations in kind or extent of community are established by differences in (1) kinds of relationships among people, (2) characteristics of networks of those relationships, and (3) extent of autonomous social control. In brief, relationships may be stronger or weaker, networks may be knit more or less densely and systematically together, and a population may be more or less able to run its own affairs without outside intervention.[59] Community constrains the range of free choice of individuals by committing them to specific, long-term social relationships. Such commitments make it possible for members of communities to act with considerable certainty as to what their fellows will do. Relatedly, because their activity is kept largely within the grounds of established relationships, members of communities are able constantly to reproduce a traditional culture without introducing wide variation in interpretation. Traditional communities, thus, are closely knit, largely autonomous collectivities which share a vital common culture.

Traditional communities are important bases of radical mobilization. Community constitutes a pre-existing organization capable of securing the participation of individuals in collective action. Communities provide a social organizational foundation for mobilization, as networks of kinship, friendship, shared crafts, or recreations offer lines of communication and allegiance. People who live in well-integrated communities do not need elaborate formal organization in order to mount a protest. They know, moreover, whom to trust and whom not to trust. Communal relations are themselves important resources to be "mobilized" for any insurgency (though they are frequently neglected by "resource mobilization" analyses). This is part of the reason why peasant, craft, and other popular revolts are generally much stronger at the local level than at the national. Indeed, such movements generally fall apart or else are taken over by special-interest groups when they extend much beyond the range of direct, person-to-person communal ties. When speaking, for example,

---

[58] Direct relationships include not just the extremely close and intimate, but those that sociologists sometimes call "secondary". They do not include those constructed through the mediation of bureaucracy or (for the most part) space-transcending communications technology. Relationships which lack personal recognition and face-to-face constitution I would call "indirect": Calhoun, "New Information Technology, Large Scale Social Integration and the Local Community", *Urban Affairs Quarterly* 22 (1986), 329–49.

[59] C. Calhoun, "Community: Toward a Variable Conceptualization for Comparative Research", *Social History* 5 (1980), 105–29. Communities may also vary in the clarity of the boundaries defining their membership. Such clarity of who "we" are as against others may be an important predisposition to collective action in some circumstances (see Calhoun, "Industrialization and Social Radicalism").

of rebellious peasants in revolutionary France (in either the First or Second Republic), we may describe a class similar in external characteristics, but we would do well to avoid the conclusion that peasants *acted* as a class. They acted on the basis of numerous local communities, with consequent variations in local strategies, demands, and strengths.[60] They may have been a class *in* itself but they were only communities *for* themselves.[61]

Traditional communities give people the "interests" for which they will risk their lives – families, friends, customary crafts, and ways of life. Popular revolts take place either when (1) external pressures on a still-coherent way of life are threatening to destroy it or (2) new opportunities appear to put old goals within reach. Thus tradition is not in itself insurrectionary. On the contrary, it is a conservative force. Much the same can be said for community. In ordinary times, the deep-rootedness of traditional understandings and communal relationships makes them conservative and provides for the reproduction of culture and social relations. But in times of rapid change, this very conservatism may make traditional communities politically radical, even revolutionary.[62] In reaction to the incursions of capitalist industry, for example, handloom weavers and other craftsmen in England and France attempted to defend their traditional crafts and communities against disruption. It did not matter that handloom weaving, especially in England, had drawn thousands of new practitioners during the early years of industrialization, degrading the craft. Industrialization continually expanded or created handcrafts at bottlenecks in the production process, only to destroy them later.[63] While these handworkers were relatively weak, compared with many better-paid and better-organized artisanal groups, their weakness does not alter the centrality of the fact that they frequently lived, worked, and revolted in traditional communities.[64] As I have argued, it is not antiquity which defines such a mode of social and cultural organization. Weavers were thus like more privileged artisans in that they fought to defend what they already had. As Sewell has shown, the language of artisans' defense included new ideas among the traditional elements as it

[60] Maurice Agulhon, *La Republique au Village* (Paris: Plon, 1970), pp. 305–406; Price, *The French Second Republic*, esp. p. 121.
[61] This understanding of the peasantry is implicit in Marx's description of peasants as resembling potatoes in a sack ("The Eighteenth Brumaire", p. 239). Marx grasped the importance of social foundations for collective action (e.g., *The Poverty of Philosophy*, p. 211) even though he failed accurately to identify the implications of different social foundations.
[62] Moore describes in detail the role of traditional communities in producing tolerance for injustice and also suggests the importance of conservatism in popular mobilization during the German revolution of 1848 (*Injustice*, chapter 8, pp. 126–33, 158).
[63] Samuel, "Workshop of the World".
[64] See Calhoun, *The Question of Class Struggle*, pp. 43–8, 78–83, 195–8.

developed from the Old Regime to 1848.[65] Traditional corporatism remained, however, a central organizing theme. New, more recognizably socialist ideas either developed out of corporatism or were incorporated to the extent that they could be fitted into the traditional structure of thought and action. Much of the change was not in the traditions themselves but in their context. What had been conservative in the eighteenth century became radical with the introduction of new technologies and patterns of capitalist economic organization. And it was largely these new patterns of capitalism which turned some workers from the defense of the rights of particular groups against other workers to an increasing focus on the similar situation of all who labor.

Not all who labored were equally interested in this radical reaction to capitalism. Some workers were directly benefiting. Accordingly, in the revolution of 1848 in France, employees of factories and modern capitalist establishments were relatively uninvolved.[66] Younger workers, excluded from the artisan corporations, were often among the first to enlist in the *garde mobile*, in which they played a leading role in the repression of the workers' rising of June 1848.[67]

Peasants were also somewhat different in orientation from urban artisans. On the one hand, most famously, it was peasants who gave the Bonapartist regime its strongest popular backing. Conservative in outlook, they backed the party of order and authority. But even the Bonapartist regime was still, initially, a version of republicanism; peasants were not hostile to all change. On the contrary, when the February revolution demonstrated the weakness of government repression, peasants immediately acted to seek redress for traditional grievances and to realize traditional goals. As Zeldin puts it: "In the first days after the revolution, they were aware only that the government had gone. Their first reactions were not political. They invaded the commons and forests, claiming back the traditional rights they had lost to the rich: they sacked the houses of those who resisted them; they drove tax collectors and policemen into hiding; they refused to pay taxes and tolls."[68] Zeldin goes on to describe this collective action of peasants as similar to that which took place in towns, "where textile handloom weavers destroyed

[65] Sewell, *Work and Revolution*.
[66] Price, *The French Second Republic*; Tilly and Lees, "The People of June"; Traugott, "Determinants of Political Organization" and *Armies of the Poor*.
[67] Theodore, Zeldin, *France 1848–1945: Politics and Anger* (New York: Oxford University Press, 1979), p. 125; see also Agulhon, *La Republique au Village*; J.M. Merriman, *The Agony of the Republic: The Repression of the Left in Revolutionary France, 1848–1851* (New Haven, Connecticut: Yale University Press, 1978); T.R. Forstenzer, *French Provincial Police and the Fall of the Second Republic: Social Fear and Counterrevolution* (Princeton, New Jersey: Princeton University Press, 1981).
[68] Zeldin, *France 1848–1945: Politics and Anger*, p. 127.

machines which were threatening their livelihoods and where carriage drivers and boatmen burnt railway stations and tore up the track of the new invention that was ruining them."[69]

But there were some important differences between the peasants and the urban workers, as well as much similarity. The peasants were not just Luddites, acting defensively. New taxes and mortgages were on their minds; they were the bearers of ancient grudges; yet they acted also with ancient ambitions. They sought the material benefits of access to more land and the social benefits of independence within their communities and especially from outsiders. They sought a new realization of traditional values. They were thus open to new political ideas which fitted with their existing culture and communities, and the Red Republicans made impressive gains among the peasants. Though the latter are more famous for voting for Louis Napoleon in 1848, a large number turned to Ledru-Rollin and the socialists in 1849.[70]

There is no contradiction between the two sorts of radicalism I have argued to be based on traditional communites. It is important to recognize both the defense of traditional practices and the demand for the practical implementation of traditional goals long unrealized. Noting the latter helps to explain the disproportionate radical involvement Wolf finds in the twentieth century among relatively prosperous "middle" peasants.[71] Such peasants get involved in potentially revolutionary struggles, not because they have completely new ideas about how the world should be run, but because they have old ideas about how their own lives should be run.[72] Peasants, like both urban and rural craftsmen, are a potent radical force because (a) they often have the resources with which to engage in struggle; (b) they have a sense that, during periods of upheaval and weakness of the state apparatus, goals for which their ancestors had struggled for centuries are all but within their reach; and (c) they have much more to lose if they do not succeed in controlling their own destinies than do those already poverty-stricken or forced out of traditional com-

---

[69] Ibid.

[70] T. Margadant has shown that the politics of peasant communities varied by region, with the southwest accounting for most of the peasant involvement in the 1851 insurrection: *French Peasants in Revolt: The Insurrection of 1851* (Princeton, New Jersey: Princeton University Press, 1979).

[71] Eric R. Wolf, *Peasant Wars of the Twentieth Century* (New York: Harper, 1969), p. 292.

[72] Perhaps the most important description of these ideas is the notion of a "moral economy" which E.P. Thompson has brought into prominence. See especially "The Moral Economy of the English Crowd in the Eighteenth Century", *Past and Present*, 50 (1971), 76–136. See also J. Scott, *The Moral Economy of the Peasant* (New Haven, Connecticut: Yale University Press, 1976) for an application of the concept to recent Asian peasant movements. The long tradition of *taxation populaire* reveals similar concerns in France.

munities and into the less solidary populations of early industrial wage laborers.

Traditional communities, I have suggested, give their members the social strength with which to wage protracted battles, the "selective inducements" with which to ensure full collective participation, and a sense of what to fight for that is at once shared and radical. This sets traditional communities apart from the modern working class.[73] The solidarity of such traditional communities may also give their members a better ability to recognize collective enemies. The very closed nature of such communities, their resistance to outsiders, may appear "backward" to us and yet be part of the basis of their occasional reactionary radicalism. Communal organization provides for a considerable degree of self-regulation. Where small localities and specialized crafts are involved – as in most of Old Regime Europe and much of the Third World today – the boundaries of a community are fairly clear, and inside them social relationships are largely autonomous and self-regulating. Borrowing White's (unpublished) notion of a "CATNET", Tilly has suggested the importance of being both categorically distinct from outsiders and strongly knit together internally in a social network.[74] Such groups, he argues, find mobilization easier.

In four important ways this is characteristic of traditional communities and helps to explain their ability to mobilize directly, instead of through the formal organizations so important to the modern working class. First, the members of such a community will find it relatively easy to identify collective enemies. If, as happened during the processes of industrialization and central state formation in much of the world, elites choose to cut themselves off from local communities, they become outsiders and potentially set apart as enemies. Conversely, the integration of elites into local communities decreases the likelihood of action against those elites. Second, a largely self-regulating system may be upset by any sort of intrusion. Thus, even well-intentioned efforts to improve the lives of the poor can threaten the communal lives of artisans, peasants, and others. If permitted to continue, such efforts displace communal autonomy by offering a new source of resources. Quite often, however, communities rebel against all disruption, including that of "do-gooders". Third, to the extent that a community is self-regulating, it has good reason to visualize a society in which it and other communities like it are entirely autonomous

---

[73] Parts of the modern working class may also be united in traditional communities – ethnic enclaves, heavily concentrated in a single industry, for example, like Poles in the U.S. steel industry – but this is not the basis for class-wide solidarity, and this is not at the heart of Marxist conceptions of the modern working class.

[74] C. Tilly, *From Mobilization to Revolution* (Reading, Mass.: Addison-Wesley, 1978), pp. 62–4.

and free from elite interference and exploitation. Thus, traditional artisanal and peasant control of the labor process is matched by communal
control over social life – in contrast to the experience of members of the
modern working class, who are subjected to the constant intervention of
formally trained "experts" in both work and personal life.[75] Fourth, the
autonomy of communities gives then a strong foundation for mobilization
outside the purview of the intended targets of collective action, a free
"social space". The need to work through formal, non-communal organizations means that modern workers' movements must always be exposed
to ideological counter-attacks.

The social foundations of radical collective action

The fact that the working class of advanced capitalist countries has tended
to pursue reforms of many kinds but not to organize "spontaneously" for
revolutionary overthrow of capitalism has long been noted.[76] This
phenomenon, of course, contradicts one of Marx's expectations. The real
question, though, is how one is theoretically to accommodate the evidence. The fact that revolution has not yet occurred in a major industrial
country does not, of course, prove that it will not occur; as a rebuttal to

[75] Cf. G. Palm, *The Flight from Work* (Cambridge: Cambridge University Press, 1977); David
Stark, "Class Struggle and the Transformation of the Labor Process: A Relational
Approach", *Theory and Society*, 9, no. 1, (1980), 89–128; Christopher Lasch, "Democracy
and 'The Crisis of Confidence'" *Democracy*, 1 (1981), 25–40.

[76] The debates over "revisionism", "left deviationism", "opportunism", and the like in the
turn-of-the-century Second International and early twentieth-century Marxist movement
provide the *locus classicus* for his observation. Bernstein in *Evolutionary Socialism*,
translated by E.C. Harvey (New York: Schocken, [1889] 1961, p. 221) held that the
conditions in which workers lived precluded an immediate demand for socialist
transformation and necessitated reformism. Lenin (*What Is to Be Done?* in R. Tucker (ed.),
The Lenin Anthology (New York: Norton, [1920] 1975), p. 24); *Left-Wing Communism: An
Infantile Disorder*, in Tucker (ed.), *The Lenin Anthology* (New York: Norton, [1920] 1975,
p. 609) agreed that workers could not spontaneously go beyond reformist "trade union
consciousness" but insisted that a vanguard party could introduce class consciousness
itself. Luxemburg, *The Mass Strike, the Political Party and the Trade Unions* (London:
Merlin, [1906] this edn n.d.), esp. pp. 15–16, 63, denied the proposition that the workers
could not directly produce revolution; immediate mass collective action would, she
thought, school the workers in revolutionary class consciousness even without the
interventions of a vanguard party. Gramsci, in Q. Hoare and G.N. Smith (eds.),
Selections from the Prison Notebooks (London: Lawrence and Wishart, [1949] 1971) in some
ways bridged this opposition with his distinction of "the war of position" from "the war
of manoeuver", suggesting that counter-hegemonic struggle might have to take place for
years before the opportunity for more directly revolutionary action presented itself, but
also that such quiet struggle need not be reformist. Anarchists were, at the same time,
arguing that revolution need not depend on the workers at all; they have a modern-day
echo in some "Third World Marxisms". Populist pessimists like F.F. Piven and R.A.
Cloward, *Poor People's Movements* (New York: Vintage, 1978) also reject the reformist
workers in favor of "the poor", though they are not so sanguine about the prospects for
revolutionary transformation.

Marxism the postponement of the revolution lacks theoretical force, however practically relevant it may be. What one wants to know are the causal factors which need to be discarded from Marx's theory as invalid, or those which must be added as intervening or basic variables. This chapter has so far considered the previously neglected importance of tradition and community in providing for radical movements. I wish now only to suggest a few social characteristics of the modern working class which are thrown into relief by contrast to reactionary radicals of various kinds. In particular, problems have arisen from a confusion of revolutionary zeal, revolutionary interests, and revolutionary capacity.

Enthusiasm for revolution has been much more widespread among intellectuals and other groups generally cut off from the main body of workers than it has been among the working class. In revolutions that have occurred, such groups have been crucial – especially as the agents of state building and central organization *after* the destruction of Old Regime authority. Such intellectuals have seldom been the prime movers in creating revolutionary movements, even when they have given them their major ideological orientations. A central question raised by this observation is whether revolutionary intentions are good predictors of revolutionary activity. This issue has two components. First, many revolutionary ideas are incorporated into the ideology of groups that do not seek revolution – indeed, the leaders of many authoritarian states claim to be revolutionary. Second, key actors in revolutionary insurrections often have sought simple redress of wrongs or reforms; it has been the objective inability of elites to mitigate their grievances that has led to both increasing radicalization of the insurgents and the revolutionary impact of their claims. More generally, it needs to be questioned whether the intention to engage in revolution or even to be particularly radical is necessary to producing a radical mobilization. Traditionalist, anti-capitalist claims may be presented in the most moderate and reformist manner and still confront elites with demands to which they can make no meaningful concessions.

In dealing with the modernization of demands by workers in advanced capitalist countries and with the preponderance of precapitalist classes in actual revolutions, Marxists have introduced various arguments. Lenin stressed both imperialism and especially the limits of spontaneous working-class consciousness and action and the need for intellectual leadership from outside to go beyond mere trade unionism.[77] More recently, an important body of literature has addressed problems in the definition of the potentially revolutionary proletariat. Such writers on class structure have been concerned (a) to indicate those workers and

[77] Lenin, *What Is to Be Done?*, p. 24.

members of the petty bourgeoisie whose interests may be contradictory within modern capitalism and (b) to show the potential importance to proletarian struggles of workers (e.g., in sales and clerical occupations) who do not, strictly speaking, produce surplus value.[78] A central assumption in this line of analysis is that workers (like others) respond rationally to their objective interests. Class interests are emphatically distinguished from the empirical concerns of particular members of the proletariat or even the whole proletariat.[79] Though this approach has been effective in showing the complexity of the modern capitalist class structure and the applicability of Marxist categories in studying it, to draw revolutionary political conclusions from this analysis implies a combination of wishful thinking and willful resistance to empirical evidence. Its proponents have taken a very rationalistic position which ignores (or relegates to the status of a separate and secondary question) both the concrete ideological orientations of real workers and the organizational difficulties of collective action.[80]

Faced with the failure of workers to seek their "objectively" defined interests, these writers have been obliged to fall back on the notion of false consciousness. In such an argument, both the conditions of immediate existence and the active ideological efforts of elites are held to impede recognition of the true class interests.

Class interests in capitalist society are those potential objectives which become actual objectives of struggle in the absence of the mystifications and distortions of capitalist relations. Class interests, therefore, are in a sense hypotheses: they are hypotheses about the objectives of struggle which would occur if the actors in the struggle had a scientifically correct understanding of their situations.[81]

The notion of true as opposed to false class interests is problematic in itself.[82] Most often noticed is the arbitrariness by which external analysis

[78] See, e.g., S. Mallet, *La Nouvelle Classe ouvrière* (Paris: Seuil, 1963); Andre Gorz, *Strategy for Labor* (Boston: Beacon, 1967); N.M. Poulantzas, *Classes in Contemporary Capitalism* (London: New Left Books, 1974); E.O. Wright, *Class, Crisis and the State* (London: New Left Books, 1978) and *Classes*.

[79] See also Marx, *The Holy Family*, p. 37.

[80] The greatest exception to this is Adam Przeworski's work, esp. *Capitalism and Social Democracy* (Cambridge: Cambridge University Press, 1985), chapter 2, which is discussed below.

[81] Wright, *Class, Crisis and the State*, p. 89. In *Classes* (esp. chapters 1 and 3) Wright has modified this view somewhat, largely under the influence of John Roemer. His newer, more subtle, conceptualization both recognizes a diversity of class interests not simply subject to ordering on the basis of scientific truth value, and treats of non-class interests as genuine, rather than merely the result of mystifications (though Wright still does not know what to do with them).

[82] It is fashionable among non-Leninist Marxists to use Gramsci's notion of hegemony rather than that of false consciousness to explain the diversion of workers' attention from "ultimately rational" ends. In this context the difference is fairly slight, and consists primarily of putting greater stress on elite ideological forces producing mistaken understandings rather than intrinsic limits to workers' consciousness.

of objective interests is granted priority over the subjective awareness actors have of their own interests.[83]

Marxists who have employed the notion of class interest have encountered great difficulty in giving it a precise empirical meaning . . . In a theory of rational action, "interest" may be assigned an exact meaning as part of a definite game, applying to a number of clearly demarcated social situations, on the market and elsewhere. But when used in more complex contexts to denote "long-term", "objective" or "true" interests – that is to say, something other than factual preferences – the notion seems to provide a spurious objectivity to essentially ideological evaluations.[84]

The notion of interests employed by Wright in his equation of revolutionary class consciousness and recognition of true interests is based on extremely rigorous and unrealistic assumptions. In particular, he assumes that there are no conflicts among true interests for members of the proletariat, though he recognizes that some people are in contradictory class positions.[85] Moreover, contrary to the best indications of collective action theory, he assumes that rational recognition of interests directly implies the rationality of action in pursuit of those interests.[86] This latter problem remains an issue even for his more recent formulation which partially alleviates the preceding concern.[87]

When Marx proposed that revolution was the only rational course of proletarian action, he was simultaneously maintaining that workers had nothing to lose but their chains. In other words, revolution was rational in Marx's account because there were no more moderate, less risky ways for workers to improve their situations. This condition must be maintained

[83] Defense of such "empiricist" concerns as to what real members of the working class may think or have thought has been central to Marxist social history in opposition to at least the structuralist variant of Marxist theory. It is an important part of the basis for Thompson's polemic against Althusser: *The Poverty of Theory* (New York: Monthly Review Books, 1979). Thompson's willingness to consider the concerns of real workers has led him to recognize some of the reformist implications of the existence of numerous competing interests and the "imbrication of working-class organizations in the *status quo*": "We need not necessarily agree with Wright Mills [Mills, "The New Left", in I.L. Horowitz (ed.), *Power, Politics and People: The Collected Essays of C. Wright Mills* (New York: Oxford University Press, 1963), p. 256] that this indicates that the working class can be a revolutionary class only in its formative years; but we must, I think, recognize that once a certain climactic moment is passed, the opportunity for a certain *kind* of revolutionary movement passes irrevocably – not so much because of 'exhaustion' but because more limited, reformist pressures, from secure organizational bases, bring evident returns" ("The Peculiarities of the English", rev. edn in *The Poverty of Theory*, p. 281). Though I agree with Thompson's argument about modern politics, I argue here in contrast to Thompson, *The Making of the English Working Class*, that this is due to a profound discontinuity in workers' history. See also Calhoun, *The Question of Class Struggle*.
[84] G. Therborn, *What Does the Ruling Class Do When It Rules?* (London: New Left Books, 1978), p. 146.
[85] Wright, *Class, Crisis and the State*, pp. 61–87.
[86] See Olson, *The Logic of Collective Action*; Moe, *Organization of Interests*.
[87] Wright, *Classes*.

for the rationality of revolution to be argued successfully. It is not enough to hold that a socialist society which could only be achieved through revolution would be better than the capitalist society which will remain in the absence of revolution. Such quantitative difference in possible benefits cannot outweigh the differences, both quantitative and qualitative, in costs and risks. In order to argue the case for a rationalist theory of interests as the basis for revolutionary action, one must maintain in some fashion either that no alternatives are available to members of the potentially revolutionary class or that the available alternatives are irrelevant. In this connection Marx described in some detail the conditions he thought would so polarize capitalist society and immiserate workers that they would have no reasonable alternative. Confronting the same issue, Wright simply maintains that class interests cannot be reduced to individual interests, thus holding that the existence of alternatives for individuals is irrelevant.[88] False consciousness becomes largely the primacy of individual consciousness over class consciousness, but it is hard to see how Wright can escape hypostatizing the class. The problem is that a good account of class structure, if it is relevant at all to political analysis of class formation, should show structure to have some determinate impact. But if one assumes that structural position is a necessary and normally sufficient condition for class formation, then one is driven to a series of more or less *ad hoc* and contingent accounts to deal with the manifest failure of class formation to proceed as predicted.

Przeworski criticizes Wright's argument about "contradictory class positions" (essentially all those placing people between polarized notions of pure proletariat and bourgeoisie) in just these terms:

The problem of the relation between objectively defined classes and classes qua historical actors will not be resolved by any classification, whether with two or many objective classes, with or without contradictory locations. The problem persists because such classifications, whether made in party headquarters or within the walls of academia, are constantly tested by life, or more precisely, by political practice. Wright's "contradictory locations" are contradictory only in the sense that his assertions about the "real interest in socialism" are not borne out by the consciousness and the organization of those who are supposed to have this interest. On paper one can put people in any boxes one wishes, but in political practice one encounters real people, with their interests and a consciousness of those interests.[89]

Among "analytic Marxists" Przeworski is unusual in his concentration on historical analysis. His historical account of the beginnings of class theory and questions of proletarianization suffers, however, from assuming that:

[88] Wright, *Class, Crisis and the State*, pp. 87–90; A. Levine and E.O. Wright, "Rationality and Class Struggle", *New Left Review*, 123 (1980), 47–68, esp. pp. 56–8.
[89] Przeworski, *Capitalism and Social Democracy*, pp. 65–6.

In 1848 one simply knew who were the proletarians. One knew because all the criteria – the relation to the means of production, manual character of labor, productive employment, poverty, and degradation – all coincided to provide a consistent image. . . . the theoretical connotation of the concept of proletariat, defined in terms of separation from the means of production, corresponded closely to the intuitive concept of proletariat conceived of manual, principally industrial, laborers.[90]

In other words, he does not consider the extent to which Marx's concept of the proletariat embodied from the beginning a confusion between expectations of political radicalism based on observation of movements in which proletarians were a relatively marginal force, and an economic theory properly forecasting the increasing generation of propertyless laborers. Przeworski sees ambiguity as arising only because historical conditions began to deviate from a mid-nineteenth-century pattern which corresponded closely to theory. Nonetheless, his main suggestion of historical tendency is well taken: the separation of workers from the means of production is not the same as the creation of jobs as industrial workers, and thus the two senses of proletarianization diverge.[91] Class formation is indeed never a finished process, because capitalism continues to change and to change the underlying structural conditions of class formation. Moreover, there is no reason why only those who conform to a narrow structural definition of the proletariat should either "live, think and act like the proletarians" or be a part of a socialist or other radical mobilization.[92] Class is neither the sole explanation of radical collective action, nor solely determined by structures of places in a system of production. Rather, for Przeworski, class is a relationship between the category of individuals occupying such places and concrete episodes of collective action.[93] Classes are formed as the effects of struggle; class is also a large part of what the large-scale socio-political struggles of the capitalist era are about. But in the end, however sensible this formulation, Przeworski does not offer either a theoretical or a concretely historical account of how "places in a system of production", cultural or ideological identities, previous political experiences and present social relations come together to constitute collectivities capable of risky but concerted collective action in pursuit of improbable outcomes and distant goals. Instead, because his interest is in the history of social democracy and the workings of capitalist democracy, he turns his attention to formal organizations such as workers' political parties. In examining them he sheds light on the

[90] Ibid., pp. 354–5.
[91] Ibid., p. 60.
[92] Ibid., pp. 63–4, 79–80.
[93] Ibid., p. 81.

continuing struggle for the reform of capitalism and the creation of democratic socialism, but not on revolutions.

When Wright revises his formulation using Roemer's game-theoretic model (exploitation defines classes wherever an alliance of "players of a society's game" have an interest in quitting the game) he seems to switch to a much less holistic notion of classes as collections of individuals.[94] At this point, classes are defined directly in terms of interests – those which would, in the absence of confounding conditions, result in a particular aggregate action – rather than as the basis for interests. The place of individuals in the structure of exploitation relations determines the interests of those individuals, which may include non-class interests. Of course, this is still an abstract analysis of interests dictated by structural position, and therefore false consciousness may still be adduced to explain failure to act correctly.

Whatever questions may remain about the content or orientation of action, Wright's new formulation does suggest the necessity of an analysis of problems of collective action (though this is not his concern). In general, if one refuses to grant the absolute irreducibility of class interests, their existence quite separate from any interests or expressed preferences of the individuals composing the class, then one must confront collective action as problematic. Olson's argument posed the fundamental questions. Olson presumes both complete rationality and perfect information, so mystification is not his explanation for failure to act collectively. On the contrary, he suggests that "unless the number of individuals in a group is quite small, or unless there is coercion or some other special device to make individuals act in their common interest, *rational self-interested individuals will not act to achieve their common or group interests*".[95] The reason for this finding, surprising when first offered, was simple. Olson held that individuals were not totally subsumed into collectivities but had numerous interests, sharing only a few. The rational course of action was to pursue individually achievable and enjoyable interests because in the absence of coercion one could not depend on one's fellows, and in large groups, without a high rate of participation, one's share in the proceeds of action would not be matched by the costs of one's own contributions. Moe has suggested that Olson's theory underestimates the importance of direct political inducements; in other words, people are more interested in political values relative to economic values than Olson had thought.[96] But Moe's analysis does not remove the problem of getting from individual

[94] Wright, *Classes*, chapter 3; J. Roemer, *A General Theory of Exploitation and Class* (Cambridge: Mass. Cambridge University Press, 1982).
[95] Olson, *The Logic of Collection Action*, p. 2.
[96] Moe, *Organization of Interests*.

interests to collective action; instead, it introduces a broader treatment of individual interests, one which better fits the goals of interest group politics. Marxist analyses based on rational recognition of objective interests offer no substantial argument for the radical precedence of class over individual interests which they assert. This is true not only of scientific versions of Marxism, such as Wright's, but of historicist versions such as Lukacs's.[97]

I suggest that the problems posed by Olson can be met in large part by my analysis of traditional communities. Not only does the sharing of tradition predispose individuals to similar analyses of their situations, but embeddedness in communal relations also produces an interdependence of interests among individuals. Taking individuals seriously (as opposed to hypostatizing class) does not mean treating individuals as identical, universal rational actors, but rather recognizing (a) qualitative variation among people and especially (b) that individuals do not exist in isolation or in themselves, but in socio-cultural relations which are the very condition of their individuality. Communities are not necessarily an additional good to be valued beyond other selfish interests, but in many cases a condition of continuous selfhood for their members. In a village of handloom weavers, for example, most of the handful of non-weavers – greengrocer, publican, shopkeeper – were likely to be as dependent on weaving for their prosperity as were the weavers themselves. A network of debts may be as important as one of sentiments; between the two it seems quite understandable that each should identify his or her interests with all.

There are certainly limits to the role which this kind of social organization can play in producing bases for collective action. Limits of scale are among the most obvious.[98] Larger groups not only obscure the contributions (or lack thereof) from particular individuals and spread the proceeds of action over a larger pool of beneficiaries, they also make it less likely that communal relations of great density will be formed. Arguments

---

[97] G. Lukacs, *History and Class Consciousness* (Cambridge, Mass.: M.I.T. Press, [1924] 1971). In Lukacs' case, to be precise, there is a strong argument for the analytic power of the "standpoint of the proletariat" but none for the sociological formation of the proletariat as a class actor.

[98] It should also be the case that the more complex the strategy needed to realize a set of shared interests, the less likely a mobilization based on traditional communities will be to succeed. Nonetheless, traditional communities offer definite advantages. To cite only one area, both Olson and Moe find the decision to join an interest group in the first place requires explanation within their theories. But both, especially Moe, are concerned primarily with formal organizations, self-consciously created and joined by their members. Traditional communities exist before any particular mobilization over any particular set of interests. Instead of incurring a cost by creating an organization, members of traditional communities are presented with a major resource in the shape of precisely that social organization and shared set of values they are seeking to protect.

concerning group size and capacity for collective action are at the heart of Olson's original theory. He suggested that beyond very small groups (about a dozen actors) some manner of formal organization and coercion would be necessary to secure participation in collective action among rational actors who do not have sufficient resources and interests to provide collective goods by themselves. Here I try to show that group-size arguments can have implications for the effectiveness of different types of social organization in producing collective action.[99]

The concept of "class" is, at bottom, an individualistic one – or, at least, the Marxist notion of "class-in-itself" is. A number of individuals are classified together on the basis of common attributes or positions. To conceive of such a class as a collective actor, however, requires a modification of this individualistic starting-point. It is not enough that the various members of the class stand in the same relationship to another class or to capital in the labor process. The individuals must be related to each other. This mutual social relationship may be taken as ontologically given, or treated as the result of individuals' social action. Regardless of one's interest in preserving methodological individualism, the latter approach has the advantage of suggesting an analysis of the variable extent of integration or solidarity within a class.

If one assumes, for example, a constant or random rate of interrelation, and a random propensity and opportunity for people to relate to each other, it is obvious that (*ceteris paribus*) the density of relationships within a population is a declining function of size. The more people within a population aggregate, the less likely it will be that any one of them will be related to any other, or set of others, and the smaller will be the proportion of total possible relationships actualized. Not only does net density decline, but its evenness declines. The larger a group, the more likely it is to be divided into clusters. Where people's relations with each other are shaped by various structural patterns which encourage in-group association – for example, sharing a place of work – the tendency is intensified. Even within the limits of this fairly simple, formalistic presentation, this argument has three important implications.

[99] The roots of group size arguments are as old as Montesquieu and classical foundations can be found in Michels and Simmel, but the crucial modern source is P. Blau, *Inequality and Heterogeneity* (New York: The Free Press, 1977). In the following discussion, I shall accept not only Blau's methodological individualism and assumptions of rational action, but his attempt to argue without reference to culture. While each of these presents potential problems for a general theory (and I would reject each as a definite position), I do not believe that they seriously impair my argument here. In one sense they may strengthen it. Arguments for the importance of traditional community are apt to be presented as arguments for sentimental attachments as against rational interests. I hope to show that community relations may in fact serve rational interests (though perhaps they may not do so for people who think and act in the rootless ways individualistic rational choice theory ascribes to everyone).

First, the larger a population aggregate (such as a class) is, the more the relationships among its members will be clustered into subgroups. In other words, it is inconceivable that all members of the class will be related to each other, and unlikely that relationships will be spread evenly throughout the whole class. If the latter were true, the class's potential for collective action would be weakened. There would be no strong groups, small enough to knit people together directly, and composed entirely of members of the larger class. Class-wide collective action, thus, may well depend on strong intermediate associations within the class. Without such intermediate associations, the possibility of class action is replaced by, at most, the simultaneous action of a number of mobs sharing common external characteristics.[100] Such intermediate associations may be formally organized or communal, but a class (or other similar large population aggregate) which lacked them would offer its members only a minimal basis for participation in collective action.[101] Subgroupings within a class, therefore, are important to its collective action, even though they may be the source of fragmentation. The collective action of the whole class cannot readily be achieved by direct identification of each member with the whole, but depends upon intermediate associations which are not as such universally and exclusively identified with the whole class. Machine-spinners are members of the working class through being machine-spinners, plumbers through being plumbers. And of course, occupational groupings (which are, perhaps, "proto-working class") are not the only sort of intermediate associations which may be important. Spatial communities, religious congregations and fraternal orders may all form intermediate associations important to the collective action of the members of the working class. The internal composition and ideology of each may make it more or less conducive to class-wide mobilization, more or less at odds with the interests which potentially unify the members of the class. Minimizing these sectional idenfications and groupings may in some ways be *opposed* to class solidarity. The task of class leaders is thus not to minimize sectional identities, but to mobilize such intermediate associations to serve the common cause. This, of course, requires cross-cutting linkages among the smaller groups (it may also be an advantage for intermediate associations to be hierarchically

---

[100] Still assuming a random or constant rate of social relatedness, an even distribution of in-class relationships would not only deprive the class of intermediate associations; it would also make it likely that such relatively small groupings of direct relationships (e.g. communities) into which members of the class were knit would be formed on the basis of non-class identities and include significant proportions of members of other classes. Only people with no stable group of friends, relatives or comrades could simultaneously avoid both in-class sectionalism and membership in largely non-class networks.

[101] C. Calhoun, "Democracy, Autocracy and Intermediate Associations".

inclusive, each incorporating those below it). During the early nineteenth century, English workers attempting class action ran into problems on this score, not only with craft exclusiveness, which has often enough been noted, but with the inability to transcend local community bonds effectively. Thus the Luddites were strong in their communities but were unable to mount concerted action even regionally, let alone as a national working class, however political (or state-focused) their intentions might have been. The Blanketeers in Lancashire marched with (increasingly despairing) expectations of being met by fellow rebels at each turn of the road. Similarly, the Pentridge rebels were duped by Oliver the Spy into believing that they were part of a national rising, information they would have doubted if they had had strong social relationships beyond their immediate vicinity.[102] The limits of an account which stresses motives or attitudes on the one hand, or position in the relations of production on the other, to the exclusion of consideration of structures of interpersonal social relations should be obvious.

Secondly, the tendency of relationships within large populations to cluster may, in some cases, help to knit non-workers into intermediate associations which can be mobilized for the pursuit of workers' interests. Briefly, if a population is divided into two groups of unequal size, any given rate of relationship across their boundaries will be proportionately greater for the smaller group. If a West Riding village, for example, were to contain 200 handloom weavers and 10 shopkeepers, and there were 50 relationships (of some specific sort, e.g. personal friendship, kinship or religious association) across group lines, then there would be a mean of 5 relationships per shopkeeper and 0.25 per weaver. In a village dominated by weavers, but having also several coalminers, shopkeepers, and others, the latter groups would be much more densely tied to the weavers than the weavers would be to them. This factor was of considerable importance in securing community-wide concertedness of action in villages and small towns during the industrial revolution.

Thirdly, clustering has an impact on power and control within groups. Just as it is formally demonstrable that, given random interrelatedness, the density of bonds, and hence presumably the likeliness to participate in collective action, is a decreasing function of group size, so, conversely, is the narrowness of oligarchic control an increasing function of size. This had important implications for both the argument concerning the role of

---

[102] Of course, a key reason why intercommunal relationships were so weak has to do with the minimal development of transportation and communications infrastructure. When the Blanketeers marched, it still took the fastest coach two days to get from Manchester to London under the best of road conditions. See C. Calhoun, "Class, Place and Industrial Revolution", in P. Williams and N. Thrift (eds.), *Class and Space: The Making of Urban Society* (London: Routledge and Kegan Paul, forthcoming).

labor aristocracy in defusing a potential English popular revolution and the nature of organization for collective action among such large groups as classes. The larger a collectivity, the more concentration of power is likely within it.[103] Moreover, if the proportionate size of the lowest strata in a collectivity increases at the expense of the highest, net inequality within the total collectivity increases.[104] While this is in accord with Marx's expectation of a growing concentration of wealth within capitalist society as a whole, it raises the initially unexamined problem that a privileged stratum is formally likely to emerge within the working class. This came to be seen as the problem of the labor aristocracy, the interests of which diverge from those of the rest of the working class.

Is working-class action likely to be organized by a relatively narrow elite, or is it likely to be the direct action of the mass of workers? Purely on the basis of the present argument from size, the former seems more likely. To the extent that the working class in question is defined externally by common position in the relations of production, and is thus viewed as made up of individuals, it shows an overwhelming vulnerability to oligarchical control. This control may take several forms. Michels' notion of the "iron law of oligarchy" is the most famous.[105] Leninist substitutionism is formally similar. The vulnerability of large, minimally differentiated crowds to demagogic leadership is another version. During the early nineteenth century, whenever popular activity extended beyond the local community and craft level, demagogues tended to intervene as the only means of leadership. The alternative – formal organization – did not begin in a significant way until the 1820s and especially the 1830s (and even then remained fairly rudimentary for decades). Formal organization does not in itself solve the problem of oligarchic control. What is generally does, and for the most part began to do in England in the middle third of the nineteenth century, is to replace independent demagogues with those who can run organizations. During the Chartist period, these people were still often charismatic figures, for the organizations were not yet strong enough to stand wholly on their own. The Chartist leaders had to combine

---

[103] B.H. Mayhew and T. Levinger, "On the Emergence of Oligarchy in Human Interaction", *American Journal of Sociology*, 81 (1976), 1017–49. This is somewhat contrary to expectations that the working-class movement should be radically democratic and equally participatory, and that it should herald an age of declining oligarchy and increasing self-organization with the "withering away of the state". Such a view is only plausible on the assumption that large-scale social organization is for the most part abandoned (to the extent it must depend on formal organization) and for the remainder structured through innumerable webs of social control through direct interpersonal relationships. The informality of such control would not render it any less close or constraining, though it would maximize participation.

[104] Blau, *Inequality and Heterogeneity*, pp. 70–1.

[105] Robert Michels, *Political Parties* (Glencoe, Illinois: Free Press, [1915] 1963).

fiery oratory with the more bureaucratic skills which would predominate in trade unionism. The tendency toward oligarchy is mitigated primarily by strong intermediate associations. A political party or union, for example, with strong regional and local organization, may be seen on the national level as composed of subgroups, not individuals. The number of actors is the formal underpinning of the push toward oligarchy; such corporate actors as local branches are necessarily fewer than are individuals.[106]

In short, for an entire class, or even any very large proportion of one, to be mobilized, for collective action, a hierarchy of intermediate associations is an invaluable social basis for steering the mobilization between the extremes of oligarchy (even autocracy) and complete disorganization. Such intermediate associations may be local communities, specific craft groupings, or competent segments of national formal organizations. In the last case, however, it is important that such groups be able to command considerable amounts of commitment from their members, and be able to act with a fair degree of autonomy and self-regulation. If they do not meet these conditions, which strong pre-existing communities generally do, then they will be unable to mediate effectively between individuals' private interests and the specific interests or aims of the oligarchy. Democracy, in such an organization, depends not so much on getting rid of an oligarchy as on providing means for ordinary members to act through their intermediate associations to choose and/or control the oligarchy itself. Generally, in a very large population (such as a class) which lacks strong organization, no individual will have sufficient control of what goes on or enough confidence in the outcome to risk much of his material resources, time, effort or safety. In order to take such a risk, individuals generally require some assurance that others will contribute their share and some reason to believe that action will be successful.

As this chapter began by observing, revolutionary class action is

[106] Conversely, changing scale of social organization may contribute to revolutionary movements by making an aristocracy both more narrowly oligarchic and less closely connected to the rest of the population at the same time. As various authors have shown, crowd control in the immediate pre-industrial period depended largely on the authority of local elite figures who knew as individuals many members of the crowds they faced and, at the same time, had personal connections to government officials; see, e.g., J. Bohstedt, *Riots and Community Politics in England and Wales, 1790–1810* (Cambridge, Mass.: Harvard University Press, 1983); also Calhoun, *The Question of Class Struggle*, pp. 161–74. The concentration of power in a capital city and the changing scale of population aggregates everywhere meant that traditional local authority deteriorated because it depended on interpersonal relationships across levels in the social hierarchy. A similar account could be given of the particular proneness to revolution of those regimes which made the most stringent division between elites and common people. Perhaps the extreme case is those settings where social revolutionary mobilization is bound up with national liberation movements against foreign occupiers and domestic elites which collaborate with them.

particularly problematic. Its success depends on the participation of a great many people, and the taking of a great many risks. Messianic fervor might well convince potential participants that success is guaranteed, thus making them willing to risk their lives and resources. Messianic fervor might also convince each one that all others will soon share his willingness to participate. Messianic fervor is not, however, the rational basis for revolution which Marx and most Marxists have had in mind. But in the absence of such fervour, there are weighty reasons why an individual would not participate. In order for it to be rational to do so, a person must either be so desperate that any outcome is preferable to the continuation of his or her present circumstances, or he or she must believe that there is some reasonable probability of success. It we assume that the repressive power (and internal solidarity) of elites and government is not sufficient unconditionally to prevent revolution, then a critical issue becomes whether or not the revolutionaries can command sufficient participation. Let me rephrase the question: did the two hundred or so Derbyshire men involved in the abortive Pentridge "Levellution" of 1817 have reason to believe that they could succeed in toppling the government of England, were they so desperate that anything was worth a try, or were they acting irrationally? My answer is that a considerable measure of desperation and relative isolation in their local communities made these men willing to believe bad predictions of their eventual success. They were not so much irrational as remarkably misinformed. Let us look at the case for a moment not from the point of view of the Pentridge Rising's failure to find a corresponding national rising but from the point of view of an individual participant. This man has reason to believe that almost everyone he knows will participate in the rising. Further, he is knit together with these people by a complex network of social bonds. This provides him with some assurance that they will not betray him and with considerable coercion to act in concert with them and not against them.

The amount of external force which would have to be applied to recalcitrant individuals to equal the strength of a community's inducements for the collective actions of its members would be vast. Communities may, indeed, even mobilize people for collective action over long periods of time, in pursuit of highly uncertain goals and at high personal costs. This is an essential strength of guerilla warfare, as many a Western military commander has learned with difficulty and regret. But the greatest weakness of guerilla warfare is the absence of an "end game". And so it is with revolutions which draw their destabilizing force from traditional communities. These may provide for both shared interests and the capacity to act on them, at least at the local level. But after the collapse of the old regime, they do not offer their members the means for taking direct control of government or even, in most cases, of their own lives.

The non-radical working class

The previous section focused on the social strength which traditional communities offered to potential collective action. But the modern working class is also capable of collective action, in some ways stronger action, primarily through such formal organizations as trade unions and political parties. We need now to make explicit the reasons why the collective action of "reactionary radicals" was more likely to be radical than that of the "modern" working class.

The first reason is that the sorts of goals sought by reactionary radicals (at least in cases like those under examination here) were fundamentally incompatible with such existing trends as the rise of industrial capitalism. They were radical not in themselves, in the abstract, but, rather, in relation to what goals other people were pursuing and what concessions governments or privileged groups were prepared to make. Thus certain radicals of late eighteenth-century Europe sought what Thompson calls "the moral economy",[107] the right to sell their products rather than their labor,[108] a "just price" in markets, especially for food,[109] the right to raise their own children and support their wives, to labor at home or in small workshops instead of in factories, to continue producing by hand and with craft skills rather than be replaced by machines or forced to produce "cut-rate" goods, to petition their "betters" for redress of wrongs, to use common lands for grazing or gathering firewood, to be paid in specie instead of paper money.

This was hardly a Marxist rationalist's list of class interests, and indeed there were several more rationalistic contemporary partisans of the working class or the common people who despaired of popular traditionalism. John Wade complained, for example:

One thing is certain, that these ancient laws have been a real stumbling block in the way of the Reformers; they have been the subject of endless unmeaning altercation; they have filled the heads of the people with nonsense, and covered their advocates with contempt and ridicule. That our leaders should continue to stick to these follies, is both provoking and astonishing. Can they bring nothing to bear against the old rotten borough-mongering system but the musty parchment, black letter and Latin quotations?[110]

---

[107] Thompson, "The Moral Economy of the English Crowd'".
[108] Reddy, "Skeins, Scales, Discounts, Steam".
[109] C. Tilly, "Food Supply and Public Order in Modern Europe", in C. Tilly (ed.), *The Formation of National States in Western Europe* (Princeton, NJ: Princeton University Press, 1975), pp. 380–455.
[110] *The Gorgon*, 20 June, 1818, p. 35.

Despite this traditionalism, despite an ideology which seldom got beyond a vague populism, the demands of the members of traditional communities were indeed radical. Handloom weavers could not be granted their continued peaceful existence without stopping the advance of technological innovation and capital accumulation. When Parisian artisans resisted the division of labor, they were attacking the industrial revolution itself. Capitalist industrialization did not mean just a lower standard of living for these workers, it meant the eradication of the communities in which, and the traditions by which, they lived and worked. There was little that capitalism could offer in return. No ameliorative reforms, no welfare system would speak to the fundamental complaints of these insurgents. Such concessions would have been nice (and the rich and powerful did precious little to soften the hard lot of the poor), but they would have left untouched the radical incompatibility of the economic and social basis of the populists' lives – traditional crafts and communities – with the new order.

So, however mild and peaceful their intentions, the reactionary radicals presented a very serious challenge to public order and nascent capitalism. Already in the early nineteenth century their cousins in the modern industrial workforce could organize unions and pursue their interests without posing such a challenge. They were born of capitalism and could compete within it for various distributive gains without fundamentally threatening the new order.

The second reason why members of traditional communities undertook radical actions, which most modern workers would not, lies in their capacity for action. The workers of early nineteenth-century France and England were defeated, of course.[111] But they had more in common with those who in other times and places have participated in successful revolutions (whether or not they have liked the resulting states) than do the workers of modern capitalism. Skocpol has noted the existence of stronger and more autonomous peasant communities in France and Russia as key reasons for the more rapid progress of their agrarian revolutions than China's. She and Tilly, Tilly, and Tilly have rightly stressed both the importance of weaknesses in state power to revolutionary success and the long-term trend of strengthening state apparatuses.[112] This increasing power, with its improved capacity for government repression of revolution, certainly helps to explain the predominance of

---

[111] The stories are told well by Thompson, *The Making of the English Working Class*, and I. Prothero, *Artisans and Politics in Early Nineteenth Century London* (Folkestone: Dawson, 1979) for England (though see also Calhoun, *The Question of Class Struggle*), and by Price, *The French Second Republic*, and Sewell, *Work and Revolution*, for France.

[112] Skocpol, *States and Social Revolutions*, pp. 148–9; Charles Tilly, L. Tilly, and Richard Tilly, *The Rebellious Century* (Cambridge, Mass.: Harvard University Press, 1975).

reformist movements in recent Western history. But another finding of Tilly *et al.* suggests a change in the strength of the mobilizations themselves. They found that violent protests became larger and more "proactive" between 1830 and 1930 as urban proletarians replaced artisanal and rural communities as the protagonists. But these protests also became shorter, less sustained and concerted efforts. I suggest that the change in social foundations from traditional communities to formal organizations of individual workers is a central reason.[113] When traditional communities were mobilized, they were able to stay mobilized over long periods of time in the face of considerable privations. Like the "true believers" found at the core of millenarian movements by Festinger, Riecken, and Schachter,[114] the reactionary radicals were integrated into a social organization which kept their beliefs and ambitions alive. As already noted, they did not have to pay high costs for maintaining a special purpose organization. They also had few other directions in which to turn for improvement of circumstances.[115]

Where communities do not already link potential insurgents to each other, formal organization becomes more important. This in itself exerts a pressure against truly radical popular actions. Strictly maintained formal organization may be central to Leninist theory and practice, but it is precisely a substitute for mass revolutionary mobilization (though it arguably never succeeds without the latter). As Piven and Cloward, among others, have noted, the existence of formal organizations often contributes to a sense that someone else is carrying the burden of protest, and one need not sacrifice one's own resources.[116] Formal organizations, moreover, are prone to the problems of oligarchical control, noted early on by Michels.[117] The larger the organization (or population to be organized), the more acute this problem becomes.[118] Such oligarchy gives the leaders of the organizations both an interest in preserving the organization itself rather than serving the needs of their constituents, and cuts the leadership off from the larger population, minimizing the likelihood of widespread

---

[113] This argument is consonant with Tilly *et al.*, *The Rebellious Century*, though it is not posed in their analysis; Charles Tilly does suggest something similar in "Did the Cake of Custom Break?", in J.M. Merriman (ed.), *Consciousness and Class Experience in Nineteenth Century Europe* (New York: Holmes and Meier, 1979), p. 38. See also Calhoun, "Industrialization and Social Radicalism", for a comparison of popular struggle in Britain and France at mid-century.

[114] Leon Festinger, H.W. Riecken, and S. Schachter, *When Prophecy Fails* (New York: Harper, 1956).

[115] Migration, especially to the United States, was probably the main alternative; it was immense among the generation of 1848 in continental Europe: see A. Whitridge, *Men in Crisis: The Revolutions of 1848* (New York: Scribner's, 1949), pp. 238–326.

[116] Piven and Cloward, *Poor People's Movements*.

[117] Michels, *Political Parties*.

[118] Mayhew and Levinger, "On the Emergence of Oligarchy".

participation. Even for those outside an organization's elite, investment in the organization gives members an interest in preserving it rather than risking it in revolutionary action.[119]

Finally, the need to work through formal organizations creates the possibility for competition among organizations. To be sure, communal ties can also create competition among subgroups, and examples abound of residential communities split in contests between kin groupings and single crafts rent by struggles between competing organizations (e.g., the various trade corporations of Old Regime France).[120] Such cases do not, however, produce quite the same likelihood of fractious "splitting" among ideologically defined groups as formalization can produce. And eighteenth-century *compagnonnages* were in any case formal organizations overlapping with informal craft communities. Their very formal structure was part of the reason for their decline, as it remained rigid in the face of socioeconomic change and gave masters insupportable, largely heredi- tary, privileges at the expense of the growing numbers of journeymen. It was, for the most part, the traditions of mutuality and the value of labor, and the crafts-based communities, which carried forward into the nascent socialism of the Second Republic, not the formal organizations.

Though organization-building is not antithetical to radical action, and indeed is necessary to securing enduring gains, formal organizations do militate against the sorts of radical movements that have provided most frequently the initial revolutionary destruction of old regimes. Most workers in the major capitalist nations of the West lack the sociocultural foundations for radicalism which traditional communities gave the artis- ans of the early nineteenth century. This is not to say that modern workers are conservative; on the contrary, it is to suggest that modern workers are not so conservative as to be forced into radical opposition to social change. They may be extremely left-wing, but a reformist strategy will nearly always be rational for them while radical strategies appear unsupportably risky.

Although a number of social scientists have stressed that working-class community has not completely dissolved into mass society, even their work shows some important differences in the nature and extent of community. Kornblum, for example, shows blue-collar workers focusing a great deal of attention on community politics and working through

---

[119] Thompson has commented on "the truly astronomic sum of human capital which has been invested in the strategy of piece-meal reform", "The Peculiarities".
A.O. Hirschmann, *Exit, Voice and Loyalty* (Cambridge, Mass.: Harvard University Press, 1970) offers the leading general attempt to describe the options open to members of organizations who have made such commitments.

[120] See Sewell, *Work and Revolution*.

primary groups and local unions.[121] His study of South Chicago shows a cluster of diverse ethnic enclaves but finds processes through which competing groups are also establishing some integration at the level of "community". Yet they are doing so largely through formal organizations, including many over which they have far less than complete control, and some – such as the Democratic party machine – the specific aim of which is to secure a share of resources disbursed elsewhere. The steel mills in which they work are owned by distant corporations; collective action to confront such employers requires organization far beyond the level of face-to-face relationships. The degree of craft control such workers have over their jobs is generally slight, and the extent of political self-regulation they can achieve is limited by their greater integration into the larger society and indeed the international economy.

This is not to deny the existence of community; I would even suggest that urban ethnic groups should be at least as important as rural villages in our images of community. But though primary ties still exist and are important to individuals, in many places they are no longer able to organize much of public life. They are less eradicated, in other words, than compartmentalized. The communities of early industrial Europe were in transition and do not represent the extreme of traditionality – perhaps tribal societies structured through kinship and descent do. But the traditional communities of early nineteenth-century France and England – and of Russia in 1917 and China in 1949 – were different from South Chicago. They were smaller, more densely knit, more autonomous, more able to produce and reproduce the cultural medium of their social solidarity through their everyday interactions. They learned of their common past and developed their dreams for the future, not in schools or from television, but in families and from each other.

In capitalist societies, driven by a totalistic pressure for capital accumulation, integrated largely by the indirect ties and abstract mediation of commodities and bureaucracies, community life is not a microcosm of the whole but a compartment. Centralization and individualism – the two sides of Tocqueville's coin – predominate.[122] Large-scale organizations may or may not be rooted in local communities and/or conducive to internal communities and other intermediate associations. At the largest level, however, ties cannot be solely communal.[123] This is a problem

121 William Kornblum, *Blue Collar Community* (Chicago: University of Chicago Press, 1974).
122 Alexis de Tocqueville, *Democracy in America*, 2 vols. (New York: Schocken, [1840, 1844] 1961).
123 The great social revolutions of Russia and China, for example, obviously knit together an enormous number of people beyond the bounds of local communities. Nonetheless, local communities in many settings provided the social basis for the revolts which eventually proved destabilizing. The revolutions were not made solely by organizations

which attempts to build a new radical populist mobilization today sometimes fail to confront. Neither the economy nor the state can be run solely
through direct interpersonal relationships. New technologies only add to
the capacity of capitalist corporations and government apparatuses. In
Manuel Castells' words:

So when people find themselves unable to control the world, they simply shrink
the world to the size of their community. Thus, urban movements do address the
real issues of our time, although neither on the scale nor terms that are adequate to
the task.[124]

This failure to confront the difference between local community and
large-scale organization is, in fact, a central element of right-wing populism. It enables a figure like President Reagan to draw support from
people worried about the deterioration of local communities while
backing the very multinational capitalist economic organization which
produces that deterioration. It projects images of community where no
close-knit web of relationship exists to support them (as, indeed, the use
of communal language in a rhetoric of nationalism often does). It
enhances the power of the state even while it proclaims the virtues of
decentralization, not least of all because it does little to foster the building
of intermediate associations through which ordinary people might
organize for collective action in challenge to the central government. Yet
the very strength of sentiment which right-wing populism can tap reveals
the potency which remains in some traditional values and visions, and the
importance many people attach to community even when they are unable
to maintain much of it. Both community building and populist mobilization on communal bases may indeed play a crucial role in resistance to
further extensions of central power. Together with efforts to revitalize
potentially oppositional traditions, they may be an important of any
eventual radical challenge to present-day social organization and political
and economic power. But they cannot be the whole of a successful
challenge.[125]

of individuals detached from immediate communities, though the cadres at the top of
the hierarchy may have fitted this model somewhat.
[124] M. Castells, *The City and the Grassroots* (Berkeley: University of California Press, 1984),
p. 331.
[125] Among other things, it must be recognized that reinvigorating community does not
directly mean revitalizing public discourse. Communities are crucial supports for direct
social participation and collective action, but, in a large-scale society, public life depends
upon the ability of strangers, members of different communities, to speak to each other
and decide issues together in the absence of communal bonds. Public life depends
largely on "secondary relationships" which are not intimate, seldom very
multidimensional, and often episodic or ephemeral. Moreover, while community
remains largely spatially constrained by the need for relatively intimate, face-to-face
interaction, public life (not to mention bureaucracy and other forms of large-scale
organization) has changed substantially with new space-transcending communications

The greater scale and lesser organization of much of everyday life in modern capitalist societies make formal organizations necessary. Acting through such organizations makes reformism more likely, both producing problems of motivation and militating against extremely radical – especially democratic – actions. The working class as it now exists lacks the unifying social basis for collective action which community structure provided (and in some cases continues to provide) to those who would resist the extension of capitalist relations of production and social forms. To mobilize effectively at the level of the modern state and/or capitalist economy, workers require not just formal organizations but an elaborate infrastructure of transportation and communication. Yet capital and existing political elites have recurrent headstarts in using each new infrastructural technology. Working-class struggle depends on such an infrastructure but, once again, its very conditions predispose workers to reformism and a low intensity of commitment.[126] Perhaps most important, the modern working class is potentially able to secure ameliorative reforms within capitalist society. This does not alter any interests workers might have in socialism, or even in a socialist revolution, but it implies that revolutionary or other radical action is not *necessary*, but only one option. One does not even have to hold that it is easier for capitalism's opponents to split the ranks of workers or mystify them with ideology, though that may be true as well. Even if these things were not true, the sociocultural foundations on which modern workers act do not make really radical mobilization as rational or as effective as traditional communities made it for artisans and peasants during the transition to capitalism.

Conclusion

Marx thought that revolution would be no risk, but rather the result of desperation, when workers had nothing to lose but their chains. I have argued that, on the contrary, revolutionary and other radical mobilizations take place when people who do have something to defend, and do have some social strength, confront social transformations which threaten to take all that from them and thus leave them nothing to lose. I have held that traditional communities are a crucial source of such radical mobilizations. I have not maintained that traditional communities are always radical or even remarkably forward looking in ideology. On the contrary, under most conditions they are bulwarks of the existing order, the social

technologies (see Calhoun, "New Information Technology"). Binary oppositions of community to association, traditional to modern, etc., are not able to grasp the various dimensions of change which have perhaps covaried somewhat but should not be conflated.
[126] See Calhoun, "Class, Place and Industrial Revolution".

foundations of deference and quiescence. During times when the existing order seems deeply threatened, including especially such great periods of transition as the industrial revolution, such communities may find that they can be traditional only by being radical. Whether their radical mobilizations lead to revolutions depends on much else – on the strength of the states which they confront, for example, and on whether or not educated elites and formal organizations stand ready to turn insurrection into real social transformation and new state power. Reactionary radicals have seldom, if ever, been able to gain supremacy in revolutions. But, at the same time, revolutions worthy of the name have never been made without them.

Part II

5 Workers' welfare and the socialization of capital*

Michael Wallerstein and Adam Przeworski

Introduction

Does workers' pursuit of their long-term material interests necessarily entail the revolutionary demand that private ownership of the means of production be abolished? An affirmative answer to this question has been the hallmark of the socialist movement since its inception. Marx's argument, as presented for example in *Wage Labour and Capital*, goes as follows: the material interests of workers and capitalists are irreconcilable. Wages and profits are in "inverse proportion".[1] This is obviously true for a fixed product that is divided into wages and profits. But Marx did not think that the antagonism between the material interests of workers and capitalists was in any way mitigated by economic expansion. The growth of capital, Marx reasoned, enlarges the power of capitalists, hastens the division and simplification of labor, accelerates the substitution of machinery for workers, and intensifies the competition among workers for increasingly scarce jobs.[2] Thus, even under the most favorable circumstances, workers in capitalist societies continue to lose ground. In an address before the General Council of the First International delivered in 1865 and later published as *Value, Price and Profit*, Marx warned that workers struggling to raise their wages with strikes and demonstrations were fighting "the general tendency of capitalist production [which] is not to raise, but to sink the average standard of wages, or to push the value of labour more or less to its minimum limit".[3] Full success would only be attained when instead of asking for "A fair day's wage for a fair day's work", workers demand "Abolition of the wages system".[4]

Two features of Marx's argument bear emphasizing. The first is that

* An earlier draft of this paper entitled "Revolutionary Demands" was delivered at the Annual Meeting of the Midwest Political Science Association, Chicago, April 1986. This draft has benefited from the comments of Stephen Weatherford and Jeff Frieden.
[1] R.C. Tucker (ed.), *The Marx–Engels Reader* (New York: Norton, 1972).
[2] *Ibid.*, pp. 180–90.
[3] Karl Marx, *Value, Price and Profit* (New York: International Press, 1935), p. 61.
[4] *Ibid.*

Marx, in these texts, views workers' interests as primarily economic. Workers will be driven to demand the socialization of capital as they attempt to increase their income under capitalism and find themselves blocked, not by the greed of individual capitalists nor even the collective greed of the capitalist class, but by the system of capitalist production. Secondly, workers are seen as fundamentally rational. Learning takes time, but workers will eventually realize that satisfaction of their material interests requires collective ownership of the capital stock.

Marx's reasoning has been attacked by non-Marxists ever since. Marx, it is claimed, failed to see that capitalism allows for the continual improvement in workers' standard of living. Marx was too concerned with the grimy side of history to see that capitalism in fact constitutes a non-zero sum game in which workers are best off cooperating with capitalists to increase the size of the pie rather than demanding capitalists' share.[5] Outside intellectuals, according to Selig Perlman, were the ones responsible in the labor movement for raising the demand of nationalization of the capital stock.[6] Workers, when left to themselves, demanded only control over their jobs. The alleged deradicalization of the labor movement is offered as conclusive proof that workers' pursuit of their material interests leads no further than demands for higher wages, social insurance, and full employment.

Many on the left have also recoiled from Marx's purported economic determinism in the face of the manifest stability and the limited use of coercion in advanced capitalist democracies. Some critics of social democracy, drawing inspiration from theorists as diverse as Michels, Luxemburg, and Trotsky, accuse the workers' party and union leaders of betraying and stifling the spontaneous revolutionary impulses of the rank and file. Others, locating the lack of revolutionary sentiment primarily in the rank and file itself, emphasize instead the difficulty of overcoming the ideological hegemony of those who own the "means of mental production" as well as the "means of material production".[7]

Yet all of these arguments in opposition to Marx's original position, Marxist and non-Marxist alike, embody a retreat from Marx's assumption that workers are fully rational. Granted that workers in advanced capitalist societies have experienced an enormous improvement in their material well-being over the last century, why should workers be satisfied if they could be even better off under socialism? Why, in other words, should workers collectively be satisficers rather than utility maximizers? Why would workers continue to follow leaders who are perpetually

[5] K. Boulding, *A Primer on Social Dynamics: History as Dialectics and Development* (New York: Free Press, 1970).

[6] S. Perlman, *A Theory of the Labor Movement* (New York: Augustus M. Kelley, 1949).

[7] R. Miliband, *Marxism and Politics* (Oxford: Oxford University Press, 1977), p. 50.

betraying their cause? Why do workers not discount information by its source and seek out the views of those who are not committed to upholding private ownership of capital?

Moreover the question of the relationship between workers' material interests and revolutionary strategies remains important politically as well as intellectually. With the exception of the first year of the Mitterand government, public ownership has grown in Western Europe in the past decade as a by-product of government bailouts of failing industries, not as a socialist strategy. But while expanding state ownership has declining support, indeed in many countries the movement is toward privatization, plans for workers' ownership of capital in wage-earner funds have been placed on the agenda by the unions in Sweden, Denmark, Germany and the Netherlands.[8] As Esping-Andersen has written (perhaps overoptimistically) of the present position of the Swedish Social Democratic Party:

> More collectivization of investment is held as indispensable for guaranteed full employment, equalization, and democracy . . . The 1975 program of the Swedish Social Democratic party proclaimed that, the struggle for political and social democracy having been completed, the time had come to bring full democratic citizenship rights into economic life. The Swedish party, along with other European socialist movements, is currently on the threshold of a fundamental programmatic shift in which the organization of capitalist production will once again be challenged.[9]

In the current period of increased international competition, slower growth, lower real wages and higher unemployment, the debate over the socialization of capital has reappeared with new vigor.

In this chapter we approach the question of revolutionary demands on Marx's original terms. The theory asserted that workers would have to socialize the means of production in order to maximize their material well-being. To the extent that workers were satisfied with material improvements which did not bring into question the ownership of capital, to the extent that workers voluntarily did not attempt to push beyond reforms, workers were claimed not to be behaving rationally.[10] The central

---

[8] In the original Meidner plan, 20 percent of profits would be transferred annually to the wage-earner funds in the form of stock ownership. It was predicted that effective majority ownership of the most major corporations would be attained between 25 and 50 years. See G. Esping-Andersen, *Politics Against Markets: The Social Democratic Road to Power* (Princeton: Princeton University Press, 1985), p. 298. See also R. Meidner, "Our Concept of the Third Way", *Economic and Industrial Democracy*, 1 (1980), 343–69, and S. Johansson, "When is the Time Ripe?", *Political Power and Social Theory*, 3 (1982), 113–43.

[9] Esping-Andersen, *Politics Against Markets*, pp. 290–1.

[10] The issue here is not one of a divergence of individual rationality and collective rationality, as argued by M. Olson, *The Logic of Collective Action* (Cambridge, Mass.: Harvard University Press, 1965), chapter 4. In spite of the dilemma of collective action, workers have been able to establish in all capitalist democracies collective organizations, albeit with highly varying centralization and coverage. The question is whether workers would want their collective organizations to pursue revolutionary or reformist strategies.

claim is that the best workers can do under capitalism is strictly inferior to workers' welfare in a society in which profits were eliminated and workers collectively determined the allocation of income between consumption and investment. Let W^c be the maximal utility attainable by workers when capital is privately owned and W^s be the utility workers could enjoy if capital were collectively owned. The claim that rational workers will adopt revolutionary demands unless facing repression rests on the premise that:

$$W^c < W^s.$$

This is the assertion we investigate in this chapter.

The question is defined narrowly. Workers may prefer socialism to capitalism because they are maximizing non-material objectives: a sense of empowerment, participation in decision-making or personal freedom. Here we only examine the consequences of workers' maximization of the utility derived from their consumption. Moreover, Marx and Engels thought that the growth of productivity would greatly increase as the fetters of capitalist relations of production were lifted. Non-Marxists have argued just the opposite: that property rights, including private owner-ship of capital, can be tampered with only at the cost of reducing economic efficiency and the incentive for innovation. Here we assume no difference between the productivity of capitalism and socialism. If workers chose, they could rent their collectively owned capital to the highest bidder and duplicate all the efficiency properties of competitive markets.[11]

The issue is theoretical, not empirical. The best workers can do under capitalism is not equivalent to what workers in capitalist societies have achieved so far. Even less can workers' welfare in a society in which workers collectively determine the rate and allocation of investment be equated with workers' welfare in actually existing socialist societies where such decisions are made by unelected managers and central planners. Our approach is analytic: we posit formal assumptions and explore the conclusions that follow. Analytic results do not often conclusively settle important substantive issues, but they can clarify the arguments and direct attention to the assumptions from which the results follow.[12]

In the next section, preliminary assumptions regarding production, the

---

[11] There is an interesting and growing literature on the economic behavior of worker-owned firms operating in competitive markets. For institutional designs of what could be called market socialism which have the same efficiency properties as competitive capitalist economies, see the papers collected in M.R. Sertel, *Workers and Incentives* (Amsterdam: North-Holland, 1982).

[12] This paper represents a continuation of a series of papers we have written on workers' strategies and material interests. See A. Przeworski, *Capitalism and Social Democracy* (Cambridge: Cambridge University Press, 1985), chapter 5. In contrast to our previous work, we can now examine the difference it makes for workers' welfare under capitalism when organized workers can influence public policy as well as their private wages.

distribution of output and individual preferences are introduced. Subsequently, we derive workers' bliss point: the outcome which workers would choose if they not only controlled their wages but also the rate of investment. This outcome is then compared with the best workers can do without owning the capital stock (a) when workers control their wages and the government is passive and (b) when, in addition to controlling their wages, workers can also exercise political influence and obtain transfer payments financed by a tax on profits. This leads to our central proposition that as workers' influence in the government approaches its logical limit, workers' welfare under capitalism approaches workers' welfare under socialism. We follow with a discussion of the generality of our results – the extent to which assumptions can be relaxed or altered without changing our proposition – and caveats that apply. Finally, we conclude with reflections on the consequence of our analysis for the long-standing debate over reformist versus revolutionary strategies.

In the text that follows, the discussion is limited to assumptions and results. The intermediate mathematical steps have been relegated to an appendix in order not to burden the reader who cares little for the technical details. For readers who wish to follow the mathematical steps of the argument, the appendix is complete and self-contained.

Preliminary assumptions

Society is assumed to be composed of two classes: workers and capitalists. Workers consume all of their income and, hence, own no capital. The only source of savings is profit. Capitalists are people whose primary source of income is profits (including top managers whose compensation is based on profits earned). Firms are assumed to be perfect agents, which is to say firms allocate profits between new investment and dividend payments in the manner which maximizes the utility of their shareholders.

In the case without taxes and transfer payments, national income is divided into three categories: wages, profits, and new investment. Since there is no money in this model, all savings imply the purchase of real assets, or investment. Savings and investment will be used interchangeably. Also, for simplicity of exposition and without loss of generality, all quantities are defined to be net of depreciation. Writing wages, $W(t)$, profits, $P(t)$, and investment, $I(t)$, as shares of net national income, $Y(t)$, all at time t:

$$W(t) = rY(t),$$
$$P(t) = (1-s)(1-r)Y(t), \quad \text{and} \tag{1}$$
$$I(t) = s(1-r)Y(t).$$

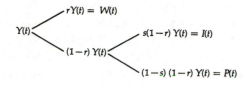

Fig. 1

Thus, r is the share of national income that workers take as wages. Capitalists receive the remainder, $(1-r)Y$, of which they invest the proportion s and consume the proportion $(1-s)$. Note that capitalists' consumption should not be interpreted too literally. From workers' perspective, any use of profits which does not add to the productive capacity of the domestic economy represents consumption out of profits, whether it be investing in foreign assets or buying consumer goods. The relationship between wages, profits and investment is presented in Fig. 1.

The parameters r and s represent the strategic choices of workers and capitalists respectively. That is, workers determine r unilaterally but capitalists choose s. Private ownership of capital means precisely that capitalists are free to do as they please with what is left after wages (and taxes) have been paid. Workers have no such legal rights over r. However, as workers gain strength through both unions and political parties, their control over wages increases. Our assumption that workers control wages absolutely serves to focus attention on the constraints that remain even as workers' power in the labor market reaches its logical maximum. While it is natural to think of r and s as bounded by zero and one, such bounds are unduly restrictive. There are times when capitalists disinvest, which is to say choose an $s < 0$. Moreover, it is possible for workers' wage demands to exceed current output, or for $r > 1$. It turns out that the relevant limits on r and s can be derived from the strategic interaction of workers and capitalists. No limits need to be imposed by assumption.

About production, we make the simplest possible assumption: output is a linear function of capital. Expressed in terms of growth:

$$Y'(t) = vK'(t) = vI(t) = vs(1-r)Y(t), \quad v > 0, \tag{2}$$

where $Y'(t)$ is the change in output at time t, $K'(t)$ is the change in capital, and v is the constant productivity of capital. The parameter v represents the amount of additional output that can be produced when an additional unit of capital is added to the capital stock. Thus, output grows at the rate of $vs(1-r)$ per year. For example, if $v = 0.25$, $s = 0.50$ and $r = 0.80$, the economy is growing at the annual rate of 2.5 percent.[13] Note that as long as r and s are constant, wages, profits, and investments grow at the same rate as output.

Both classes are assumed to be composed of homogeneous actors. Moreover, all actors, workers and capitalists alike, are assumed to share the same utility function. To arrive at an explicit solution, it is necessary to select a particular utility function to work with. In this paper we confine our analysis to the case with a logarithmic utility function:[14]

$$U(x) = \ln x. \tag{3}$$

Both workers and capitalists, however, look to the future as well as the present. What each seeks to maximize is not the utility of consumption today but the utility of present and future consumption given by:

$$X^* = \int_0^\infty e^{-\varrho t} \, U[x(t)] \, dt = \int_0^\infty e^{-\varrho t} \ln[x(t)] \, dt, \quad \varrho > 0, \tag{4}$$

where X^* equals either W^*, in the case of workers, or P^*, in the case of capitalists and $x(t)$ represents consumption in period t. The parameter ϱ is the rate at which workers and capitalists discount the future. While endowing workers and capitalists with an infinite horizon might seem unreasonable, the alternative of fixing a terminal point is hardly better. Is the appropriate horizon five years or twenty-five years? Here we let a short time horizon be represented by a high value of ϱ.

The two parameters which have been introduced, the rate at which workers and capitalists discount the future ϱ and the productivity of capital v, play prominent and symmetrical roles in the model. The productivity of capital measures the increased output that an additional unit of capital would generate. The parameter v, in other words, represents the social return from investment. The discount rate ϱ, on the other hand, represents the cost of postponing consumption. Increased income today is worth more than the promise of the same increase at some point in the future, both because there is a cost associated with waiting and because the future is, to some extent, unknown, while the present is certain.[15] Thus the ratio ϱ/v which appears throughout our results reflects, in some sense, a comparison of the cost of postponing consumption to the

[13] These figures are rough estimates for the postwar United States economy. Estimates of the productivity of capital can be found in T.P. Hill, *Profits and Rates of Return* (Paris: OECD, 1979). The others can be found in the National Income and Products Accounts published by the United States Department of Commerce.

[14] This assumption is more restrictive than necessary. See our discussion below of possible generalizations of the model.

[15] An increase in income today will be worth more than an increase in the future for a third reason which is independent of the discount rate, ϱ, if income is growing over time. With diminishing marginal utility, the value of an increment of consumption declines as consumption increases.

social return from the investment that postponing consumption makes possible.

Workers' bliss point

Before deriving the outcome of class conflict with and without taxes and transfers, it is useful to consider first the promise of socialism. Socialism is defined as a society in which workers alone decide through democratic means the allocation of resources between consumption and investment. In terms of our model, socialism is a society in which workers can choose both s and r. These two choices can be considered separately. Assume, for the time being, that the rate of saving out of profit, s, is fixed. We can then find workers' optimal choice of wage share by finding the value of r which maximizes workers' welfare $W(r, s)$. We call the maximizing value of r, which depends on s, workers' best reply, written $r^*(s)$. In other words, the best workers can do when faced with a particular value of s is to receive wages equal to $r^*(s)$ of the total product.

With workers' welfare, W^*, being defined by (4), it is shown in the appendix that workers' best reply takes a particularly simple form:

$$r^*(s) = \varrho/vs. \tag{5}$$

Intuitively, workers are choosing between present consumption and growth. The higher the rate at which the future is discounted, ϱ, the greater the share of the product workers would want to receive today. Conversely, the greater the share of savings out of profits, s, and the greater the growth of output which new investment makes possible, v, the more workers will prefer to postpone consumption into the future. In fact, the product (vs) represents workers' rate of return. Each unit of investment has a physical rate of return equal to v while s is the proportion of non-wage income which is invested. Workers' best reply consists of a comparison of their rate of return with the cost of postponing consumption, ϱ. Workers will only choose to "invest", or select an $r < 1$, if their rate of return exceeds the discount rate. If very little was saved out of profits, that is if s approached zero, workers' choice of r would approach infinity.

Workers are always better off with higher rate of savings out of profits. Any value of s less than unity represents income that neither adds to the productive capacity of the economy nor to workers' current consumption. Such income is simply lost from the workers' point of view. Workers may have to allow this loss in order to induce investment under capitalism, but not under socialism. Workers' optimal s is simply $s = 1$. Thus, under socialism, all profits would be invested and workers would choose to consume the proportion

$$r^*(1) = \varrho/v \tag{6}$$

of output. When all that is not paid in wages is invested, workers compare their discount rate with the rate of return to the economy as a whole or the productivity of capital. If $\varrho > v$, workers would not voluntarily refrain from consuming the entire product under any circumstances. But if $\varrho < v$, workers would leave $(1 - \varrho/v)$ of the output for investment which would allow the economy to grow at the rate of $(v - \varrho)$. Given the parameters ϱ and v, this is the best possible situation for workers, or workers' bliss point.

Workers and capitalists without taxes and transfers

In a capitalist society, however, it is the owners of capital who have the right to decide on the allocation of profits between consumption and investment. To determine how capitalists would choose, we find the best reply of capitalists to a fixed wage share. That is, when faced with a particular level of wage demands, r, capitalists would choose the rate of saving s which maximizes the present value of their consumption stream, $P^*(s, r)$. The maximizing value of s, or capitalists' best reply, can be written:

$$s^*(r) = 1 - \frac{\varrho}{v(1 - r)} . \tag{7}$$

(See appendix.) Again we see a comparison of rate at which the future is discounted, ϱ, and a rate of return on investment, $v(1 - r)$. But this rate of return – the increase in output which investment makes possible multiplied by the fraction of the increased output which will be left over after workers have taken their share – is the rate of return capitalists receive from investing. Capitalists will always choose a rate of saving less than one (provided $r < 1$). Capitalists will choose a positive rate of savings only if their rate of return exceeds the discount rate, that is if and only if $(1 - r)v > \varrho$. Otherwise they will disinvest. Moreover, as workers' wage demands increase, $s^*(r)$ declines or $ds^*/dr < 0$. As workers' wage demands approach the level at which profits are confiscated, or as r approaches unity, $s^*(r)$ goes to negative infinity.

Two solution concepts are frequently used in models of this sort. The first and most common are the Nash equilibria (there is often more than one) defined to be all pairs of strategies such that each is best against the other. The Nash equilibria of this model are the values of r and s such that both workers and capitalists are selecting their best reply strategy simultaneously. That is, a pair (r^i, s^j) qualifies as a Nash equilibrium if and only if $r^i = r^*(s^j)$ and $s^j = s^*(r^i)$. Both classes are doing as well as they can given the strategy chosen by their opponent. In this game there is always one Nash equilibrium, the point of maximum militancy and maximum disinvestment. Given confiscatory wage demands, capitalists' best reply is to disinvest and, facing capitalists who are disinvesting at the maximum rate, workers' best reply is to confiscate profits and as much of the capital stock as possible. If ϱ/v is sufficiently low, there also exist one or two additional Nash equilibria at values of r less than unity and s positive.[16]

But there is an unreasonable aspect to the concept of Nash equilibria in the context of this model. It demands that workers react as if s were independent of r when, if capitalists are following their best reply, capitalists' rate of saving is a negative function of r. If workers know that increasing their share of income will cause capitalists' rate of investment to fall, workers will anticipate the reaction of capitalists in choosing r. The alternative solution concept, the Stackelberg solution, is based on the notion that one player, called the Stackelberg leader, anticipates the best reply of the other. When workers behave as the Stackelberg leader, they choose the value of r which maximizes their welfare given capitalists' predictable response. In mathematical language, workers would seek to optimize $W^*(r, s^*(r))$, not $W^*(r, s)$.

When workers anticipate that capitalists will respond to r with $s(r)$, workers' optimal strategy is not given by r^* but by

$$r^{**} = \varrho/v. \tag{8}$$

(See appendix.) Workers behave as if the rate of saving were fixed at unity. Compare (8) with (6). But capitalists are *not* investing all of their profits. Capitalists' best reply to $r = \varrho/v$ is:

$$s^*(r^{**}) = 1 - \frac{(\varrho/v)}{1 - (\varrho/v)}. \tag{9}$$

As long as $\varrho < v$, $s^*(r^{**}) < 1$. (And if ϱ were not less than v, workers' demands would be confiscatory and capitalists would disinvest as fast as possible.) Thus, given capitalists' rate of savings, workers would prefer a greater share of the output. In mathematical notation, $r^*(s^*(r^{**})) > r^{**}$. Workers do not increase their wage demands in accordance with their best reply strategy because workers anticipate the negative effect on investment which a wage increase would occasion. Workers are induced to moderate their militancy by the threat of reductions in investment. In fact, workers find it optimal to set their wage demands as if capitalists saved and invested all of their profits when s actually falls short, even far short, of unity.

---

[16] In particular if $\varrho/v = 1/4$, $r = s = 1/2$ is a Nash equilibrium. If $\varrho/v < 1/4$, there exist two additional Nash equilibria.

In the Stackelberg equilibrium, the share of output going to capitalists' consumption is:

$$P/Y = (1 - s^*)(1 - r^{**}) = \varrho/v, \qquad (10)$$

the same as to workers. The share going to investment is:

$$I/Y = s^*(1 - r^{**}) = 1 - 2(\varrho/v). \qquad (11)$$

One way to consider the relative weakness of workers *vis-à-vis* capitalists is to consider the conditions under which workers and capitalists will choose strategies which leave room for positive rates of growth. If $\varrho > v$, workers would attempt to confiscate all profits while capitalists' rate of saving would go to negative infinity. Or, looking at equations (8) and (10), both workers and capitalists would each try to consume more than the available output. In such a world there is no room for compromise. The conflict is a pure zero-sum game over who is to consume society's wealth. If, however, $\varrho < v < 2\varrho$, workers would not demand the entire product, but capitalists would still choose a negative rate of saving. Workers would voluntarily relinquish some of the product to capitalists even as capitalists are disinvesting and the economy is declining. The reason is that if workers increased their demands, the rate of disinvestment would accelerate, making workers even worse off. In the case in which $2\varrho < v$, both workers and capitalists would choose moderate strategies. Workers would choose an $r < 1$, capitalists would choose an $s > 0$ and the economy would expand. But note the asymmetry between workers and capitalists. Workers offer positive profits as long as $\varrho < v$. Capitalists, on the other hand, offer positive savings only when $\varrho < v/2$. The allegiance of capitalists to the compromise is more fragile than workers. Capitalists seek to move their investments out of the economy long before workers seek to confiscate capitalists' profits.

The divergence between workers' Stackelberg strategy and their best reply strategy can create a collective action problem for workers. Each union local would prefer to raise its wage demands up to the level of its best reply. But if all the local units increased their wages, investment would decline leaving all workers worse off. There is an inherent tension between more militant union representatives at the local level with more moderate union leaders at the top, due not to the isolation of the top leadership from the rank and file but to the divergence of local from global optimizing strategies. In Norway and Sweden, countries in which collective bargaining is national in scope, local agreements to raise wages above the level specified in the contract of wage drift comprise as much as 50 percent of aggregate wage increases.[17]

[17] R.J. Flanagan, D.W. Soskice and L. Ulman, *Unionism, Economic Stabilization, and Incomes Policies: European Experience* (Washington D.C.: Brookings Institution, 1983), p. 313.

Moreover, it is the collective action problem inherent in being the Stackelberg leader which prevents capitalists from occupying that position. Workers must organize to press wage demands. Firms choose their rate of investment individually. For capitalists to anticipate the effects of their rate of investment on workers' wage demands, capitalists would have to collectively invest more than is optimal for each individually. Unions can collectively demand less than is optimal for each local by requiring all to honor a wage contract (even if compliance is far from perfect). For firms to invest more than their best reply, investment decisions would have to be subject to collective controls. This is a case in which power resides in the lack of effective organization. Capitalists are in the more advantageous position precisely because workers are forced to anticipate the response of capitalists to their choice of strategy and not vice versa.[18]

Workers and capitalists with taxes and transfers

It would be incorrect to assert that now we are introducing a state. The existence of a state has been implicit all along, in the sense of a set of political and legal institutions which endow workers with the capacity to enforce wage demands and capitalists the freedom to allocate their income between consumption and savings. But now we introduce a government which can tax and spend on transfer payments. The question to be addressed is to what extent the government can alter the outcome by levying taxes and distributing the receipts when both workers and capitalists are rational actors who take the government's policy into account when choosing their strategies.

The standard answer is very little or none at all. According to one line of argument government attempts to redistribute income are undercut by private bargains anticipating the government policies. As stated in a recent study of the redistributive impact of welfare expenditures: "Redistributive policies may increase the inequality of primary income determination because in the bargaining process determining primary incomes allowances are made for the workings of the redistributive system."[19] Another line of argument asserts that government policy-makers do not attempt more than mildly redistributive policies because the government is constrained by the threat of disinvestment in exactly the same manner

---

[18] Capitalists do better as the Stackelberg follower than they would as the Stackelberg leader. However, the Stackelberg equilibrium with workers as the leader is better for both workers and capitalists than the Nash equilibrium.

[19] J.C.M. van Arnhem and G.J. Schotsman, "Do Parties Affect the Distribution of Incomes? The Case of Advanced Capitalist Democracies", in F.G. Castles (ed.), *The Impact of Parties* (Beverly Hills: Sage Publications, 1982).

as workers.[20] Thus adding the tax and spending powers of the state should alter nothing.

Both lines of argument can be shown to be correct in the context of our model if the government taxes profit at a flat rate and distributes the tax revenues to workers. Capitalists maintain their zero-tax share of consumption when profits are taxed at a flat rate by reducing their rate of savings. Workers do not gain from the transfers they receive, since they find it optimal to reduce their wage demands by an amount exactly equal to the transfers they receive in order to allow greater investment. Taxes and transfers in this case turn out to change nothing but the share of income workers receive as wages and as transfers.[21]

But constraining the tax schedule to be flat is unduly restrictive. In no country that we know of are profits actually taxed at a constant rate. Systems of profit taxation typically contain depreciation allowances which differ from the rate at which plant and equipment actually wear out, investment tax credits, cash grants for investment, special treatment of capital gains and interest payments, and double taxation of profits distributed as dividends, to name only some of the most common deviations from a flat profit tax.[22] Clearly governments have more tax instruments than a single flat rate allows and when more complicated tax schedules are analyzed, the result that the government is unable to alter the outcome when its policies are anticipated no longer holds.

Rather than attempt to capture the full complexity of the tax code in any existing country, it suffices to consider a tax schedule only slightly more complicated. Here we will assume that the government taxes uninvested profits, rather than total profits, at a flat rate. Such a tax could be achieved, for example, by the combination of a flat tax on income from capital with immediate expensing (a depreciation allowance which permits the deduction of 100 percent of all investment on plant and equipment within the first year of purchase). This tax schedule is given by:

$$Z(t) = zP(t) = z(1-s)(1-r) Y(t), \tag{12}$$

where z is now the tax rate on consumption out of profits. The taxes received from capitalists are distributed as transfer payments to workers. Thus capitalists now consume $P(t) - Z(t)$ which equals $(1-z)(1-s)(1-r) Y(t)$ while workers consume $W(t) + Z(t)$ or $[r + z(1-s)(1-r)] Y(t)$.

[20] See C. Lindblom, *Politics and Markets* (New York: Basic Books, 1977) and F. Block, "The Ruling Class Does Not Rule", *Socialist Revolution*, 3 (1977), 6–28.

[21] A. Przeworski and M. Wallerstein, "Structural Dependence of the State upon Capital", University of Chicago and University of California, Los Angeles: manuscript, 1986.

[22] See M.A. King and D. Fullerton, *The Taxation of Income from Capital* (Chicago: University of Chicago Press, 1984), for a comparison of the system of profit taxes in the United States, United Kingdom, Sweden and West Germany.

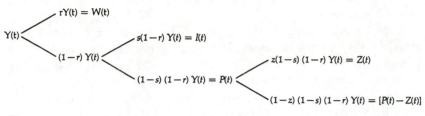

Fig. 2

Again, the division of the product between wages, profits, taxes and investment are best grasped by reference to Fig. 2.

With taxes levied on uninvested profits, capitalists' best reply is still given by the expression:

$$s^*(r, z) = 1 - \frac{\varrho}{v(1-r)} \tag{13}$$

(See appendix.) The tax on consumption out of profits does not enter in the firm's investment decision. Firms will invest at the same rate as if there were no taxes, as can be checked by comparing (13) with (7). Taxing consumption out of profits, unlike taxing aggregate profits, does not alter the terms of capitalists' choice between consumption today and in the future. All consumption, whenever it occurs, is simply reduced by the fraction $(1 - z)$.

Such taxes do alter workers' choice of strategy. Workers who anticipate receiving tax revenues and capitalists' best reply to their choice of r maximize their welfare with the strategy:

$$r^{**}(z) = (1 - z) \varrho/v. \tag{14}$$

(See appendix.) Increasing the tax on uninvested profits reduces the share of the output which workers demand in private wages.

Since taxes on consumption out of profits do not alter capitalists' best reply to any particular r while reducing workers' optimal r, the rate of savings must actually increase. Capitalists' best reply to r^{**} is:

$$s^*[r^{**}(z)] = 1 - \frac{\varrho}{v - (1-z)\varrho} \tag{15}$$

which is a positive function of z. Without taxes capitalists would not choose a positive rate of investment unless $v > 2\varrho$. Now capitalists will invest rather than disinvest as long as $v > (2 - z)\varrho$.

With taxes on uninvested profits workers are receiving less in wages than with no taxes, but they are receiving transfer payments. Workers' total share of the output remains unchanged:

$$(W + Z)/Y = r^{**} + z(1 - s^*)(1 - r^{**}) = \varrho/v. \tag{16}$$

But capitalists are saving at a higher rate, which implies more is being invested:

$$I/Y = s^*(1 - r^{**}) = 1 - (2 - z)(\varrho/v), \tag{17}$$

and the economy is growing more rapidly. Moreover, since more is being invested, capitalists must be consuming a smaller share of the product:

$$(P - Z)/Y = (1 - z)(1 - s^*)(1 - r^{**}) = (1 - z)\varrho/v. \tag{18}$$

The effect of a tax on uninvested profits is : (1) to shift workers' income from private to "public" wages, and (2) to shift capitalists' income from consumption to investment. As for the first effect, workers are indifferent in this model. But the second effect of the tax schedule will have a powerful impact on workers' welfare unless the rate at which workers discount the future is very high. With the imposition of taxes on consumption out of profits, workers receive the same share of an economy which grows at a faster rate. The higher the tax on uninvested profits, the higher the rate of investment and the better off workers are:

$$dW^*/dz = 1/\varrho > 0. \tag{19}$$

(See appendix.)

Capitalists' consumption is reduced in the short run by increases in z although, as the economy grows exponentially at a faster rate, capitalists' consumption will eventually surpass what they would have been able to consume if the tax rate had not increased. Nevertheless, the long-run gains in consumption are not sufficient to compensate for the immediate loss (assuming that $0 < z < 1$):

$$\frac{dP^*}{dz} = -\frac{z}{\varrho(1 - z)} < 0. \tag{20}$$

(See appendix.)

Taxes on uninvested profits have real effects even after workers and capitalists have adjusted their strategies. Workers' consumption, as a proportion of national income, is unaffected by the tax. Workers' gains in transfer payments are exactly offset by a reduction in workers' private wage demands. But capitalists are induced to consume less and invest more. When workers try to increase their income by raising private wages, the rate of investment declines. Thus gains in wages today come at the expense of the potential wage increases in the future. But a pro-worker government which sought to finance transfer payments by a tax on uninvested profits can do so without altering the rate of investment. If, as in the model we analyze here, workers have sufficient power to uni-

$$G^* = (W^*)^\mu (P^*)^{1-\mu}$$

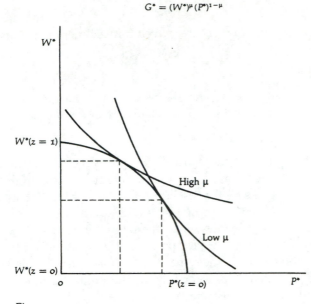

Fig. 3

laterally determine their wage rates, workers will maintain their target income share by reducing private wage demands as public transfer payments are provided. Then, as taxes on uninvested profits are substituted for private wages, claims on profits which do not cause a fall in investment replace claims on profits which do and the aggregate rate of investment raises. With a tax on consumption out of profits, investment increases and capitalists' consumption share declines simultaneously.

All increases in investment must come at the expense of the consumption of someone. But whether the trade-off is between workers' consumption share and investment or capitalists' consumption share and investment depends on the particular policy instrument chosen. Private ownership of the capital stock does not, in itself, dictate that it must be workers who accept sacrifices if investment is to be increased.

The political support maximizing tax

So far, the tax rate has been treated as an exogenously given parameter to which workers and capitalists react. We have established that the government has the means, via tax and spending policies, to increase the rate of investment without reducing workers' income share. But what remains to be established are the conditions, if any, under which such policies would be adopted.

Assume, as has become commonplace in economic analyses of political behaviour, that governments which face electoral competition choose policies to maximize their political support.[23] In addition, suppose the political support a party received depended on the level of welfare of both workers and capitalists according to the formula:[24]

$$G^* = (W^*)^{\mu} (P^*)^{1-\mu}, \quad 0 < \mu < 1, \tag{21}$$

where μ is the weight attached to workers' welfare and $1 - \mu$ is the weight attached to capitalists' welfare. Thus an μ equal to zero would imply that the government looks only to capitalists for support while an μ of unity indicates a government which cares only about workers' welfare. Any μ in between zero and one implies a government which is concerned, to some extent, with the welfare of both classes.

There is a simple geometric exposition of the government's optimal choice, as illustrated in Fig. 3. It follows from equations (19) and (20) that the trade-off between the welfare of capitalists and workers as z is increased (for $0 < z < 1$) is equal to:

$$\frac{dP^*/dz}{dW^*/dz} = -\frac{z}{1-z} \tag{22}$$

which is a concave function as drawn in Fig. 3. This represents the feasible set from which the government selects a point by choosing a tax rate. The government's objectives, as defined in (21), produce conventionally shaped indifference curves representing the political trade-off between material gains for workers versus gains for capitalists, also as drawn. The best the government can do is to pick the tax rate which allows it to reach the highest indifference curve, or the point at which an indifference curve is tangent to the feasible set. If μ is close to zero, the government's indifference curves will be almost vertical lines and the government's choice will be close to capitalists' most preferred outcome. As μ increases, the indifference curves flatten and the outcome for workers improves. In the limit, as μ approaches one, the indifference curves approach horizontal lines and workers' welfare approaches its maximum.

Algebraically, it is shown in the appendix that the political support maximizing tax rate is given implicitly by the equation:[25]

[23] J. Schumpeter, *Capitalism, Socialism and Democracy* (New York: Harper and Row, 1942). S. Peltzman, "Toward a More General Theory of Regulation", *Journal of Law and Economics*, 19 (1976), 211–40.

[24] F.A.A.M. van Winden, *On the Interaction Between State and Private Sector: A Study in Political Economics* (Amsterdam: North-Holland, 1983).

[25] Both P^* and W^* contain z so, contrary to appearances, z is not isolated on the left-hand side of (23).

$$z = \frac{\mu P^*}{\mu P^* + (1 - \mu) W^*} . \tag{23}$$

Thus, as long as μ lies between zero and one, the government will choose to tax uninvested profits at a rate also between zero and one. Moreover, the more a party cares about the support of workers, the higher will be the party's preferred tax rate, or $dz/d\mu < 0$ as shown in the appendix. Finally, as μ approaches unity, z also approaches unity.[26] As the weight given to the support of workers approaches one and the weight given to the support of capitalists approaches zero, the optimal tax on uninvested profits will approach one.

Workers' welfare under capitalism and socialism

The results of the analysis can be summarized by restating the income shares going to workers' consumption, capitalists' consumption and investment in each of the cases that has been considered.

Socialism:

$$
\begin{aligned}
W/Y &= \varrho/v \\
P/Y &= 0 \\
I/Y &= 1 - (\varrho/v)
\end{aligned}
\tag{24}
$$

Capitalism without taxes and transfers:

$$
\begin{aligned}
W/Y &= \varrho/v \\
P/Y &= \varrho/v \\
I/Y &= 1 - 2(\varrho/v)
\end{aligned}
\tag{25}
$$

Capitalism with a tax on uninvested profits and transfers:

$$
\begin{aligned}
(W + Z)/Y &= \varrho/v \\
(P - Z)/Y &= (1 - z)\varrho/v \\
I/Y &= 1 - (2 - z)\varrho/v
\end{aligned}
\tag{26}
$$

Capitalism without taxes and transfer is inferior for workers to a society in which workers owned the capital stock and determined the rate of investment. Workers receive the same share of the output in both but under socialism all that workers do not consume is invested. There is thus less investment and slower growth when the rate of investment is left to the market. The outcome with transfers to workers financed by a tax on uninvested profits lies in between socialism and capitalism without taxes

---

[26] This statement does not automatically follow from (23) since P^* and W^* also contain z. It does follow with a little additional argument which is given in the appendix.

or transfers. Workers' share remains the same but capitalists are induced to invest more and consume less than they would in the absence of the tax and transfer policy.

Workers' welfare is determined completely in this model by the share of the product which workers consume and the share which is invested (which determines the rate of growth). Under socialism, workers' welfare is given by:

$$W^*(r, s) = W^*(\varrho/v, 1) = W^s. \tag{27}$$

Under capitalism, workers' welfare depends on the tax and transfer policy of the government, which in turn is dependent upon the weight given by the government to workers' interests. Writing the rate of investment as a function of μ, and recalling that workers' share with transfers is equal to $[r + z(1 - s)(1 - r)]$, workers' welfare under capitalism can be written as:

$$W^*[r + z(1 - s)(1 - r), s] = W^*[\varrho/v, s(\mu)] = W^c(\mu). \tag{28}$$

As μ approaches one, capitalists' consumption share approaches zero and the investment share approaches all that remains after subtracting the wage share. In other words, as μ approaches one, s also approaches one which implies that workers' welfare approaches the level associated with socialism. As this is our central result, it deserves to be stated formally:

As $\mu \rightarrow 1$, $W^c(\mu) \rightarrow W^s$.

If workers, through political action, gain a preponderant influence over governmental policy, workers can attain a level of welfare arbitrarily close to their welfare under socialism using means no more radical than transfer payments financed by taxes on uninvested profits.

Caveats and generalizations

A number of restrictive assumptions were used to obtain these simple results but many can be relaxed without changing the final conclusion. It is obvious that the same conclusion could have been derived using a more complicated and realistic profit tax schedule. Adding more tax parameters simply increases the ability of the government to alter economic outcomes. Our assumption of a logarithmic utility function is also more restrictive than necessary. The same results can be derived using any of the family of utility functions with a constant elasticity of marginal utility.[27] The logarithmic function proved to be the most simple to work with.

---

[27] This is the family of utility functions given by $U(x) = (1 - b)^{-1}x^{1-b}$, $b > 0$, for b not equal to one and $U(x) = \ln x$ for $b = 1$. The parameter b is the elasticity of marginal utility.

There are only two points at which our model diverges significantly from the usual neo-classical framework. The first is in our assumption that workers collectively determine their wage share. (We do not assume that capitalists act collectively. Each firm is independently following its best reply strategy.) The second is our assumption of a linear production function. In a previous note we have analyzed the same taxes on profits within the more common framework in which wage rates are fixed exogenously and additions to the capital stock yield positive but diminishing returns.[28] In such a model one is led to study, not the rate of investment, but the profit-maximizing level of capital stock. Our results there were perfectly compatible with the results presented here: taxes on uninvested profits reduce after-tax, net-of-investment income from profit without altering the optimal level of capital. Tax schedules with even more generous relief for investment can generate tax revenue and raise the profit-maximizing level of capital simultaneously.

On the other hand, it could be argued that our model is too neoclassical in its neglect of unemployment. Marxists have traditionally claimed that unemployment is a necessary feature of capitalism and can only be eliminated with central planning and public ownership of capital. Yet there is no reason to believe that the tax system or other policies could not be used to alter the employment decisions of firms as effectively as firms' investment decisions.

Another modification of the model is to allow the discount rate of workers to differ from that of capitalists. If ϱ is replaced by ϱ^w and ϱ^c for workers and capitalists respectively, the conclusion does change somewhat. As workers' weight in the government's objective function and the tax on uninvested profits approach one, capitalists' consumption share approaches zero as before. But now workers' share under capitalism approaches ϱ^c/v and the share going to investment approaches $1 - \varrho^c/v$, while under socialism workers are consuming the share ϱ^w/v with the remainder going to investment. If $\varrho^w > \varrho^c$, workers in the best of all capitalist worlds would be forced to restrain their present consumption more than they would prefer.

Profits are not the only source of investment funds in capitalist economies. In some countries public investment is significant. In others, pensions are a major source of investable funds. Such alternatives to profits as the source of investment which are controlled by the government or even unions only weakens the dependence on profits and strengthens the argument of the paper. Of course our argument implies that such direct controls are not necessary.

[28] A. Przeworski and M. Wallerstein, "Comment on Katz, Mahler and Franz", *American Political Science Review*, 79 (1985), 508–10.

Tax policies which reduce capitalists' consumption share, however, would make a country less attractive to foreign investors. Note that foreign investments by domestic capitalists or domestic affiliates of foreign companies can be treated as consumption by the tax system. Capital flight can be discouraged as readily as actual consumption of income from profit. The existence of multinational corporations or international capital mobility does not makes taxes any less capable of inducing domestic capitalists to invest at home or of inducing foreign firms to reinvest their local earnings in the local economy.[29] Such policies cannot induce investments out of profits earned abroad, but neither will a policy of nationalization.

Finally, the government may not be a perfect agent of workers, even when workers' interests predominate. Our assumption that workers value income received as transfer payments just as much as wage income might reasonably be questioned.[30] Some of the income will be skimmed off by the bureaucracy which collects the taxes and distributes the transfer payments. In addition, the government might use the tax revenues to purchase collective consumption goods, such as health care, which are valued less by workers than private income. Moreover, in using the tax system to induce greater investment, the potential for inefficiencies in the allocation of investment due to differing effective tax rates on different kinds of investment arises. Neutral tax incentives – tax incentives which do not favor one kind of investment over another – may be difficult to implement in the presence of efforts by particular industries to obtain special consideration. Yet one must be careful not to compare socialist blueprints with the reality of democratic capitalism. Imperfections of the state as an instrument for the implementation of popular preferences provide equally telling arguments against visions of socialism which increase the role of the government in economic decisions.

---

[29] See J. Freeman, "The Welfare Consequences of Mixed Economies", paper presented at the Annual Meeting of the American Political Science Association, New Orleans, 1985, and R.H. Bates and D.D. Lien, "A Note on Taxation, Development, and Representative Government", *Politics and Society*, 14 (1985), 53–70, for arguments to the contrary.
J. Frieden, "Debt, Development and Democracy: Five Latin American Borrowers from Boom to Bust and Back", manuscript, University of California, Los Angeles, 1986, claims that most investments by multinational firms in Latin America are financed locally and thus do not represent inflows of capital from abroad. The conclusion of Bates and Lien that owners of more mobile assets have greater control over public policy depends, however, on their restriction of feasible taxes to those with a flat rate on income. A government which, in their words, could tax "defections" from the market, would not be so constrained.
[30] And was questioned by Stephen Weatherford when this work was presented at the Annual Meeting of the Midwestern Political Science Association.

Conclusions

We have posed the question of whether the best workers can do in a capitalist society is strictly inferior to the welfare workers could attain if private ownership of capital were abolished, or whether $W^c(\mu) < W^s$. Strictly speaking, our answer is positive. Workers under capitalism can never attain exactly the level of welfare associated with collective ownership of capital. A tax rate equal to unity is incompatible with private ownership of capital (and with the existence of a solution to capitalists' maximization problem). But the difference between workers' welfare under socialism and capitalism, $W^s - W^c(\mu)$, becomes negligible as the weight given workers' welfare by the government, μ, approaches one.

This is the social democratic strategy of "functional socialism" whereby the functions of capital ownership are brought under government control while leaving ownership itself untouched.[31] The great advantage of this strategy is the possibility of obtaining the benefits of control over the allocation of capital in gradual steps without the risks inherent in strategies which directly challenge the right of capitalists to their property. The risks inherent in challenging private ownership of capital are twofold: popular mobilization and government preparations for the socialization of capital may heighten the uncertainty of capitalists, even those whose property is meant to be exempt, and produce rapid disinvestment. In the context of this model capitalists will disinvest when $\varrho^c/v > 1$ at any positive value of r. Such capital flight requires no conspiracy. It occurs as a result of each capitalist following his or her best reply strategy. For this reason, Oskar Lange recommended that the capital stock be nationalized as quickly as possible to reduce the period of disinvestment.[32] But a strategy of socializing the capital stock in one stroke with no forewarning is not feasible. The period of disinvestment may be shortened by bold initiatives but not eliminated. Secondly, there is always the danger that a serious threat to the private ownership of capital may provoke a counter-revolution in which capitalism is preserved, democracy is destroyed and the labor movement is suppressed. As Adler-Karlsson eloquently argued:

Let us avoid the even more dangerous contests which are unavoidable if we enter the road of formal socialization. Let us instead grip and divest our present capitalists of one after another of their ownership functions. Let us even give them a new dress, one similar to that of the famous emperor in H.C. Andersen's tale. After a few decades they will then remain, perhaps formally, as kings but in reality as naked symbols of a passed and inferior stage of development.[33]

[31] Esping-Andersen, *Politics Against Markets*.
[32] O. Lange, "On the Economic Theory of Socialism", in B. Lippincott (ed.), *On the Economic Theory of Socialism* (New York: McGraw-Hill, 1938).
[33] Quoted by Esping-Andersen, *Politics Against Markets*, p. 23.

Why, then, have the Swedish unions and others raised again the demand for the socialization of capital in wage-earner funds? In large part, we surmise, because of disappointments with the political feasibility of functional socialism. Workers' welfare may never attain the preponderance in the government's objectives that our results demand. After all, workers, defined as manual wage-earners in manufacturing, mining and agriculture, nowhere constitute a majority of the electorate. In order to win a majority, therefore, parties which represent workers must seek votes from non-workers as well. Social Democratic or Labor Parties which win elections do so as parties of the "people" with promises to satisfy diverse sets of interests.[34] Secondly, even if workers can prevail in the formulation of policy, workers may not be able to effectively monitor the government bureaucracy. Workers might prefer direct ownership over both public ownership and indirect control exercised through taxes and transfers because of the limitations of the state as agent of any single group in society. The socialization of capital may occur as a means of restraining rather than enhancing the role of the government in the economy.

Mathematical appendix

Model without taxes

The basic model consists of an economy in which income is allocated among three uses – consumption by workers, $W(t)$, consumption by capitalists, $P(t)$, and investment, $I(t)$ – according to the formulas:

$$W(t) = rY(t),$$
$$P(t) = (1-s)(1-r)Y(t), \quad \text{and} \qquad \qquad \text{(A1)}$$
$$I(t) = s(1-r)Y(t).$$

The growth of aggregate income, $Y(t)$, is assumed to be a linear function of the growth of the capital stock or investment:

$$Y'(t) = vI(t) = vs(1-r)Y(t), \qquad \qquad \text{(A2)}$$

where v is the (constant) productivity of capital. This last equation can be solved to yield:

$$Y(t) = Y_o \, e^{vs(1-r)t}, \qquad \qquad \text{(A3)}$$

with Y_0 representing the initial level of output. Workers seek to maximize their utility over present and future consumption, given by the expression:

[34] A. Przeworski and J. Sprague, *Paper Stones: A History of Electoral Socialism* (Chicago: University of Chicago Press, 1986).

$$W^* = \int_0^\infty e^{-\varrho t}\, U[W(t)]\, dt = \int_0^\infty e^{-\varrho t}\, \ln[W(t)]\, dt, \tag{A4}$$

where ϱ is the rate at which workers discount the future, $\varrho > 0$.

Workers' best reply is defined to be the value of r, denoted $r^*(s)$, which maximizes W^* holding capitalists' choice of s fixed. To find $r^*(s)$, we substitute (A1) and (A3) into (A4) and carry out the integration:

$$W^* = \int_0^\infty e^{-\varrho t}\, \ln[rY(t)]\, dt$$

$$= \ln(rY_0)\int_0^\infty e^{-\varrho t}\, dt + vs(1-r)\int_0^\infty t\, e^{-\varrho t}\, dt$$

$$= \frac{1}{\varrho}\left[\ln(rY_0) + \frac{vs(1-r)}{\varrho}\right]. \tag{A5}$$

The optimal r is given by the first-order condition:

$$\frac{\partial W^*(r,\, s)}{\partial r} = (1/\varrho)\,[(1/r) - (vs/\varrho)] = 0, \tag{A6}$$

which implies:

$$r^*(s) = \varrho/sv. \tag{A7}$$

The second-order condition for a maximum is met everywhere as can be readily seen from (A6).

Capitalists' best reply is defined in parallel fashion to be the value of s which maximizes capitalists' welfare, P^*, for a given r. Capitalists' objective function is given by the expression:

$$P^* = \int_0^\infty e^{-\varrho t}\, U[P(t)]\, dt = \int_0^\infty e^{-\varrho t}\, \ln[P(t)]\, dt$$

$$= \int_0^\infty e^{-\varrho t}\, \ln[(1-s)(1-r)\, Y(t)]\, dt$$

$$= \ln[(1-s)(1-r)\, Y_0]\int_0^\infty e^{-\varrho t}\, dt + vs(1-r)\int_0^\infty te^{-\varrho t}\, dt$$

$$= \frac{1}{\varrho}\left\{\ln[(1-s)(1-r)\, Y_0] + \frac{vs(1-r)}{\varrho}\right\}. \tag{A8}$$

To find capitalists' best reply function $s^*(r)$ we proceed as usual, differentiating P^* and solving for s:

$$\frac{\partial P^*(s,\, r)}{\partial s} = \frac{1}{\varrho}\left[\frac{v(1-r)}{\varrho} - \frac{1}{1-s}\right] = 0, \tag{A9}$$

which yields:

$$s^*(r) = 1 - \frac{\varrho}{v(1-r)} \, . \tag{A10}$$

Again, it is easily verified by looking at equation (A9) that the second-order condition for a maximum is met.

To find workers' best choice of strategy given capitalists' response of $s^*(r)$, substitute (A10) into (A5) and take the derivative:

$$\frac{dW^*[r, s^*(r)]}{dr} = (1/\varrho)\,[(1/r) - (v/\varrho)] = 0, \tag{A11}$$

which gives

$$r^{**} = \varrho/v \tag{A12}$$

as the solution. Following their best reply (A10), capitalists will choose

$$s^*(r^{**}) = 1 - \frac{(\varrho/v)}{1 - (\varrho/v)} \, . \tag{A13}$$

Model with taxes and transfers

Uninvested profits are assumed to be taxed at a flat rate z:

$$Z(t) = z(1-s)(1-r)\,Y(t) \tag{B1}$$

with the tax revenues given to workers as transfer payments. In this case the allocation of income between workers' consumption, capitalists' consumption and investment is given by the formulas:

$$\begin{aligned} W(t) + Z(t) &= [r + z(1-s)(1-r)]\,Y(t), \\ P(t) - Z(t) &= (1-z)(1-s)(1-r)\,Y(t), \quad \text{and} \\ I(t) &= s(1-r)\,Y(t). \end{aligned} \tag{B4}$$

The expression for $I(t)$ and, therefore, the equations for the growth of output (A2 and A3) remain unchanged. Workers' objective functions is:

$$\begin{aligned} W^* &= \int_0^\infty e^{-\varrho t}\,\ln\{[r + z(1-s)(1-r)]\,Y(t)\}\,dt \\ &= \frac{1}{\varrho}\left\{\ln(Y_0) + \ln[r + z(1-s)(1-r)] + \frac{vs(1-r)}{\varrho}\right\}. \end{aligned} \tag{B3}$$

Capitalists' objective function is:

$$\begin{aligned} P^* &= \int_0^\infty e^{-\varrho t}\,\ln\{[(1-z)(1-s)(1-r)]\,Y(t)\}\,dt \\ &= \frac{1}{\varrho}\left\{\ln[(1-z)(1-r)\,Y_0] + \ln(1-s) + \frac{vs(1-r)}{\varrho}\right\}. \end{aligned} \tag{B4}$$

To find capitalists' best reply, we maximize P^* with respect to s with r held constant:

$$\frac{\partial P^*(s, r)}{\partial s} = \frac{1}{\varrho}\left[\frac{v(1-r)}{\varrho} - \frac{1}{1-s}\right] = 0, \tag{B5}$$

which yields:

$$s^*(r) = 1 - \frac{\varrho}{v(1-r)}, \tag{B6}$$

exactly the same as without taxes (A10).

Workers choose the value of r which maximizes W^* given capitalists' best reply $s^*(r)$:

$$\frac{dW^*[r, s^*(r)]}{dr} = \frac{v}{\varrho}\left[\frac{1}{vr + z\varrho} - \frac{1}{\varrho}\right] = 0. \tag{B7}$$

Solving for r^{**}:

$$r^{**} = (1 - z)\varrho/v. \tag{B8}$$

Capitalists' best reply to r^{**} is:

$$s^*(r^{**}) = 1 - \frac{(\varrho/v)}{1 - (1-z)(\varrho/v)}. \tag{B9}$$

The share of output being invested is given by:

$$\begin{aligned} I/Y = s^*(1 - r^{**}) &= [1 - (1-z)(\varrho/v)] - (\varrho/v) \\ &= 1 - (2 - z)(\varrho/v). \end{aligned} \tag{B10}$$

The share of workers' consumption is:

$$\begin{aligned} (W + Z)/Y = r^{**} + z(1 - s^*)(1 - r^{**}) \\ = (1 - z)\varrho/v + z\varrho/v = \varrho/v. \end{aligned} \tag{B11}$$

The proportion of output which capitalists consume is:

$$\begin{aligned} (P - Z)/Y &= 1 - (W + Z + I)/Y \\ &= 1 - \varrho/v - [1 - 2(1-z)(\varrho/v)] = (1-z)\varrho/v. \end{aligned} \tag{B12}$$

Using (B10) and (B11), W^* can be rewritten as:

$$W^* = (1/\varrho)\{\ln[Y_o(\varrho/v)] + v/\varrho - 2 + z\} \tag{B13}$$

from which it follows immediately that:

$$dW^*/dz = 1/\varrho > 0. \tag{B14}$$

Similarly, P^* can be rewritten:

$$P^* = (1/\varrho)\{\ln[Y_0(\varrho/v)] + \ln(1-z) + v/\varrho - 2 + z\} \tag{B15}$$

from which it follows that:

$$\frac{dP^*}{dz} = -\frac{z}{\varrho(1-z)} < 0 \tag{B16}$$

for $z < 1$.

Letting the government's objective function be defined as:

$$G^* = (W^*)^\mu (P^*)^{1-\mu}, \quad 0 < \mu < 1, \tag{B17}$$

we can find the tax rate which the government would choose. Taking the derivative:

$$\frac{dG^*}{dz} = (W^*)^{\mu-1}(P^*)^{-\mu}\left[\mu(P^*)\frac{dW^*}{dz} + (1-\mu)(W^*)\frac{dP^*}{dz}\right] = 0.$$

Substitute (B14) and (B16) and rearrange terms to obtain the expression:

$$\mu(1-z)P^* - (1-\mu)zW^* = 0 \tag{B18}$$

which implicitly determines the optimal choice of z. Note that both P^* and W^* contain z. Nevertheless, it is useful to isolate z on the left-hand side:

$$z = \frac{\mu P^*}{\mu P^* + (1-\mu)W^*}, \quad \text{for } z < 1. \tag{B19}$$

From (B19) it can be observed that $0 < z < 1$ (since $0 < \mu < 1$). Moreover, from (B13) it can be seen that W^* does not explode as μ approaches one. Thus $(1-\mu)W^*$ approaches zero and z approaches one as μ approaches one. Finally, from (B15) it can be verified that P^* does not explode as μ approaches zero. Therefore, as μ approaches zero, so does z. To determine the effect of μ on z for $0 < \mu < 1$, we differentiate (B18) implicitly to obtain:

$$\frac{dz}{d\mu} = \frac{(1-z)P^* + zW^*}{\mu P^* + (1-\mu)W^* + z/\varrho} > 0. \tag{B20}$$

6 Marx, revolution and rational choice*

Jon Elster

I. Introduction

There are two perspectives on politics in Marx's writings. On the one hand, politics is part of the superstructure and hence of the forces that oppose social change. The political system stabilizes the dominant economic relations.[1] On the other hand, politics is a medium for revolution, and hence for social change. New relations of production are ushered in by political struggles. To see the relation between the two functions of politics, they must be seen in the wider context of historical materialism. This theory affirms that new relations of production emerge when and because the existing ones cease to be optimal for the further development of the productive forces: this is the ultimate explanation of a change in the economic relations. In this transition, political struggle has no independent causal force. It acts as a midwife, bringing about what is doomed to come about sooner or later.[2]

When the new relations have come about, the political movement that brought them into being is solidified into a political system which contributes to keeping them in place. When performing this stabilizing function politics is initially progressive, but later becomes reactionary. It is progressive as long as the relations of production remain optimal for the development of the productive forces; it becomes reactionary when new, superior relations appear at the horizon. In the latter stage, the political system can no longer be explained by its ability to stabilize economic relations which, themselves, are further explained by their ability to promote the productive forces at an optimal rate. In its reactionary stage, the political system becomes an independent social force. It now keeps alive what formerly kept it alive, namely, a system of property rights that

---

* This chapter draws upon and extends the arguments in my *Making Sense of Marx* (Cambridge: Cambridge University Press, 1985).

[1] For this view, see notably G.A. Cohen, *Karl Marx's Theory of History* (Oxford: Clarendon Press, 1978), chapter 8.

[2] For the problems raised by this phrase, see G.A. Cohen, "Historical Inevitability and Human Agency", forthcoming.

no longer can rest on its progressive economic function. It can only, however, give them a stay of execution. The political movement corresponding to the new relations of production will, inevitably, win out.

These general propositions are supposed to apply to all societies, from the Asiatic model of production through slavery, serfdom, capitalism up to communism. (There is one difference: the political movement that leads up to communism does not, after its victory, solidify into a new political system, but rather proceeds to the dismantling of politics.) Actually, Marx and later Marxists have applied them to a much more limited set of problems: the rise and fall of capitalism. At the center of Marx's political writings is the capitalist state in its stabilizing function. He believed that he wrote at a time when the capitalist relations of production, from being optimal, were turning suboptimal. Correspondingly, the capitalist state was in the process of going from its progressive to its reactionary stage. This is the overriding concern of his political theory: how does the state maintain and support capitalist relations of production in the face of the rise of communism as a potentially superior system?

He also made numerous observations on the political processes at both sides of capitalism: the political transition from feudalism to capitalism and from capitalism to communism. While often suggestive, these are much less coherent than his theory of the capitalist state. They are also much less plausible, since they depend too heavily on the teleological framework of his theory of history. Marx never offers anything remotely resembling an argument for his view that individuals or classes will engage in political struggle for the sake of relations of production which will enable the productive forces to develop at an optimal rate. The extent to which he neglected microfoundations, and instead simply put his faith in history, is brought out in his irritation at the petty-minded German burghers during the 1848 movement, when they refused, contrary to the general movement of history, to enter into an alliance with the working class. Had he been more willing to entertain the idea that they were rational political actors, instead of puppets of their historical destiny, he would have understood that if *he* could see that this alliance would ultimately benefit the workers in their struggle against capitalism, the burghers could also see what lay in store for them if they accepted it.

The argument of this chapter is as follows. Section II is a brief survey of Marx's theory of the capitalist state. Sections III and IV consider, respectively, Marx's theory of the revolutionary transitions from feudalism to capitalism and from capitalism to communism. Section V offers a conclusion and some generalizations.

II. The capitalist state

Marx had not one, but two or three theories of the capitalist state. Prior to 1848 he held a purely instrumental theory, usually thought of as *the* Marxist theory of the state, according to which it is "nothing but" a tool for the common interests of the bourgeoisie. After 1848, when this view became increasingly implausible, he substituted for it an "abdication theory" to the effect that capitalists abstain from political power because they find their interests better served this way. Finally, if one removes from the second theory all that is sheer stipulation or unsubstantiated assertion, a more plausible account emerges. This is the view that the state is an independent actor on the social arena, and that the interests of the capitalist class serve as constraints rather than goals for its actions.

In the *Communist Manifesto* Marx tells us that "the executive of the modern State is but a committee for managing the common affairs of the whole bourgeoisie".[3] In other pre-1848 writings he is somewhat more careful. He recognizes that in most countries the state is not yet fully capitalist in nature, but adds that it must inevitably become so if economic progress is to continue. "Bourgeois industry has reached a certain level when it must either win an appropriate political system or perish",[4] where by "appropriate" he meant a system in which the bourgeoisie directly assumes the political power. It was when Marx had to give up this basic premise that he developed the abdication theory of the state.

The instrumental theory has two sides to it. On the one hand the state solves the collective action problems of the bourgeoisie; on the other hand it blocks the cooperative solution to the similar problems faced by the workers. Of these, the first task is more fundamental, and actually includes the second, since an unorganized working class is a public good for the capitalists. In one sense Marx stands in the Hobbesian tradition that views the state as a means for enforcing cooperative behaviour in a Prisoner's Dilemma.[5] The crucial difference is that while Hobbes thought of the relevant Prisoner's Dilemma as one involving the war of all against all, Marx restricted it to the internal war among members of the economically dominant class. In the only place where Marx refers to the function of the state in providing genuinely public goods, he adds that with the development of capitalism these will increasingly be provided by

---

[3] *The Communist Manifesto*, in Marx and Engels, *Collected Works* (London: Lawrence and Wishart), vol. 6, p. 486. (Hereafter referred to as CW, followed by a number indicating the volume.)

[4] *Neue Rheinische Zeitung*, 22 November 1849. The newspaper articles referred to here and below can be easily retrieved in the chronologically arranged CW.

[5] See especially M. Taylor, *The Possibility of Cooperation* (Cambridge: Cambridge University Press, 1987).

private industry.[6] It is a puzzle why he should think that, say, basic research or defense against external enemies could profitably be undertaken by private firms; most probably he did not have a clear understanding of the problem.

Among the tasks of the capitalist state, Marx cites expropriation of private property when it is in the interest of the capitalist class as a whole;[7] legal regulation of the length of the working day;[8] and enforcement of competition.[9] Of these, the last two are especially interesting. It is sometimes argued that the task of the state, rather than enforcing competition, is to save firms from the ravages of competition.[10] If firms in an industry are unable to form a cartel, because of the free-rider problem involved, the state can force them to act in their collective interest. There have been quite a few instances of such forced cartellization in the history of capitalism, especially during the Great Depression. Marx argued that the state had to take the long view. In the long run, the viability and hence the legitimacy of capitalism depend upon the spur of competition. Similarly, he argued that the Ten Hours Bill of 1848 was introduced to protect capitalists against their short-term greed. By overexploiting the workers, for the purpose of short-term profits, they were threatening the physical reproduction and survival of the class which formed the very condition for profit.

This argument presents a puzzle. If the state can act in the collective, long-term interests of the capitalist class, will it not also anticipate and prevent the communist revolution? Would not a state which does *not* say "Après nous le déluge" try to pre-empt any revolutionary social movement by reformist concessions? Marx did not confront this issue, except by a fiat to the effect that it would not arise, but on his behalf one might offer the following considerations. The natural response of ruling classes is to meet social unrest by repression rather than pre-emption. If it turns out that repression does not work, or has the very opposite effect of what was intended, by unifying the forces it was supposed to crush, the rulers may turn to concessions as a fall-back strategy. In that case they will find, however, that this is a difficult technique to deploy. To be effective, concessions must be given before the demand for them has even arisen, since otherwise they will be taken as a sign of weakness and provoke still further demands. It remains true, nevertheless, that both repression and reform sometimes do work. The principle that would guide a rational

[6] *Grundrisse* (Harmondsworth: Penguin, 1963), pp. 524ff.
[7] *Capital I* (New York: International Publishers, 1967), p. 239.
[8] *The German Ideology*, CW 5, pp. 355ff.
[9] Ibid.
[10] For a valuable discussion, see J. Bowman, "The Politics of the Market", *Political Power and Social Theory*, 5 (1985), 35–88.

ruling class is either to give no concessions or to pre-empt the claims by giving more than is demanded.[11]

Events in Europe between 1848 and 1852 showed that the bourgeoisie, far from reaching out towards political power, turned away from it. The English capitalists dismantled the successful Anti-Corn Law League, instead of using it as a stepping-stone to power. Having defeated the landowners over this particular issue, they showed no interest in dethroning them from power generally, to Marx's frustration and puzzlement. In France and Germany the revolutionary movement of 1848–9 was not the uninterrupted march forward of the bourgeoisie that Marx had predicted. Instead, it took the form "One step forward, two steps backward". The final outcome of the bourgeois struggle against feudal, absolutist or bureaucratic regimes was not their dissolution, but their further entrenchment. To remain consistent with his general theory of history, Marx had to argue that these non-capitalist regimes could ultimately be explained by the interests of the capitalist class.

This argument was provided by what I have called the abdication theory of the capitalist state, formulated by Marx in writings on French and English politics around 1852. ("Abdication" is used here in a somewhat extended sense, which includes abstaining from taking the power which is within one's reach as well as giving up the power which one has.) There are three steps in the argument. First, like several other writers, Marx argued that at this particular juncture in history the bourgeoisie benefited from having a state that was not the immediate extension of their class interest. Next, unlike these other writers, he claimed that the existence of this non-capitalist state could actually be explained by these benefits. As usual, Marx had difficulties in accepting the idea that there can be accidental, non-explanatory benefits in social life. Finally, he argued that since the presence of a non-capitalist state could be explained by its value to the capitalist class, its autonomy was only an apparent one. This step is also questionable, since it neglects important strategic elements of the situation.

Many writers have been struck by the apparent paradox that England, the foremost capitalist country in the nineteenth century, was governed by a resolutely aristocratic elite, whose economic basis was ownership of land rather than capital. In earlier history, cumulation of economic and political superiority had almost invariably been the rule. The bourgeoisie was the first property-owning class which was not also the governing class.[12] The most natural explanation of this fact, at least to a non-Marxist,

---

[11] The argument in this paragraph derives, more or less directly, from Tocqueville's writings on the revolutions of 1789 and 1848.

[12] P. Veyne, *Le Pain et le Cirque* (Paris: Editions du Seuil, 1976), p. 117.

is that the aristocracy had a traditional monopoly on government which was not easily broken. In the words of S.M. Lipset, the aristocracy "continued to maintain its control over the governmental machinery because it remained the highest status group in society".[13] The alternative explanation, favored by Marx, is that the bourgeoisie shied away from power because it was not in their interest to take it.

Various writers have argued that the English bourgeoisie benefited from having a non-capitalist government. An editorial in *The Economist* from 1862, possibly written by Walter Bagehot, argued that "not only for the interest of the country at large, but especially for the interest of its commerce, it is in the highest degree desirable that the Government should stand high above the influence of commercial interest". The implication seems to be that a purely "commercial" or capitalist govern-ment would be too myopic or greedy on behalf of capital, thus undermin-ing its long-term interest. In a related argument Joseph Schumpeter claimed that the bourgeoisie "needs a master", not because they are too greedy but because they are too incompetent, "unable not only to lead the nation but even to take care of their particular class interests".[14] In a quite different vein G.D.H. Cole remarks that the English bourgeoisie "were too occupied with their own affairs to wish to take the exercise of political authority directly into their own hands".[15]

The benefit cited by Marx was quite different. He argued that were the capitalists to take political power, the two enemies of the working class – Capital and Government – would fuse into one, creating an explosive social situation. As long as the workers had to fight a two-front war against economic exploitation and political oppression their combativity and class consciousness would lack a clear focus. Conversely, "when political dominion and economic supremacy will be united in the same hands, when, therefore, the struggle against capital will no longer be distinct from the struggle against the existing Government – from that very moment will date the *social revolution of England*".[16] Recognizing this, the English bourgeoisie cleverly stayed away from power. Marx applied the same analysis to France. The revolution of 1848 led to the formation of the Second Republic and brought the bourgeoisie into political power. Yet they soon recognized that the July Monarchy had been a better arrange-ment from their point of view, "since they must now confront the

[13] S.M. Lipset, "Social Stratification: Social Class", in *The International Encyclopedia of the Social Sciences* vol. 15 (New York: Macmillan, 1968).
[14] J. Schumpeter, *Capitalism, Socialism and Democracy* (London: Allen and Unwin, 1961), p. 138.
[15] G.D.H. Cole, *Studies in Class Structure* (London: Routledge and Kegan Paul, 1955), pp. 84–5.
[16] *New York Daily Tribune*, 25 August 1852.

subjugated classes and contend against them without mediation, without the concealment afforded by the crown".[17] Hence there was a need for a new blurring of the class lines, providentially ensured by Louis Napoleon. Marx interpreted Bonaparte's *coup d'état* of December 1851 as the abdication from power of the French bourgeoisie, just as he saw the dismantling of the Anti-Corn Law League as a deliberate stepping back from power by the English capitalists.

Marx, then, wanted to explain the presence of a non-capitalist state by the interests of the capitalist class. The explanation is not supported by the historical record. There is no evidence to suggest that the capitalists, individually or as a class, were motivated by such considerations. In the absence of subjective intentions, the objective benefits do not in themselves provide an explanation. Nor is it clear that the benefits cited by *The Economist* or by Schumpeter provide an explanation for the political passivity of the English bourgeoisie. A simpler explanation is provided by the logic of collective action. The free-rider problem ensures that capitalists will keep out of politics, unless intolerably provoked by state measures that go strongly against their interests. This fits in with Cole's argument: although all capitalists would make more money if they all made some political effort, each individual capitalist would rather stay in business. It may then well be true that what capitalists do out of individual self-interest also, by a happy coincidence, benefits their class as a whole, but this fact is no part of the explanation of why they do it.

A variant of the argument can be applied to the French case, where the capitalists first had power and then lost it. Marx often suggests that the French bourgeoisie was weakened by internal dissensions among its several fractions and that this is what allowed Louis Bonaparte to take power. The observation suggests that the French bourgeoisie had not overcome their free-rider problems, that is, that they were not yet a stable collective actor. Hence they had little resistance to offer to the *coup d'état*. This fact, combined with the (alleged) benefits they derived from having a non-capitalist state, could be seen as justifying the view that they deliberately opted for the latter and abdicated from their own rule.

To see that the view is not justified, consider an analogy. A fugitive from justice may allow himself to be captured out of sheer exhaustion. It may turn out, moreover, that he does better for himself in prison than he would have done had he remained in liberty. These two facts, clearly, do not entitle us to say that he abdicated from liberty out of long-term self-interest, nor that the explanation of his being captured lies in the benefits he derived from being in prison. Writing about Germany, Marx does actually refer to the "Babylonian captivity" of the bourgeoisie in the

[17] *The Eighteenth Brumaire of Louis Bonaparte*, CW 11, p. 129.

decade following the 1849 counter-revolution, claiming that their lack of political power made them into the effective economic power in the land.[18] In this case, however, he refrained from suggesting that their captivity was explained by those economic benefits.

Although there is little evidence that capitalists abstained from power because they saw that this best served their interests, there could well be some truth in this view. It could be that the lack of political ambitions on the part of individual capitalists was reinforced by the perception that even were they to overcome their free-rider problem, they might not be well served by doing so. Evidence about individual motivations for abstaining from action is, by the nature of the case, hard to come by. Let us explore, therefore, the possibility that the benefits cited by *The Economist*, Schumpeter and Marx did in fact enter into the explanation for the capitalist abstention from power. Marx claimed that if the presence of a non-capitalist state could be explained by such benefits, it would prove that the state was "really" or ultimately a capitalist one.

I shall argue against this view. Marx held a narrow, *pre-strategic* conception of power that prevented him from recognizing that the states he observed had autonomy in a real sense and not only as a fief from the capitalist class. To see this, observe first that there are two ways in which group interests can shape state policies: by serving as the goal which those policies try to promote, or by serving as a constraint on them. On first glance, it is tempting to argue that if the choice between the feasible political alternatives is always made according to the interest of one group, then it has all power concentrated in its hands. On reflection, however, it is clear that power – real, as opposed to formal – must also include the ability to define the set of alternatives, to set constraints on what is feasible. The following scenario is intended to bring out the relations between these two ways of wielding power. It is constructed so as to apply to nineteenth-century European politics, as a strategic game between Capital and Government with the working class as an important background variable. In modified form, it could also apply to aspects of twentieth-century politics.

There are two agents: *A* ("Capital") and *B* ("Government"), initially facing a given number of alternatives. *B* has the formal power to choose among the feasible alternatives, *A* may have the power to exclude some of the alternatives from being considered. We assume that in *A*'s judgment some alternatives are very bad, to be avoided at all costs. Among those remaining, some are judged better than others, but none is outstandingly superior. If the bad alternatives can somehow be excluded from the feasible set, it might not matter too much which of the remaining ones is

18 *The New York Daily Tribune*, 1 February 1859.

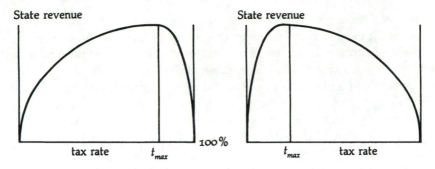

Figs. 1 and 2

chosen by *B*. It may not even be necessary for *A* to take any steps to exclude the inferior alternatives. *B*, acting on the "law of anticipated reactions", may abstain from choosing any of these, knowing that if he does *A* has the power and the motive to dethrone him. Moreover, to the extent that what is bad for *A* is also bad for *B*, perhaps because *B*'s affluence depends on that of *A*, *B* might not want to choose an inferior alternative even could he get away with it. On the other hand, *A* might actually welcome the fact that *B* does not choose the alternative top-ranked by *A*, for example if *A* does not want to be seen having power or if he deplores his own tendency to prefer short-term over long-term gains. Or, if he does not welcome it, he might at least tolerate it as the lesser evil, compared to the costs involved in *taking* the formal power (as distinct from the costs involved in *having* it). In either case *B* would be invested with some autonomous power of decision, although its substance might be questioned. Marx would say that the autonomy is only apparent, since ultimately it is granted by *A*. *B* has autonomy as a fief.

Consider, however, the same situation from *B*'s perspective. He will correctly perceive his power as deriving from the cost to *A* of having or taking it. To be sure, *B*'s power is limited by the fact that there are certain bounds that he cannot transgress without provoking *A* into taking power for himself, perhaps also by the need to avoid killing the goose that lays the golden eggs. But, conversely, *A*'s real influence is limited by his desire not to assume formal, political power unless provoked. Both actors, in fact, have power, of an equally substantive character. How much power they have, depends on the further, specific features of the situation, as may be seen by comparing Figs. 1 and 2. (Needless to say, the following argument is extremely stylized – it is intended to be suggestive, not demonstrative.)

Each curve shows the amount of tax revenue to the state as a function of the tax rate. If the tax rate is 0, there is no tax income; if the tax rate is 100, no taxable activity will be forthcoming, and again there is no tax revenue. Somewhere in between there must be a tax rate, t_{max}, that maximizes government income. Let us assume, for simplicity, that this is the only interest of the government: to raise as much tax revenue as possible.[19] The interest of the capitalist class is, to simplify again, that the tax rate be as close to 0 as possible.[20] Depending on various economic factors, as well as on the form of tax collection, the optimal tax rate may be high, as in Fig. 1, or low, as in Fig. 2. In the former case, the government has substantial freedom to act against the interests of the capitalist class,[21] whereas in the latter it is constrained to track very closely what is optimal policy from the capitalist point of view.[22] *It is a purely empirical question* whether, in any given case, something like Fig. 1 or something like Fig. 2 obtains. No amount of conceptual juggling or a priori reasoning can prove the structural dependence of the state upon capital.

We have seen some of the reasons why *A* might not want power. One is that *A* might know that if in power his decisions will be motivated by short-term gain to himself, and that he wants to prevent this by letting the power remain safely outside his reach. From the point of view of *A*'s long-term interest it may be better having the decisions taken in accordance with *B*'s interest, although not, of course, as good as if *B* would take them to promote *A*'s long-term interest. Another reason could be the presence of a third actor *C* ("Labour"), who is already opposed to *A* and who also tends to oppose whoever has the formal power of decision. For *A* it might then be better to leave the formal power with *B*, so that some of *C*'s attention and energy, should be directed towards *B* and diverted from *A*. From this perspective *A* might positively desire that *B* should not consistently decide in accordance with *A*'s long-term interest, since otherwise *C* might perceive that the distinction between *A* and *B* is quite spurious.

Finally, *A* has reasons for not wanting to take power, as distinct from his reasons for not having it. To go into politics is like a costly investment that only bears fruit after some time while requiring outlays in the present. If one's interests are reasonably well respected in the present, the prospect

---

[19] The government may also have an interest in a high growth rate for the economy, for instance if it believes that economic growth is necessary to stave off popular unrest.

[20] The capitalist class may have a collective interest in some taxation, for the provision of public goods.

[21] Assuming that the capitalist class is unable or unwilling to take power for itself – that is, that there is no political constraint operating.

[22] The latter case is, implausibly, taken to be typical in P. van Parijs, *Evolutionary Explanation in the Social Sciences* (Totowa, N.J.: Rowman and Littlefield, 1981), pp. 183ff, arguing that the level of economic activity and governmental revenue are maximized by the same set of state policies.

of a future in which they might be even better respected need not be very attractive, considering the costs of transition. Myopia – a high evaluation of present as opposed to future income – might prevent *A* from wanting to take power, just as his knowledge of his own tendency to act myopically might prevent him from wanting to have it. These facts also create an incentive for *B* to make the transition costs as high as possible, and to ensure that *A*'s interest is just sufficiently respected to make them an effective deterrent.

In more concrete language, the state has an interest in maximizing tax revenue, the bourgeoisie in maximizing profits. How the state further uses its revenues does not concern us here. The substantive goals of the state can range from enriching the bureaucracy to promoting cultural expansion, imperialism or social welfare. The fact that such activities are pursued by the state operating in a capitalist society does not prove that they are "really" in the interest of capital. Even if it is in the interest of capital to have a state with sufficient autonomy to pursue *some* such goals, the specific goals being pursued need not reflect that interest.

We saw above that if we only consider the short-term economic constraint which the state faces – the need to keep alive the goose that lays the golden eggs – the government may have wide-ranging freedom to impose its interests on the capitalist class. These are not, however, the only relevant considerations. The goose should not just be kept alive: it should be healthy and thriving. The state has an interest in future tax revenue, not just in current income from taxation. If it maximizes income from taxes in the short run, there will be less left over for capitalist profit, investment and the creation of future taxable income. The state as well as the capitalist class can be the victim of myopia.

There is, furthermore, a political constraint. If the state imposes a very high tax rate, which is optimal from the point of view of tax revenue, the capitalists might not sit still and take it. They have the resources and the motivation to overthrow the government if their interests are not sufficiently respected. Although the presence of a potentially dangerous working class may make them pull their punches for a while, they will not do so indefinitely. Knowing this, a rational government might not want to impose the tax rate which maximizes tax revenue. The binding constraint may be the political rather than the economic one. Fear for loss of power in the short run may accomplish what fear for loss of income in the long run does not.

A distinction can be made between states according to whether the economic or the political constraint is the binding one. Broadly speaking, the political constraint seems to have been binding in most precapitalist societies and remains so in many developing countries today. Before the government approaches the tax level at which further tax increases would be self-defeating, it encounters the organized political opposition of the taxable classes. By contrast, I conjecture that in mid-nineteenth-century England the economic constraint was the binding one. Out of a self-interested concern for tax revenue the government kept well within the bounds of what the capitalist class could accept. In part, this may have been so because the English government, to a higher extent than most precapitalist states, was moved by *long-term* self-interest and hence abstained from confiscatory measures that would have a negative impact on long-term growth.

Clearly, Marx underestimated the complexity of the situation he was discussing. The view that the English, French and German governments had power simply as a fief from capital cannot be upheld. The basic flaw in Marx's analyses derives from a limited view of what constitutes a political resource. On his conception, power grows out of the end of a gun – or, more generally, out of money and manpower. Yet the power base of a political actor can also be his place in a web of strategic relationships. The capitalists' fear of the working class, for instance, gives a lever to the aristocratic government that has little to do with the physical resources which it actually has at its disposal. Similarly, incumbent officeholders have an edge on their rivals which, again, does not derive from any prepolitical power base. Related phenomena in other domains are the general advantage of the defense over the offense in military matters, and the disproportionate power that may accrue to a political party that happens to be in a pivotal position between the two major political blocs.

Marx argued that the presence of an autonomous, non-capitalist state could be explained by the structure of capitalist class interests. It is not clear that he was right. It is at least as plausible to explain the political abstention or abdication of the capitalists in terms of their individual interests. Even if he was right, however, it does not follow that the autonomous policy decisions of the state can also be explained by these interests, or that the autonomy was an illusory one. A state which can consistently impose policies very different from those that capitalists would prefer and promote interests very different from theirs is a paradigm of autonomy. It does not become less so by the fact that the capitalist class may prefer this state over any feasible alternative.

III. The revolutionary transition to capitalism

Marx never wrote extensively about precapitalist politics. His views on the absolutist state and on the classical bourgeois revolutions must be reconstructed from a large number of brief texts, scattered around in his writings. The conception that emerges is surprisingly un-Marxist, in the sense that politics appears as anything but derivative. The decisive force in the shaping of modern history was not capitalism, but the strong nation-states that emerged in the sixteenth and seventeenth centuries. For them, "plenty" was a means to "power" and subservient to power. The bourgeois revolutions of 1648 and 1789 brought the capitalists towards power, but not all the way to power. Their rise was arrested, for the reasons set out above, and the state once again became a dominant, independent actor.

Unlike some recent Marxist historians, Marx did not argue that absolute monarchy was the political superstructure over feudalism. Perry Anderson writes, for example, that it was a "feudal monarchy" whose seeming "distance from the class from which it was recruited and whose interests it served" was in fact "the condition for its efficacy as a state".[23] This amounts to saying that absolute monarchy was for the feudal aristocracy what in Marx's view the Bonapartist state was for the bourgeoisie – a tool, but at one remove. Marx did not, however, apply his theory of indirect class representation to the absolutist state. He argued that absolute monarchy was a competitor to the aristocracy and the bourgeoisie, not a tool, however indirectly, of either. In *The German Ideology* he refers to the period of absolutism as one in which "royal power, aristocracy and bourgeoisie are contending for domination and where, therefore, domination is shared".[24] Elsewhere he suggests that the winner in this contest for the power was the state, at least in the early modern period. By mediating between the classes and playing them off against each other, the state could prevent either from getting the upper hand.

In *The German Ideology* Marx also asserts, without much argument, that the independence of the absolutist state was transitory and illusory. In later writings this view is spelled out in a more interesting way. Here he suggests that the independence of the state is self-defeating, since it cannot promote its interest without also strengthening one of its rivals, the bourgeoisie.[25] The state does not stand in the same relation to the bourgeoisie as it does to the feudal nobility. The state and the nobility compete over the division of a given surplus, created by the exploited peasantry. The state can only gain by reducing the power of the nobility. By contrast, the state will hurt its own economic interests if it interferes too much with the bourgeoisie, which is creating the "plenty" which the state needs to promote its "power". Up to a point the state will, out of its self-interest, further the interests of the bourgeoisie. By promoting the

---

[23] P. Anderson, *Lineages of the Absolutist State* (London: New Left Books, 1974), pp. 18, 108.
[24] *The German Ideology*, p. 59; see also pp. 90, 195.
[25] *Deutsche Brüsseler Zeitung*, 18 November 1847.

mobility of capital, labor and goods and by creating a unified system of money, weights and measures, the state allows the bourgeoisie to fill their own coffers as well as those of the state. The creation of competition and of a national market was not the quasi-automatic effect of foreign trade, as Marx suggests elsewhere.[26] It required very deliberate state intervention against the numerous feudal barriers to mobility. Unlike the state in the Asiatic mode of production, the absolutist state actively reshapes the pattern of economic activities. Where it does not, as in Spain, Marx suggests that it is in fact to be ranged with Asiatic rather than European forms of government.

Beyond a certain point, this dependence on the bourgeoisie creates a dilemma for the state. If the state continues to encourage trade and industry, it will create a formidable internal rival. If it tries to hamper the bourgeoisie, it will reduce the economic and hence the military strength of the country, thereby laying it open to foreign rivals. "If . . . growth is destabilizing, so is no growth, when a political–economic unit exists in a world of competing political–economic units."[27] (Marx does not actually make the last argument. The international dimension of absolutist policies is a major lacuna in his writings on the topic.) It would look, therefore, as if the state is in a fix: damned if it does and damned if it doesn't. What is strength with respect to the internal enemy is weakness with respect to the external, and vice versa. A balance may be found, but not easily. In particular, the attempts by many absolutist rulers to encourage industrialization without a general modernization of society have not been successful.[28] Usually, they have got the worst of both worlds, not, as they hoped, the best of both. The equilibrium can be stabilized only by the emergence of an enemy of the internal enemy – by the rise of the working class that drives the bourgeoisie to ally itself with its former opponent against the new one.

What is the role, in this general picture, of the classical bourgeois revolutions? Almost all Marx has to say about the English Revolution of 1640–88 is contained in a book review of Guizot's *Discours sur l'Histoire de la Révolution d'Angleterre*, which also offers a few comparisons with the French Revolution of 1789.[29] His numerous remarks on the French Revolution are all very brief, except for a slightly more extended discussion in *The Holy Family*. Although the main characters and events of the

---

[26] *Grundrisse*, p. 256.
[27] D. North, *Structure and Change in Economic History* (New York: Norton, 1981), p. 29.
[28] For a brilliant analysis of such policies (and their failures) in China, see J. Levenson, *Confucian China and its Modern Fate* (Berkeley: University of California Press, 1968). For the Russian version of the same problem, see B. Knei-Paz, *The Social and Political Thought of Leon Trotsky* (Oxford: Clarendon Press, 1977).
[29] CW 10, pp. 251ff.

French Revolution were part of his mental universe and shaped the categories through which he interpreted current events, he never subjected it to a systematic analysis.

The two classical bourgeois revolutions had some features in common. They were transitions from absolute to constitutional monarchy, with a republican interlude. It would be misleading to focus on the transition from absolutism to republic as *the* revolution, since it is only the first stage in a process whose overall pattern is "Two steps forward, one step backward". In both revolutions this republican phase was accompanied by the formation of communist movements, which – following the revolutionary logic of going to extremes – wanted to take a third step forward. Marx suggests that the events of 1794, which he construed as a premature bid for power by the French proletariat, was part and parcel of the bourgeois revolution. There was a need to make a clean sweep of the past before the bourgeois order could be constructed. This historical task was, unbeknownst to themselves, performed by the workers.[30] As usual, Marx could not resist the temptation to find a *meaning* in these aborted attempts.

The main difference between the two revolutions concerns the structure of the alliances that carried them out. "In 1648 the bourgeoisie was allied with the modern aristocracy against the monarchy, the feudal aristocracy and the established church. In 1789 the bourgeoisie was allied with the people against the monarchy, the aristocracy and the established church."[31] Specifically, Marx suggests that the English Revolution was carried out by an alliance of the bourgeoisie and the big landowners. The latter provided the former with the labor force they needed to operate their factories, while also benefiting from the general economic development which the bourgeoisie set in motion. The suggestion of a divided gentry appears to lack empirical support,[32] and in any case the argument as a whole is a piece of blatantly anachronistic teleological thinking. In 1640 there were no actual or anticipated factories in need of workers. Also, Marx's characterization of the coalition structure behind the French Revolution does not appear to stand up in the light of later research. French landed property was probably more integrated with bourgeois property than Marx thought.[33]

Marx, however, thought that the explanation of the revolutions could be found in their achievements rather than in their causes. In an extravagantly teleological remark, he writes that the bourgeois revolutions

[30] *Deutsche Brüsseler Zeitung*, 11 November 1847; *Neue Rheinische Zeitung*, 15 December 1848.
[31] *Neue Rheinische Zeitung*, 15 December 1848.
[32] L. Stone, *The Causes of the English Revolution* (London: Routledge and Kegan Paul, 1972), p. 56.
[33] F. Furet, *Penser la Révolution Française* (Paris: Gallimard, 1978), pp. 137ff.

"reflected the needs of the world at that time rather than the needs of those parts of the world where they occurred, that is England and France".[34] The "needs of the world" amounted, essentially, to the abolition of feudal privilege and the creation of a regime of free competition. Whatever the revolutionaries may have thought they were doing, this is what they achieved.

This argument, however, presents a puzzle. On the one hand Marx insisted on the progressive function of the absolute monarchies in creating a national market and abolishing barriers to competition. On the other hand, we now find him saying that these were the achievements of bourgeois revolutions directed against these very monarchies. The puzzle can be resolved by recalling the self-defeating character of absolutism. On the one hand the absolutist state finds that it is in its interest as an autonomous agent to strengthen industry and hence the bourgeoisie. On the other hand, the protection of the material power of the bourgeoisie also tends to generate its political power and hence to threaten the autonomy of the state. The state, therefore, will be somewhat halfhearted in its defense of the bourgeois interests, trying, perhaps, to achieve industrialization without all the concomitant social and political reforms. At some point the state will want to stop further liberalization. At that point, however, the bourgeoisie may already be too strong to be stopped. If so, the bourgeois revolution will occur to complete the process begun by the absolute monarchy.

Although a rational absolutist ruler might want to stop the process just before the bourgeoisie gathers the strength needed for a revolution, he is not likely to succeed in doing so, for three reasons. First, although we can, with the benefit of hindsight, perceive the internal tensions in the absolutist state, it is not clear that the absolutist rulers themselves were in a position to do so. Secondly, the need to fortify the country against external enemies may in any case have been more pressing. Thirdly, depriving the bourgeoisie of the means to take political power would also deprive them of much of their economic usefulness. The only thing that will keep an economically vigorous bourgeoisie away from power is lack of motivation to take it.

Marx's analyses of the German Revolution of 1848–9 can also be read in this perspective. In the initial stage of the revolution he appears to have believed that the pattern of the French Revolution would largely be reproduced. The alliance structure would be the same, except that the workers would play a more active part than merely carrying out the dirty work of the bourgeoisie, to be repressed as soon as their historical mission was fulfilled. Also, when the revolution made slower progress than

[34] *Neue Rheinische Zeitung*, 15 December 1848.

expected, Marx put his trust in a repeat of the counter-revolutionary wars of the French Revolution. Russia would intervene against Germany and ignite the revolutionary struggle.

Gradually, however, it dawned upon Marx that his adversaries could read the situation as well as he. If *he* could perceive that a bourgeois regime would set up conditions which, further down the road, would undermine it, a rational bourgeoisie, reading the same signs, would keep away from power. If *he* could anticipate that Russian intervention would unleash the forces of revolution, a rational tsar would remain passive. If *he* could learn from history, so could his adversaries. Marx sinned against a main rule of political rationality: never make your plans strongly dependent on the assumption that the adversary is less than fully rational. (Since he tended to emphasize teleology rather than rationality, he rarely sinned against another: never make your plans strongly dependent on the assumption that the adversary is fully rational.) Later Communist leaders have been victims of the same hubris, most notably in the sequence of events that led up to the Shanghai massacre of Chinese Communists in 1927. Although the C.C.P. (or the Comintern) believed they could ally themselves with Chiang Kai-shek for a while and discard him when his usefulness was exhausted, the manipulators ended up as the manipulated.

IV. The revolutionary transition to communism

There are two central questions which ought to be faced by any theory of the communist revolution.[35] First, under which conditions would a rational working class want to undertake a revolution? Secondly, how could a rational capitalist class or a rational government allow these conditions to arise? Failing plausible answers to these questions, a theory of revolution must invoke political irrationality on the part of workers, capitalists or government. Marx, to be sure, did not state the problem in these terms. Since, nevertheless, they seem to correspond to the reality of the situation, we must see whether his views can be restated within a framework of this type.

It follows from the central propositions of historical materialism that the communist revolution will occur *when* and *because* communist relations of production become optimal for the development of the productive forces. Let us first see whether this view can be defended, and then examine the weaker versions that arise if we drop the causal or the chronological parts of the claim.

Marx argued that under capitalism the productive forces develop at an

---

[35] On these questions see also John Roemer's contribution to this volume.

ever faster rate. Yet at some level of their development communist relations of production will allow for an even higher rate of their further progress. Hence the communist revolution will not be caused by technical stagnation, but by the prospect of an unprecedented technical expansion. The idea that communism will bypass capitalism with respect to the rate of innovation is itself highly implausible, but that is not our concern here. Rather we must ask if this prospect can plausibly motivate the workers to carry out a revolution.

Rational workers might, in the first place, be subject to a free-rider temptation that would block the efficacy of the motivation. Even if we assume that workers are able to act collectively to promote their common interests, a rational working class would still, in the second place, take account of the costs of transition and, moreover, be subject to some degree of myopia and risk-aversion.[36] It is not reasonable to expect workers to sacrifice what they have – a dynamic, efficient capitalism – for the sake of a remote and uncertain possibility of a system that will perform even better. Having much more to lose than their chains, they will be reluctant to throw them off.

A first retreat from this highly implausible view is to drop the causal implication of historical materialism while retaining the chronological one. On this view, what will motivate the workers to revolution is not the esoteric thought-experiment just sketched. Rather, they will be driven to revolt because of directly observable features of capitalism: alienation, exploitation, waste, inefficiency, trade cycles. It just so happens that the time at which these ills become so grave as to create the subjective conditions for a communist revolution is also the time at which communism becomes objectively superior as a framework for developing the productive forces. The communist revolution occurs when, but not because, capitalism becomes a brake on further technical progress.

This view, too, is implausible. In Leon Trotsky's words, "societies are not so rational in building that the dates for proletarian dictatorship arrive exactly at that time when the economic and cultural conditions are ripe for socialism".[37] Indeed, Trotsky's own work supports a stronger statement. Societies are systematically so irrational in building that the objective conditions for communism and the subjective conditions for a communist revolution never coincide. Theory suggests and experience confirms that communist revolutions will only take place in backward countries that are nowhere near the stage of development at which they could overtake capitalism. Russia around the turn of the century was a breeding-ground

---

[36] See also A. Przeworski, *Capitalism and Social Democracy* (Cambridge: Cambridge University Press, 1985), chapter 5.
[37] L. Trotsky, *A History of the Russian Revolution* (London: Pluto Press, 1977), p. 334.

for revolution because her backwardness created the proper economic and ideological conditions. Being a latecomer to economic development, Russian factories were free to employ techniques of large-scale production, requiring huge numbers of workers. Such concentration facilitates class consciousness, which is further helped by the absence of a reformist tradition and the possibility of drawing on the stock of advanced socialist ideas developed in the West.[38]

For Marx's argument to be plausible, the ruling classes would have to be somewhat irrational. Since the development of the productive forces creates the material conditions for a general improvement in the standard of living, including protection against unemployment, he must assume that capitalists or government fail to deploy these means to pre-empt a communist revolution. Or, at the very least, he must assume that they deploy them irrationally and inefficiently, by combining stick and carrot in a way that only incites the revolutionary energy of the workers. Revolution is more likely to occur in a society where the level of development has not reached the stage where widespread concessions to the workers are affordable – but at that stage a communist revolution will also be premature, as far as the ability to develop the productive forces is concerned. These problems were at the root of the controversy between Mensheviks and Bolsheviks in the Russian socialist movement. The former wanted the workers to pull their punches in the struggle with the capitalists, so that capitalism could have the time to reach the stage at which a viable communism could be introduced. The latter argued, more realistically, that by postponing the revolution one would take it off the agenda for good.

Most of the time Marx seems to have assumed that the first communist revolution will occur in the most advanced capitalist country. In some writings, however, he anticipated Trotsky's "theory of combined and uneven development" according to which the center–periphery dimension of capitalism is crucial for the possibility of revolution. In *The Class Struggles in France* he wrote that although England is the "demiurge of the bourgeois cosmos" and the ultimate cause of capitalist crises, revolutions first occur on the European Continent. "Violent outbreaks must naturally occur rather in the extremities of the bourgeois body than in its heart."[39] Some thirty years later he suggested, in correspondence with Russian socialists, that Russia might enjoy "advantages of backwardness" that would allow it to bypass the capitalist stage and go directly on to communism.

[38] Trotsky, *A History of the Russian Revolution*, p. 33; also Knei-Paz, *Social and Political Thought*.
[39] *The Class Struggles in France*, CW 10, p. 134.

This argument suggests that the subjective and the objective conditions for communism will be developed in different parts of the capitalist world system. The objective conditions emerge in the advanced capitalist countries, the subjective ones in the backward nations. How could the two sets of conditions be brought together? Around 1850 Marx argued, as did Trotsky after him, that revolution, once it had occurred in the capitalist periphery, would spread to the center. Again he put his hope in counter-revolutionary intervention as the mechanism that would ignite the general revolutionary conflagration; again he failed to see that a rational capitalist government would, for that very reason, abstain from intervening. Thirty years later he emphasized the diffusion of technology from West to East, rather than the diffusion of revolution in the opposite direction. This argument also fails, however, since it is much more difficult to borrow technology than Marx thought. The use of advanced industrial technology requires education and mental habits which cannot themselves be borrowed.

We must conclude, therefore, that Marx's theory of the communist revolution assumes that workers, capitalists or governments of capitalist nations must behave irrationally. Since he did not provide any arguments for this assumption, his theory fails. The point is not that events could not conceivably develop according to one of these scenarios. Irrational behavior can be an extremely powerful political force. Rather, the point is that Marx provided no rational grounds for thinking that events would develop as he hoped. His scenarios were, essentially, based on wishful thinking, not on social analysis.

V. Conclusions and some extensions

Marx's writings on nineteenth-century European politics have limited applicability today. Even regimes at comparable levels of economic development are not really comparable. In the world-economic context they are relatively backward, whereas the countries Marx studied were in the forefront of economic development. The events which have taken place since Marx's time include an explosive economic and technical development, the rise and fall of colonialism, the rise of totalitarian ideologies and regimes, the rise of the welfare state, the rise of the middle classes, the rise of managerial capitalism, the rise of the Third World, and increased international mobility of capital and labor. Also, workers in the capitalist countries have to come to grips with the massive fact that so far communism has not been introduced from below in any advanced industrial country. Clearly, any mechanical application of Marx's theories, even when cleansed of teleology, is unthinkable.

The case has been made, nevertheless, for a close analogy between the Bonapartist state as analyzed by Marx and twentieth-century fascism.[40] The peculiarity of Bonapartism, according to Marx, was that it had both a manifest and a latent class basis. The manifest or active class support came from the peasantry, which, unable to organize and represent itself, had to be represented from above. The latent or permissive support came from the capitalist class, which perceived that a non-capitalist state was in their interest at this particular stage. Similarly, the argument goes, fascism enjoyed the active support of the petty bourgeoisie and the tacit support of the bourgeoisie.   At first glance, the analogy seems more plausible than the original. In Germany around 1930 there existed what was conspicuously lacking in France around 1850: a numerically strong industrial proletariat. Hence it would seem to make sense for the bourgeoisie to leave power to a strong independent state in order to avoid confrontations with the workers. At second glance, it is just as implausible, although for the opposite reason. The fascist state arose against the background of an actual class struggle between a well-organized working class and the capitalist class: it was not a pre-emptive strike to forestall class struggle. Bonapartist theories of the state have maximal plausibility when the numerical and organizational strength of the workers is at an intermediate level – greater than in France around 1850 and smaller than in Germany around 1930. The rise of Bismarck's *Sozialstaat* probably offers a better example. A strong working class must be accommodated or repressed; a weak working class can be ignored; a moderately strong working class can be thrown off balance by pre-emptive concessions.

More convoluted arguments have been proposed by writers like Hirsch, Poulantzas and O'Connor to show that modern democracies and welfare states essentially conform to Marx's analyses.[41] The common idea is that the apparent independence of the state from capital masks a deeper dependence, and in fact is a condition for the latter, since "too intimate a relation between capital and state normally is unacceptable or inadmissible to the ordinary person".[42] The view ignores the possibility of a simpler explanation: state and capital appear as independent from each other because they are independent from each other, in the sense of having different substantive goals. Needless to say, this does not exclude that in another sense they are mutually dependent on each other, since they are involved in a game of mixed conflict and cooperation. Each party, to

---

[40] See notably A. Thalheimer, "Über den Faschismus" (1930), reprinted in W. Abendroth (ed.), *Faschismus und Kapitalismus* (Frankfurt a.M.: Europäische Verlagsanstalt, 1970).

[41] J. O'Connor, *The Fiscal Crisis of the State* (New York: St Martin's Press, 1973), pp. 69–70; J. Hirsch, *Staatsapparat und Reproduktion des Kapitals* (Frankfurt a.M.: Suhrkamp, 1974), p. 54; N. Poulantzas, *Pouvoir Politique et Classes Sociales* (Paris: Maspero, 1968), p. 310.

[42] O'Connor, *The Fiscal Crisis of the State*, p. 69.

realize its interest, must ensure that the other can do so as well, at least to some minimal extent.

Instead of lingering over the autopsy of the classical Marxian theory of the state, let us consider what a reconstructed theory might look like. We can no longer apply a model in which the main social actors are, first, an active government; secondly, a capitalist class in self-imposed political passivity; and thirdly, a working class whose passivity is imposed by others, through repressive or pre-emptive measures. In Western capitalist countries both capitalists and workers are organized, politically no less than economically. In the economic arena this gives rise to a three-person non-cooperative game between Government, Capital and Labor. The government can choose the tax rate and the tax relief rate on investment; the capitalist can choose the rate of reinvestment out of profit; and the workers can choose a particular rate of militancy which translates into a particular wage rate as proportion of the net product.[43] Or, alternatively, the problem may be seen as a nested or hierarchical principal–agent problem, with Capital being both the agent of Government and the principal of Labor.

In the political arena, the main change since Marx is the introduction of universal suffrage, which substitutes a different kind of political constraint for the one Marx had in mind. Contemporary governments in advanced capitalist societies do not fear that workers or capitalists will make a revolution if their interests are not sufficiently respected: they simply fear that they will be voted out of power. Any government that wants to be re-elected must to some extent accommodate the interests of the major classes. Although the capitalist class is numerically small, their voting power is strengthened by large numbers of upwardly mobile voters who, by anticipatory socialization, share their values. Moreover, they use their superior economic resources to support candidates who on past performance can be expected to favor their interests.

It remains an open question how much scope for autonomous action is left for the state after the operation of these constraints. The sheer complexity of the strategic interactions, of which I have only mentioned the most salient ones, together with the lack of consensus over macro-economic theory, tends in any case to reduce the interest of the problem. The situation is characterized, minimally, by the presence of three strategic actors, interacting in two interlocking arenas, in a doubly time-dependent way,[44] with very imperfect knowledge about what out-

---

[43] Przeworski, *Capitalism and Social Democracy.*

[44] Present decisions have consequences for future payoffs to the agents, via the impact on investment; in addition, in any iterated game among the same agents present choices influence later choices.

comes will follow from any given set of values of the control variables at the agents' disposal. It is, in other words, a situation in which rational-choice theory has little power to tell us what the actors will do.[45] Marx faced a much simpler problem. In the mid-nineteenth century there was essentially only one actor capable of full-blown strategic behaviour, since workers and capitalists remained largely passive. Moreover, there was essentially only one arena that mattered, if I am right in thinking the economic constraint to have been the binding one. Under such conditions, which to some extent prevail in the developing countries today, strategic analysis can help us assess the scope for autonomous state action and the conditions under which revolution becomes a rational option. In advanced capitalist democracies we might do better to turn to Keynes, and explain the overall strategies of Government, Capital and Labor by their animal spirits.

[45] For a discussion of the conditions under which rational-choice theory has little prescriptive or explanatory power, see my editorial introduction to *Rational Choice* (Oxford: Blackwell, 1986).

7 Rationalizing revolutionary ideology: a tale of Lenin and the Tsar

*John E. Roemer**

Introduction

Revolutions have been thought of by social scientists, for the most part, as inexplicable or irrational events, events exogenous to the jurisdiction of the models we build to explain economic and social behavior. (Historians, being less enamoured of models, have placed revolutions more centrally in the purview of their discipline.) The hurdle for economists and political scientists in explaining revolutions is the collective action problem: why should any individual join a revolutionary movement, when the costs to him of participation are potentially very high, and the benefits, if the revolution succeeds, will be enjoyed by him even without his participation? Rosa Luxemburg was not unaware of the problem of explaining mass action (she wrote on the psychology of the mass strike); in modern jargon, she could be translated as saying that in certain situations, the preference structure of the Prisoner's Dilemma game does not characterize the way people think about participating or not participating in the mass movement – they have, instead, what are called "assurance game" preferences, in which each person derives more utility from participating if others do than from defecting or scabbing if others participate. Saying this does not make it so, and we must ask: what explains the switch in preferences from those which characterize the "individualistic" Prisoner's Dilemma, to those of the "cooperative" assurance game, facilitating the possibility of mass action?

In this chapter, I sidestep this central question. Too often, I think, in economics we fail to study phenomena because they do not make sense given our way of thinking about things. Or, worse, we deny that a phenomenon exists because we cannot explain it. The attitude of many economists towards mass unemployment is such a casualty of our scientific method. And while no one denies the existence of revolutions, they tend not to be studied because our models of individual behavior are

* I am grateful to Roger Howe and Karl Vind for invaluable mathematical discussion on this topic.

not convenient for explaining them. It is not a big step to conclude, as a consequence of this failure of theory, that revolutions are aberrations, or exogenous, like earthquakes. I have avoided calling upon the *deus ex machina* of "paradigm myopia" to explain the non-study of revolutions, because I do not wish to suggest that the "other" so-called paradigm, Marxism, has all the answers regarding them. Certainly for Marxism revolution occupies a central place, but I do not think Marxists have answered very well the important questions of collective action and revolutionary dynamics.

I choose to sidestep the question of collective action because there are many other aspects of revolutions that are important to study, aspects which can be discussed while holding in abeyance the microfoundations of collective action. In particular, I am interested in what one might call revolutionary ideology. Ideology is usually conceived of as an irrational or unfounded commitment which a person has to a set of ideas. One might think of an ideology as affecting the utility function of the agent; but I propose here to conceive of an ideology as a self-imposed limitation placed on one's feasible set. An agent has a set of possible strategies in a situation; ideology causes him to rule out a certain portion of that set as beyond the pale, perhaps for ethical reasons. An important question is: can we explain why people have the ideologies they do?

We frequently attribute certain actions of actors in revolutionary situations to their ideologies. Here are two examples. Think of a revolution as a competition between the present ruler (whom I shall call the Tsar), and a revolutionary entrepreneur, whose name is Lenin. Lenin and the Tsar are competing for support of coalitions of the population, in a way which will become precise below. Frequently, in such situations, we observe that the Tsar imposes very harsh penalties on the poor for participating in revolutionary activity, and somewhat lighter penalties on the more well-to-do who have abandoned their comfortable stations in life and joined Lenin. (An example is provided by the elections in El Salvador several years ago: non-participation was viewed, by the regime in power, as a kind of revolutionary protest. The severity of the penalties imposed for not voting was inversely proportional to wealth. The poorest people who did not vote were beaten up and lost their jobs, while middle-class people were censured in some fairly innocuous way.) This behavior of the ruler might be viewed as ideologically (in the sense of irrationally) motivated: he hates the poor and feels more friendly to the rich. The second example: Lenin, in trying to overthrow the Tsar, usually proposes a progressive redistribution of income: he promises to take from the rich and give to the poor. This behavior is viewed as the consequence of Lenin's egalitarian ideology.

I would like to provide rational foundations for these ideologies. For instance, I will show that if Lenin wants to overthrow the Tsar – by *any* means necessary – it will be in his interest to adopt a progressive redistribution of income. And if the Tsar wants to preserve the present regime against Lenin's onslaught, his best strategy will entail assigning penalties for revolutionary participation which are inversely proportional in severity to the income of the participants. My purpose is twofold: (1) to encourage social scientists to think of revolutions as events which are amenable to rational analysis, and (2) to make the same point, more generally, about ideology: that we should not rule out of court certain kinds of behavior as ideological, but seek to explain the evolution of ideology using rational choice models.

Although the work described is quite technical, I will try to avoid most mathematical detail, and will concentrate on the general lessons from this tale of Lenin and the Tsar. The interested reader can get the full story elsewhere.[1]

Revolution as a two person game

My stylized view of revolution, for the purpose of studying the ideology reflected in revolutionary strategy, is as a two person game between the ruler Tsar and the revolutionary entrepreneur Lenin. The population enter only passively, as its members form coalitions whose support Lenin and the Tsar are vying for. This is the appropriate set-up for the questions I pose, because the strategies which Lenin and the Tsar will choose in their contest reflect what one can call revolutionary and reactionary ideology, respectively. Think of the current regime as an income distribution $z = (z_1, \ldots, z_n)$ among a population of size n. In his attempt to overthrow the Tsar, Lenin can propose redistribution of the fixed pie of income. Thus Lenin's *strategies* consist of the set of all possible redistributions $y = \{(y_1, \ldots, y_n) \mid \Sigma y_i = \Sigma z_i, y_i \geq 0\}$. People will join Lenin if they stand to gain in the new distribution. The Tsar wishes to deter people from joining Lenin. To this end, he announces a list of *penalties* $d = (d_1, \ldots, d_n)$ which define what each agent who chooses to join Lenin will forfeit, should the revolutionary attempt fail. A person's penalty can be no less than zero and no greater than his income. Thus the domain of feasible penalties is $D = \{(d_1, \ldots, d_n) \mid 0 \leq d_i \leq z_i\}$.

The essential element in the contest between these two is a stochastic one: each possible coalition S of the population has only a probability of succeeding in making the revolution, conditional upon its deciding to

[1] John E. Roemer, "Rationalizing Revolutionary Ideology", *Econometrica*, 53 (January 1985), 84–108.

form and fight. For the moment, call this probability p_S. Suppose the Tsar has announced penalties $\mathbf{d} = (d_1, \ldots, d_n)$, and Lenin has announced the promised income redistribution $\mathbf{y} = (y_1, \ldots, y_n)$. What coalitions are likely to form to try and fight for this revolution? Take a coalition S. I propose to call S *formable* for the pair of strategies $(\mathbf{d}, \mathbf{y})$ if the expected income of every member of the coalition exceeds his present income, that is:

$$\text{for all members } i \text{ of } S, \quad p_S y_i + (1 - p_S)(z_i - d_i) > z_i \tag{1}$$

This model, however, is not sufficiently rich to present the Tsar with any strategic problem: for it will be in his interest to announce the highest possible penalties, to set penalties equal to income for everyone. That would dissuade people from joining Lenin, and there would be no cost to the Tsar. And so I introduce this complication: each coalition has a *probability function* $p_S(d_1, \ldots, d_n)$, where the probability of the coalition's succeeding in revolution is a non-decreasing function of the penalties announced against the population. I will motivate this assumption shortly; for the moment, simply observe that now the Tsar faces a strategic problem, for there is a trade-off in raising penalties. On the one hand, raising penalties makes it more costly for an individual to join Lenin, but, on the other hand, raising penalties increases the probabilities of a coalition's succeeding, and so the Tsar might defeat his own purpose by proposing too high a penalty structure.

Indeed, I will need for most of this analysis only three assumptions, which embody revolutionary behavior in the properties of the probability functions:

Coalition Monotonicity: If coalition S contains T, then for any given penalty vector $\mathbf{d}$, $p_S(\mathbf{d}) \geq p_T(\mathbf{d})$.

Penalty Monotonicity[2]: For any given coalition S, if $\mathbf{d'} \geq \mathbf{d}$, then $p_S(\mathbf{d'}) \geq p_S(\mathbf{d})$.

Lean and Hungry: Let S be a coalition not containing two agents i and j, and suppose $z_i \leq z_j$. Then $p_{S \cup i}(\mathbf{d}) \geq p_{S \cup j}(\mathbf{d})$. That is, adding a poor person to a coalition raises the probability of its revolutionary success at least as much as adding a richer person does.

Coalition Monotonicity need hardly be motivated. Revolutionary potential increases as the coalition adds new members. Penalty Monotonicity is more controversial; I mean it to reflect the *psychology of tyranny*. The probability of a coalition's succeeding in revolution, should it form, is in part the degree to which the Tsar is perceived as a tyrant. My postulate is that his degree of tyranny is perceived to increase as penalties are increased, since incomes z_i are constant. Penalty Monotonicity states that the conditional probabilities of revolution do not decrease, and perhaps

---

[2] For vector orderings, $\mathbf{d'} \geq \mathbf{d}$ means $\mathbf{d'_i} \geq \mathbf{d_i}$ for all components j.

increase, as penalties are raised. Perhaps people in the coalition fight harder, perceiving the Tsar as more tyrannical; perhaps they receive more support from those sitting on the sidelines who do not join the revolution, but would stand to gain if the revolution wins (remember the phrase about a guerilla being a fish in a sea of supporting peasantry). The third assumption, Lean and Hungry, states something about what characterizes revolutionary psychology in this model: the poorer people are, the harder they fight. Now one might like to make precisely the opposite assumption, that the financial resources of a coalition have a *positive* effect on its probability of success. Frankly, Lean and Hungry is what Imre Lakatos calls a proof-generated assumption: it is needed to derive interesting results; and I do think it describes an interesting and perhaps very large class of revolutionary situations. Note that Lean and Hungry is a weaker assumption than Symmetry, which says:

Symmetry: For any $\mathbf{d}$, the probability of revolution depends only on the size of the revolutionary coalition. $p_S(\mathbf{d}) = p_T(\mathbf{d})$ if $|S| = |T|$.

Symmetry means revolutionary power is characterized by "one revolutionary, one gun"; all that counts is size. Since Lean and Hungry is implied by Symmetry, all of the results in this model hold if we wish to assume that each revolutionary brings one gun to the revolution, and revolutionary power flows out of the proverbial barrels.

The first fact is: for any pair of strategies $(\mathbf{d}, \mathbf{y})$ proposed by the Tsar and Lenin, there is a unique maximal formable coalition. This is a coalition that is willing to form, according to the expected income calculations, given by (1), and it includes as a sub-coalition every other formable coalition. Hence, it has the largest probability of success at this pair of strategies. Call this the *maximal formable coalition* at the strategy pair $(\mathbf{d}, \mathbf{y})$. Now Lenin's strategic and *non-ideological* behavior is this: facing a given penalty list $\mathbf{d}$ from the Tsar, he proposes that income distribution $\mathbf{y}$ which maximizes the probability of success of the associated maximal formable coalition. Lenin only wants to overthrow the Tsar, he has no other precommitments with respect to income distribution – in that sense he is non-ideological concerning income distribution. The Tsar, knowing Lenin will behave this way, proposes that penalty vector $\mathbf{d}$ which minimizes the probability of revolution when Lenin acts optimally. Thus, for a given pair of strategies $(\mathbf{d}, \mathbf{y})$, let $\mu(\mathbf{d}, \mathbf{y})$ be the probability that the maximal formable coalition at those strategies succeeds. For any $\mathbf{d}$, Lenin chooses $\mathbf{y}$ to

$$\max_{\mathbf{y}} \mu(\mathbf{d}, \mathbf{y})$$

and hence the Tsar, knowing this, chooses $\mathbf{d}$ to

$$\min_{\mathbf{d}} \max_{\mathbf{y}} \mu(\mathbf{d}, \mathbf{y}).$$

The solution to this min-max problem is a certain optimal penalty list $\mathbf{d}^*$ proposed by the Tsar, an optimal income distribution $\mathbf{y}^*$ proposed by Lenin, and an associated revolutionary coalition S^* which forms as the maximally probable coalition at those strategies. $\mu(\mathbf{d}^*, \mathbf{y}^*)$ is called the *instability of the regime*. It is the probability of revolution when both revolutionary actors act optimally. My problem is now to describe the properties of these three objects, $\mathbf{d}^*$, $\mathbf{y}^*$, and S^*, given the assumptions on revolutionary behavior embodied in the probability functions.

Before proceeding, a note is required on where the problem of mass action has been ignored. The critical assumption was that Lenin can succeed in recruiting to the revolution any coalition all of whose members stand to gain, according to inequality (1). But an individual in such a coalition might reason: granted, I expect to gain by sticking in this coalition, but if I drop out and all the others fight, I stand to gain much more. For I will get the same income Lenin has promised me whether or not I fight and I do not take the risk of paying the penalty if the revolution fails. With this reasoning revolutionary coalitions will unravel. There are several possible resolutions to this revolutionary Prisoner's Dilemma problem. I think the most realistic one is to ignore it in this informed way: Lenin's job is to overcome the Prisoner's Dilemma psychology, to convince members of coalitions that if they think in this way, then the project will fail, and they will all be worse off. So I recognize the problem of mass action, I do not wish to study it here, and I endow Lenin with a charisma which enables him to convince people to behave cooperatively, so long as that action is at least in the self-interest of each in the sense of increasing each one's expected income, as inequality (1) stipulates.

Tyranny does not pay

The first question one must ask of this model is whether a solution pair of optimal strategies always exists. This turns out not to be *pro forma*; first of all, the payoff function $\mu(\mathbf{d}, \mathbf{y})$ which gives the probability of revolution is discontinuous in the strategies due to the finite population I have stipulated. I therefore choose to have the Tsar move first, by publishing his constitution of penalties, and then Lenin reacts by proposing his income distribution. Secondly, the rather complicated nonlinear program which characterizes Lenin's optimization problem when facing the Tsar's penalty proposal has some open inequalities in it (due to the open inequality which defines the formability of coalitions). Therefore, it is not automatic that a solution exists. Nevertheless, optimal solutions always do exist, so long as the probability functions are continuous in the penalties. We may discuss without further ado the solution to this game, when the Tsar moves first.

Define a Tsar to be *tyrannical* if he has an optimal set of penalties at which penalties are set equal to incomes. Recall that if the penalty function for each coalition is in fact *insensitive* to the penalties proposed, then the Tsar always has an optimal strategy which is tyrannical. (Insensitivity means for each coalition S, $p_S(\mathbf{d})$ is a constant function on $\mathbf{D}$.) Now introduce a little bit of sensitivity into the probability functions, that is, there *is* an active psychology of tyranny. If the Tsar raises penalties, the probability of revolution for each coalition increases, if only by the tiniest amount. One might expect that since an insensitive regime always has a tyrannical solution, then in regimes which are only the least bit sensitive, a tyrannical solution will still obtain. That is, one might expect that although the Tsar incurs a potential cost in raising penalties, that cost is more than compensated for by the benefit of deterrence which higher penalties provide. But this is not the case. The first theorem of Tsarist strategy is:

Theorem 1: Tyranny never pays in sensitive regimes.

Under the three assumptions on probability functions, a sensitive regime never has a tyrannical Tsar. I find this a bit surprising.

I will prove this result, in order to give some feeling for the structure of the problem and the kind of reasoning involved. First, notice that the following inequality is a necessary and sufficient condition for a coalition S to be formable at penalty vector $\mathbf{d}$, for *some* income distribution proposal by Lenin:

$$\frac{p_S(\mathbf{d})}{1 - p_S(\mathbf{d})} > \frac{d^S}{n - z^S} \tag{2}$$

Here, $d^S \equiv \sum_{i \in S} d_i$, $z^S \equiv \sum_{i \in S} z_i$, and n is total income, $n = \sum_{i \in N} z_i$. To recruit S to form, Lenin must be able to promise them an expected increase in their individual incomes which more than compensates for their expected penalties, should the revolution be routed. The additional income Lenin has to promise members of S can come only from its complement, and is $(n - z^S)$ in amount. By cross-multiplying the terms in inequality (2), notice (2) is precisely the required condition. Lenin can propose an income y which will recruit S to form if and only if (2) holds.

Notice the left-hand side of (2) is simply the *odds of victory* for S at penalties $\mathbf{d}$. Call the odds function $\beta_S(\mathbf{d}) \equiv [p_S(\mathbf{d})/1 - p_S(\mathbf{d})]$. Now we can represent every coalition as a point in the space indicated in Figure 1, and I claim that at the solution of the revolutiuonary game the picture looks something like that shown in the figure.

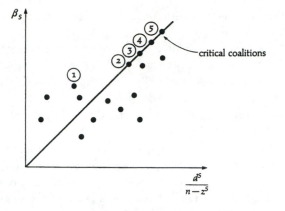

Fig. 1

Every formable coalition lies strictly above the 45° line by inequality (2). The revolutionary coalition S^* is labelled ①, since that is the formable coalition of maximum winning probability. What is important to note is the existence of several coalitions, here labelled ②, ③, ④, ⑤, which have higher odds of winning and are just on the boundary of being formable. They must exist at the optimum in a sensitive regime with some positive penalties. For suppose not. Then the Tsar would lower some positive penalty by a small amount, which would decrease the probability of victory for S^*, and no other coalition with higher odds of winning would become formable. What prevents him from so lowering penalties? Only the existence of a coalition, like ②, that has higher odds of winning than S^*, and will suddenly become formable if the Tsar lowers a penalty. I call the coalitions which are just on the verge of becoming formable at the optimum the *critical* coalitions; they are the blocking coalitions, so to speak, which prevent the Tsar from further lowering the penalties from $\mathbf{d}^*$ and hence prevent him from lowering the odds of revolution.

There are quite a few critical coalitions: in fact, *every agent with a positive penalty is in one*. For suppose agent i has a positive penalty but is in no critical coalition. Then lowering d_i to $d_i - \epsilon$ will cause every point on the 45° line associated with a critical coalition to drop below the line, by sensitivity, since β_S will drop but $d^S/n - z^S$ will remain unchanged. The Tsar *could* then lower d_i, thus lowering $\beta_{S'}$, and he would not have been at the optimal penalties. So agent i must be in some critical coalition.

Suppose the Tsar has a tyrannical solution and $d_i = z_i$ for all i. In particular, the richest agent, call him Max, is in some critical coalition S by the previous paragraph. But I claim *every* agent must then be in S, which is impossible, since critical coalitions are all *proper* sub-coalitions of N. For suppose some agent i is not in S. Then consider the coalition $\hat{S}$ defined:

$$\hat{S} = S - \text{Max} \cup i$$

That is, replace Max by i in S. Since $z_i < z_{max}$, it follows that $\beta_{\hat{S}} \geq \beta_S$ by Lean and Hungry. But $d_i < d_{max}$, which implies that

$$\frac{d^{\hat{S}}}{n - z^{\hat{S}}} < \frac{d^S}{n - z^S} \tag{3}$$

Hence

$$\beta_{\hat{S}} \geq \beta_S = \frac{d^S}{n - z^S} > \frac{d^{\hat{S}}}{n - z^{\hat{S}}}$$

and so the point in Fig. 1 associated with $\hat{S}$ must lie *above* the 45° line, meaning $\hat{S}$ is formable, an impossibility, since $\hat{S}$ has odds of winning greater than S^*.

This proves that tyranny never pays in a sensitive system, even if it is "nearly" insensitive. I have actually proved, if you examine the argument, a stronger result: that in a sensitive regime, *the richest agent never is assessed the highest penalty by the Tsar*. We have, then, our first result on Tsarist ideology. Rasputin will advise the Tsar not to be a blind tyrant. This is, so far, a weak result, as it refers only to the richest person. But I shall describe next how we can extend this Tsarist softness towards the rich a good deal farther.

To further articulate the Tsar's behavior, a second-order assumption is required concerning the psychology of tyranny. Recall the first-order assumption is called Penalty Monotonicity: that for any coalition, the conditional probability of success is a non-decreasing function of the penalty vector the Tsar proposes. I now wish to propose how people evaluate the *relative* severity of penalties assigned to different people. Suppose, at a given vector of penalties, Tom is being more severely penalized than Harry. Penalty severity might be measured in a number of ways – for instance, people might consider severity to be reflected by the ratio (d_i/z_i), the penalty rate. I will allow penalty severity to be measured by any function $\sigma(d_i, y_i)$ of the penalty and income which is increasing in the penalty and decreasing in income. The *Assumption of Relative Severity* is now this: that if the Tsar raises Tom's penalty by a little bit, the probability of revolution increases more, for all coalitions, than if he raises Harry's penalty by the same little bit.

Relative Severity If $\sigma(d_i, z_i) > \sigma(d_j, z_j)$ where σ measures perceptions of penalty severity then

$$\text{for all } S, \quad \frac{\partial p_S}{\partial d_i} > \frac{\partial p_S}{\partial d_j}.$$

This is like a second-order condition on the psychology of tyranny: people are more incensed by a Tsar who increases the severity of penalties against those already heavily penalized than they are by a Tsar who metes out penalties in a more equally severe fashion. I reiterate that I do not impose any particular measurement of penalty severity on this population: I simply propose that however they measure severity, by some function $\sigma(d_i, z_i)$ which behaves as I said, the odds of revolution respond as described. We now have:

Theorem 2: Assume Penalty Monotonicity, Relative Severity, and Lean and Hungry. If j is penalized more severely than i at the solution, then j is poorer than i.

$$\sigma(d_j, z_j) > \sigma(d_i, z_i) \Rightarrow z_j < z_i.$$

This result is not too difficult to establish. At the equilibrium penalties $\mathbf{d}^*$, let j be more severely penalized than i. Now consider these perturbed penalties: the Tsar reduces j's penalty by ϵ and increases i's penalty by ϵ. By the Assumption of Relative Severity, all coalition revolutionary probabilities decrease; in particular, the probability of success of the revolutionary coalition decreases. Why doesn't the Tsar perturb the penalties in this way? Because some critical coalition must become formable with the proposed change in penalties. Recall Fig. 1, and notice the only critical coalition that could have become formable with these perturbed penalties is one which contains j and does not contain i. All the critical coalitions containing j which also contain i drop below the 45° line in Fig. 1 with the perturbed penalties. Thus: *if $\sigma(d_j, z_j) > \sigma(d_i, z_i)$ then there must be a critical coalition S containing j but not i.*

Now suppose $z_j \geq z_i$, contrary to what we wish to prove. Since j is richer than i and also more severely penalized it follows that $d_j \geq d_i$, since the penalty severity function σ is increasing in d_i and decreasing in z_i. So

$$(z_j, d_j) \geq (z_i, d_i) \tag{4}$$

with strict inequality in at least one component. Now consider the critical coalition S of the last paragraph, and form

$$\hat{S} = S - j \cup i.$$

By Lean and Hungry, $\hat{S}$ has at least as great a probability of winning as does the critical coalition S. But

$$\frac{d^{\hat{S}}}{n - z^{\hat{S}}} < \frac{d^S}{n - z^S}$$

by inequality (4).

Hence $\hat{S}$ is formable and beats the revolutionary coalition in probability, an impossibility. This contradicts the supposition that $z_j \geq z_i$ and so *Theorem 2* is established.

Thus, the severity of the optimal penalties is monotone decreasing in incomes! (This does not say that richer people face a *smaller* penalty, but they face a *less severe* penalty, taking account of their income.) A rudimentary intuition for the result is this. It is the poor whom Lenin can recruit relatively easily, because he does not have to promise them as much income to make it worth their while to fight as he would have to promise the rich. Furthermore, by Lean and Hungry, the poorer a person is, the more helpful he is to the revolutionary coalition. Hence the Tsar, who wants to economize on the penalties he doles out because of Penalty Monotonicity, will not waste penalties on the rich: he will tend to penalize the poor more to dissuade them from Lenin's proposals. It is not intuitively clear, to me at least, that optimal penalty severity will actually be monotone decreasing in income, which I take to be a non-trivial conclusion about Tsarist ideology. When we observe the Tsar proposing increasingly severe penalties as people become poorer, we might have thought that was a consequence of his hatred of the poor and his sympathy for his class brothers, the rich, a consequence, that is, of his "ideology". Decreasing penalty severity with wealth, however, is just good strategy, it need not come from any precommitment the Tsar has in regard to how people should be treated.

When is Lenin progressive?

I now turn to discussion of aspects of Leninist ideology. Call an income redistribution *progressive* if it takes from the rich and gives to the poor. A rather weak notion of progressivity is: there exists an income level w, such that anyone with a higher income than w has his income reduced under Lenin's proposal, and anyone with a lower income has his income increased. Question: when will Lenin's optimal strategy be a progressive redistribution of income? We tend to observe revolutionaries proposing progressive redistributions: is that necessarily a consequence of ideology, or is it just good strategy, if Lenin's goal is simply to overthrow the Tsar, by any means necessary?

Suppose the revolutionary coalition turns out to be *poor-connected*: by this I mean it consists of all agents who have income less than some amount. Then it is easy to see Lenin has a progressive strategy. He can simply take as much income as he requires to recruit these poor revolutionaries, at the Tsar's stated penalties, from the richer coalition of non-revolutionaries. Hence I ask: when is the revolutionary coalition poor-connected, for that is a sufficient (although not necessary) condition for Lenin to be progressive in his choice of strategy.

Unfortunately, the easiest result to prove is that the revolutionary coalition is poor-connected if optimal penalties are monotone increasing in income. But we know for sensitive regimes, this is *never* the case (for recall, in particular, the richest agent is never assessed the largest penalty). However for insensitive regimes, where the probabilities of revolution are constant for each coalition, we know there is an optimal penalty vector which is monotone increasing in incomes: namely, the tyrannical solution of setting penalties equal to incomes. Hence, we have the more-or-less complete story for insensitive regimes, where the psychology of tyranny is degenerate, so to speak:

Theorem 3: If the population is insensitive to increasing penalties, then (1) the Tsar is tyrannical, (2) the revolutionary coalition is poor-connected, and (3) Lenin is progressive.

Furthermore, it is possible to do some comparative instability analysis for insensitive regimes. It turns out that:

Theorem 4: Let **z** and **z'** be two income distributions for the same population, who behave insensitively towards penalties. If the Lorenz curve of **z** lies everywhere on or below the Lorenz curve for **z'**, then **z** is at least as unstable as **z'**. (That is, the probability of revolution at the optimal strategies is at least as great for the income distribution which is more inegalitarian.)

This is the only result I have which compares stability across regimes.

For the case of sensitive regimes, the interesting case, I want to know whether there is any hope for establishing that the revolutionary coalition is poor-connected, even though penalties are never increasing income. It turns out that there is. I will present a pictorial argument. For the rest of the discussion, the stronger *Symmetry* assumption will replace *Lean and Hungry*. I will show that at the optimum, there are always three income classes: a class of poor people, all of whom are in the revolutionary coalition; a class of rich people, none of whom are in the revolutionary coalition; and a middle-income class between these two, whose members may or may not be in the revolutionary coalition.

Call the revolutionary coalition S^*, and the optimal Tsarist penalties the vector **d**, and let β be the odds of revolution for S^* at **d**. Then, to recruit the coalition S^* to form, Lenin must offer each of its members an income somewhat more than he is currently receiving. It is immediate to calculate from (1) that the *reservation income* of each member i of S^* is given by:

$$\bar{y}_i = z_i + \frac{1}{\beta} d_i \tag{5}$$

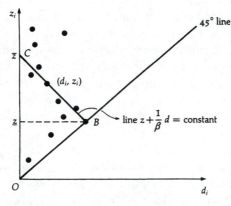

Fig. 2

Now we can represent every agent in the population as a point in Fig. 2. (This figure has nothing to do with Fig. 1: we are in a different space.) Each agent is represented by a point on or above the 45° line, since penalties cannot exceed incomes.

Consider lines in this plane of the form

$$z + \frac{1}{\beta} d = \text{constant}$$

When we pass such a line through any "agent", its intercept on the z axis is the reservation income of that agent, according to equation (5). Suppose the size of the revolutionary coalition is 6. Then it must consist of the six agents with smallest reservation incomes: for all coalitions of six people have equal odds of winning, by *Symmetry*, and Lenin must economize on the incomes he promises to the revolutionaries. So he promises each of the six agents with the smallest reservation incomes a little more than his reservation income. Geometrically, Lenin locates these six revolutionaries by pushing out the line of slope $-1/\beta$ from the origin until he has gathered up six points. Fig. 2 shows a typical configuration, where the points in the triangle OBC comprise the revolutionary coalition. From Fig. 2, we can immediately observe the Class Decomposition Theorem I stated:

Theorem 5: Everybody with income below z must lie in triangle OBC, so those people must be in the revolutionary coalition. Everybody with income above $\bar{z}$ necessarily lies outside the triangle OBC, and hence is not in the revolutionary coalition; and agents with income between z and $\bar{z}$ can lie either inside our outside the triangle: hence their status as revolutionaries is not determinate, from this analysis.

Notice this Class Decomposition Theorem is not enough to guarantee that S^* is poor-connected: for it may be that some relatively poor member of the middle class is not in the triangle, and some richer member is. I have drawn this possibility in Fig. 2. I wish I could say I have ruled out this possibility, but I have not. I do not know whether it can happen. But at least I do know that everybody who is sufficiently poor, with income below z, is surely a revolutionary, and everyone sufficiently rich is surely not revolutionary.

There is an asymptotic result, however, which states that for sufficiently high probabilities of revolution, the revolutionary coalition is poor-connected, and therefore Lenin is progressive. I can indicate this with the aid of Fig. 2. Notice the band of incomes associated with being in the middle class gets smaller as the slope of the line $\overline{BC}$ get less steep. Now the higher the odds β of revolution, the flatter is the line $\overline{BC}$. Hence, if the revolution is sufficiently highly probable, the middle-income class all but disappears, and in this case it can be shown the revolutionary coalition is indeed poor-connected. To summarize:

Theorem 6: For a given income distribution z, there is a number q less than 1, such that if the probability of revolution is at least q, then: (1) the revolutionary coalition is poor-connected, (2) Lenin is progressive.

The important observation is that the number q is independent of the probability functions p_S. So we can think of a comparative statics experiment, in which due to changing attitudes of the population, let us say, all probability functions gradually increase over time. Eventually a time comes when the revolutionary coalition has probability of at least q of winning, in which case *Theorem 6* asserts that Lenin is progressive, and the population is polarized between the poor revolutionaries and richer non-revolutionaries. Moreover, this reasoning indicates that the more unstable a regime is, the more likely it is that Lenin is progressive, and the more likely it is that the population is polarized into two income classes, with the disappearance of the middle class.

Finally, I would like to mention an "equal treatment theorem", which has some bearing on how we might think about the development of class consciousness. It turns out that at the solution, every member of the poor income class (those with income less than z) has identical severity of penalty.

Theorem 7: Assume Relative Severity, Penality Monotonicity, and Symmetry. Then all agents with income below z have $\sigma(\mathbf{d}, \mathbf{z})$ = constant.

We already know from *Theorem 2* that penalty severity can only decrease as income increases; we now know that everyone in the poor class suffers the same severity of penalty, which is the maximal severity in the population. It might be that such homogeneous, severe treatment by the Tsar of the members of S^* fuels the emergence of their class consciousness – and, among other things, thereby enables them to overcome the free rider problem which I referred to at the beginning. Perhaps Lenin appeals to them not to defect from the coalition on the grounds that they suffer a common and harsh fate. Of course, such remarks are strictly off the record, they have no place within the model, as I have defined it. There are, indeed, other results about homogeneous treatment: if the revolutionary coalition is poor-connected, then all its members suffer the same and maximal penalty severity, including the middle-class members. So poor-connectedness of the revolutionary coalition, which implies that Lenin will be a progressive revolutionary organizer, is associated as well with homogeneous, severe treatment of the revolutionaries by the Tsar, which might in a meta-model contribute to the formation of class consciousness and cohesiveness among the revolutionaries. The problem with making this statement rigorous is that *if*, indeed, homogeneous treatment of revolutionaries adds to their cohesiveness then the Tsar will have an additional incentive to treat people non-homogeneously, which in this model he does not. So to be honest, I must simply observe that homogeneous, harsh treatment of the revolutionaries is a fact in this model, but no feedback from this fact to revolutionary behavior can be acknowledged, unless we say the Tsar is unaware of the feedback effect, and therefore will not take it into account in formulating his strategy.

Conclusion

I conclude by first reviewing some of the results of this tale:

(1). In a regime where the conditional probabilities of revolution by coalitions are insensitive to the penalties announced, the Tsar might as well be a tyrant, and announce maximum penalties for everyone. However, once the least bit of sensitivity to penalties exists, because of the psychology of tyranny, the clever Tsar will never be tyrannical.

(2) Under the assumption of relative severity on the psychology of tyranny, the severity of optimal penalties is a non-increasing function of income. The Tsar treats the poor harshly and lets the rich off lightly.

(3) Lenin can propose a progressive redistribution of income as his optimal strategy if the revolutionary coalition is poor-connected; it will be poor-connected for insensitive regimes, and for sensitive regimes which are sufficiently unstable, the revolutionary coalition is poor-connected.

(4) Highly probable revolutions are highly polarized revolutions: the population is divided between a coalition of poor people all of whom are

revolutionaries and who suffer an equally harsh penalty severity, and a richer class, with lower severities of penalty.

(5) In fact, the revolutionary coalition is poor-connected if and only if all its members suffer the same penalty severity. This suggests in an imprecise way what perhaps could be developed in a more ramified model, that the development of class consciousness is equivalent to a highly unstable regime.

In what sense do I claim this exercise "rationalizes revolutionary ideology?" Do I think that an actual revolutionary entrepreneur, like Lenin, does not have a precommitment to a progressive redistribution of income, that he only chooses such a strategy because it is clever behavior, which he adopts to pursue his non-ideological and power-hungry goal of overthrowing the Tsar? Some people might use the model for this sort of cynical inference, but I think that would be incorrect. What the model tells us is that if Lenin has an ideological precommitment *against* progressive redistributions, then he will not be a very successful revolutionary leader, he will relegate himself to low-probability strategies. That is, the revolutionary entrepreneurs we tend to see, the ones who succeed, are the ones who are willing to be progressive. If you wish, it is a selective adaptation for a revolutionary entrepreneur to be progressive, for the would-be Lenins who are ideologically committed against progressive redistribution will not succeed, according to this model.

Similarly, there is a natural selection of Tsars, so that the ones we tend to see maintaining their power with greatest success are those who penalize the members of the population in inverse severity to their wealth; they do not act as complete tyrants, and so on. I must take pains to distinguish this position from what might be called a vulgar materialist one, which would maintain people adopt the ideologies they do in order to be successful. I believe, on the contrary, that ethical and moral opinions are important in forming ideologies, in constraining them in appropriate ways, and these opinions are not adhered to *because* they are "efficient" in the sense of entailing successful strategies in life's struggles. Rather, for an ethic or morality to achieve visibility, to last, it must be relatively efficient, although that is not the reason people adopt it. Lenin would not be a very charismatic revolutionary leader if he did not have an independent ethical commitment to progressive redistribution. But there may be equally committed retrogressive revolutionary entrepreneurs who do not make history, because of the handicap their ideology imposes upon them.

8 The logic of relative frustration*

Raymond Boudon

This text, theoretical in nature, is intended as a contribution to a particular debate. This debate is concerned with the paradox in there being a relation between both inequality and satisfaction *and* material plenty and satisfaction. In fact classical sociology is full of paradoxical statements of this sort. For Tocqueville greater equality tends to produce envious comparisons: as they become more equal individuals find their inequality harder and harder to bear. C. Wright Mills has also taken up this theme. For Durkheim individual happiness does not increase in direct ratio to the quantity of available goods. The relation between happiness and goods has the form of a reversed U-shaped curve: on this side of and beyond a particular optimum satisfaction decreases. Again, for Tocqueville, dissatisfaction and frustration may grow when each person's opportunities begin to open out and improve. In *Marienthal*, Lazarsfeld observes the converse of Tocqueville's theorem: when an individual's future is blocked, recriminations against the social system may well be weak. Stouffer's works show that individuals may well grow more discontented with the social system to which they belong as it offers them what are, on average, better opportunities for success and promotion.

In short Tocqueville, Durkheim, Lazarsfeld, Stouffer and also Merton, Runciman and Hyman, authors who surely differ massively in their various methodological, theoretical and political orientations, agree to acknowledge the complex and (since there is no need to reject the word when it is given an exact meaning) *dialectical* character of the relation between material plenty and equality on the one hand, and between material plenty and individual satisfaction on the other.

By contrast there are many more recent authors who interpret this relation in a manner than would seem to have no other virtue apart from its simplicity: some clearly think that an intolerable and potentially explosive situation is created as soon as the poorest 5 per cent have a salary that is less than half the national average. There are others who

* From: *The Unintended Consequences of Social Action* (London: Macmillan, 1982).

think that a reduction in inequalities is invariably positive, regardless of the context.

The following text reaffirms its links with the sociological tradition. It argues that the paradoxical relationships that the classical works of sociology point to can be deduced from simple models inspired by game theory. The basic virtue of these models lies in their ability to show that (among other things) there is no simple way in which one can associate a particular degree of collective happiness, frustration or satisfaction with the various possible distributions of goods. The simple models presented here bring out complex effects of composition (which may account for the paradoxical appeal of the propositions referred to above).

Now let us consider the effect of this public prosperity on the private happiness of citizens. First of all, if these riches are distributed equally, it is certain that they will not long remain in this state of equality, or that, if they did, they would be as if non-existent for those who possessed them. For, in everything beyond immediate necessity the advantages of fortune only make themselves felt in terms of differences.   Jean-Jacques Rousseau, *Political Fragments*

The notions of relative deprivation and of reference group together make up a conceptual whole whose success is doubtless attributable to the way in which it allows one to account – with the help of commonsense propositions – for paradoxical observations. As Runciman notes, the two notions derive from a familiar truism, namely "that people's attitudes, aspirations and grievances largely depend on the frame of reference within which they are conceived".[1] Observation in fact shows that in most cases it is impossible to understand why an individual *A* will feel envious of *B* but not of *C* if one does not know "the frame of reference" of *A*. How is one to explain why it is that *A* envies his right-hand neighbour's Peugeot if one does not know that *A* can hope to raise himself up to his right-hand neighbour's level but not to that of his left-hand neighbour? Suppose we use the excellent definition of relative deprivation proposed by Runciman: "A strict definition is difficult. But we can roughly say that *A* is relatively deprived when (i) he does not have *x*, (ii) he sees some other person or persons, which may include himself at some previous or anticipated time, as having *x* (whether or not this will in fact be the case), (iii) he wants *x* and (iv) he sees it as feasible that he should have *x*. Possession of *x* may of course mean avoidance of or exemption from *y*."

The difficulty with this definition, as Runciman acknowledges, is the notion of *feasibility*: people only desire what they can plausibly hope to obtain. But what rules determine the things that one can or cannot obtain? Does *A*'s envy of *B* decrease in ratio to the feasibility of *A* obtaining the

---

[1] W.G. Runciman, *Relative Deprivation and Social Justice* (Berkeley: University of California Press, 1966).

object *x* that *B* possesses? Suppose I take this argument a little further. By defining the notion of relative deprivation in terms of the concept of *feasibility* is one not setting up a kind of vicious circle? I understand that the Jaguar owner does not belong to *A*'s reference group, a group that includes the Peugeot 504's owner. I also understand that *A* envies the second but not the first. But the first proposition sheds no light on the second: the notion of reference group is simply a rephrasing of the proposition that has it that *A* feels envious of the Peugeot 504 owner but not of the Jaguar owner.

I do not propose to analyze here the important literature to which the two notions of reference group and relative deprivation have given rise. I think however that it is fair to say that the following two propositions contain the most comprehensive summary of this literature:

1. The two notions make it possible to account for certain fundamental social phenomena. Take, for instance, Tocqueville's famous law. This law holds that the improvement of the condition of all may well increase rather than diminish the general sense of discontent. When prosperity increases, Tocqueville writes, "people seem, however, more uneasy and anxious in their minds; public discontent is aggravated; hate against all the old institutions increases . . . What is more, the parts of France which must be the principal focus for this revolution are the very ones in which progress is most apparent . . . it could fairly be said that the French have found their position increasingly unbearable as it became better."[2]

One can clearly also postulate a link between the notions of reference group and relative deprivation and the law of Durkheim's that has it that the satisfaction that the individual experiences depends less on the plentiful supply of goods that are at the collectivity's disposal and more on the tendency the collectivity has to instil desires in the individual that are limited to what he can hope to obtain:

Under this pressure, each, in his own sphere, becomes vaguely aware of the furthest point to which his ambitions may reach, and aspires to nothing beyond it if, at least, he is respectful of rules and has a docile attitude to collective authority, i.e., if he has a healthy moral constitution, he feels that it is not right to demand more. A goal and a limit are thus marked out for the passions. But this determination doubtless has nothing rigid or absolute about it. The economic ideal assigned to each category of citizens is itself understood to have certain limits, within which desires may freely move. But it is not without these limits. *It is this relative limitation, and the moderation that it entails, which makes men happy with their lot, while at the same time stimulating them, within reason, to improve it*; and it is this average contentment that gives rise to that feeling of calm and active joy, that

---

[2] A. de Tocqueville, *L'Ancien Régime*, trans. M.W. Patterson (Oxford: Basil Blackwell, 1933) pp. 185–6. See also James C. Davies, "Toward a Theory of Revolution", *American Sociological Review*, 27 (1962), 5–19.

pleasure in being and living which, for societies as for individuals, is what characterises health.[3] (My italics)

Lastly, I will call to mind the famous conclusion of *The American Soldier*, the book that marks the beginning of the literature on relative deprivation and on reference groups. Military policemen, who belong to a group in which promotion is rare, declare themselves satisfied with the system of promotion that governs their lives. Pilots, on the other hand, though belonging to a group in which promotion is frequent, declare themselves to be unsatisfied with the system of promotion.[4] Everything happens as if an objectively greater upwards mobility brought with it weaker overall satisfaction.

2. There is no doubt that the apparently paradoxical phenomena covered by Tocqueville's, Durkheim's or Stouffer's laws are fundamental ones. But that would clearly be the second conclusion that one would draw from an analysis of the literature, that is, however useful the concepts of reference group and relative deprivation are, they only enable one to grasp very imperfectly the logic underlying these laws.

In the notes that follow I hope to show that the sociological notions of collective relative deprivation and reference group may be more clearly defined if one has recourse to simple models derived from game theory. These simple models suggest that the appearance of relative deprivation phenomena is, in some situations anyway, the "natural" product of structures of interaction (of competition) within which individuals are located. In other words it would seem that some structures of competition incite a more or less significant proportion of individuals to participate in "rivalries" from which some amongst them must necessarily emerge as losers. This proportion and, consequently, the general rate of deprivation, varies with the properties of these structures. I will devote the rest of this chapter to a presentation of these elementary structures of competition and to an analysis of certain of their logical properties. As the reader will observe, even extremely simple structures of competition give rise to relatively complex analyses. It is incidentally worth noting that the *counter-intuitive* character of the properties of these structures of competition may well explain their capacity to fascinate: the consequences that

---

[3] E. Durkheim, *Suicide*, trans. John A. Spaulding and George Simpson, edited with an introduction by George Simpson (London: Routledge and Kegan Paul, 1970) p. 287.

[4] Samuel A. Stouffer, *The American Soldier*, vol. 1 (New York: Wiley, 1965); R.K. Merton and A.S. Rossi, "Contributions to the Theory of Reference Group Behaviour", in R.K. Merton (ed.), *Social Theory and Social Structure* (Glencoe, Illinois: The Free Press, 1957). Along with Durkheim, Tocqueville and Stouffer, one could cite the Danish sociologist, Kaare Svalastoga, who, in *Prestige, Class and Society* (Copenhagen: Gyldendal, 1959), defends the notion of a curvilinear relation between social mobility and individual satisfaction.

they entail correspond to data that are often observed but only with some difficulty explained.

On a theoretical plane the simple models developed below make it possible to specify the purchase that Tocqueville's, Durkheim's and Stouffer's "laws" enjoy, to demonstrate that it is not a question of universally valid laws, as Durkheim thought, but of propositions which may be conditionally true. In other words it is not true that in general an increase in the opportunities or goods offered to individuals will in every case bring about the higher degree of dissatisfaction observed by Tocqueville. On the other hand it is true that the phenomenon can, in certain cases, occur. By "certain cases" I mean as a function of modifications in the structures of competition that the increase in opportunities or goods offered to individuals by the "social structure" has provoked.

We therefore arrive at a completely different interpretation of his law than Durkheim himself does. In *Suicide*, and perhaps even more clearly in *The Division of Labour*, Durkheim has recourse to propositions that are well established in the psycho-physiology of the period in order to explain that dissatisfaction may grow with the increasing number of goods on offer: "Indeed, it is a truth generally recognised today that pleasure accompanies neither the very intense states of conscience nor those that are too weak. There is a pain when the functional activity is insufficient, but excessive activity produces the same effects . . . . This proposition is, besides, a corollary of Weber's and Fechner's law. It is not without reason that human experience sees the condition of happiness in the *golden mean*."[5]

The reader will see below that this interpretation rests on hypotheses that are both needlessly ponderous and probably false.

As Runciman suggests, in the text quoted above, there is relative deprivation when there exists a good x that A possesses and that B does not have. The notion of relative deprivation does, in other words, imply the notion of competition for a good.

Imagine a simple competition model in which there is a group comprising N individuals. "Society" proposes the following option to each of the N individuals: (1) They can either reap a profit B ($> C$) for a stake C, with a probability that diminishes as the number of competitors rises; (2) or they can choose not to participate in the competition. This very general structure characterizes a whole number of situations in which there is competition: should I "invest" in order to try and be promoted to the rank of office head, given that the majority of my colleagues are doubtless driven by the same objective? I would like to make it clear that throughout

---

[5] E. Durkheim, *The Division of Labour in Society*, trans. George Simpson, (London: Collier-Macmillan, 1964), p. 235.

the first part of this chapter I shall assume individuals are equal and regard each other as such. This hypothesis will be abandoned in the last part of the chapter.

It is worth introducing a methodological proviso at this point: I am aware that in many situations of competition individuals are not equal and do not consider themselves as such. It is clear enough that, through sociology, a statistical correlation between social origins and a whole range of other characteristics could be elicited. One is nevertheless entitled, from the methodological point of view, to neglect this fact during the first stages of the analysis. This strategy has the added advantage of highlighting in all its purity the *perverse* character of the effects of composition that structures of competition generate. In the last part of the analysis I will openly abandon the egalitarian hypothesis in order to postulate the existence of groups that tend to be endowed with different levels of resources. These groups can be called classes. One will not of course obtain identical perverse effects when one advances an essentially unrealistic hypothesis – that all are equal – as when one admits that classes do exist, but in either case one will still observe them. They tend, *ceteris paribus*, to be more marked when the egalitarian hypothesis is posited.

Quite apart from its methodological interest, recourse to the fiction of equality allows one to obtain a sociologically significant result, namely, that equality of opportunity does not necessarily lead to deprivation being minimalized. We thus come back to another of Tocqueville's classic themes, and one that C. Wright Mills later revives: that equal conditions tend to stir up rather than to curb envy. I will come back to these points later.

In order to fix these ideas in the reader's mind and in order to make the logic of interaction shown by the preceding model more concrete I propose to give its parameters an arithmetical value. Let N therefore equal 20: the set of individuals to whom the option is available comprises twenty individuals. Let us also imagine that stake and profit are quantifiable, which is clearly not always the case in social life, and that C, the stake, equals £1, while B, the profit, equals £5. Finally we will only allow $n = 5$ winners. Thus if fifteen out of twenty persons decide to put down a stake, only five of these fifteen will draw a profit of £5. The other ten will lose their stake. We will presume that the distribution between winners and losers is random and occurs through drawing lots (it would naturally be possible to construct more complex examples but there is some interest in beginning with the analysis of the simplest cases). What will happen? How many of the twenty potential players will in fact decide to re-enter the game? How many losers or frustrated people will the game create? In this example the answers to these questions are not difficult to provide. If we take just one of the twenty players and presume that he is perfectly well informed about the situation, he will make the following calculations:

1. If I suppose that I, Jones, am the only person playing, I know that in staking £1 I am absolutely certain to get back £5. I will therefore make a bet;
2. This also applies if one, two, three or four colleagues play. In each case I am assured of a net profit of £4 (£5 profit less my stake of £1) since there are five winners;
3. If five of my colleagues play: there are six of us competing for the five winners' places. I have therefore five out of six chances of winning £4 (£5 profit less a stake of £1) and one chance of losing my stake, that is, of obtaining a negative profit, or as one would be more likely to put it, a loss of £1. My "expectations" of a profit therefore stand, in statistical terms, at $(5/6) (4) + (1/6) (-1) = 3.2$. I clearly run the risk of losing my stake but I have a good chance of winning £4. It is likely that I will decide to make a bet;
4. If six of my colleagues play, my expectations of a profit will then be: $(5/7) (4) + (2/7) (-1) = 2.6$. I therefore make a bet;
5. If 7, 8, 9, 10 . . . . 16, 17, 18 of my colleagues play, my expectations of a profit will diminish accordingly but will still be positive: the value of my possible profit, multiplied by the probability of obtaining it, exceeds the value of the possible loss incurred, multiplied by the possibility of suffering it. I have five out of nineteen chances of winning £4 and fourteen out of nineteen of losing £1. My expectation of profit is therefore $(5/19) (4) + (14/19) (-1) = 0.3$. Supposing I consider it quite reasonable to make a bet when my expectation of profit is positive: I will then bet on the assumption that the number of other gamblers is equal to eighteen. If everyone bets, my expectation of making a profit is still positive: $(5/20) (4) + (15/20) (-1) = 0.25$. I will therefore make a bet.[6]

We are therefore dealing with a structure of competition in which each person, regardless of the behaviour of others, reckons that it is in his interests to bet. As a result there will naturally be fifteen losers. The example simulates a situation of competition in which each of the group's members feels justified in entering the lists. Nothing forces potential players to rejoin the game, except the encouragement given by the fact that expectations of profit are positive irrespective of the number of players. The players therefore invest in the game not because of any constraint but because a good understanding of their individual interests inspires them to do so. Now the combined effect of these interests is to turn three-quarters of the group's members into losers. The structure generates a collective deprivation that can be measured in terms of the

[6] The hypothesis implicitly adopted here, according to which an expectation of a gain of a given value is seen as equivalent to an assured gain of the same value, is clearly a simplification, which is meant to place my argument in terms of the simplest examples. In fact, it is generally admitted (cf. Arrow, *Essays in the Theory of Risk-Bearing* (Amsterdam: North Holland, 1971) that a lottery where there is an expectation of gain X offers the individual an assured gain to the value of $X - h$ (where h is positive). It is obvious that, by supposing individuals to be indifferent to the risk involved ($h = 0$), one maximizes the rate of frustration.

number of losers: in the above game, fifteen out of twenty individuals appear to be so deprived. Their contribution was the same as that of the five winners. It was no more unreasonable for them to bet than it was for those who came out of the game without losses. These individuals cannot help adopting the five winners as a reference group and therefore feeling *relatively deprived* in relation to them. In this case the structure helps to generate a level of dissatisfaction typical of the upper level. It perhaps helps to throw some light on Stouffer's observations: when promotions are relatively numerous it is in everyone's interest to bet on promotion. But all those not promoted (the majority in this case) are then deprived. Ease of promotion generates a considerable degree of overall frustration.

The previous game brings to mind the case of the aviators who figure in Stouffer's famous analysis. The game's structure offers individuals objective opportunities for profit – or, in another language, for promotion or increased mobility – that are by no means negligible. But it therefore encourages an excessive number of players and consequently a considerable collective deprivation.

Before proceeding any further I will introduce a new methodological proviso. In the previous model I used a fairly unpopular version of *homo sociologicus*. Sociologists tend to recoil from the idea of assimilating *homo sociologicus* to a calculating individual intent on pursuing his own interests. In fact the model does not at all imply such a narrow representation of the determinants of his behaviour. Although it would make my mode of exposition and argument far more ponderous, I could eliminate the apparently shocking nature of the hypotheses used. I could for instance suppose that individuals were moved not only by the idea of profit but by other motives (pleasure at playing, for example), or that some work out the lottery's value, in a more or less confused way, before deciding, whilst others decide to take part in the game because they believe their luck is in, or decide to abstain because they are plagued by ill fortune (I will leave to one side the question raised by the unrealistic hypothesis of *equality* between individuals, which, once again, will be taken up again below). I could put forward hypotheses as to the frequency with which individuals decide as a function of their own interests. It is not hard to see that, under a wide range of conditions (i.e., if one supposes that social agents do *on average* tend to follow their own interests rather than setting them to one side), my previous conclusions hold good, in the sense that a perverse effect will invariably appear. The brutal simplification implicit in positing a rational *homo sociologicus* does have the considerable methodological advantage of making the exposition and demonstration less ponderous. It would be purely and simply a misunderstanding to interpret this hypothesis as an ontological statement. It is also incidentally worth noting that if one postulates a minority of individuals who fail to recognize their own best interests and make their decision on the basis of irrational sentiments (ill luck, chance etc.), the collective level of deprivation will, paradoxically, be attenuated.

Suppose we now simulate the second case presented in Stouffer's classic analysis, that of the military police. Here promotion is, objectively speaking, rare. This feature can be represented by supposing that the number n of winners no longer equals 5, as before, but equals 2, for example.[7] Thus, the proportion of winners to group members is no more than two out of twenty. For the rest, I will keep the parameters of the previous example and consider military policeman Jones's line of reasoning:

1. If I, Jones, make a bet, and if at the most one of my colleagues also bets, I have a guaranteed win of £4.
2. If two colleagues bet, I have two in three chances of winning £4 and one chance in three of losing £1. My hope of winning is then: $(2/3) (4) + (1/3) (-1) = 2.3$.
3. If 3, 4, 5, 6, 7, 8, 9 colleagues bet, my chances of winning are progressively reduced and in the final case, become nil. In fact $(2/10) (4) + (8/10) (-1) = 0$.
4. If more than nine colleagues bet, my expectations of winning are negative and the "hoped for" loss will rise in ratio to the number of people who bet. Then, for fifteen people betting altogether, Jones's expectation of winning is $(2/15) (4) + (13/15) (-1) = -0.33$. When there are twenty people altogether who bet, Jones's chance of winning amounts to: $(2/20) (4) + (18/20) (-1) = -0.50$.

What will Jones do? Imagine that he has no information about the possible behaviour of the others and that the same goes for them: each must then decide whether to participate or not in the game, given a totally solipsistic context.[8] In this case Jones and each of his colleagues reckon that, if there turned out to be 11, 12, 13 . . . 20 people betting in all, this would result in an unfavourable situation in which expectations of profit would be negative (expectations of loss). Beyond solipsism a sort of solidarity must then be introduced: with no one having control over the

[7] One thus supposes that the objective opportunities offered to individuals are weaker than in the previous case. Another way of simulating the deterioration in objective opportunities would consist in reducing the amount of gains offered by the society or by the organiser of the game.

[8] There is a considerable difference between the two structures corresponding to my first two examples. In the first case, each player has a dominant strategy, and therefore has no need for any information about the behaviour of the other. In the second case, on the contrary, Ego's interest in each of his strategies depends on the number of others adopting the same strategy as him. If the group in question was a face to face one, the emergence of a structure of this sort would give rise to *negotiations* between the actors. In the case I am considering here, although, in order to simplify the analysis, I took it that $N = 20$, I presume that individuals cannot negotiate with each other. This is a characteristic situation, for instance, in educational behaviour or in behaviour affecting mobility.

behaviour of others, each will do everything in his power to ensure that the total number of people betting does not exceed ten.

It is worth giving this point some thought, for, in spite of the fact that the model's hypotheses tend to simplify things, the structure of interdependence that it generates is of extreme complexity. Let me repeat the proposition that I have just formulated: "Each will do everything in his power to ensure that the total number of people betting does not exceed ten". In reality, although it is in everyone's interest to obtain this result, no one can assume responsibility for it, since it clearly depends on the collaboration of all. But a collaboration of this sort was ruled out by definition. Suppose we imagine that the lottery simulates a choice that the educational system offers a public of potential students: those who play clearly cannot, in such circumstances, confer amongst themselves. What should one do in such a contradictory situation? If Ego assumes that each will take his chance, it is in his interests to abstain. But everyone might reason like this. In reality Ego stands to gain most if, in the hope that the others will do likewise, he allows himself one chance in two of participating in the game.[9] If everybody acts thus, the number of participants will be of the order of a dozen. Interestingly enough the structure of interdependence commits the players to a form of tacit cooperation that I defined above in terms of the notion of quasi-solidarity. It is worth making at this point a methodological observation of the sort I had made above, although in a different context: the model attributes to policeman Jones the capacity to make subtle calculations. But it is important to recognize that the relevance of the hypothesis is purely *methodological*. In other words it is a caricature of the more realistic proposition that, in a situation in which upwards mobility is rare, the potential players will hesitate more

[9] One could well contest the "solution" of the game in this example. The maximin strategy could be defended. The "solution" employed here relies on the following observation: if each player employs the strategy that consists in giving himself x chances out of N of participating in the game, in the case where a number of players greater than x entails a negative expectation for each, this combination of strategies results in an *equilibrium*. In fact, a player who would unilaterally abandon this strategy, in order to give himself a greater chance than x/N of participating in the game, would be punishing himself. What would happen if $x = 10$? Suppose that all the players decide to allow themselves $x/N = 1/2$ chances of participating in the game. Each person's expectation is then $1/2[(2/10)(4) + (8/10)(-1)] = 0$. In choosing unilaterally to participate in the game when he is certain, the player lowers his own expectations, since the sum between brackets becomes negative. On the other hand, if all the players allow themselves a probability p lower than $x/10$ of participating in the game, it is in the interests of each to choose a value higher than p. The solution here is naturally far more difficult to determine than in the previous example. But the important thing to note is that the difference in structure, with respect to the preceding example, must entail a corresponding fall in participation. If, like Rapoport, one admits that, when no dominant strategy exists for anyone, and multiple Pareto equilibria exist, "rationality" consists necessarily in minimizing risks, participation is zero. The "solution" envisaged here corresponds to a less marked fall in participation.

before investing their energies in the search for a difficult promotion. In hesitating thus they will, without wishing to and perhaps without knowing it, be manifesting a behaviour of *quasi-solidarity*.

Let us now return to the model and suppose that each will allow his own bet to be decided by the toss of a coin. Let us suppose that Jones and the others employ this strategy. Each will then hope to gain: $(1/2) (0) + (1/2) [(2/10) (4) + (8/10) (-1)] = 0$.

This clearly is not a brilliant result but it is preferable to the one that Jones could hope to obtain by deciding, for instance, to allow himself more than a 1/2 chance of participating in the game. The term in brackets does in this case become negative, since the coefficient of 4 would then be lower than 2/10 and that of (-10) higher than 8/10. Jones therefore imposes on himself, and consequently on the others, a negative expectation of profit.

One can in short admit that, in a situation of this sort, the behaviour of a rational player can broadly be described by supposing that he will allow a toss of the coin to decide his participation in the game. There will then be ten people betting (if we admit, for the sake of simplicity, that the twenty tosses of the coin will give heads ten times and tails ten times).[10] Once again a result like this is only a semblance of what one actually observes. But, at the same time, it is not entirely unrealistic. One often enough finds that an individual who wants to obtain a good but perceives, more or less clearly, that the number of individuals who desire it makes his chances of obtaining it purely "random" uses a dice throw to decide whether or not to participate in the game.

Once this process of *self-selection* has occurred, we find that the situation for ten people betting is analogous to the first situation examined; out of the ten, eight will emerge losers and two as winners, since it was stated that only two individuals could win the £5 prize.

---

[10] I have applied this type of formalization to problems in the politics of education, thus giving rise to an interesting reaction on the part of Jon Elster, in "Boudon, Education and Game Theory", *Social Sciences Information*, (1976) no. 15, 733–40. Jon Elster asks if one may realistically apply game theory to situations of competition in which hundreds of thousands of students in a country like France are placed, *volens nolens*. This strikes me as being a thoroughly interesting question, and one that calls for comments that I cannot give in full here. The value of N does, naturally, play a vital role here. Consider, for instance, the second of the examples analysed above. If N is large, a player who unilaterally allows himself a probability higher than x/N of participating in the game hardly affects his expectation of gain. Thus, the strategy of eliminating oneself is only justifiable when N is not too large. It is also the case when N is large but one is dealing with a latent group of the federative type (in Olson's sense). The overall number of pupils who finish is, for example, a group of this type. I have the impression that out of the 20 pupils involved, only 2 will have anything to gain from "investing" in (for instance) a class preparing them for a *Grande École*. Self-eliminating strategies will probably be seen to emerge. The fact that there are a significant number of last-stage classes does not alter this situation 'n any way. In other words, the conclusions that may be drawn from the preceding examples may, in certain circumstances, be taken also to refer to cases in which N is large.

The game that corresponds to the second example – the one simulating the result given in *The American Soldier* for the military police – can in short be summed up as follows:

1. Ten potential players do not take part in the competition game. They win nothing, but lose nothing. Their non-participation in the game is the result of a considered and reasonable procedure. I have shown how this abstention can be interpreted as a result of the *quasi-solidarity* imposed by the structure of competition.
2. Two players bet and win.
3. Three players bet and lose.

What sort of consequences does this result lead to, with respect to frustration? The two winning players do of course have no reason to feel frustrated. As for the eight players who have made bets and lost, they will probably be tempted to compare their fate to that of the two winners, that is, to consider them as their reference group: their *contribution* is equal to that of the winners, their *reward* less. This difference in treatment received will tend to be perceived as illegitimate, and frustration is in this case the most likely response to the situation. The case of the ten players who have abstained and have therefore won nothing has to be considered separately. The situation is different from that of the two other groups of players, for the zero value of their reward is the proper remuneration for the zero value of their contribution. From another angle their abstention only appeared to them to be a reasonable strategy because of the existence of the structure of interdependence. They can therefore consider themselves to be frustrated. Nevertheless frustration is very probably more likely here than when the players have lost their stake out of a feeling of resignation. I will define their reaction in terms of the notion of *resigned* frustration. One can conclude from this that the collective frustration engendered by the lottery is lower in this case than in the preceding model. More precisely, the number of individuals who are likely to feel frustrated and cheated at the outcome of the game, and who will therefore contest its legitimacy, will doubtless be lower in this case than in the preceding example. This can therefore be summarized by saying that a frustration leading to *quarrels* will be least frequent in the latter case. It is worth noting, incidentally, that the model, in spite of the simplicity of the original psychological hypotheses, generates complex distinctions regarding the situations in which individuals find themselves at the start of the game, and therefore regarding the sentiments which ought to correspond to these situations. We have in short to deal with a situation that is objectively less favourable than the first one was for the potential players. In the first situation the number of potential winners was five, whereas in the second it is two. But, on the other hand, the first situation incites each player to participate in the game, while in the second it would be quite reasonable for each player to decide whether to participate in the game by tossing a coin. The first situation thus generates fifteen cases of frustration *leading to quarrels* in a group comprising twenty persons, while the second only produces eight cases of this type. In this latter case we therefore have a situation comparable to that of the military police analyzed by Stouffer: there is less chance of promotion there than in the air force, but the general level of frustration produced by the system of promotion is much weaker. To be more exact, frustration *leading to quarrels* is less likely to appear.

To conclude I will recall an important methodological observation: in the two cases analysed above, I presumed that individuals would evaluate in the same way a fixed profit and a lottery linked to expectations that are, mathematically, of equivalent value. In actual fact it tends to be the case that individuals only treat a lottery and a fixed profit identically when the expectations of profit linked to the lottery are higher than those in the case of the fixed profit.[11] In applying this principle to the results of the two examples above, I would conclude that my analysis gives a maximum estimate of the rates of frustration for both. But, whatever hypothesis one retains as to the value of the difference between the fixed profit and the expectation of profit, it is important to realize that the rate of frustration leading to quarrels is higher in the first case, although individuals' objective opportunities are greater.

It is of some interest to formalize the above argument. I will posit a group of N persons, who are then offered a possible win of B_1 for a stake $C_1(B_1 > C_1)$ or B_2 for a stake $C_2(B_2 > C_2)$, with $B_1 > B_2$, $C_1 > C_2$. If $B_2 = C_2 = 0$, one again finds the two situations cited in the previous section (either one tries to obtain B_1 with a stake C_1 or one does not participate in the game). Let n_1 and n_2 be the numbers of winners of lots B_1 and B_2 respectively (supposing $n_1 + n_2 = N$). It is worth noting, incidentally, that the fact of introducing positive values for B_2 and C_2 is of more interest at the level of sociological interpretation than at the formal level. In fact, in the case of B_2 and C_2 not being nil, the game amounts to proposing to the players an additional stake $C_1 - C_2$, with the clear option of abstaining, that is, in this case obtaining nil (additional) profit as against nil (additional) stake.

When $x_1(> n_1)$ players stake C_1, the expectation of profit $E_1(x_1)$ of a player also betting C_1 is:

$$E_1(x_1) = (B_1 - C_1)\frac{n_1}{x_1} + (B_2 - C_1)\frac{x_1 - n_1}{x_1}$$

[11] Cf. Arrow, *Essays in the Theory of Risk-Bearing.*

$$= (B_1 - B_2) \frac{n_1}{x_1} + B_2 - C_1 \tag{1}$$

The expectation of profit $E_2(x_1)$ of a player betting C_2 when $x_1(> n_1)$ players stake C_2, is, however:

$$E_2(x_1) = B_2 - C_2 \tag{2}$$

Thus when $x_1(> n_1)$ players stake C_1, a player is advised to stake C_1 rather than C_2 if:

$$E_1(x_1) > E_2(x_2)$$

or

$$(B_1 - B_2) \frac{n_1}{x_1} + B_2 - C_1 > B_2 - C_2 \tag{3}$$

More simply, it is advisable to stake C_1 if:

$$(B_1 - B_2) \frac{n_1}{x_1} \geq C_1 - C_2$$

or

$$\frac{B_1 - B_2}{C_1 - C_2} \geq \frac{x_1}{n_1} \tag{4}$$

I will now apply this relation to the two examples given in the previous section. In the first example, $B_2 = C_2 = 0$. Potential players are in effect offered the possibility either of trying to win $B_1 = 5$ by betting $C_1 = 1$, or of not playing. Resolution (4) here becomes:

$$B_1/C_1 > x_1/n_1 \tag{5}$$

In other words so long as the relation B_1/C_1 – which amounts to $5/1 = 5$ in the example given – is higher than x_1/n_1, it is reasonable for a player to stake C_1. Since x_1 cannot be higher than the total number of members of the group ($N = 20$ in the first example), and given that n_1 equals 5, x_1/n_1 cannot be higher than $20/5 = 4$. The example is therefore structured in such a way that inequality (5) is always satisfied for all possible values of x_1. It is therefore reasonable for each player to stake C_1.[12]

In the second example x_1/n_1 is higher than B_1/C_1, once x_1 is higher than 10, since $n_1 = 2$. The reader will recall that a player's expectation of profit does in fact become negative if the number of people betting exceeds ten.

This simple formalization makes it easier for us to analyse the consequences of the system $\{B_1 - B_2; C_1 - C_2; n_1; N\}$. Suppose, for instance, we study the variations in the level of overall frustration, as defined by the

[12] If we still presume that the players wish to maximize their expectation of gain, and that they are indifferent to the structure of the lottery proposed.

proportion of individuals who find themselves in the tiresome position of acquiring at the high price C_1 the lot of least value, B_2.[13] If lot B_1 is considerably more attractive than lot B_2, or, to be more exact, if the difference between them is much greater than the difference in cost, to the effect that $(B_1 - B_2)/(C_1 - C_2) > N/n_1$, all potential players will stake C_1 and the rate of frustration will amount to $(N - n_1)/N$. If, on the other hand, $(B_1 - B_2)/(C_1 - C_2)$ amounts to $k/n_1 < N/n_1$, the number of individuals staking C_1 will be k and the rate of frustration will amount to $(k - n_1)/N$.

In order to study the relation between the structure of competition and the phenomenon of frustration, I have drawn up two tables. Table 1 gives the percentage $100x_1/N$ of players considered as a function of the relation between the additional advantage $B_1 - B_2$ and the cost of the additional stake $C_1 - C_2$ on the one hand and the percentage of winners $100n_1/N$ on the other. Table 2 gives the proportion of frustrated members considered in relation to the different values holding between the stake $(B_1 - B_2)/(C_1 - C_2)$ and the percentage $100n_1/N$ of winners. Table 2 brings out the complex manner in which the overall rate of frustration depends, on the one hand, on the individual being given back $(B_1 - B_2)/(C_1 - C_2)$ an increase in his investment, and on the frequency of high-level lots on the other. When $100n_1/N = 100$, the number of lots of high value is the same as that of the members of the group. Each person invests C_1 and receives a lot B_2. In this case none of the group's members is frustrated (last column in the table). When $(B_1 - B_2)/(C_1 - C_2) = 1$ (first line of the table) the number of investors will be exactly n_1: the first line of the table corresponds to a situation in which the number of individuals choosing the investment C_1 corresponds to the number of lots of value B_1. None of the group's members is frustrated, since the group is here divided into two categories: those who make a high investment C_1 and receive B_1 in return, and those who make a low investment C_2 and receive B_2 in return. One ends up here with a stratified system without relative frustration.

In every other case a proportion of the group's members appears to be frustrated. Thus when the rise in profit is twice as rapid as the rise in cost (second line of the table) and the number of lots of value B_1 amounts to 30 per cent of the number of players N (fourth column of the table), for those making a bet to avoid an expectation of negative profit the percentage of betters $100x_1/N$ must be lower than $100 (n_1/N) (B_1 - B_2)/(C_1 - C_2)$, that is, in this case, $30 \times z = 60$. Each individual will thus stake C_1, with a probability 6/10, from which it follows that six out of ten individuals will stake (on average) C_1. As there are only three lots of value B_1 for ten individuals, three individuals out of ten will end up being frustrated.

---

[13] In what follows I have only considered what I termed above *quarrelsome* frustration.

Table 1. *Percentage of players as a function of the relation between the stake and the percentage of winners*

expected gain $= \dfrac{B_1 - B_2}{C_1 - C_2}$	Percentage of winners: $100\ \dfrac{n_1}{N}$										
	0	10	20	30	40	50	60	70	80	90	100
1	0	10	20	30	40	50	60	70	80	90	100
2	0	20	40	60	80	100	100	100	100	100	100
3	0	30	60	90	100	100	100	100	100	100	100
4	0	40	80	100	100	100	100	100	100	100	100
5	0	50	100	100	100	100	100	100	100	100	100
6	0	60	100	100	100	100	100	100	100	100	100
7	0	70	100	100	100	100	100	100	100	100	100
8	0	80	100	100	100	100	100	100	100	100	100
9	0	90	100	100	100	100	100	100	100	100	100
10	0	100	100	100	100	100	100	100	100	100	100

Table 2. *Percentage of frustrated people as a function of the relation between the stake and the percentage of winners*

expected gain $= \dfrac{B_1 - B_2}{C_1 - C_2}$	Percentage of winners: $100\ \dfrac{n_1}{N}$										
	0	10	20	30	40	50	60	70	80	90	100
1	0	0	0	0	0	0	0	0	0	0	0
2	0	10	20	30	40	50	40	30	20	10	0
3	0	20	40	60	60	50	40	30	20	10	0
4	0	30	60	70	60	50	40	30	20	10	0
5	0	40	80	70	60	50	40	30	20	10	0
6	0	50	80	70	60	50	40	30	20	10	0
7	0	60	80	70	60	50	40	30	20	10	0
8	0	70	80	70	60	50	40	30	20	10	0
9	0	80	80	70	60	50	40	30	20	10	0
10	0	90	80	70	60	50	40	30	20	10	0

The rest of table 2 may be reconstituted by applying (4) in an analogous way.

What general propositions can we deduce from these tables?

1. If we follow the lines in table 2 down the page we find situations in which the profits distributed to the group's members attain a greater and greater overall importance. The rate of frustration grows along with the

hopes raised by investment, that is, with the formal equivalent of those Durkheimian considerations as to the link between individual happiness and the limitation of desires: when n_1/N, for instance, amounts to 20 per cent, it is preferable, where the general rate of frustration is concerned, that the profits obtained by an additional investment should be weak rather than strong.

2. The highest levels of frustration occur in cases in which high-value lots are distributed among small minorities.

3. Moderate lots $(B_1 - B_2)/(C_1 - C_2)$ have the advantage of generating a moderate level of frustration, except when they are generously distributed.

4. Equivalent levels of frustration are obtained by distributing important lots parsimoniously or less important lots generously. Note, for instance, that when $100n_1/N = 30$ and $(B_1 - B_2)/(C_1 - C_2) = 3$, the overall rate of frustration is 60, and that the same rate is attained when the return on the additional investment amounts to 7 but the lots are parsimoniously distributed ($100n_1/N = 10$).

5. Generally speaking the curves corresponding to identical degrees of frustration have a complex trajectory. Comparison of tables 1 and 2 does nevertheless bring out the general shape of the phenomenon: in that part of the table representing the situation in which everyone bets ($x_1 = 10$) we find a linear progression of the overall rate of frustration, which is inversely related to the rate of winners. This "plateau" is eroded at the point at which constraint is no longer operative (the "slope's line of change" is the mode of distribution of each line in the table), and this *curve of maximum discontent* expresses a balance: expected gain $= k$/probability of winning.

The two preceding sections provide us with a general model through which we can formally define the different classes of situations of competition and study the proportion of individuals who, in each case, decide to enter the lists at such and such a level. Analysis confirms the basic intuition; namely that, in the vast majority of cases, the structures of competition determine the appearance of frustrated players, whose number, *b*, varies according to the characteristics of the structure. The preceding model is therefore a sort of theoretical machine that allows one to simulate, by simplifying them, the more complex structures of competition that one encounters in social life. The model's interest also lies in the fact that it provides a simple explanation for certain phenomena sometimes considered paradoxical in classical sociology. Thus by scanning, for example, lines 2, 3 or 4 of table 2 from left to right, one obtains a simple simulation of Stouffer's famous example: given the same relation of additional investment, overall frustration grows as the number of winners increases (up to a certain point, at any rate). It is therefore not at all surprising that satisfaction, with regard to promotion, is greater in a system in which it is in fact rare: in this case it is irrational to invest and consequently absurd to complain if one does not get any dividends. On the other hand in situations of competition in which it is rational to invest (frequent promotion, significant chances of mobility), the fact that for some dividends are nil is necessarily felt not merely to be frustrating but to be illegitimate: this resembles Homans' notion regarding the balance between contribution and reward.[14] But it so happens that situations of competition that culminate, at the individual level, in a balance between contribution and reward, are special ones (margins of table 2). In the majority of cases structures of competition determine whether participation in the competition is excessive or insufficient. These excesses are, moreover, a means normally used to select individuals with regard to the collective interest, it being left up to the collectivity to create the legitimacy of the selection thus effected.

It would now be of interest to ask what happens when individuals are no longer presumed equal or perceive themselves to be equal, as was the case in previous sections of this chapter, but have, for instance, different resources. To simplify, let us imagine that competitive games are presented to two categories of potential players, whom I will call the rich and the poor. I am, in other words, using the very simplest hypothesis that one could advance with respect to the structure of a system of stratification: there exist two social classes. And, in order to avoid vicarious connotations, I use banal terms. One can then imagine that the difference in resources finds expression in the poor being more hesitant in taking risks. Thus it is not enough for them to know that applying a particular strategy gives a negative or positive expectation of profit. They also take into account the structure of the lottery that is offered to them. Thus one can imagine that the value of a lottery giving them an expectation of profit G is equal to G for the rich and, for the poor, lower than G, in that the risk of losing is all the greater. Whatever definition one finally adopts here, there will still be less probability of the poor person making a high bet than of the rich person doing so.

Consider, for instance, the structure

$$n_1/N = 1/6, (B_1 - B_2)/(C_1 - C_2) = 4, N = 20$$

and imagine that there are six rich people and fourteen poor people. Suppose the rich person reckons one strategy as being at least of equal

14 George C. Homans, "Social Behaviour as Exchange", *The American Journal of Sociology*, 62 (1958), 697–706. See also W.G. Runciman, "Justice, Congruence and Professor Homans", *Archives Européennes de Sociologie*, 8 (1967), 1, 115–28, and Lucien Karpik, "Trois concepts sociologiques: le projet de reference, le statut social et le bilan individuel", ibid., 6, 2.

value to another if the expectation of profit associated with it is at least equal, and that a poor person adds to this condition a maximin-type condition: that the probability of losing should not be higher than r. To make this more concrete, imagine $r = 40$ per cent. That means that the poor person prefers the certainty of a nil profit to a lottery in which he would have fifty chances out of a hundred of winning £2 and fifty chances out of a hundred of losing £1. Even though the expectation of profit associated with the second strategy is positive, the poor person is presumed to prefer the first. Suppose we analyse this structure.

The strategy of "investing" (betting C_1) gives, through (4), a positive expectation of profit if a maximum of 2/3 potential players take part in the game (bet C_1). The rich will therefore (if they are ignorant of the behaviour of the poor) bet C_1 with a probability of 2/3. Consider now the case of the poor. Given that $n_1 = 3$, the probability that a player will lose his bet exceeds 2/5 = 40 per cent, once the number of people betting is higher than five. The result of these hypotheses is that the poor will bet C_1 with a probability of 5/20 = 1/4.[15] Thus between three and four poor persons, on the one hand, and four rich persons, on the other hand, will bet C_1. Stratification therefore has the effect: (1) of attenuating the general rate of frustration; (2) of determining effects of self-reproduction of classes: the rich are the beneficiaries of the relatively more intense withdrawal of the poor.

One could introduce any number of further complications into the models outlined above. There is probably no point in doing more here than suggest those that are possible at the present stage in the argument.

1. Let us simply recall the family of variants that have just been outlined. It rests on the hypothesis of a preliminary *stratification* between potential players, this stratification having the effect of differentiating the players' attitudes with regard to risk.

2. One could also complicate things by making B_1 a function of n_1: by introducing, for example, the hypothesis that B_1 decreases with n_1. This sort of hypothesis is clearly useful for simulating those processes of competition for the acquisition of goods whose value, as is the case with prestige, sinks perceptibly with the rise of the number of people to whom they are distributed. This observation suggests that the logic of relative frustration may be thought to change with the nature of the good considered (prestige, money . . .).

3. In order to refresh the reader's memory, I will simply mention variants of a more mechanical nature, such as the one that consists of offering players the choice of three options: C_1, the necessary but not the

---

[15] Where the hypothesis is that the members of each of the two categories reckon that those of the other will behave as they do.

sufficient condition for obtaining B_1; C_2, the necessary but not the sufficient condition for obtaining B_2; C_3, the necessary but not the sufficient condition for obtaining B_3 (with $B_1 > B_2 > B_3$, $C_1 > C_2 > C_3$).

4. Instead of supposing that a stake, C_1, is the necessary (but not sufficient) condition for the acquisition of a lot of value B_1, one may suppose that the stake C_1 allows access to a lottery characterized by a particular distribution of lots, the stake C_2 allowing access to another sort of lottery.

5. It is worth noting, incidentally, that the model also provides the logical skeleton for a research project in experimental social psychology that would probably lead to some very instructive results and would perhaps put one in a better position to understand phenomena like envy.

What I have tried to suggest is that simple competition models can readily provide an account of effects which have for a long time perplexed sociologists. They clearly show that the level of overall frustration does not necessarily decrease along with the diffusion of hopes of profit: an increase in opportunities for promotion for all may in fact lead to a still more rapid increase in the obstacles to promotion. The model's advantage lies in its clearly showing the sort of conditions under which this occurs, and its results make it possible to formulate more exactly the intuitive propositions advanced, in various forms, by Tocqueville, Durkheim and by those authors who used the notions of reference group and of relative deprivation, that is, Hyman, Merton and Stouffer.

The model confirms Tocqueville's analysis of the effects of the differences between individuals being attenuated. Everything else being equal, when differences in individual resources are attenuated, one observes an increase in the number of cases of frustration of the sort that leads to quarrels. In other words the attenuation of distances between social "strata" must, *ceteris paribus*, increase the level of frustration leading to quarrels. One should however insist on the limiting clause of *ceteris paribus*: if distances between individuals decrease, if, in other words, equality of opportunity increases, the general level of frustration tends – as an effect of this change – to grow; but this effect can be reinforced or, on the other hand, limited, as table 2 shows, when opportunities open to individuals grow as much as when they lessen. Consider, for example, line 8 of this table. There one sees that, when the number of winners goes from 10 per cent to 20 per cent, the rate of frustration shifts from 70 per cent to 80 per cent; but when the number of winners goes from 20 per cent to 30 per cent the rate of frustration falls from 80 per cent to 70 per cent. If one combines this result with the effect of a diminution or of an increase in the inequality of opportunities, it is clear that all possible configurations can in theory be observed. In other words an increase in the number of winners or, to shift from the language of games to that of sociology, an increase in social mobility may coincide with either an increase or a diminution in the overall frustration. It may also coincide with a constant level of overall frustration, in the hypothetical case of an increase in mobility and a simultaneous diminution in the inequality of opportunity having effects that would compensate for each other at the level of collective frustration.

One of the model's essential virtues therefore lies in the fact that it allows one to clarify the logical status of those results in classical sociology that I have cited throughout this chapter. It does, for instance, show that the proposition of Tocqueville's that has it that the attenuation in differences between individuals must increase frustration and envious comparison is, *ceteris paribus*, true. On the other hand the proposition linking increase in mobility to the level of frustration is only valid if one presents it as a possibility: it is *possible* (but not necessary) that the increase in mobility should provoke an increase in the overall level of frustration. The model thus has a double advantage: it completely eliminates the mystery contained in Tocqueville's paradox; it is sufficient to posit individuals preoccupied with the pursuit of their interests and to confront them with a lottery having a determined structure, in order to simulate Tocqueville's proposition. But from another angle the model shows that one can observe an inverse correlation between mobility and general level of frustration. That does not mean that one is faced with an independence between the two phenomena. They are, on the contrary, closely dependent on each other, but the direction of the dependence depends on the properties of the structure of interdependence linking the individuals.

The model does of course show, in the same way, that Durkheim's "law" *may* in certain cases give the impression of being valid but in other cases may not be so. Applied to Stouffer's example, the analysis likewise shows that one could in other circumstances expect to find an inversion in the links observed. I mean that, as the model shows, one *may* encounter situations in which weaker promotion opportunities are associated with *greater* dissatisfaction, just as one *may* encounter the situation described in *The American Soldier*, in which a *lesser* dissatisfaction is associated with weaker promotion opportunities. This does not mean, let me stress once more, that opportunities for mobility and satisfaction are phenomena without any relation one to another, but that the structures of interdependence are different in the two cases.

These remarks have a corollary whose importance I would emphasize. It is in vain to wonder if, *in general*, an increase in mobility or in the accessibility of these *goods*, whatever the nature of the goods, or in the equality of opportunity, produces an increase in individual satisfaction.

The question is not liable to a general answer. Not because individual satisfaction is a random phenomenon, and one that is independent of the individual's social position and of the opportunities that the collectivity offers him, but because the direction of the dependence in question rests on structures of interdependence.

The above notes are clearly just a sketch. But they do indicate a possible direction for research that could turn out to be important. They show that it is possible to construct a theory allowing one, for instance, to link the rate of overall satisfaction with the characteristics of situations of competition. They also show that it is possible, on the basis of the model that was fleetingly invoked in the final section, to analyse the problem of the reproduction of inequalities and handicaps by means of a "light" model, that is, one that does not imply the unwieldy and banal hypothesis which crops up so often in the work of certain sociologists, which has it that the persistence of inequalities is the effect of a dominant group oppressing a dominated one. Generally speaking it may be that the neo-individualist perspective[16] adopted here allows one to reiterate certain questions bearing on the study of social stratification. The models outlined above do clearly define the reference groups imposed on actors because of the conditions of interaction. They lead to definitions of the different types of frustration and envy and include, in filigree, a theory of *envy* in which this sentiment would not be the consequence of every single occurrence of inequality, as many sociologists implicitly admit, but a response to particular situations generated by definite structures of interdependence.

One could further complicate the preceding models by questioning the legitimacy of the structures of competition thus introduced: thus, if it is a question of choosing future doctors, a structure characterized by $(B_1 - B_2)/(C_1 - C_2) = 1$ is perhaps satisfying to the extent that it minimizes the overall frustration. On the other hand it is definitely not the sort that will lead to the best and most motivated candidates being selected.

From another angle consideration of the theory – defended by authors like Jencks and Easterlin – that has it that industrial societies automatically generate phenomena of generalized envy and frustration suggests that, in terms of the perspective in use here, it is perhaps unnecessarily pessimistic.[17] As the present chapter indicates, it is not self-evident that every

---

16 As regards this notion, see François Bourricaud, "Contre le sociologisme une critique et des propositions", *Revue Française de Sociologie*, 16 (1975), supplement, 583–603.

17 Christopher Jencks, *Inequality, a Reassessment of the Effect of Family and Schooling in America* (New York: Basic Books, 1972); Richard A. Easterlin, "Does Money Buy Happiness?", *The Public Interest*, 30 (1972), 3–10. See also Victor R. Fuchs, "Redefining Poverty and Redistribution of Income", *The Public Interest*, 8 (1967), 88–95. This article perhaps dispenses once and for all with the doctrine according to which there exists a maximum tolerable dispersion of the distribution of goods.

difference between two individuals generates envy and frustration. One must at least distinguish between that situation in which two individuals receive different rewards, each having made a similar contribution, and that situation in which each has made a different one. It is not certain that industrial societies, by improving the situation of all while at the same time maintaining and sometimes even aggravating relative differences, do for that reason generate frustration. Nor is it certain that, as Jencks would claim, overall frustration is narrowly tied to the distribution of goods being dispersed.

Finally the model developed above makes it reasonable to suggest that the real relation between the objective opportunities that society offers individuals and the level of collective satisfaction may be a negative one, as Durkheim and Tocqueville propose. The profound intuition of these two authors is quite opposed to the simplicity of the theory presented by Easton: "We can expect that direct satisfaction of demand will at least generate specific support; and the longer such satisfactions are felt, the more likely it is that a higher level of political good will develop."[18] In fact the preceding models show that one can only guarantee that a system will bring about a weak or a non-existent level of frustration if one advances the absurd hypothesis that it could eliminate every institution of competition. For the rest one must be prepared for the eventuality that, having succeeded in *increasing* and *levelling out* the opportunities of all, it will nevertheless see its audience decrease, because this improvement in the lot of all will have increased the general level of frustration leading to quarrels.

[18] David Eason, *A Systems Analysis of Political Life* (New York and Amsterdam: Wiley, 1965).

Index